9.2.99

Programming Web Graphics
with Perl and GNU Software

Programming Web Graphics with Perl and GNU Software

Shawn P. Wallace

O'REILLY®

Beijing · Cambridge · Köln · Paris · Sebastopol · Taipei · Tokyo

Programming Web Graphics with Perl and GNU Software
by Shawn P. Wallace

Published by O'Reilly & Associates, Inc., 101 Morris Street, Sebastopol, CA 95472.

Editor: Richard Koman

Production Editor: Jane Ellin

Printing History:

     March 1999:   First Edition.

This book is printed on acid-free paper with 85% recycled content, 15% post-consumer waste. O'Reilly & Associates is committed to using paper with the highest recycled content available consistent with high quality.

ISBN: 1-56592-478-9   [3/99]

Table of Contents

Preface

Welcome to *Programming Web Graphics with Perl and GNU Software*! In this book we will focus on two areas: generating web graphics "on the fly," and creating web graphics using a scripting language (Perl) to simplify mundane or repetitive tasks. Intermediate and advanced web users will probably get the most out of this book, though hopefully it will demystify the manipulation of graphics files for newcomers as well.

Programming Web Graphics takes a practical approach to the material. It is not a book about the design or aesthetics of web graphics; its focus is on writing programs that manipulate graphics files to be published on the Web. The examples in the book use Perl as a scripting language, although the concepts are applicable to any programming language. Perl is well-suited for web graphics programs for several reasons:

- Perl is ubiquitous on the Web.

- Perl has many free, reusable modules for generating web graphics, such as the GD and GIFgraph modules described in Chapters 4 and 6.

- Perl has interfaces to more powerful image manipulation tools, such as ImageMagick (Chapter 5) and the Gimp (Chapter 7).

- Perl has a bevy of well-developed modules for various web applications that support the cause of programming web graphics. The popular CGI module (Chapter 2) allows you to easily create CGI scripts, for instance.

- Perl is easily integrated with high-performance web servers. The mod_perl extension to the Apache web server, for example, offers a significant performance improvement over other implementations.

- Perl is a fast, well-documented, and popular scripting language.

Most of the topics in this book are applicable to any platform (NT, Linux, Unix, even MacOS), with the exception of the chapter detailing the Gimp (Chapter 7), which (for now) exists primarily on Linux and Unix systems. The focus is always on free software, when it is available.

Contents of This Book

The book is divided into three parts. Part I, *Introduction to Web Graphics*, provides a survey of the current state of web graphics:

Chapter 1, *Image File Formats*
> In which the "black box" of the three predominant web graphics formats (GIF, JPEG, and PNG) is opened, explored, and accompanied by a discussion of web graphics concepts such as transparency, compression, interlacing and color tables. Chapter 1 is supplemented by Appendix A, which details a simple implementation of a PNG decoder script written in Perl.

Chapter 2, *Serving Graphics on the Web*
> In which we present the standard ins and outs of creating CGI scripts that generate dynamic images, and take a look at the HTML tags that embed images in web pages.

Chapter 3, *A Litany of Libraries*
> In which we briefly tour some of the more useful free graphics libraries available on the Web. The average end user will probably not use these resources directly, but a number of them (the Independent JPEG Group's libjpeg and the PNG libraries, for example) are used by most web browsers to implement graphics support, so it is good to know about them.

Part II, *Graphics Programming Tools*, is dedicated to documenting several tools for generating web graphics:

Chapter 4, *On-the-Fly Graphics with GD*
> In which we discover the GD module and explore its use in CGI applications. The GD module is a collection of functions for reading, manipulating, and writing color GIF files. GD is great for quick and dirty scripts that are fast and not all that dirty, but it is limited in that it can only read and write GIF files.

Chapter 5, *Industrial-Strength Graphics Scripting with PerlMagick*
> In which we are introduced to ImageMagick and its Perl interface. ImageMagick is a collection of functions and a transparent interface for reading and writing over forty different graphics file formats. It is a great "Swiss army knife" for image conversions, scaling, cropping, and color management. It can handle file formats that contain multiple images in a single file, such as GIF89a. ImageMagick is (of necessity) a bit bulky, however, and may not be suited for all CGI programming tasks, though it certainly can be used for a lot of them.

Chapter 6, *Charts and Graphs with GIFgraph*

> In which we use GIFgraph to create graphs from data provided by an HTML form. GIFgraph is a Perl module that extends the GD module by offering a number of functions for creating many types of graphs and charts. For quite a while, almost all of the financial graphs or web server load graphs that you would find on the Web were generated by CGI scripts using GIFgraph to generate the images.

Chapter 7, *Web Graphics with the Gimp*

> In which we learn how to use the Gimp-Perl module to create custom plug-ins for the GNU Image Manipulation Program. The Gimp started out as a free "Photoshop-like" program. It would be inaccurate to call the current version of the Gimp a Photoshop clone, however, as the Gimp has surpassed Photoshop in certain areas, and has marked out new territories for image manipulation. The Gimp has a sophisticated scripting interface (several, actually). In this chapter we use the Gimp-Perl interface to write Gimp plug-ins. Chapter 7 is supplemented by Appendix B, which provides a reference guide for the Gimp, and Appendix C, which provides a reference to the procedures available to Gimp-Perl scripts.

Part III, *Dynamic Graphic Techniques*, focuses on specific web-based graphics applications:

Chapter 8, *Image Maps*

> In which we discuss client-side (and server-side) image maps and create an example script that generates image map regions on the fly from data retrieved from a database.

Chapter 9, *Moving Pictures: Programming GIF Animation*

> In which we are presented with seven easy GIF animation scripts using ImageMagick, and are introduced to a home-brewed language called GIF-script that describes the structure of animated GIF files.

Chapter 10, *Web Graphics Cookbook*

> In which we are presented with a number of common web graphics recipes, with reusable code examples written in Perl.

Chapter 11, *Paperless Office? Not in Our Lives: Printing and the Web*

> In which we are introduced to the PostScript page description language, and develop a framework for easily generating PostScript code to leap the separation between the Web and the printed page.

Part IV, *Appendixes*, supplements Chapters 1 and 7.

Conventions Used in This Book

The following font conventions are used in this book:

Italic

>   Is used to indicate URLs, folders, directories, functions, methods, options, commands, variables, and menu names, as well as to introduce new terms.

`Constant Width`

>   Is used to indicate code sections, attributes, parameters, and HTML tags.

`Constant Width Italic`

>   Is used to indicate replaceable text within code.

How to Contact Us

We have tested and verified all the information in this book to the best of our ability. If you have an idea that could make this a more useful study tool, or if you find an error in the text or run into a question on the exam that isn't covered, please let us know by writing to us at:

>   O'Reilly & Associates
>   101 Morris Street
>   Sebastopol, CA 95472
>   1-800-998-9938 (in the U.S. or Canada)
>   1-707-829-0515 (international/local)
>   1-707-829-0104 (FAX)

You can also send messages electronically. To be put on our mailing list or to request a catalog, send email to:

>   *nuts@oreilly.com*

To ask technical questions or comment on the book, send email to:

>   *booktech@oreilly*

If you would like to contact the author, he has set up a web page to support users of the book at:

>   *http://www.as220.org/shawn/pwg.html*

This web site contains the source and working versions for most of the longer examples in the book, as well as an errata sheet and other tidbits.

Acknowledgments

This book is dedicated to my wife Jill, of course, and to my parents Bob and Paula, sister Erin, and Grammy Alice.

The very first person I have to thank is Brian Jepson. I am indebted to Brian for many things, only a few of which have to do with this book. The original idea of creating a book about generating dynamic web graphics was his, and he has provided enough technical support over the past several years that I considered getting him an 800 number for Christmas. Brian deserves a paragraph to himself so I will stop this one here.

Thanks to everyone at O'Reilly, including editor Richard Koman, editorial assistant Tara McGoldrick, illustrator Robert Romano, production editor Jane Ellin, quality controllers Nicole Gipson Arigo, Sarah Jane Shangraw, and Sheryl Avruch, and everyone else "behind the scenes." I'd also like to thank Andy Oram, Andrew Schulman, Linda Mui, and Katie Gardner for helping out early on, and Gina Blaber and Brian Jepson (again) for nice references.

Thanks to the prestigious group of technical reviewers who took a lot of time to help us remove all* the typos, technical goofs, and boldfaced lies from the text: John Cristy, brian d foy, Bob Freishanham, Shishir Gundavaram, Mark Hershberger, Brian Jepson, Marc Lehmann, Randy J. Ray, Greg Roelofs, Lincoln Stein, and Martien Verbruggen.

Thanks to all my co-workers in the AS220 office for putting up with me for the past eight months and picking up the proverbial slack and dropped balls while I worked on The Book. They are: Umberto Crenca, Sheri Francine VanAntwerp, Geoff Griffin, Lizzie Araujo, Jill Colinan, Joe Auger, Chris Kilduff, Richard Goulis, Susan Kavanaugh, Mark Pedini, Kim Kazan, Lauren Brooke, and Scott Lapham. And of course, members of the SMT Computing Society (Josh Marketos, Scott Schoen, Jim Bray, Eric Moberg, and Geoff Griffin in particular) from whom I have learned the ins and outs (mostly the outs) of the Web over the past several years. Several artists allowed me to use their work in some of the examples herein: thanks to Winsor Pop for the cat in Chapter 5, Keith Munslow for various drawings, Jonathan Thomas for letting me use his head throughout, John Everett for the drawing in Chapter 9, Angel Dean for the photo in Chapter 1, and Umberto Crenca for the crow in Chapter 1.

Since a good deal of this book documents pieces of software created by others, I owe these good people a great debt for their efforts. I would like to thank Tho-

---

* This is actually a typo itself; it is impossible to remove *all* typos from a book. Check out the web site for an up-to-date errata listing.

mas Boutell for giving us the GD libraries and Lincoln Stein for the Perl version. Thanks to John Cristy who created (and tirelessly maintains and improves) ImageMagick, and Martien Verbruggen who created the GIFgraph module. Thanks to Marc Lehmann for crafting the Gimp-Perl interface. Some people still can't believe that quality software can be produced by a group of people who are not being paid to write it. An oft-quoted response to this is that one of the motivations of free software developers is the all-too-infrequent "pat on the back." Thus, I would like to pat all of the programmers who contibuted to Gimp 1.0, including: Spencer Kimball, Peter Mattis, Manish Singh, Adrian Likins, Federico Mena Quintero, Xach Beane, Adam D. Moss, Sven Neumann, Misha Dynin, Chris Gutteridge, Peter Kirchgessner, Shuji Narazaki, Jens Lautenbacher, Tim Newsome, Eiichi Takamori, Scott Goehring, Seth Burgess, Michael Sweet, Josh MacDonald, Daniel Risacher, Andy Thomas, Brian McFee, Hirotsuna Mizuno, Karl-Johan Andersson, Miles O'Neal, Nick Lamb, Albert Cahalan, Alexander Schulz, Erik Nygren, Francisco Bustamante, Hrvoje Horvat, Jens Restemeier, Martin Edlman, Michael Taylor, Raphael Francois, Gordon Matzigkeit, Scott Draves, Brian Degenhardt, David Koblas, Thorsten Schnier, Torsten Martinsen, Reagan Blundell, Andrew Donkin, Andrew Kieschnick, Brent Burton, Edward Blevins, Daniel Cotting, Eric L. Hernes, Alan Paeth, John Schlag, Stephen Norris, Simon Budig, Graeme W. Gill, Jochen Friedrich, John Beale, Michael J. Hammel, Jörn Loviscach, Jens Restemeier, Kevin Turner, Lauri Alanko, Marcelo de Gomensoro Malheiros, Morten Eriksen, Norbert Schmitz, Owen Taylor, Sean Cier, Ed Mackey, Rob Malda, Tracy Scott, Thomas Noel, Tim Rowley, Tom Bech, Daniel Skarda, Vidar Madsen, Wolfgang Hofer, and Xavier Bouchoux (hopefully I haven't left anyone out, but I'm sure I have; thanks to you too!).

I hope that this book will contribute to the free software cause, a phenomenon which I believe is a manifestation of an innate, timeless human instinct to share with others and contribute to the greater community of earthlings.

I

Introduction to Web Graphics

1

Image File Formats

Because graphics files are stored as binary data and are unreadable by humans (actually, parts of graphics files *are* readable by humans, if you know what you're looking for), most people are intimidated into not looking under the hood at the internals of image file formats. Of course, it is a Good Thing that as a web author you can think of an image as a "black box" that somehow understands its own image-ness. But image file formats are not necessarily inscrutable objects if you really want to know how they work, and understanding the structure of the files that you work with on a daily basis can help you remember the vagaries of image manipulation. Knowing how a GIF file is formatted, for example, will help you answer these questions:[*]

- Why isn't a GIF with 129 colors smaller than one with 256 colors?
- Can a multi-image GIF have more than one transparent color?
- What is the maximum color depth of a GIF?
- How does a decoder program know that a file is a GIF?
- How can I make the smallest possible multi-image file?

Hopefully this chapter will help demystify image file formats and help you feel more at home with the binary black boxes called GIFs, PNGs, and JPEGs.

Network Graphics Basics

Creating graphics file formats for distribution over variable speed communications networks (such as the Internet) poses a number of problems. Each end user's

---

[*] Answers to these questions are given in the GIF section later in this chapter.

computer may be connected at speeds as slow as 14.4 bits per second or as fast as several megabits per second, and you would like them all to be able to download and display graphics at some sort of reasonable speed. The Internet started as a place where the common coin was text. ASCII text is easy; one byte* per character keeps the average missive to a size where near-instantaneous communication is possible. Graphics, however, are much more information-intensive. The proverbial picture worth a thousand words can actually translate into hundreds of thousands of words when it comes to sending that picture over the Internet. To deal with network graphics, people have developed a toolkit of structuring conventions and compression tricks that make possible the graphics-intensive Web that we know and love. This section will provide an overview of this vocabulary and point out how GIF, PNG, and JPEG (what we will call the *web graphics formats*) actually implement these concepts.

Fields and Streams

No, this section is not about hunting and fishing. Web graphics formats can be thought of as data streams broken up into fields (so much for the outdoor activity metaphor). Everything that is transferred over the Web may be thought of as a data stream—a series of data packets received one at a time and assembled into a sequential data structure. This data structure is in turn divided into fields. The GIF and JPEG formats call these fields *blocks*, and PNG calls them *chunks*. Fields are a fixed, predictable data structure stored within an image file whose layout is defined by the file format specification. Typically a field will contain information about an image's dimensions, how the colors are defined within the image, special information needed by a display device to properly render the image, etc. These fields of information are often structured so that it is easy for a program displaying the image to quickly extract all the information it needs.

Image transmission is always a tradeoff between two limiting factors: the time it takes to transfer the image over the network versus the time it takes to decode the image. JPEG, for example, is a highly compressed format that allows for small files and quick transmission times but requires longer to decode and display. The format works very well because generally the network is the bottleneck, with the average desktop computer perfectly able to perform the necessary decoding operations in a reasonable amount of time. Of course, the ideal is a very small file that is very easily decoded. In practice, it is always a tradeoff.

---

* Modern character sets are getting bulkier, however; the UC2 Unicode set is two bytes per character and Unicode UTG8 is 8 bytes per character.

Color Tables

An image with a color depth of 24 bits per pixel (or more) is known as a *truecolor* image. Each pixel in the image is saved as a group of three bytes, one for each of the red, green, and blue elements of the pixel. Each of the RGB elements can be represented as one of 256 (2^8) values, which gives us 256^3 or 16,777,216 possible colors: 8 red bits + 8 green bits + 8 blue bits = 24 bits. This also means that a 200×200 pixel truecolor image saved in an uncompressed format would take up 120K for the image data alone, and a 500×500 pixel image would take up 750K. Both of these images would be too large to put on a web page, which is a reason that some image formats store color information in color tables that make for a far smaller image file size (see the section "Compression" later in this chapter).

The PNG format allows you to save color images with a depth of up to 48 bits per pixel, or grayscale images at 16 bits per pixel. This is actually beyond the display capacity of most consumer video hardware available today, where 24-bit color is the standard. JPEG will also let you store images with a color depth of up to 36 bits.

An image with a color depth of 8 bits is sometimes called a *pseudocolor* or *indexed color* image. Pseudocolor allows at most 256 colors through the use of a *palette*, which is sometimes also referred to as a *color index* or a *Color Lookup Table* (CLUT). Rather than storing a red, green, and blue value for each pixel in the image, an index to an element in the color table (usually an 8-bit index) is stored for each pixel. The color table is usually stored with the image, though many applications should also provide default color tables for images without stored palettes.

To save a "real world" image (i.e., something with more than 256 colors) as a pseudocolor image, you must first *quantize* it to 256 colors. Quantization alone will usually give you an image that is unacceptably different than the source image, especially in images with many colors or subtle gradients or shading. To improve the quality of the final image, the quantization process is usually coupled with a dithering process that tries to approximate the colors in the original by combining the colors in various pixel patterns. Figure 1-1 shows an original image, the same image quantized to an "optimal" 256 colors (the 256 colors that occur most frequently in the image), and the image quantized and dithered with the Floyd-Steinberg dithering process.

Creating indexed color images for use on the Web has a number of pitfalls, which are discussed in Chapter 2, *Serving Graphics on the Web*.

The GIF file format is an indexed color file format, and a PNG file can optionally be saved as an indexed color image. A GIF file will always have at most 256 colors in its palette, though multiple palettes may be stored within a multi-image file,

Figure 1-1. A 24-bit image (top) must be quantized to 256 or fewer colors to save it as an 8-bit indexed image (left). Usually, dithering is applied (right) to improve the image quality.

so the 256-color limit is only applicable to one image of a multi-image sequence. A PNG may also have a 256-color palette. Even if a PNG image is saved as a 24-bit truecolor image, it may contain a palette for use by applications on platforms without truecolor capability.

Transparency and Alpha

Transparency in web graphics allows background colors or background images to show through certain pixels of the image. Generally, transparency is used to create images with irregularly shaped borders (i.e., non-square images). The three primary file formats have varying degrees of support for transparency.

Right off the bat, we should note that transparency is not currently supported in JPEG files, and it will most likely not be supported in the future, because of the particulars of the JPEG compression algorithms and the niche at which JPEG is aimed.

The GIF file format creates transparency by allowing you to mark one index in a color table as the transparent color. The display client should use this transparency index when displaying the image; pixels with the same index as the transparency index should simply be "left out" when the image is drawn. Each image in a multi-image sequence can have its own transparent index.

A single transparency index takes up one byte in the GIF file, as part of a *Graphics Control Extension Block,* described in the GIF section (later in this chapter). The PNG format allows for better transparency support by allowing more space for describing the transparent characteristics of the image (see Figure 1-2), though the full range of its capabilities are not necessarily supported by all web clients. PNG images that contain grayscale or color data that has been sampled at a rate between 8 and 16 bits per sample may also contain an *alpha channel* (also called an *alpha mask*), which is an additional 8 to 16 bits (depending on the image color depth) that represents the transparency level of that sample. An alpha level of 0 indicates complete transparency (i.e., the pixel should not be displayed) and an alpha value of $2^n - 1$ (where n is the color depth) indicates that the pixel should be completely opaque. The values in between indicate a relative level of semi-transparency. Again, the actual implementation of the display of these semi-transparent pixels is left to the display client, and robust web browser support for the full range of possibilities presented by a full alpha channel has been spotty in the past. Consult your favorite browser's documentation for the details of its alpha support.

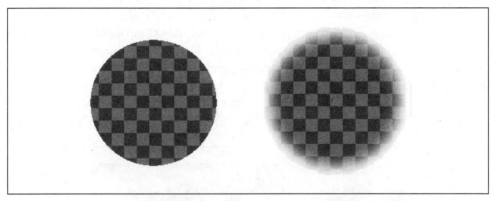

Figure 1-2. A GIF with a single transparent color (left) versus a PNG with a full alpha channel (right)

In a PNG with a color table, alpha values can be assigned to one or more entries in the table through the use of a tRNS chunk, described in the "Portable Network Graphics (PNG)" section of this chapter.

Compression

For the purposes of high-level web graphics programming, we only need to understand a couple of high-level concepts about data compression. One is the distinction between "lossy" and "lossless" compression formats, and the other has to do with intellectual rights and freedoms.

People generally interpret the term "lossy" compression to mean that there is information lost in the translation from source image to compressed image, and that this information loss results in a degraded image. This is true to a point. However, you could also argue that there is information lost in the process of creating a GIF (a so-called "lossless" storage format) from a 24-bit source image, since the number of colors in the image must first be reduced from millions to 256. A more accurate definition of lossy would be something like "a compression algorithm that loses information about the source image during the compression process, and repeated inflation and compression will result in further degradation of the image."

JPEG is an example of a lossy compression format. PNG and GIF are both examples of lossless compression. A lossless compression algorithm is one that does not discard information about the source image during the compression process. Inflation of the compressed data will exactly restore the source image data.

The distinction between these two methods of compressing image data actually affects the way you do your everyday work. Suppose, for example, you have created a number of images for a web site, which are meant to be served as JPEGs (a lossy format) because they contain nice gradients that would look less-than-spiffy as GIFs (and you haven't explored the possibility of PNG yet). Suppose you created all these images in Photoshop (or even better, the Gimp) and saved them as JPEGs, but neglected to save the original source files. Then suppose that your client wanted the images cropped slightly differently and you had to reopen those JPEGs, edit the images, and re-save them. This would be a very painful way to learn the meaning of the term lossy compression, because the resulting images would most likely be less than presentable, as you can see in Figure 1-3.

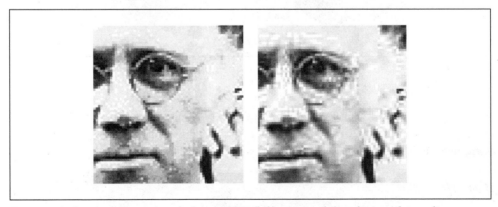

Figure 1-3. Once an image is saved as a JPEG (left), repeated decoding and encoding can result in information loss and poor image quality (right)

Generally a JPEG can be decoded and re-encoded and, as long as the quality setting is the same, you will not get visible degradation of the image.* If you change any part of the image, however, the changed part of the image will lose even more information when it is re-encoded. If an image is cropped or scaled to a different size, the entire image will lose more information.

 A quick aside about saving images: Proper procedure is to keep a copy of the original artwork in a format that retains all of the image's information. If you are using an image manipulation program like Photoshop or the Gimp, you will probably want to save it in the program's native format (PSD and XCF, respectively) to preserve information about layers and channels and whatnot. Or save it as a PNG. PNG is in general a superior file format for multiple-purpose images, as we will see later in this chapter.

The other important bit of information to know about image compression is more of a legal issue than a technical one. "Do I have to pay licensing fees?" is one of the more frequently asked questions about the GIF file format. In a nutshell, GIF is not free and unencumbered software because CompuServe, the creators of GIF, used the LZW (Lempel-Ziv-Welch) *codec* (compression-decompression algorithm) to implement its data compression. The patent for the LZW algorithm† is owned by the Unisys Corporation, which requires a licensing fee for any software that uses the LZW codec. The GIF file format does not allow the storage of uncompressed data, or data compressed by different algorithms, so if you use GIF, you must use LZW. There is some confusion as to exactly what uses are covered by the patent, but Unisys *has* taken the matter to court a number of times. The LZW patent has been called (by Unisys) "one of the most broadly licensed patents in history." I am not a lawyer so I will not attempt to offer an opinion on the matter. However, there has been much discussion of this topic on Usenet by people with a lot of opinions.

Because of this patent and the tendency of the software world toward open standards and open source, an "anti-GIF" movement has been prevalent on the Web for quite some time, though it has been thus far unsuccessful‡ because of the momentum gathered by GIF early on, and the relatively slow adoption of browser support for other graphics formats.

The PNG file format was developed as an alternative to GIF. The compression algorithm used by PNG is actually a version of the Deflate algorithm used by the

---

* Actually, there is a form of lossless JPEG, but it not been implemented in the world of web clients.

† U.S. Patent No. 4,558,302

‡ "Unsuccessful" in the sense that virtually every web page has at least one GIF on it.

pkzip utility. Deflate is, in turn, a subset of the LZ77 class of compression algorithms (yes, that's the same L and Z as in LZW compression). PNG's compression method does not use any algorithms with legal restrictions, however. This is one of its major selling points.

The JPEG file format uses JPEG compression. That may seem like a tautologous statement, but it's not. We'll get to the semantics of JPEGs in a little bit.

Interlacing

All three of the standard web graphics formats support a means for providing the progressive display of an image as it is downloaded over the network. Why further complicate an image file to support progressive display? It offers a big perceptual gain in download speed. The idea is that partial information about an entire image may be shown and the display may be refined as the image downloads, rather than displaying a refined image one row at a time. Progressive display is achieved by *interlacing,* a technique in which pixels are saved in a nonconsecutive order and then drawn in the order they are received from the stream. The result is an image drawn as a grid of pixels that is progressively filled in with more information. Interlacing is implemented differently by different file formats.

It should be noted that interlaced files tend to be slightly larger than non-interlaced files (except for Progressive JPEGs, which tend to be slightly smaller). This is because most compression schemes make certain assumptions about the relationships of adjacent pixels in an image, and the interlacing process can disrupt this "natural" ordering of pixels that work well with compression algorithms. Interlacing can more than make up the slight difference in file size with a perceptual download speed up, however.

GIF interlacing

The image data for a GIF file is stored by the row (or *scanline*), with one byte representing each pixel. A non-interlaced GIF will simply store each scanline consecutively in the image data field of the GIF file. An interlaced GIF will still group pixels into scanlines, but the scanlines will be stored in a different order. When the GIF file is encoded, the rows will be read and saved in four passes; the even-numbered rows (using a 0-based counting system) will be saved in the first four passes, and the odd-numbered rows will be saved in the final pass. The interlacing algorithm is, in words:

> **Pass One**: Save Row 0, then save every 8th row thereafter (0, 8, 16...).
> **Pass Two**: Save Row 4, then save every 8th row thereafter (4, 12, 20...).
> **Pass Three**: Save Row 2, then save every 4th row thereafter (2, 6, 10, 14, 18...).
> **Pass Four**: Save every odd row.

Graphically, with each pixel coordinate labeled with the pass on which it is saved and rendered, GIF interlacing would look like this:

```
1 1 1 1 1 1 1 1
4 4 4 4 4 4 4 4
3 3 3 3 3 3 3 3
4 4 4 4 4 4 4 4
2 2 2 2 2 2 2 2
4 4 4 4 4 4 4 4
3 3 3 3 3 3 3 3
4 4 4 4 4 4 4 4
```

When the image is later reconstituted, the display client (the web browser) will usually temporarily fill in the intervening rows of pixels with the values of the nearest previously decoded rows, as you can see by looking at the progressive stages in an interlaced GIF display shown in Figure 1-4. The interlacing approach taken by the GIF format displays after one pass a version with one-eighth vertical resolution of the entire image, one-quarter resolution after two passes, one-half resolution after three, and the complete image after the fourth. In many cases the user can interpret the image after only the first or second pass.

Figure 1-4. Interlacing provides a perceptual increase in download speeds by presenting a distribution of pixels as the image comes across the network

PNG interlacing

PNG uses a slightly different interlacing scheme than GIF. While GIF completes the interlacing in four passes, where the first three passes count even scan lines, PNG uses a seven-pass scheme called Adam7 (named after its creator, Adam M. Costello), where the first six passes contribute to the even rows of pixels, and the seventh fills in the odd rows. Because PNG files do not necessarily have to store pixels in a contiguous scanline, each pass contains only certain pixels from certain scanlines. In words, the interlacing algorithm (which reads like a Fluxus poem or a word problem from a Mensa test in spatial visualization) is:

Pass One: Save every 8th pixel (starting with Pixel 0) on every 8th row (starting with Row 0).

Pass Two: Save every 8th pixel (starting with Pixel 4) on every 8th row (starting with Row 0).

Pass Three: Save every 4th pixel (starting with Pixel 0) on every 8th row (starting with Row 4).

Pass Four: Save every 4th pixel (starting with Pixel 2) on every 4th row (starting with Row 0).

Pass Five: Save every even pixel on every 4th row (starting with Row 2).

Pass Six: Save every odd pixel on every even row.

Pass Seven: Save every pixel on every odd row.

Graphically, this looks like the grid below, where each pixel in an 8×8 block is labeled with the pass on which it appears on the screen:

```
1 6 4 6 2 6 4 6
7 7 7 7 7 7 7 7
5 6 5 6 5 6 5 6
7 7 7 7 7 7 7 7
3 6 4 6 3 6 4 6
7 7 7 7 7 7 7 7
5 6 5 6 5 6 5 6
7 7 7 7 7 7 7 7
```

This scheme leads to a perceptual speed increase over the scanline interlacing used by GIF. After the first pass, only 1/64th of the image has been downloaded, but the entire image can be drawn with 8×8 pixel resolution blocks. After the second pass, 1/32nd of the file has been transferred, and the image can be drawn at a 4×8 pixel block resolution. Small text in an image is readable after PNG's 5th pass (25% of the file downloaded) which compares favorably with GIF's interlacing gains, where small text is typically readable after the 3rd pass (50% of the file downloaded).

JPEG interlacing: Progressive JPEGs

JPEG files may also be formatted for progressive display support. Progressive JPEG is considered an extension to the JPEG standard and progressive display is not fully implemented by all web clients.

The scanline interlacing techniques used by GIF and PNG are not applicable to JPEG files because JPEGs are a more abstract way of storing an image than a simple stream of pixels. (It is more accurate to call a JPEG file a collection of Discrete Cosine Transform coefficients that describe a pixel stream, but more on that later.) Essentially, a Progressive JPEG that is displayed as it is transferred over the network would first show the entire image as if it had been saved at a very low quality setting. On successive passes the image would gradually resolve into the complete image, at the quality level at which it was saved.

Progressive JPEGs are not yet the most efficient means of progressive display, as the entire image must be decoded with each subsequent pass; however, the JPEG format offers such substantial compression that progressive display is not as important as for other file formats.

GIF, PNG, JPEG: Which to Use When?

For quite a while, the only file formats that could be used on the Web for general-purpose images were GIFs and JPEGs. Each format has applications at which it excels and applications at which it, in the popular parlance, sucks. The adoption of PNG as a standard format has made the question of what to use when a bit fuzzier. In general, PNG is intended as a replacement for GIF, but there are some applications for which PNG can be used effectively instead of JPEG, and there are still applications where GIF must be used. To start with, we should summarize some of the details discussed in the previous section. Table 1-1 provides an overview of the formats.

Table 1-1. File Format Comparison

Category	GIF	PNG	JPEG
Truecolor support	No	Yes	Yes
Color table support	Yes	Yes	No
Maximum size of color table	256	256	--
Maximum color depth	8-bit indexed	8-bit indexed 16-bit grayscale 48-bit RGB +16 bits w/alpha	12-bit grayscale 36-bit "RGB" 32-bit CMYK
Transparency support	Yes	Yes	No
Alpha channel	No	Yes	No
Max alpha channel depth	--	16 bit	--

Table 1-1. File Format Comparison (continued)

Category	GIF	PNG	JPEG
Maximum image size (pixels)	64K×64K	2Gig×2Gig	64K×64K
Multiple images per file	Yes	No	No
Byte ordering	Little-endian	Big-endian	Big-endian
Compression	LZW	Deflate	JPEG
Compression ratio	3:1 to 5:1	4:1 to 10:1	5:1 to 100:1
Compression method	Lossless	Lossless	Lossy
Progressive display	Yes	Yes	Yes
Interlacing style	Scan line	Adam7	PJPEG

What follows is a kind of "consumer reports" for web graphics formats, suggesting appropriate formats for various applications. All of the comparative images started from the same RGB source image. They were all created with the Gimp (GNU Image Manipulation Program, which is described in Chapter 7, *Web Graphics with the Gimp*) and saved with the default settings for each format. The default quality rating for JPEGs is .75 and the default compression setting for PNG is 9.0.

Circular or irregularly shaped images

Only the GIF and PNG formats support transparency, which is required to create irregularly shaped images. If you use PNG, be aware that full alpha support is not included in most browsers. Figure 1-5 shows a circular image saved in the three formats.

Figure 1-5. GIF (left) and PNG (center) support transparency, while JPEG (right) does not. In this example, the GIF version compresses to 7K, less than half the size of PNG's 15.8K.

Photographs

In general, photographs should be saved as JPEGs, which will allow a greater compression ratio and maximum image quality. Photographs in PNG are much larger. If the photograph is irregularly shaped or requires transparency, you may have to compromise with GIF, which will reduce the quality but still achieve a file size that is easily transferable (see Figure 1-6).

Figure 1-6. Three reduced versions of a 5x3 photograph. The GIF version (left) weighs in at 74.9K, and with dithering it represents the image pretty faithfully. The PNG (center) is 187.1K, and the JPEG (right) is a mere 17K.

Images with text

GIF or PNG should be used for images with text. If the image is a graphical menu and is larger than a few kilobytes, save it as an interlaced PNG, which will allow the user to read the menu after only a quarter of the file has downloaded. JPEG encoding does not deal with sharp edges very well and will introduce artifacts that will mar the appearance of the text (see Figure 1-7).

Figure 1-7. GIF (left) and PNG (center) both handle the sharp edges of text well, while JPEG (right) introduces artifacts and takes twice as many bytes

Grayscale images

Grayscale images with 256 or fewer levels should be saved as GIFs or PNGs. Even grayscales with more than 256 levels do not necessarily need to be converted to JPEGs; for most applications, 256 levels of gray is sufficient, and the GIF or PNG will give you lossless compression that is not too different than JPEG's grayscale compression (see Figure 1-8).

Figure 1-8. At 10.1K, the GIF (left) is roughly the same quality as the PNG (center), which is much smaller at 4.3K. The 9.5K JPEG (right) shows artifacts missing from the other images.

Line drawings

For line drawings with 256 colors or less, GIF or PNG should be used. For line drawings with more than 256 colors, PNG should be used. JPEGs are not designed to handle line drawings (see Figure 1-9).

Figure 1-9. Line drawings compress down to a small 3.7K in the GIF version (left) and 3.8K for the PNG version (center). The JPEG (right), containing artifacts, is 6.3K.

Animated images

Until MNG files (Multiple-Image Network Graphics, a multi-image–capable version of PNG) becomes widely supported, you'll have to go with GIF89a for animated images, since neither PNG nor JPEG support multiple images within a file. Figure 1-10 shows the frames of a multi-image GIF89a file.

Figure 1-10. So far, animated GIFs are the only widely supported multi-image file format

With that overview of the strengths and weaknesses of the different formats, the next three sections delve into the nitty-gritty of the actual file formats themselves. These sections will be especially instructive if you have never peeked into the "black box" before.

Graphics Interchange Format (GIF)

At the beginning of this chapter, I posed five questions about the GIF file format. Well, before we delve into the inner workings of the GIF format, here are some answers:

- Why isn't a GIF with 129 colors smaller than one with 256 colors?

  This is because the number of entries in the color table is not directly stored within the GIF file; it is actually calculated from the number of bits used to represent each index in the table. The total number of entries in the color table is calculated by raising 2 to the power of the number of bits per entry; thus if the number of bits used per index is 8, there are a maximum of 256 entries in the table (2^8). A 129-color palette requires 8 bits per entry (because $2^7 = 128$), which means that a 256-color palette will be allocated, even if only 129 colors are actually used.

- Can a multi-image GIF have more than one transparent color?

  Yes, each image in a multi-image sequence may have its own local palette, which may contain its own transparent color index. The transparent index for a color table is defined in the *Graphics Control Extension* (described later). According to a strict interpretation of the GIF specification, only one graphic control block is allowed per image, so each image can have its own unique transparent color.

- What is the maximum color depth of a GIF?

  The maximum color depth of a GIF is 256 colors, because each pixel is represented as a single byte, which can be an index to at most $2^8 = 256$ colors.

- How does a decoder program know that a file is a GIF?

  The first 3 bytes of the GIF file are always the hexadecimal string "0x47 0x49 0x46" which is the string "GIF" in ASCII characters. Bytes 4–6 are either the hex string "0x38 0x37 0x61" or "0x38 0x39 0x61," which is either "87a" or "89a" in ASCII, depending on the version of encoding used. Unfortunately, some applications (such as certain web browsers) determine the content of the file solely by the extension used on the filename.

- How can I make the smallest possible multi-image file?

  This is a loaded question, but one way would be to make sure that your image manipulation software is using global palettes when color tables can be shared by more than one image. Each image may have its own local palette, which (for a 256-color palette) can add 768 bytes per palette. That's actually not that much, but every bit counts. Also, the GIF format allows you to provide an offset (and to choose a "disposal" method) for each image in a file; the size of the file may be reduced by removing redundant data (either by creating a bounding box around the changed area and cropping away the rest, or by analyzing the image on a pixel-by-pixel basis and setting unchanged pixels to transparent) and allowing underlying frames to show through. An example is given in Chapter 9, *Moving Pictures: Programming GIF Animation*, and the Gimp (described in Chapter 7) provides an Animation Optimizer that automates this technique.

The GIF file format is pretty easy to decode. The specification is not the best general purpose file format description. For instance, the format of each type of block is inconsistent, which makes it a bit harder to parse. The standard unit for the fields in a GIF file is the byte, though in a couple of cases GIF uses a packed byte structure to store multiple fields within a single byte. Because of these structural decisions GIF does not have much room to grow as a file format. It is, however, a perfectly fine, robust specification as it is. In fact, CompuServe has recognized PNG as the official successor to GIF, so there won't be any more official GIF revisions, at least not from CompuServe.

A GIF file always starts with the three-byte signature "GIF" and ends with the byte (in hex) "3B," which indicates the end of the data stream. There is no built-in error-checking for determining whether the data in the file has been corrupted or not. The signature is part of the *header* block of information.

The Header Block

The header block of the GIF file contains a signature that identifies it as a GIF of version 87a or 89a, and a *Logical Screen Descriptor* block, which contains information about the minimum requirements of the device needed to display the image as intended by the creator. The header also contains information about the global color table included in the file, if any. The header is 13 bytes in length, consisting of the following fields:

Signature (3 bytes)
    Always GIF.

Version (3 bytes)
    Always 87a or 89a.

Screen Width and Screen Height (2 bytes each)
    The minimum screen dimensions required on the display device to properly render the image without scaling to fit the screen. These fields are often set to 0 for general purpose images.

Color Table Information (1 byte)

The next byte describes attributes of the global color table. The eight bits in this byte contain the following fields:

Bits 0–2

The number of bits used for each color table entry minus one; if the color table has 256 entries, each entry would require an 8-bit index, so this field would contain 7 (111 in binary). This number is used to calculate the number of entries in the color table.

Bit 3

This bit is set to 1 if the elements in the table are sorted in order of decreasing occurrence in the image.

Bits 4–6

A number from 0 to 7, indicating the significant bits per sample of each color in the table, minus one.

Bit 7

The Global Color Table flag, which is 1 if the file contains a global color table.

Background Color (1 byte)

A byte that contains an index for the color in the Global Color Table to be used as the border and background colors of the file.

The Global Color Table Block

A GIF file may optionally contain a global color table. If it does, the table will immediately follow the header in the data stream (that is, it will start on byte 14). This color table will contain 2, 4, 8, 16, 32, 64, 128, or 256 entries and will take up from 6 to 768 bytes. Each element of the color table consists of three bytes: one for each of the red, green, and blue components of the color.

Each *Image* block (described later) can also contain its own local color table, which would take precedence over the global color table. If every image block has its own local color table, the file does not need a global color table. If a file does not have a global color table and does not have local color tables, the image will be rendered using the application's default color table, with unpredictable results. Local color tables have the same form as the global color table.

The GIF specification suggests that the first two elements of a color table be black (0) and white (1), but this is not necessarily always the case.

The Image Block(s)

A GIF file can contain an unlimited number of images. Each image is stored in its own block, which consists of two or three parts: the *Local Image Descriptor*, an optional *Local Color Table*, and the compressed *Image Data*.

Local Image Descriptor

The Local Image Descriptor always consists of 10 bytes that contain the dimensions of the image and information on which color table to use and how the image data is stored. The fields of the Local Image Descriptor block are:

Separator (1 byte)

Always the hex value 2C, which identifies this as a Local Image Descriptor block.

Left, Top (2 bytes each)

Each of these is a number in the range 0 to 65,535, which indicate the x, y coordinate within the image frame at which the upper-left corner of the image should be offset when it is displayed. See the bouncing ball example in Chapter 9 to see how these fields may be used effectively to reduce the size of a multi-image GIF.

Width, Height (2 bytes each)

These fields provide the width and height of the image, in pixels.

Color Information (1 byte)

The last byte of the Local Image Descriptor contains 8 bits describing the following fields (starting with the least significant bit):

Bit 0

This bit is set to 1 if the Image Block contains a Local Color Table that should be used when rendering the image.

Bit 1

This bit is set to 1 if the image data is stored in an interlaced format.

Bit 2

This bit is set to 1 if the local color table is sorted in order of decreasing occurrence.

Bits 3–4

These bits are reserved for use by future versions of GIF.

Bits 5–7

The number of bits used for each entry in the Local Color Table.

Local Color Table

The Local Color Table is in the same form as the Global Color Table—i.e., between 2 and 256 entries of one-byte triplets for each RGB value. If bit 0 of the Local Image Descriptor is set to 0, there is not a local color table, and the Image Data will immediately follow the Descriptor block.

Image Data

The Image Data for each image is always stored in the LZW compressed format. It is not stored as a continuous stream of LZW encoded data, but rather as an arbitrary number of shorter sub-blocks from 1 to 255 bytes in length. These sub-blocks each start with a count byte that is the number of bytes in the sub-block, which is followed by the encoded data. Each of the sub-blocks must be sent to the LZW decoder individually before they are assembled to form the decoded image data. A count byte of 0 indicates the end of the image data block.

Once the sub-blocks have been read and decoded, we must know whether the pixels of the resulting block of image data are stored in an interlaced or noninterlaced form. Each pixel value is stored as a single byte in the decoded data block, regardless of the size of the color table. If the data is stored in a non-interlaced form, it may be read in linearly, with each scanline read consecutively after the previous. If the data is interlaced, it must be read according to the interlacing algorithm described earlier in the chapter.

The Extension Block(s)

The GIF89a specification adds four extension blocks to the original GIF87a format. Two of these extension blocks are used to implement common features of web graphics such as transparency and animated loops. The four extension blocks are the *Graphics Control, Application, Comment,* and *Plain Text Extensions.* Of these we will cover the Graphics Control Extension and the Application Extension, which are used in web graphics. The Plain Text Extension is not used in web graphics applications. The Comment Extension is often used to store copyright information for the image, but it is generally ignored by web clients.

An extension block may appear anywhere in a GIF file between the Global Color Table (if there is one) and the trailer. All extensions begin with an identifier byte which is always 0x21 to identify the block as an extension block. This is followed by an extension type byte, which indicates the type of extension. The codes for the Graphics Control and Application extensions are 0xF9 and 0xFF, respectively.

The Graphics Control Extension

The Graphics Control Extension contains information that can tell an application how to deal with transparency in the image and how to dispose of images when displaying a multi-image GIF. It is 8 bytes long and contains seven fields:

Introducer (1 byte)
> This byte is always 0x21, indicating an extension block.

Extension Label (1 byte)
> this byte is always 0xF9, indicating a Graphics Control Extension.

Block Size (1 byte)
> This is always 0x04, because there are four more bytes of information before the extension block terminator.

Control Information (1 byte)
> This packed byte consists of the following three fields:

> *Bit 0*
>> Transparent color flag. This is 1 if the images referred to by this block are to contain a transparent color.

> *Bit 1*
>> User Input Enabled. This flag is not implemented by web browsers.

> *Bits 2–4*
>> Disposal method. This is a number from 0–4 that indicates the way the application should display the next image in a multi-image file:
>>
>> 0   Not specified
>>
>> 1   Do not dispose between frames
>>
>> 2   Overwrite frame with background color from header
>>
>> 3   Overwrite with previous frame

> *Bits 5–7*
>> Reserved.

Delay Time (2 bytes)
> This field contains the number of hundreths of a second the display client should wait before displaying the next image in a multi-image sequence. This allows very fine control of the delay time, which can be from 0 to 655.35 seconds.

Transparent Color Index (1 byte)
> If the transparency bit is set, the color with this index should be made transparent when the image is rendered (i.e., it should not be drawn). This index applies to the current color table. It will continue to be the transparent index

for every image until another Graphics Control Extension turns transparency off or changes the index.

Extension Terminator (1 byte)
This is always 0.

The Application Extension

The Application Extension Block allows GIF files to be customized for particular applications. Netscape took advantage of this feature to supplement the graphics control block with an application extension block that would tell a web browser how many times to display a sequence of images in an animated GIF before stopping. This became known as the *Netscape Looping Extension,* and it may as well be part of the GIF specification (though it isn't). This is ironic because the GIF specification specifically notes that GIF was not intended as a platform for the delivery of animations, yet Netscape's modification made GIF the *de facto* animation standard on the Web.

A Netscape looping extension follows the format of a generic application extension and looks like this:

Introducer (1 byte)
This byte is always 0x21, indicating an extension block.

Extension Label (1 byte)
This byte is always 0xFF, indicating an Application Extension.

Block Size (1 byte)
This is always 0x0B, because there are eleven more fields of information before the extension block terminator.

Identifier (8 bytes)
This is a human-readable 8-character string. For the Netscape looping extension, this field is always "NETSCAPE."

Application Authentication Code (3 bytes)
This field contains a 3-byte code that may be used to uniquely identify the application that created the file. In this case, the field will be "2.0."

Application Data (4 bytes)
In general, an application data field can contain a variable number of sub-blocks, the first of which is the number of bytes of sub-blocks remaining in the Data field. For a looping extension this number is always 3, of which only the second two are used to represent the number of times the animation should loop. Because it is 2 bytes (16 bits) long the possible range of values is 0 to 65,535. A value of 0 indicates that the animation should loop forever. Absence of a looping extension is generally interpreted as a value of 1.

Extension Terminator (1 byte)
This is always 0.

Portable Network Graphics (PNG)

In the "GNU's Not Unix" tradition of recursive acronyms, PNG may unofficially be taken to stand for "PNG's Not GIF." PNG was designed as an open standard alternative to GIF, and it plays that role very well. PNG will not completely replace GIF, however, if only because PNG can only store one image per file* and there are a million web pages out there that are full of GIF images.

A PNG file is assembled as a series of chunks which, for all intents and purposes, are the equivalent of GIF's blocks. PNG just has a friendlier name for the structure. The 1.0 PNG specification defines a number of standard chunks, of which four are considered "critical chunks." At least three of the critical chunks must be present in every valid PNG format file. The non-critical standard chunks are sometimes called "ancillary chunks." The critical and ancillary chunks, along with a short description of each, are listed in Tables 1-2 and 1-3. Critical chunk codes begin with a capital letter; ancillary chunks begin with a lowercase letter.

Table 1-2. Critical Chunks

Name	Description	Code
Header chunk	Global information about the image	IHDR
Palette chunk	A palette (optional)	PLTE
Image Data chunk	The compressed image data	IDAT
Image End chunk	The end-of-file marker	IEND

Table 1-3. Ancillary Chunks

Name	Description	Code
Background Color chunk	Defines a background color index in palette or a background shade for a grayscale or RGB image.	bKGD
Primary Chromacities chunk	Stores information that accounts for color differences on different output devices to allow for color correction.	cHRM
Gamma chunk	Stores information about the gamma value of the image relative to its creation environment.	gAMA
Image Histogram chunk	Stores data on the frequency of occurrence of each color in the palette.	hIST
Physical Pixel chunk	Indicates the resolution at which the image should be displayed.	pHYs
Significant Bits chunk	Stores the bit depth of the original source image.	sBIT
Text Data chunk	Stores text in the Latin-1 character set.	tEXt

---

* A PNG variant capable of storing multiple images is in the works. More information about the Multiple-image Network Graphics (MNG) format may be found on the MNG home page at *http://www.cdrom.com/pub/mng/*.

Table 1-3. Ancillary Chunks (continued)

Name	Description	Code
Time Modified chunk	Stores the time that the image was last changed.	tIME
Transparency chunk	For indexed color images, this chunk stores 1–255 alpha values. For RGB/grayscale images, it can describe a shade or color to be made transparent.	tRNS
Compressed Text chunk	Stores compressed text.	zTXt

For the purpose of getting a grasp of the PNG format, we will only describe the format of the four critical chunks in this section. See Appendix A for an example of a simple PNG decoder written in Perl.

At the very beginning of each valid PNG file is an 8-byte signature that identifies it as PNG-formatted. This signature is not considered a part of any particular chunk. The signature is 8 bytes long, of which the first byte is always the hexadecimal value 0x89 and the remaining 7 bytes are:

```
PNG\r\n^Z\n
```

This signature communicates more information than the signatures of other file formats. Each byte provides an added layer of information about the format and integrity of the data that follows.

Byte 0: 0x89

The first byte of the file indicates that the file is in binary form (a text file would only contain ASCII characters in the range 0x00 to 0x7F). It also allows the decoder to detect data corruption if the file had been transferred in text mode, in which case the eighth bit would be stripped from each byte and the first byte would be 0x09 instead of 0x89.

Bytes 1–3: PNG

A human-readable (as opposed to machine-readable) ASCII display of the file format.

Bytes 4–5: \r\n

Transfers between different operating systems can sometimes cause problems with newlines and carriage returns. Converting a file from Unix to Win32 can add a \r to a lone \n, conversion from a Win32 system to Unix may strip the \r, and conversion to MacOS may convert \n to \r.

Byte 6: ^Z

If the file is displayed on the Win32 command line with the TYPE command, the ^Z code will halt the listing of the file.

Byte 7: \n

> Some file transfer modes on some systems have problems with carriage returns and newlines.

Unlike GIF, every PNG chunk is laid out in a standard form. A consistent chunk format makes it easy to parse PNG files and allows room for future expansion of the file format. Each chunk in a PNG data stream starts with an 8-byte chunk header and ends with a 4-byte trailer. This chunk header consists of two 32-bit fields, the first of which is the length (in bytes) of the data in the chunk (not including the header or the trailer), and the second is a 4-byte code that identifies the type of the chunk. The codes for the standard chunks are all readable ASCII characters. The standard chunk codes that would be found in this field are listed in Table 1-2.

The header is followed by the chunk data fields, which vary for each type of chunk. The data fields for each critical chunk are described later in their respective sections.

Each chunk ends with a 4-byte trailer called the CRC field, which refers to Cyclic Redundancy Check method of error checking. This field contains a CRC-32 value, which is computed when the file is created and may be compared to the data in the chunk to determine whether or not the data has been corrupted. A sample CRC algorithm is appended to the PNG specification (referenced at the end of this chapter).

The header chunk

The header chunk (IHDR) describes the overall attributes of the PNG image. It is 13 bytes long (not including the 8-byte chunk header and 4-byte CRC trailer) and consists of seven fields:

Width, Height (4 bytes each)

> The dimensions of the image. Four bytes are used to represent each dimension, but only 31 bits are used because some languages have trouble with unsigned 4-byte values. Thus the maximum size of a PNG image is approximately 2 Gigapixels $\times$ 2 Gigapixels, which at a standard screen resolution of 72 pixels per inch could store an image approximately 470 miles $\times$ 470 miles. This would allow you to save a 1:1 life size image of most of New England in a single PNG file! By comparison, a GIF file has a maximum size of 75 feet $\times$ 75 feet, which would let you store a 1:1 image of a large house. Of course, your ISP would hate you if you put either of these images on your web page.

Bit Depth (1 byte)

> This field contains the number of bits used for each index in the palette chunk or for each sample in a grayscale, RGB, gray+alpha, or RGBA image. Each

index in an indexed color image can be represented with a bit depth of 1, 2, 4, or 8. A grayscale image can have a maximum bit depth of 16.

Color Type

This field is a code that indicates the method that the image uses to represent colors. Valid values are:

0   Each pixel is a grayscale value

2   Each pixel is an RGB triplet

3   Each pixel is an index to a color table

4   Each pixel is a grayscale value followed by an alpha mask

6   Each pixel is an RGB triplet followed by an alpha mask

Compression Type (1 byte)

This field contains a code that indicates the type of compression used to encode the image data. As of Version 1.0, PNG only supports the Deflate method, so this field should be 0.

Filtering Type (1 byte)

The filter byte contains a code indicating the type of filtering that was applied to the data before it was compressed. At this time the only type of filtering supported is an adaptive filtering method described in the PNG spec, so this field should be 0.

Interlace Scheme (1 byte)

This field contains a code that indicates the type of interlacing scheme in which the data is stored. Currently the defined values are 0 (none) and 1 (two-dimensional Adam7 interlacing, described earlier in the chapter).

The palette chunk

The palette chunk (PLTE) contains a suggested color table to be used when rendering image data. It is required for PNG files that are saved as indexed color images (i.e., if the Color Type field of the header chunk is set to 3). Truecolor images do not need a palette chunk, although they may include one for use on those systems that are incapable of displaying more than 256 colors.

The data section of the palette chunk consists of a list of red, green, and blue values (one byte per color) for each entry in the table. The table may contain between 1 and 256 entries, similar to the GIF color table. Note that while GIF can only use palettes whose size is a multiple of 2, PNG will store palettes in an optimal amount of space (that is, a 129 color palette would take up 768 [256x3] bytes in a GIF, whereas it would only take up 387 [129x3] bytes in a PNG).

The Image Data chunk

The Image Data chunk (IDAT) holds the compressed data for each of the pixels in the image. Multiple Image Data chunks may be stored within the same PNG file. Because each PNG file describes only one image, multiple IDAT chunks are combined into a single image when decoded and displayed. The IDAT chunk contains the compressed data, in addition to the 8-byte chunk header and 4-byte CRC trailer.

Before displaying the data, it must be decompressed and decoded. The information in the header chunk is used to determine the number of bytes used to represent each pixel and the pixel ordering, which will vary depending on whether or not the data is interlaced.

Ancillary chunks

There are a number of ancillary chunks defined by the PNG 1.0 specification that allow you to encode a great deal of information in the image file. For example, the Gamma chunk (gAMA) contains a value representing the gamma characteristics of the device on which the image was created. This value could be used by a rendering client to adjust the gamma level to suit the display of the client, if it is being displayed on a platform with different gamma characteristics.

Most of the ancillary chunks have not been widely implemented by web browsers, although certain features have been added. Web browsers still have to make a lot of memory-versus-speed compromises, so support for such features as 16-bit alpha masks is still a goal for the future.

The PNG specification also suggests that ancillary chunks with an unrecognized type code should not cause an error for the decoder. This allows the definition of custom chunk types that can be tailored to specific applications, similar to GIF's Application Extension Block.

JPEG

JPEG stands for Joint Photographic Experts Group, which is the name of the committee set up by the International Standards Committee that originally wrote the image format standard. The JPEG committee has the responsibility of determining the future of the JPEG format, but the actual JPEG software that makes up the toolkit used in most web applications is maintained by the Independent JPEG Group (*http://www.ijg.org*).

The JPEG standard actually only defines an encoding scheme for data streams and not a specific file format. JPEG encoding is used in many different file formats (TIFF v.6.0 and Macintosh PICT are two prominent examples), but the format used on the Web is called JFIF, an acronym that stands for JPEG File Interchange Format,* which was developed by C-Cube Microsystems (*http://www.c-cube.com*) and placed in the public domain. JFIF became the *de facto* standard for web JPEGs because of its simplicity. When people talk about a JPEG web graphic, they are actually referring to a JPEG-encoded data stream stored in the JFIF file format. In this book we will refer to JFIFs as JPEGs to reduce confusion, or to further propagate it, depending on your point of view.

To create a JPEG you must start with a high-quality image sampled with a large bit depth, from 16 to 24 bits, for the best results. You should generally only use JPEG encoding on scanned photographs or continuous-tone images (see the section "GIF, PNG, JPEG: Which to Use When?" earlier in this chapter).

JPEG encoding takes advantage of the fuzzy way the human eye interprets light and colors in images by throwing out certain information that is not perceived by the viewer. This process creates a much smaller image that is perceptually faithful to the original. The degree of information loss may be adjusted so that the size of an encoded file may be altered at the expense of image quality. The quality of the resulting image is expressed in terms of a *Q factor,* which may be set when the image is encoded. Most applications use an arbitrary scale of 1 to 100, where the lower numbers indicate small, lower-quality files and the higher numbers indicate larger, higher-quality files. Note that a Q value of 100 does not mean that the encoding is completely lossless (although you really won't lose much). Also, the 1 to 100 scale is by no means standardized (the Gimp uses a 0 to 1.0 scale), but this is the scale used by the IJG software, so it is what we will use here. There are a few guidelines for choosing an optimal Q factor:

- The default value of 75 is appropriate for most purposes; a value as low as 50 is acceptable for web applications. This is a good starting point anyway, yielding a compression ratio of 10:1 or 20:1.

- The Q factor should never be set above 95. Values higher than 95 cannot be distinguished from 95. In practice, you may find images with Q factors of 75 or above nearly indistinguishable from each other in quality.

- Very-low-resolution thumbnails can have a Q value as low as 5 or 10.

- Most Progressive JPEG encoders expect a Q value in the range of 50–75. Values outside this range will not get the most out of the Progressive JPEG scheme.

A rule of thumb for estimating the effectiveness of JPEG compression is that it will save an image at 1 to 2 bits per pixel. It does this by running the data through an elaborate decoding process.

---

* PNG has a *recursive* acronym, JFIF has a *nested* acronym.

The JPEG Encoding Process

To encode a 24-bit image as a JPEG, the image goes through a four-step assembly line. Decoding the image essentially reverses the process, though rounding errors and certain assumptions made in the encoding process make JPEG a lossy form of compression. Lossy compression is when the decompression process cannot reproduce the original data exactly bit for bit. The four steps of the encoding process are:

1. Apply color space transform and downsample

2. Apply Discrete Cosine Transform (DCT) to blocks of data

3. Quantize

4. Apply Huffman encoding

Step 1. Color space transform and downsampling

The first step in the encoding process accounts for about 50% of the space savings of JPEG encoding (for color images, anyway; grayscale images pass immediately to step 2 and are thus inherently less susceptible to JPEG compression). Taking advantage of the fact that the human eye responds more to changes in levels of brightness than to changes in particular colors in adjacent pixels, this step first changes the color space of the image from RGB to (usually) YC_bC_r. The YC_bC_r color space represents an image as three components of brightness or luminance (Y) and chrominance (C_b for blue chrominance and C_r for red chrominance). Of these components, luminance is the most important, so the two chrominance components are downsampled to reduce the amount of information we need to store. Downsampling means that only one chrominance value pair is stored for each 2×2 block of pixels, rather than four pairs. This is where the 50% savings comes into play:

- A 2×2 block of R, G, B = 4 + 4 + 4 = 12 bytes

- A 2×2 block of downsampled Y, C_b, C_r = 4 + 1 + 1 = 6 bytes

From this point on, each component may be thought of as an individual channel that is encoded separately.

Step 2. Discrete Cosine Transforms

The second bit of physiological trivia taken into account by JPEG is that the eye is more sensitive to gradual changes in brightness than to sudden changes. Because of this, we can achieve another factor of compression with minimal change in the perceived image by throwing out information about the higher frequencies in the image. To separate low- and high-frequency information, we apply a *Discrete*

Cosine Transform (DCT) to 8×8 blocks of the image data. The DCT is a big intimidating formula (it's actually not that difficult to understand if you have some higher-level math skills), which we won't print here because it would scare off potential readers just thumbing through the book looking for an access counter script.* Seriously though, all you need to know about the DCT is that it gets the data into a form that makes it easy for the next step in the process to discard unnecessary information, and that it is the most time-intensive part of the encoding/decoding process.

At this point, it is not really accurate to think of the image as being stored as discrete pixels any more than you would think of a real photograph as being comprised of pixels. It is more accurate to think of the image as a table of values that refer to an abstract mathematical model that describes the image.

Step 3. Quantization

In the third step, the DCT value for each 8×8 block is divided by a *quantization coefficient*, which is stored in a table along with the image to be used in the decoding process. This quantization table is generally taken from an existing table (the JPEG specification defines a sample table) which is modified by the Q value (described earlier) that determines the quality of the resulting image. Files saved with a higher Q rating will have their DCT coefficients divided by smaller numbers, which will enable the image to be decoded more accurately, but will result in a larger file size. Files with lower Q values will have coefficients divided by larger numbers and will be smaller, but the decoding process will be less exact. This step is where most of the information loss occurs.

Step 4. Huffman Encoding

The resulting stream of divided coefficients is encoded using Huffman run-length encoding, which is well-suited to the typical data resulting from step 3 and provides an added compression factor.

A working JPEG decoder is more complicated than a GIF or a PNG decoder and would take up too much space in this chapter. There is, in fact a whole book on the topic (see "References" below). The IJG's free JPEG library described in Chapter 3, *A Litany of Libraries*, includes several utilities written in C for decoding JPEG files.

---

* Which, incidentally, may be found in Chapter 10, *Web Graphics Cookbook*.

References

The Encyclopedia of Graphics File Formats, 2nd Edition (an excellent tome covering more than 100 file formats, including GIF, PNG and JPEG):

> Murray, James D., and William vanRyper, O'Reilly & Associates, 1996

License Information on GIF and Other LZW-based Technologies:

> *http://corp2.unisys.com/LeadStory/lzwfaq.html*

The PNG Specification:

> *ftp://ftp.uu.net/graphics/png/documents/png-1.0-w3c-single.html.gz*

An explanation of compositing partially transparent pixels from the PNG specification:

> *ftp://ftp.uu.net:/graphics/png/documents/png-1.0-w3c-single.html.gz#D.Alpha-channel-processing*

The Deflate algorithm that PNG uses as its compression method:

> *ftp://ds.internic.net/rfc/rfc1951.txt*

Some information on the CRC algorithm (ISO 3309):

> *http://bbs-koi.uniinc.msk.ru/tech1/1994/er_cont/crc.htm*

MNG home page:

> *http://www.cdrom.com/pub/mng/*

JPEG home page:

> *http://www.jpeg.org/*

JPEG FAQ:

> *http://www.faqs.org/faqs/jpeg-faq/*

JPEG:Still Image Data Compression Standard (a book containing the complete ISO JPEG standards):

> Pennebaker, William B., and Joan L. Mitchell, Van Nostrand Reinhold, New York, 1993.

The comp.compression FAQ:

> *http://www.faqs.org/faqs/compression-faq/*

Greg Roelofs' PNG Page with current comparisons of PNG support by different browsers:

> *http://www.cdrom.com/pub/png/*

The description of the Image Library for the Mozilla web browser (an instructive look at how an actual "real world" web browser deals with file formats, with some discussion about the tradeoffs in features versus performance):

> *http://www.mozilla.org/docs/tplist/catCode/imagdesc.htm*

PNG: The Definitive Guide (due out in May 1999):

> Roelofs, Greg, O'Reilly & Associates, 1999.

2

Serving Graphics on the Web

When creating graphics, one should keep in mind that not all web browsers handle all "standard" HTML features in the same way. Specifically, browsers have been known to have their own idiosyncratic interpretations of the ALT attribute, client-side image maps, the USEMAP attribute, GIF89a animation, image spacing attributes, transparency, inline PNG/XBM/Progressive JPEG images, the LOWSRC attribute, borders on image links, alignment tags, and scaling tags.

In short, just about every feature that should have a standard implementation has, at one time or another, had different levels of compliance to the standard on different browsers. As of this writing, the most popular browsers implement the HTML 3.2 standards such that they can be trusted with your exquisitely crafted HTML code. However, be sure to do a little research before making your knockout web page depend on some new or proprietary feature. You may be writing off a significant portion of your potential audience who can't see it.

The same could be said for external image-viewing plug-ins. Now that we are several years into the Web Revolution, users are spending more time using the Web to get exactly the information they want and less time "surfing" the waves of information overload. Developers are also realizing the ramifications of the time and costs associated with keeping a web site going until Doomsday. If you are thinking about adding critical images (or even non-critical information, like goofy animated buttons) that require the use of a third-party extensions or external plug-ins, think about it very carefully. Assuming that your web site will be around for a while, where will this technology be in five years? Ten years? It's a pretty good bet that currently adopted standards (PNG, JPEG, even GIF) will be supported well into the future. In general, don't make your users download and install plug-ins to get to your content. Keep in mind that most people on the Web use their browsers for just that: browsing.

That said, there are a few applications that force the use of plug-ins. If you wish to participate in the web audio or streaming media scenes, you're going to have to choose one of the many competitive proprietary solutions that have yet to be universally adopted. The real purview of plug-ins and extensions is in the design of Intranets, where you, the developer, have dictatorial control over what is installed on everyone's desktop. If you have 20,000 images in RAD format that have to be seen on your corporate Intranet, by all means, require your users to use a RAD plug-in! (However, you could also write a script using Image::Magick to batch convert them to PNG files, which could also be used on your public web site, but we'll talk about that in Chapter 5, *Industrial-Strength Graphics Scripting with PerlMagick*.)

If you are interested in finding out more about the capabilities of the various browsers out there, look at *http://www.browsercaps.com*, which shows how a range of browsers responded to a battery of standardized tests, and *http:// browsers.com*, which has news, gossip, and ftp links for a bunch of browsers.

You can actually retrieve a good deal of information about the client looking at your web page directly from the client. Information that may be relevant to web graphics applications include the browser version (accessible through the HTTP_ USER_AGENT environment variable), or the MIME (Multipurpose Internet Mail Extension) types that the client will accept. Certain web servers (Apache, for instance) offer options for modifying the image request negotiation process to accommodate different browser capabilities, so that, for example, browsers that can't see PNG files will automatically be sent a GIF version instead. Consult the documentation on your web server for these features.

The Server and CGI

Generally, when people talk about a "web server," they are referring to two things: a program that accepts a request for resources (i.e., HTML pages, images, applets, DOM objects, etc.) and returns resources, and a collection of resources to return (and, I guess, a computer where they both live, if you want to get technical). When we talk about a web server, we will be referring to the program that does the serving; we assume that there is also a corresponding collection of web pages and images to be served.

The requests made to and responses returned by the web server must be in a standard form that is described by the Hypertext Transfer Protocol (HTTP). Web servers are an inherently simple concept and may be very simple programs or very complicated affairs. The popular Apache web server (*http://www.apache.org*) falls somewhere in between. Apache takes a modular design approach; it has a very fast, simple core set of operations that may be extended with other modules.

Whichever web server you are running, its primary function is the basic capability of handling requests and returning resources.

When a web browser requests an image from a server, the request is in the form of a URL, just like any other HTTP request. This URL points to a file that resides on the same computer as the web server, in its collection of resources. Generally the web server points to a specific root directory which it will use to determine the location of the requested image. For example, the URL *http://www.shemp.net/splashscreen.png* would point at a file in the Portable Network Graphics (PNG) format located in the web server's root directory. If this URL is requested by a client (and it exists), the web server determines a MIME type for the file and sends back an HTTP header to the client. The web server then reads the data in the file pointed to by the URL and immediately follows the header with a stream of data from the file.

Certain MIME types are said to be registered, i.e., clients implementing the HTTP protocol should at least recognize them as valid MIME types. Some of the registered MIME types of interest are:

`text/html`   for HTML documents

`image/jpeg` for JPEG image files

`image/gif`   for GIF image files

`image/png` for PNG image files

The HTTP header consists of the case-insensitive string "Content-type:" followed by one of the content types listed above, followed by two "Internet standard"* newlines (a carriage return followed by a line feed):

```
Content-type: image/gif

(...image data...)
```

An image may be generated dynamically by a program or script run on the server; most of this book is about dynamically generating images from scripts written in Perl. All a script has to do is generate an appropriate HTTP header, then generate valid image data. When a web client makes a request for a dynamically generated image, the web server simply runs the script specified by the URL (if it is a valid script and if the web server has been properly configured to run external scripts), retrieves the output from the script, and passes it back to the client. This interaction looks something like Figure 2-1. These scripts are generally called CGI scripts because they adhere to the Common Gateway Interface, which is simply a

---

* Technically, two "Internet Standard" linefeeds are `\r\n\r\n`, but because of widespread use of two plain newlines (`\n\n`) in HTTP headers produced by CGI scripts, most browsers will accept either form. If you are writing a CGI script, it's best to avoid the issue and use the *header()* method of the CGI or CGI_Lite modules.

standard way for the web server and external scripts to communicate. There is a module for Perl that makes this communication relatively painless.

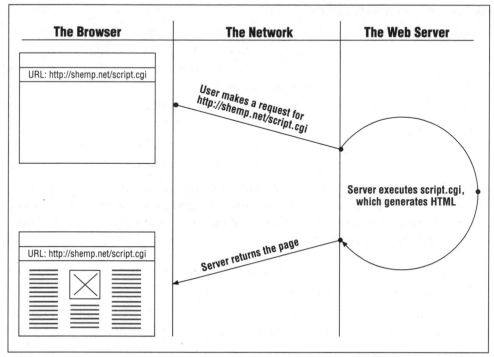

Figure 2-1. A script can return HTML, an image, or any other resource of a web server using the Common Gateway Interface and HTTP

The CGI.pm Module

The CGI.pm Perl module is a collection of object-oriented routines for creating HTML forms and parsing form submissions and writing valid HTTP headers and HTML responses. In other words, it is a tool that helps you take input from and write output to the Common Gateway Interface. Using the CGI module simplifies the process of implementing CGI scripts and will help you avoid common pitfalls and write more readable Perl code. The CGI module is used by several examples in this book to parse queries and print HTTP headers in a standardized way.

CGI.pm was written by Lincoln Stein and is available on CPAN.

The methods of the CGI module are made available to your script with the *use* function, the same as with any other module. The new method will create a new CGI object. Thus, CGI scripts using the CGI module will all have the following somewhere near the beginning of the script:

```
use CGI;
my $query = new CGI;    # create a new CGI object
```

Once you have instantiated a CGI object, you can use it to parse input to your CGI script or to create output destined for the web server.

Parsing CGI input with CGI.pm

Generally, input to a CGI script will come from a user filling out a form, though input doesn't *have* to come from a form. See the chess CGI example in Chapter 4, *On-the-Fly Graphics with GD*, for an instance of an image generation script being called with input parameters directly embedded in an <IMG> tag. In any case, input to a CGI script (generally called a *query string*) will always be encoded in a standard format. A form submission with three input fields, for example, would send a query string in the following format:

```
http://www.shemp.net/script.cgi?field1=data1&field2=data2&field3=data3
```

Rather than writing all new code (with potential bugs or security holes) each time you write a CGI script, you can use the *param* method to access each of the query parameters with an object-oriented–style syntax. To access the value for the field named *field1,* for example:

```
use CGI;
my $query = new CGI;
my $field1value = $query->param('field1');
```

If *field2* were a collection of values returned from a scrolling list in a form, simply assign it to an array and CGI will parse the query and return a list of values:

```
my @field2values = $query->param('field2');
```

To retrieve a list of all of the parameter names from the query, call *param* without an argument:

```
my @params = $query->param();        # returns ('field1', 'field2', 'field3')
```

To provide default values for the parameters that will be overridden if the value is specified by the user's form submission (allowing you to provide default values for fields that the user left empty), supply the default values as a hash when creating the query object:

```
my $query = new CGI( name => 'Anonymous',
                     address => 'No address provided' );
```

You can also get the unparsed query string (URL and all) with the *query_string* method:

```
$qs = $query->query_string();
```

Generating HTTP headers with CGI.pm

The header method provides a simple way of writing HTTP headers so you don't have to worry about the exact format of the header. You can print the header for any sort of MIME type by specifying the **-type** attribute in the call to header. To write an HTTP header for an image file, use one of the following:

```
use CGI;
my $query = new CGI;
print $query->header(-type => 'image/gif');    # for a GIF, or
print $query->header(-type => 'image/png');    # for a PNG, or
print $query->header(-type => 'image/jpeg');   # for a JPEG
```

If the content type is the only parameter being sent to *header()*, you may omit the left side of the hash and just include the content type string.

The header method also allows you to include any field that is defined by the HTTP standard in the header. You can easily include an *expires* field, for example, that will tell the browser when to remove the image from its cache. Usually, the output of CGI scripts are not cached by browsers, but you can control this behavior with:

```
print $query->header(-type => 'image/png',
                     -expires => '1d');        # remove from cache tomorrow
```

The expiration value can indicate seconds, minutes, days, months, years, or a specific date:

5s in five seconds

5m in five minutes

5d in five days

5M in five months

5y in five years

Wednesday, 21-Oct-98 12:00:00 GMT at a very specific time

To make sure that your image is not cached, use a negative value (e.g., **-1s**) or specify now for the **-expires** attribute.

To include a *Refresh* field within an HTTP header, use the **-Refresh** attribute, where the assigned value is the number of seconds the browser should wait before reloading the page:

```
print $query->header(-type => 'image/png',
                     -Refresh => '5s');
```

To redirect the browser to another URL after a certain period of time, you can specify an optional URL within the refresh value:

```
print $query->header(-type => 'image/png',
                     -Refresh => '5s; URL=http://www.shemp.net/image2.png');
```

The CGI module provides many other methods for writing CGI output, such as a clean, object-oriented way of creating the HTML for forms. These methods are

beyond the scope of this introduction; visit the CGI.pm documentation site referenced at the end of this chapter if you wish to explore its other capabilities.

Increasing Server Performance

Dealing with graphics can be a computationally intensive procedure. Generating
graphics for a medium like the Web in a time span short enough that the experience can still be called "interactive" is even more intensive. Luckily, images destined for the Web are generally small and optimized for quick transfer and display
rates. But often this is at the expense of a longer encoding rate (see Chapter 1,
Image File Formats). In addition to the actual RAM and processor resources necessary to generate web graphics, there is the additional overhead of the web server,
and (if you are using Perl as a scripting language) the Perl interpreter itself. And
the load multiplies with the number of simultaneous hits received by your server.

Perhaps I am painting too bleak a picture; most computers used as web servers
today can easily handle a moderate load of requests for image-generating CGI
scripts. For busier web sites, or sites with more intensive graphics serving needs,
there are a few options for enhancing your web server to meet the demand,
described in the following sections.

Limit the number of simultaneous requests

When it comes to web server performance, the most valuable system resource is
RAM. Each request to a web server typically takes up a certain amount of RAM,
which, for a request that also spawns an image generation CGI request, can be
anywhere from 1 MB to 32 MB or more for each request. The amount of physical
RAM on your system determines how many simultaneous requests your server can
take before it has to use whatever disk space has been allocated for virtual (swap)
memory. Once processes start using the swap, performance quickly drops off and
your server becomes quite unresponsive. To head off this problem you should
configure your web server to limit the maximum number of simultaneous requests
to be processed at one time. Additional requests beyond this limit will have to wait
as they are queued up and processed in turn, but that is preferable to an exces-
sive number of requests bogging down the server such that it is completely unresponsive.

Figure out how much RAM is typically used by one web server process for your
specific application, and limit the number of users so that the maximum number of
requests will fit within the amount of physical RAM on your system.

Install mod_perl

If you are writing scripts in Perl and running the popular Apache web server, a
fairly painless way to limit the amount of memory taken up by each process, and

thereby allow your server to process more simultaneous requests, is to install mod_perl on your server. This allows you to write Apache modules directly in Perl. For CGI developers, this means that the Perl interpreter can be "embedded" within the web server, so that multiple HTTP requests can avoid the performance cost of restarting an external instance of the interpreter with each request. Installing mod_perl also allows you to preload commonly used modules that may be shared among multiple web server processes for additional memory savings. Well-behaved CGI programs should run without modification on a mod_perl-enabled web server.

However, mod_perl does not provide any specific mechanisms for optimizing the process of generating images for the Web. It merely reduces the amount of over-head needed to serve many requests for web resources generated dynamically by Perl scripts by making the Perl interpreter persistent. For information about installing and running mod_perl, check out the Perl-Apache Integration Project link listed in the "References" section of this chapter.

"Image farming"

If you have more than one computer available, consider farming out some of the work to the other machine so that your main web server isn't bogged down. The actual SRC attributes of the images within the HTML page may be modified to point to the new URL, or the request for the image may be redirected by the server to the appropriate machine, so the actual "passing of the buck" is transparent to the web page requesting the image. The following <IMG> tag, for example, calls a CGI script that generates a PNG image as its output:

```
<IMG SRC="http://www.shemp.net/image1.cgi">
```

If the computer at *www.shemp.net* became a popular site and you decided to farm out the task of producing this image to another computer running a web server on your network named *images.shemp.net,* you could move the CGI program to the new server and change the <IMG> tag to:

```
<IMG SRC="http://images.shemp.net/image1.cgi">
```

or you could move the CGI program to the new server and replace the file *image1.cgi* with a shell script (or batch file) that prints a short HTML file, which (via a *Location* HTTP header) redirects the request to the new server. The following Unix-style shell script will do the job:

```
#!/bin/sh

echo 'Location: http://images.shemp.net/image1.cgi';
echo;
```

It may be written as a shell script to reduce the overhead of implementing such a trivial script in Perl or some other language. The redirection document must be some sort of executable file because the server has identified the file *image1.cgi* as an executable program and will attempt to execute it. Note that the second case has the additional overhead of another HTTP transaction, but this may be worthwhile if it makes maintenance of the site easier.

Other performance issues will be brought up in relevant sections of the book. Probably the most important enhancement for serving images is not a hardware or software solution at all. Make sure that you use the `WIDTH` and `HEIGHT` attributes of the `<IMG>` tag properly, so that the layout of the page by the browser is not at all dependent on the speed of execution of a CGI script. More on this in the next section.

Web Graphics and the Browser

As an example of how a web browser processes and organizes images internally, let's look at the model used by the Mozilla web browser, which is the "open source" release of the Netscape browser. This is a good object of study because the browser's code is freely available under the Netscape Public License, and the code is amply documented at Mozilla headquarters (*http://www.mozilla.org*).

Mozilla is written in C++. It is designed as a modular system with well-defined tasks handled by different modules. The layout of a page is handled by a layout engine called *NGLayout* (for Next Generation Layout). NGLayout is built on the open standards for Internet content (HTML, Cascading Style Sheets, and the Document Object Model) and it handles all the tasks associated with creating the layout of a page and rendering all of the page's components. The layout engine draws all of the geometric primitives (such as rules and table borders), places text, and renders images by interacting with a lower-level Image Library. This Image Library is what actually manages the flow, the decoding, and the eventual display of images. When the layout engine calls for an image to be rendered, the Image Library takes the following steps:

1. A URL is requested by the code that handles the layout of the page. This request could be initiated by the parsing of an `<IMG>` element or by one of the user interface options, such as the "Show Images" button on the navigation bar. This request is made with the *GetImage()* function.

2. The Image Library maintains a cache of previously requested and decoded images. With each image request, the Image Library will look for the image in the cache and, if it finds it, will draw the previously requested image from the cache. If it is not in the cache, the Library will open a data stream to get the image data, create a new image object, decompress and decode the data, and store the object in the cache, according to the pragmas that are associated

with the file. A request to the Image Library returns an *ImageReq* data structure, which consists of the decoded image data.

3. The Image Library provides an interface for the integration of multiple image decoders (in the future, this model will most likely be superseded by a COM-like component model). Each decoder must implement five functions that allow it to communicate with the Image Library:

init()

This function should allocate all necessary resources and data structures.

write_ready()

This function is needed with some image file formats to determine the maximum number of bytes to read ahead. It exists primarily as a work-around for supporting older platforms.

write()

This function should handle the decompression, color table management, and dithering tasks.

complete()

This function should let the Observer know that the image has been decoded.

abort()

This function is called when a request is aborted or at the end of a successful decode. It should clean up the resources and structures used by the decoder.

4. The decoding process is a straightforward series of steps:

a. The header info for the image is parsed and information such as the dimensions of the image is extracted.

b. If this is the first time this image has been loaded, the Image Library will add the five functions for the appropriate image decoder to its function table.

c. The target dimensions are computed, taking into account adjustments indicated in the <IMG> tag.

d. The decoded data is resized to the target dimensions as it is read, line by line.

e. The transparency mask (if any) is scaled to the target dimensions.

f. If the color depth of the image exceeds that of the browser, the image is dithered to best match the client.

5. An "Observer" is also created with each request to the Image Library. The Observer will provide status information on the progress of the image request

and will notify the layout module of information, such as when the image has been decoded or when a complete frame of a multi-image animation has loaded. This allows the browser to update the screen as the request is being processed.

6. The actual display of the image on the screen is handled by separate display code that handles the decisions necessary to render pixmaps on different platforms.

Currently, all of the decoded images in a single HTML page will be stored in memory at the same time, even though they may not all be displayed on the screen at once. This is one of the factors that contribute to the relatively large footprint of most browsers.

Now that we've looked at the underpinnings of graphics and the web browser, let's look at the HTML elements that couch images and control their placement and sizing.

Presenting Images in HTML

As of the HTML 3.2 specification, there was only one way to include an image in an HTML document, and that was with the <IMG> tag. With the HTML 4.0 standard there are two equally supported means of including images—the <IMG> tag and the <OBJECT> tag. The <OBJECT> element is intended as a more open solution to the problem of inserting inline media into web documents. The examples in this book all use the <IMG> tag, because it is very likely that 3.2 will still be the most widely implemented standard for quite some time. However, we will look at both the <IMG> and <OBJECT> forms in this chapter.

The <IMG> element embeds an image in the body of a document (it cannot be used in the head section). The element consists of a start tag without an end tag, and does not include content as such. It is formed according to standard HTML syntax, which is to say it should look like this in its simplest form:

```
<IMG SRC="someimage.png">  # include an inline png
```

In Perl, you may use the HTML::Element module to create image tags. This module is designed to let you build the nodes of an HTML syntax tree with method calls. It can be used as in the following example:

```
use HTML::Element;          # use this module

# Set attributes when creating the element...
my $img = new HTML::Element 'img', src => 'someimage.gif';

# ...or add them later with the attr() method
$img->attr('alt','This is Some Image!');
```

```
# Use as_HTML() to print the element as an html tag .
print $img->as_HTML;
```

The SRC Attribute

The SRC attribute indicates the URL of the image. This can be an absolute or relative address, and it may refer to a file to be read as data or to a script that is to be run to create the proper image output. The syntax in either case is the same:

```
<IMG SRC="images/staticfile.gif">
<IMG SRC="cgi-bin/dynamicscript.cgi">
```

In the first case, the browser reads the file at the given URL (in this case, a local file), interprets the image data within that file, and displays that data inline at the proper place in the document. In the second case, the browser requests the CGI script at the given URL, the web server invokes the script, and the script's output (whatever is written to STDOUT) will be sent to the web browser for inclusion in the web page. From the browser's point of view, we don't really care what language the script is written in, just that it adheres to the Common Gateway Interface and sends valid image data back to us. If the script fails for some reason, the image data coming back will not be in a valid image format, and the browser will display a broken image icon. The broken image icon is shown in Figure 2-2.

Figure 2-2. The broken image icon is displayed when an image data stream cannot be decoded by the client

One problem with creating images on the fly via the Common Gateway Interface is the reporting of errors. A broken image icon does not tell a user very much. Did the script crash? Is the network unreachable? Do I have an incompatible browser? It's hard to tell from the broken image icon.

One way to get around this problem is to print "wrapper" HTML around your image, so that your script is not just printing out a stream of image data (or not printing out a stream of image data, as the case may be). With this approach you can print an appropriate error message in HTML. On the server side, it is generally a good idea to use the Perl CGI::Carp module to neatly report CGI error messages in your server log file.

The following trivial script will read in a binary image file and print it to STDOUT. When this is called from a web browser as a CGI script, it will have the same

result as if *someimage.gif* had been included as the source file in the SRC attribute.
The script is called from a single line of HTML:

```
<IMG SRC = "someimage.cgi">
```

Here is the code for the script:

```perl
#!/usr/local/bin/perl

# someimage.cgi
# A trivial script for passing an image to a web browser.
#
open INFILE, "someimage.gif";
undef $/;                                # Set the file input separator
binmode(STDIN);
my $input2 = <INFILE>;                   # Now the whole file is in $input
print STDOUT "Content-Type: image/gif\r\n\r\n";  # Print the header info
binmode(STDOUT);                         # For our Win32 friends
print STDOUT $input2;                    # Write the image data to STDOUT
```

Let's say we want to see if the image file exists, and print an appropriate message
if it does not. Adding the following to the script will not work the way we want it
to:

```perl
open INFILE, "someimage.gif" || die "Image not found";
```

This is because the browser will be expecting some sort of MIME header, and will
get the string "Image not found" if the file does not exist. One way to get around
this is to do the image inclusion as a Server Side Include (SSI), or to use a "wrapper" script that will generate the entire HTML page. The wrapper method is also
useful when you want to generate a page that contains text and images that are
generated based on data provided by the user—from a form, for instance. The
server requests and responses in this case are pictured in Figure 2-3. In the case of
a page of mixed text and images, you would indicate the wrapper script in the
ACTION attribute of the <FORM> tag, and the script would embed the call to the
image generation script in an <IMG> tag, as in the following HTML page:

```html
<HTML>
<HEAD>
<TITLE>Example start page</TITLE>
</HEAD>
<BODY>
<FORM METHOD=POST ACTION="wrapper.cgi">
Enter up to 20 characters, no spaces:
<INPUT TYPE=TEXT NAME="sometext">
<INPUT TYPE="submit" VALUE="Submit"><br>
</FORM>
</BODY>
</HTML>
```

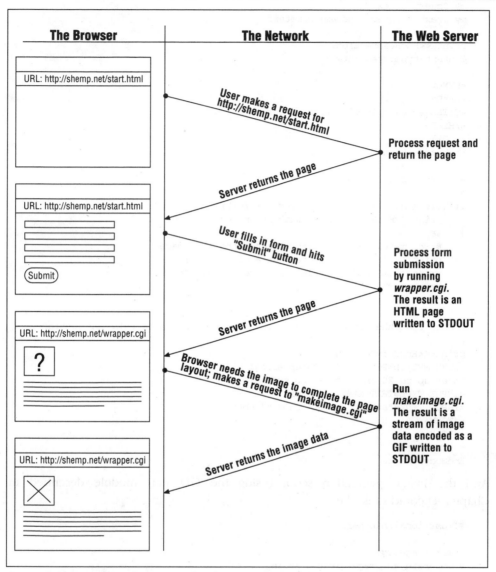

Figure 2-3. Requests and responses for the wrapper example

The wrapper script could look something like this:

```
#!/usr/local/bin/perl

# wrapper.cgi
# Generate a response to a form submission.
#
use CGI;

# Get the parameter passed into the script
#
```

```perl
my $query = new CGI;
my $text = $query->param('sometext');

print <<EndHeadSection;
Content-type: text/html;

<HTML>
<HEAD>
<TITLE>An example of a wrapper script</TITLE>
</HEAD>
<BODY>
EndHeadSection

# Do some basic range checking
#
if ((length($text) > 20) | ($text =~ / /)) {
    print "<H2>20 chars max with no spaces, please...</H2>";
} else {
    # The makeimage.cgi script creates the GIF image
    print "<H2>Here's your text as a GIF:</H2>";
    print "<IMG SRC=\"makeimage.cgi?text=$text\">";
    print "<BR>";
}

# Note that the action string in the form tag refers to this very script
#
print <<EndBodySection;
<FORM METHOD=POST ACTION="wrapper.cgi">
Enter up to 20 characters, no spaces:
<INPUT TYPE=TEXT NAME="sometext">
<INPUT TYPE="submit" VALUE="Submit"><br>
</FORM>
</BODY>
</HTML>
EndBodySection
```

And the image generation script (using the GD Perl module described in Chapter 4) could look like:

```perl
#!/usr/local/bin/perl

# makeimage.cgi
# Generate an image given a string.
#
use strict;
use CGI;
use GD;

my $query = new CGI;

# Get the parameter and its length
my $text = $query->param('text');
my $length = length($text);
```

```
# Each character is 9 pixels wide and 15 pixels high
my $image = new GD::Image(9*$length,15);
$image->colorAllocate(0, 0, 0);              # allocate a black background
my $yellow=$image->colorAllocate(255, 255, 0);  # the text color

# Draw the string on the image
$image->string(gdGiantFont, 0, 0, $text, $yellow);

# Let the CGI module print the content-type header
print $query->header('image/gif');

# Write the image to STDOUT as a GIF
binmode(STDOUT);
print $image->gif();
```

The results generated by these scripts is shown in Figure 2-4.

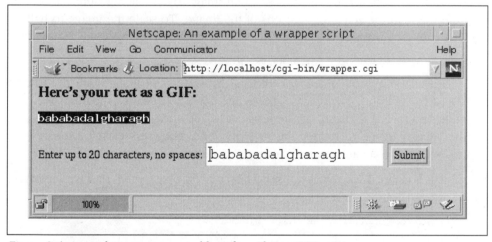

Figure 2-4. A simple image generated by a form-driven CGI script

This method can be very awkward and is one of the reasons that CGI can be so clunky to use. It works, however, which is why CGI will remain useful for quite a while. With the advent of HTML 4.0 and the <OBJECT> tag, image data can be included directly within the HTML document as part of the object's DATA attribute. While this alleviates the need for wrapper scripts in many cases, it is generally not a good practice in this sort of application because the resulting pages will be visually unreadable.

In Chapter 10, *Web Graphics Cookbook*, we will implement the BrokenImage package for generating a more informative broken image icon. Chapters 4, 5, and 6 all contain examples of generating dynamic images from form-based input from users.

The WIDTH and HEIGHT Attributes

The `WIDTH` and `HEIGHT` attributes may be added to an `<IMG>` tag to make the loading of web pages more efficient. When a web browser is loading and displaying a page, it must load all of the image files and extract information about their dimensions from the information encoded in the files. If the page contains complicated layout elements (such as tables), it can sometimes take quite a bit of time for a browser to load and compose an entire page. If the `WIDTH` and `HEIGHT` attributes are provided, however, the browser can compose the page as it loads, and fill in the images as they load. The attributes are simply included within the `<IMG>` tag; the order doesn't matter:

```
<IMG SRC="someimage.gif"  HEIGHT=200  WIDTH=300>
```

These attributes can also be used to scale an image by providing dimensions that are different than the actual dimensions of the image. To scale the image to half its size, for example, use:

```
<IMG SRC="someimage.gif"  HEIGHT=100  WIDTH=150>
```

In general it is not good practice to reduce the size of an image with the `WIDTH` and `HEIGHT` attributes. In this case, the entire 200×300 image is loaded over the network, and then it is scaled by the browser to 100×150. It is much better to create the smaller image to reduce the network load. Browsers can't necessarily be depended upon to do an adequate scaling job, either.

To create a horizontal line that is 4 pixels high and 150 pixels wide, start with a single-pixel image and use:

```
<IMG SRC="onepixel.gif"  HEIGHT=4  WIDTH=150>
```

You can also specify a scaling percentage, such as:

```
<IMG SRC="someimage.gif"  HEIGHT="50%"  WIDTH="50%">
```

where the percentages indicate a fraction of the current browser window's width and height. This method will almost certainly distort the original image, so be sure to test it under different window sizes before using it.

Next, let's write a Perl script that takes a filename as a parameter and returns a report on all of the images on the page. It will print out the width, height, file size, and an estimated download time for several different connection speeds. For a file named *smt.html* that contains 4 images, the script will print the following:

```
Information for images in the file smt.html
.........................................................
GIF Image: images/smtcharacter.gif (9.525 K) WIDTH = 150 HEIGHT = 194
   Estimated download times:
      14.4 Kbps : 5.29 seconds
      28.8 Kbps : 2.65 seconds
```

```
    33.3 Kbps : 2.29 seconds
    56 Kbps : 1.36 seconds
    1000 Kbps : 0.08 seconds

GIF Image: images/logo.gif (1.77 K) WIDTH = 312 HEIGHT = 95
  Estimated download times:
    14.4 Kbps : 0.98 seconds
    28.8 Kbps : 0.49 seconds
    33.3 Kbps : 0.43 seconds
    56 Kbps : 0.25 seconds
    1000 Kbps : 0.01 seconds

GIF Image: images/facade.gif (11.89 K) WIDTH = 125 HEIGHT = 185
  Estimated download times:
    14.4 Kbps : 6.61 seconds
    28.8 Kbps : 3.30 seconds
    33.3 Kbps : 2.86 seconds
    56 Kbps : 1.70 seconds
    1000 Kbps : 0.10 seconds

GIF Image: images/menu.gif (12.93 K) WIDTH = 600 HEIGHT = 65
  Estimated download times:
    14.4 Kbps : 7.18 seconds
    28.8 Kbps : 3.59 seconds
    33.3 Kbps : 3.11 seconds
    56 Kbps : 1.85 seconds
    1000 Kbps : 0.10 seconds

Total estimated time to download all images in this document:
    14.4 Kbps : 20.06 seconds
    28.8 Kbps : 10.03 seconds
    33.3 Kbps : 8.68 seconds
    56 Kbps : 5.16 seconds
    1000 Kbps : 0.29 seconds
..........................................................
```

This report can be useful for estimating the amount of time users will have to wait for all your images to download, or to gather information about the dimensions of images for later inclusion in the HTML tags.

Note that the script assumes that it is being run in the same directory as the target file, and that all of the images reside locally relative to the file. This could easily be extended to gather information about remote URLs with the HTTP::Request module. The assumption, however, is that you will not want to hard-code information about an image that you can't directly control. Here's the code:

```
#!/usr/local/bin/perl -w

# ListImgInfo.pl
# This script will print a list of the attributes of all of the images
# in the document given as a parameter on the command line.
#
use HTML::LinkExtor;
```

```perl
use Image::Magick;
use strict;

my $filename = $ARGV[0];
my @rates = ( 14.4, 28.8, 33.3, 56.0, 1000);
my %totaltime = ();

foreach (@rates) {
    $totaltime{$_} = 0;
}

# The LinkExtor (link extractor) module takes a callback routine as
# an argument; this routine is called for each link tag that the
# parse_file method recognizes.
#
my $p = HTML::LinkExtor->new(\&getImgSize);

if ($filename) {
    print ".....................................................";
    print "Information for images in the file $filename";
    print ".....................................................";

    # The parse_file function finds all of the links within a document.
    #
    $p->parse_file($filename);

    print "Total estimated time to download all images in this document:\n";
    foreach (@rates) {
        print "$_ Kbps : ". ( sprintf "%.2f", $totaltime{$_}) ." seconds\n";
    }

    print ".....................................................\n";

} else {
    print "You must specify a filename.\n\r";
}

# This routine defines our callback action.
#
sub getImgSize {

    # Each time the callback is invoked, it is sent the tag name and a hash of
    # arguments. In this case we are looking for 'img' tags, and the hash will
    # contain the attributes of the image (src, alt, etc.).
    #
    my($tag, %links) = @_;

    return if $tag ne 'img';    # Ignore other types of links

    my $info = Image::Magick->Ping($links{'src'});
    if ($info) {
        # Ping() returns the info as a comma-delimited string
        #
        my ($width, $height, $filesize, $format) = split /,/, $info;
```

```
            # People are used to seeing the filesize in Kbytes
            #
            $filesize = $filesize / 1000;

            print "$format Image: $links{'src'} ($filesize K)";
            print " WIDTH = $width HEIGHT = $height\n";
            print " Estimated download times:\n";
            downloadTimes($filesize);      # print a section with estimated
                                           # download times for this image
            print "\n";
        } else {

            # In this case, the image is of a type not recognized by the
            # ImageMagick library (could be an esoteric format, in which case
            # most browsers couldn't view it, or an external library may not be
            # installed).
            #
            print "Unrecognized image format: $links{'src'}\n";
        }
    }

sub downloadTimes {
    my $size = $_[0];
    foreach my $rate (@rates) {
        my $time = $size * 8 / $rate;    # size in Kb, rate in Kbit
        print "$rate Kbps : ". ( sprintf "%.2f", $time) ." seconds\n";
        $totaltime{$rate} += $time;
    }
}
```

Many HTML authoring applications provide options for automatically assigning the WIDTH and HEIGHT tags while the page is created. For those of you who like to use a plain old text editor, or perhaps for updating legacy HTML documents, you might find the following script useful. Using the HTML module (from CPAN) this script parses an HTML document, determines the dimensions of each of the local images referenced by the document, and changes the <IMG> tag's WIDTH and HEIGHT attributes to reflect the actual dimensions of each image. Note that it does not check to see if these attributes have already been set; previously defined values for these parameters will be replaced by the actual dimensions of the image.

```
#!/usr/local/bin/perl -w

# AddImgInfo.pl
# This script will try to add width and height information to the
# img tags in the document given as a parameter on the command line.
# It will output the modified web page to a file called modified.filename.

use HTML::TreeBuilder;
use Image::Magick;
use strict;

my $filename = $ARGV[0];
```

```
my $p = HTML::TreeBuilder->new;

if ($filename) {
    my $html = $p->parse_file($filename);
    open OUTFILE, ">modified.$filename";
    $html->traverse(\&analyzeHtml);
    close OUTFILE;
} else {
    print "You must specify a filename.\n";
}


# This routine defines our callback action.
#
sub analyzeHtml {
    my ($node, $startbool, $depth) = @_;

    if (ref $node) {
        # In this case, the node is some sort of markup tag; use the startbool
        # flag to determine if it is a start tag or end tag
        #
        if ($startbool) {
            if ($node->tag eq 'img') {
                # In this case we have an image tag on our hands.
                # Use the Ping() method to find the information
                # and add it to the end of the attribute string...
                #
                my $info = Image::Magick->Ping($node->attr('src'));
                if ($info) {
                # Ping() returns the info as a comma-delimited string
                  #
                  my ($width, $height, $filesize, $format) = split /,/, $info;
                  $node->attr('width', $width);
                  $node->attr('height', $height);
                }
            }
            print OUTFILE $node->starttag;
        } else {
            print OUTFILE $node->endtag;
        }
    } else {
        # In this case the node is just text; print it as is.
        #
        print OUTFILE $node;
    }
    print OUTFILE "\n";       # add a new line
    return 1;                 # continue analyzing the children of this node
}
```

These scripts use the *Ping()* method of the Image::Magick module, which is described in Chapter 5. The *Ping()* method returns information about an image's file type and geometry without decoding the entire file. Another way to find information about the dimensions of an image is with the Image::Size module, which also recognizes many file formats.

```
use Image::Size;
my $filename = "someimage.png";

# Use the imgsize method to find the dimensions of the image
my ($x, $y) = imgsize($filename);

# The html_imgsize will return the geometry as a string
# ready to be included in an HTML tag...
my $size = html_imgsize($filename);   # returns the string "HEIGHT=y WIDTH=x"
```

Layout and Spacing Attributes

The HTML 3.2 specification defines four attributes for the `<IMG>` tag that allow control over the space around an image and how the image is aligned with other elements on the page. These are the `ALIGN`, `BORDER`, `HSPACE`, and `VSPACE` tags. The coming of the HTML 4.0 specification brings with it a paradigm shift in the way HTML authors should look at the visual presentation and layout of web pages. All of these tags have been deprecated in the official 4.0 spec in favor of style sheets. However, it will take a while for programs implementing the 3.2 specification to be completely subsumed by HTML 4.0, so this chapter will discuss the use of these attributes, leaving the explanation of style sheets to other books,* as they are beyond the scope of this one.

The `ALIGN` attribute specifies how the image should be positioned on the page with respect to the elements around it. The default value is `bottom`. Both Netscape and Microsoft have created their own proprietary extensions to the `ALIGN` attribute, which we will not go into here. See "A Rogue's Gallery of Proprietary Attributes" later in this chapter for more on these extensions. The HTML 3.2 specification defines the following alignment options, which are also shown in Figure 2-5:

top

>   This indicates that the top of the image should be aligned with the baseline of the text or objects surrounding it.

middle

>   This option indicates that the vertical center of the image should be aligned with the baseline of the text or objects immediately before it. Note that Netscape and Internet Explorer implement this differently; Netscape aligns the image with the text's baseline and IE aligns the image to the absolute middle of the line of text.

---

* *HTML: The Definitive Guide* (3rd Edition) and *Web Design in a Nutshell*, both from O'Reilly, include in-depth discussions of style sheets.

`bottom`

> This option indicates that the bottom of the image should be aligned with the baseline of the text or objects surrounding it.

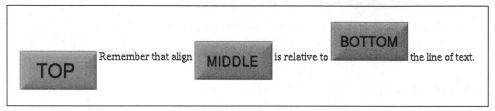

Figure 2-5. The top, middle, and bottom alignment options

`left`

> This option indicates that the image should be pushed to the left margin of the current text flow, and any text or other objects should wrap around it. This is useful for effects such as starting a paragraph with a drop cap, as in Figure 2-6.

`right`

> The right attribute indicates that the browser should push the image to the right margin of the current text flow and wrap any text or other objects around its left side. This can be used to quickly create layouts that have a newspaper feel, as in Figure 2-6.

The `BORDER` attribute allows you to set the width, in pixels, of the space around the image. If the image is within a link element, the border will be the same color as other links (as defined by the browser settings or by document-level settings in the `<BODY>` tag). For many of the Web's more visual sites, square, clunky, colored borders around the images would ruin the graphic design. If you are designing a page with, say, several interlocking transparent images that act as hyperlinks to various corners of your web site, you can turn off the image borders by setting `BORDER` to 0. Keep in mind that colored borders are a visual clue that something is a link, so if you remove an image link's border, be sure to provide some indication that it is in fact a link (and by this I don't mean JavaScript mouseovers saying "CLICK ME!").

Images as Links: ISMAP and USEMAP

Images may be used as links, in the same way as any other HTML element. Just include the `<IMG>` tag within the content of a hyperlink tag, as in:

```
<A HREF = "shempscape.html">
    <IMG SRC = "images/shempscape.gif" ALT = "Shempscape Now!">
</A>
```

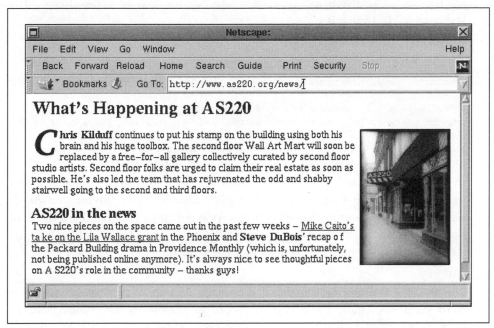

Figure 2-6. Left alignment (the drop cap) and right alignment options (the photo) allow for more dynamic layouts without using HTML tables

The HTML specification also defines two attributes which allow different hyperlinks to be assigned to different sections within an image. These images are known as image maps. An image map is constructed by defining regions that have actions or URLs associated with them. The `<IMG>` tag must also specify one of two image map attributes, `ISMAP` or `USEMAP`, depending on whether the regions are to be resolved by the server or by the client:

ISMAP

The `ISMAP` attribute indicates that the image is a server-side image map. When the user clicks on the image in the browser window, the (x, y) coordinate within the image is sent to the web server, and the URL of the map file (given by the HREF attribute) is used to determine whether a link should be followed. For example:

```
<!-- A Server-side image map -->
<A HREF = "face.map">
    <IMG SRC = "images/facemenu.gif" ISMAP>
</A>
```

The *face.map* file on the server will be used to determine which areas of the image correspond to which links. There are several different implementations for the layout of the map file, depending on the web server software. The standard NCSA format is:

```
# Image map file = face.map

# The Right Ear: upper left and lower left points of a rectangle
rect http://www.shemp.org/shawn/ear.html  252,168, 273,246

# The Nose: a polygon described by four points
poly http://www.shemp.org/shawn/nose.html  141,166, 125,236, 193,232, 164,162

# The Right Eye: A circle with a center point and a radius
circle http://www.shemp.org/shawn/eye.html  100,180,30
```

In this format, each line is either a comment or a region of the image. For example, the line beginning with "poly" associates the hyperlink *http://www.shemp.org/shawn/ear.html* with the polygon region defined by the four points specified in the coordinate list. Chapter 8, *Image Maps*, delves into the various server-side map file formats in greater detail.

USEMAP

The USEMAP attribute indicates that the image is a client-side image map. For most purposes, client-side image maps are preferable to server-side because there is no need to establish a network connection to resolve every mouse click the user makes. This is because the map file is embedded in the HTML document, and the lookup is performed locally by the browser. For example:

```
<!-- A Client-side image map -->
<IMG SRC="face.gif" USEMAP="#facemap">
```

When a user clicks on the image, the map information labeled *facemap* (which is embedded in the document) is interpreted to determine whether a link should be followed. A client-side image map definition is constructed with the <MAP> tag:

```
<MAP NAME="facemap">
    <AREA SHAPE=rect COORDS="252,168, 273,246"
        HREF="http://www.shemp.org/shawn/ear.html" ALT="Ear">
    <AREA SHAPE=poly COORDS="141,166, 125,236, 193,232, 164,162"
        HREF="http://www.shemp.org/shawn/nose.html" ALT="Nose">
    <AREA SHAPE=circle COORDS="100,180,30"
        HREF="http://www.shemp.org/shawn/eye.html" ALT="Eye">
</MAP>
```

If the browser is not capable of displaying images, the ALT attribute is used to create a text menu so that the user can still follow the embedded links. Most browsers also display the ALT text on the status bar, which gives users some idea of the locations of the image's clickable regions.

Most browsers support client-side image maps, but some do not. To accommodate those browsers, you may implement both client- and server-side image maps within the same tag. The browser will first try to determine the link reference locally and, failing that, will contact the server-side map file. This kind of redundancy looks like:

```
<!-- A Client-side image map with a server-side alternate representation -->
<A HREF = "face.map">
    <IMG SRC = "images/facemenu.gif" ISMAP USEMAP="#facemap">
</A>
<!--the document must also contain the map element described above -->
<!--the server must also have a valid map file for everyone to be happy -->
```

The current popular opinion is that client-side image maps are generally more efficient than server-side image maps. However, depending on your application, you may find that it is easier to maintain a site based on server-side image maps. Many people feel that widespread use of image maps is a snub of the "least common denominator" philosophy of the Internet, and should not be used in any application. I take the middle ground; image maps can be abused, but they also have their uses. The rule of thumb is to not use image maps when you can do the same thing with several separate images (or even text). See Chapter 8 for a complete discussion of client- and server-side image maps, and several tools for managing and creating them on the fly.

Dehanced for Lynx: The ALT Attribute

You might be surprised by how many people use text-only web browsers. In addition to being useful, low-overhead tools in the command-line world (for browsing the Web via a Telnet session, for example) and their widespread use on Free-nets and BBS's, text-based browsers have a user base that should not be ignored.

The **ALT** attribute of the **<IMG>** tag is used to provide an alternative textual representation for an image when a client cannot (or chooses to not) support graphical images. It is included within the image element as in:

```
<IMG SRC="obert.jpg" ALT= "A picture of Matt Obert.">
```

So, what should your **ALT** text say? It will not do to print something like "Please upgrade your browser to the latest version of Netscape or Internet Explorer" or "Please turn on images." It's also a good idea to avoid using irrelevant text in the **ALT** attribute. An exception to this rule of thumb is adding functional ASCII renditions of your image in the **ALT** tag, as in:

```
<IMG SRC="next.gif" ALT = ">>">
<IMG SRC="prev.gif" ALT = "<<">
```

It is also helpful to know that **ALT** text cannot contain additional HTML markup (it will be rendered as plain text). See Chapter 10 for more about formatting **ALT** tags.

Background Images

A background image for a web page may be specified with the `BACKGROUND` attribute of the `BODY` tag, as in:

```
<BODY BACKGROUND="marble.png">
```

Though animated GIFs may be used as background images, proceed with caution; it is difficult to design an animation that is suitable as a backdrop for text, and animated GIFs can consume a good amount of a client's resources.

The OBJECT Tag

Starting with HTML 2.0, the architects of the HTML specifications realized the need for a more robust means of inserting media into documents. The `<IMG>` tag was the only official way to insert inline images. Netscape extended the language with the `<EMBED>` tag, Microsoft introduced the `DYNSRC` attribute for inline AVI movies, and Sun brought the `<APPLET>` tag for including (Java) code within a document. None of these decisively address the need for a way of including generic inline media, possibly in several alternate formats. The `<OBJECT>` tag is meant to serve this purpose. It can also be used as an alternative to the `<IMG>` tag.

The `<OBJECT>` tag can be used in conjunction with an image tag to provide backwards compatibility, or if the user agent does not have the capability for rendering the data type, as in:

```
<OBJECT data="MonkeyMovie.avi" type="application/avi">
    <IMG SRC="MonkeyStill.png" ALT="A picture of some monkeys.">
</OBJECT>
```

Most importantly, the `<OBJECT>` tag has replaced the `<APPLET>` tag, which is deprecated in HTML 4.0. The primary use for the `<OBJECT>` tag is for implementing complex media objects that cannot be instantiated only on the server-side. For just representing inline images, it is perfectly acceptable to still use the plain old `<IMG>` tag.

A Rogue's Gallery of Proprietary Attributes

Over the course of the early rapid development of the Web, several companies rushed in with extensions and additional HTML attributes that filled the gaps in the various HTML specifications of the time. Because we are looking at developing web sites that will last well into the future without a dependence on proprietary technologies, this book will not use examples that depend on any of these extensions. There are useful and interesting applications for these tags, however.

Netscape tag extensions

Besides adding many tags and attributes that later became part of the HTML spec (and many that didn't), Netscape created the JavaScript scripting language. Java-Script allows many options for adding interactivity to web images. In particular, the following three attributes may be added to an <IMG> tag to associate Java-Script with the image:

NAME

> The NAME attribute will allow the image to be referenced in a JavaScript handler. The image must have a name if it is to be manipulated in JavaScript. For example,
>
> ```
> <IMG SRC="logo.gif" NAME="logo">
> ```
>
> will allow JavaScript to reference the image with the name "logo."

ONABORT

> The ONABORT attribute associates an event handler with the image that is called when the user stops the image download before it has finished. For example:
>
> ```
> <IMG SRC="beatniks.gif" ONABORT="window.alert ('Load Aborted!')">
> ```

ONERROR

> The ONERROR event handler will be called if the image fails to load because of an error. For example:
>
> ```
> <IMG SRC="beatniks.gif"
>     ONERROR="window.alert ('How distressing; an error occurred...')">
> ```

ONLOAD

> The ONLOAD event handler is invoked as soon as the image has been loaded and displayed by the user agent. For example:
>
> ```
> <IMG SRC="beatniks.gif" ONLOAD ="window.alert ('Welcome to my world!')">
> ```

See Chapter 10 for an example of using JavaScript mouse handlers to control the display of images.

Netscape also defines the LOWSRC attribute for the <IMG> tag, which can be used to provide the URL of a low-resolution version of the image indicated by the SRC attribute. Netscape will load the low-resolution image first, compose the rest of the page, and then, once the page has been fully displayed and is readable, replace the low-res images with high-res versions. Note that this approach requires you to create two versions of each image. Other browsers may simply ignore the LOWSRC attribute.

Internet Explorer tag extensions

Internet Explorer has implemented several proprietary extensions that enable the inclusion of inline AVI movies within a web page. Remember that these are not official HTML extensions; they can only be seen by Internet Explorer users, or in browsers that have taken the trouble to include Internet Explorer compatibility.

The DYNSRC extension will allow you to include inline AVI movies within a web page, audio track and all. This attribute can be used in conjunction with the SRC attribute to provide alternatives for other browsers. In the following example, the AVI movie called *movie.avi* in the local folder *movies* will be displayed inline if the page is viewed with Internet Explorer, and the GIF file called *moviestill.gif* will be displayed on other browsers:

```
<IMG DYNSRC="movies/movie.avi" SRC="moviestill.gif">
```

The CONTROLS attribute can be added to this statement to add a control bar beneath the inline AVI that will allow the user to stop, play, rewind, fast-forward, and control the volume of the movie. The presence of the CONTROL attribute acts as a Boolean value for whether the control bar should be displayed, as in:

```
<IMG DYNSRC="movies/movie.avi" CONTROLS>
```

The START attribute is another modifier for the DYNSRC attribute. It tells Internet Explorer when to start playing the AVI movie. START has three settings:

fileopen

>   If START is set to fileopen, the movie will start playing as soon as it is completely downloaded. This is the default value.

mouseover

>   In this case, the movie will play only when the user has the mouse positioned over the inline movie box.

fileopen,mouseover

>   In this case, the movie will play through once as soon as it is downloaded and then will play again whenever the user passes the mouse over the movie image.

The LOOP attribute can be set to repeat the movie a certain number of times, or to loop it indefinitely by setting the value to infinite.

Colors and the Web Browser

Images displayed on monitors with a limited number of available colors (typically 256) will be dithered when they are rendered. Netscape and Internet Explorer on Macintosh or Windows systems support a 216-color "web-safe" palette that will be accurately represented on all systems. These 216 colors are a subset of the Macintosh's 256-color system palette; the extra 40 colors are different from colors found in Win32 standard palettes. Colors not in this safe palette will be dithered to varying degrees on 8-bit systems. The 216 colors of the web-safe palette may be modeled as a 6×6×6 color cube.

Browsers running on Unix platforms running the X11 window system will sometimes use the 6×6×6 cube (216 colors), a 5×5×5 cube (125 colors), or even a 4×4×4 cube (64 colors), depending on how many colors are available to the browser. On an 8-bit system, Netscape may be run with the −install option specified on the command line to start the browser with the 216 color palette.

In later chapters, we will be writing scripts to generate graphics that are to be displayed on web browsers using this limited palette. These scripts will often need to allocate colors in the color table of the image. You may find it useful to have a utility script for computing the nearest color in the 6×6×6 color cube given a list of RGB values.

The 216 colors of the 6×6×6 color cube are those for which each of the red, green, and blue values are either 00, 33, 66, 99, CC, or FF (these numbers in decimal are 0, 51, 102, 153, 204, and 255). We'll call these our "safe" values. The following Perl script will take a list of the red, green, and blue values in decimal and will return the closest match for the color in the web-safe palette:

```perl
sub WebSafeColor {
    # Returns the closest color in the 216 color web-safe palette.
    #
    my ($red, $green, $blue) = @_;
    my (@returnlist, $max, $hex);

    # Find closest value in the 6x6x6 "web-safe" color cube,
    # algorithm described below.
    #
    foreach my $number ($red, $green, $blue) {
        LOOP: for ($max = 25; $max < 281; $max += 51) {
            if ($number <= $max) {
                push @returnlist, ($max - 25);
                $hex .= sprintf("%02X", $max - 25);
                last LOOP;
            }
        }
    }
    return (@returnlist, "#$hex");
}
```

The algorithm for *WebSafeColor()* simply makes six comparisons within the loop:

- If the number is between 0 and 25, the closest safe value is 0.

- If the number is between 26 and 72, the closest safe value is the midpoint, 51.

- If the number is between 73 and 127, the closest safe value is the midpoint, 102.

- If the number is between 128 and 178, the closest safe value is the midpoint, 153.

- If the number is between 179 and 229, the closest safe value is the midpoint, 204.

- If the number is between 230 and 255, the closest safe value is 255.

The *WebSafeColor()* subroutine takes three decimal values as input parameters because that is the format in which most of the packages described in the following chapters take their arguments. The script returns a list of the "safest" red, green, and blue values, *and* the hex representation of the color as a four-element list. Thus, you can retrieve the results in the following ways:

```
# get all values
my ($red, $green, $blue, $hex) = WebSafeColor(70, 120, 225);
# get just the return value in hex
pop(WebSafeColor(70, 120, 225))
```

Due to the wide range of possible configurations for clients who may be looking at your web pages, it can be almost impossible to guarantee *exactly* how your colors are going to be mapped to the client's display. In applications where exact color matches are important, be sure to provide a disclaimer noting the fact that the Web is an imperfect place, color-wise (I thought that the sweater that I ordered from your web catalog was *orange!*).

In the hopes of solving this problem, there has been much talk of creating a platform-independent color space. The International Color Consortium (*http://www.color.org*) has proposed the ICC profile format, which attaches an extracted "profile" to the image that will allow clients to make sure that the colors are represented properly. Hewlett-Packard and Microsoft have proposed the sRGB standard, which is a calibrated form of the RGB color space. Color calibration across platforms is a very complicated problem because it involves standardizing the treatment of color on many levels: in the operating system, in device drivers, and in the way documents are described on the Internet. It will probably be a problem for some time.

The Once and Future Browser

One of the key ingredients to the success and beauty of the Web is that it started with a set of specifications and requirements that were simple and robust enough so that anyone who wanted to could participate in publishing to the world. As we move into the world of the "Object Web" and more complicated specifications, anyone can still participate on some level, but overall the Web is not as simple a place as it once was. Once XML (eXtensible Modeling Language) is popularized, the field becomes even more cluttered.

Probably the most significant contribution of XML to the web graphics world is the possibility of representing vector graphics within the markup of a document, and allowing the client to render the graphics. Scalable vector graphics have been integrated into the Web, mostly as plug-ins or external viewers for formats such as PDF or CGM. An up-and-coming format is the Precision Graphics Markup Language (PGML), an XML application with an imaging model based on that of PostScript. Scalable graphics represented in a compact, portable vector form will truly kindle a revolution in the look and feel of the Web.

The Synchronized Multimedia Integration Language (SMIL) is another XML-based language that deserves attention. It may be used to represent media actions that may be triggered by various time controls. It will be used to make the Web a more multimedia-friendly place.

Web multimedia and vector graphics are two fields of expansion that are filled with potential. It may be some time before the standards have settled into place, but what's the rush? The Web isn't going anywhere.

References

The Official Guide to Programming with CGI.pm:
> Stein, Lincoln D., John Wiley & Sons, 1998.

Online CGI.pm documentation:
> *http://www.genome.wi.mit.edu/ftp/pub/software/WWW/*

The Idiot's Guide to Solving Perl CGI Problems:
> *http://www.perl.com/CPAN-local/doc/FAQs/cgi/idiots-guide.html*

The Perl-Apache Integration Project:
> *http://www.perl.apache.org*

mod_perl performance tuning guide:
> *http://perl.apache.org/tuning*

HTML: The Definitive Guide:
> Musciano, Chuck, and Bill Kennedy, O'Reilly & Associates, 3rd Edition, 1998.

3

A Litany of Libraries

This chapter provides a tour of some of the more useful free graphics libraries available on the Web. Most of these are implemented in C, but several also have scripting interfaces for Perl, Python, or Java. The average user will probably not use these resources directly, but a number of them (the Independent JPEG Group's libjpeg and the libpng libraries, for example) are used extensively by web browsers and by other graphics packages such as ImageMagick and the Gimp, so it is good to know about their existence. It is also interesting to follow up on some of these packages and find out how standards and libraries are developed and supported.

Image Support Libraries

The majority of the packages described in this chapter are covered by the GNU General Public License, and they are designated with GPL as their licensing scheme. A few packages have their own variations on the GPL or other Open Source licenses; these are marked "Open." This does not mean that they necessarily conform to the official Open Source Definition; it just means that they are "open" in spirit, and most likely fit the definition. In any case, this categorization is only meant as an overview. You should really read the individual licenses if you are concerned about reusing code from these libraries (see "References").

AA-lib, an ASCII Art Library

Authors: Jan Hubicka, Thomas A. K. Kjaer, Tim Newsome, and Kamil Toman
URL: *http://horac.ta.jcu.cz/aa/aalib/*
Platform: any Unix
License: GPL

AA-lib is a low-level graphics library for rendering ASCII art. It was developed by two Czech guys who wanted to be able view the Linux Penguin logo on their old Hercules monitors that weren't capable of displaying graphics. That's as good an excuse as any, and the library that they have created allows anyone to convert graphics to ASCII art, like the Linux Penguin logo shown in Figure 3-1, for example.

Figure 3-1 was created with the AA plug-in for the Gimp (see Chapter 7, *Web Graphics with the Gimp*), which uses aalib to save images as ASCII art, exporting text, HTML, or ANSI escape codes. It also has an option that will generate the HTML for inclusion of ASCII art in the `ALT` field of the `<IMG>` tag. You can get the source code for the AA plug-in via the Gimp registry at *http://registry.gimp.org/plugins/AA/*.

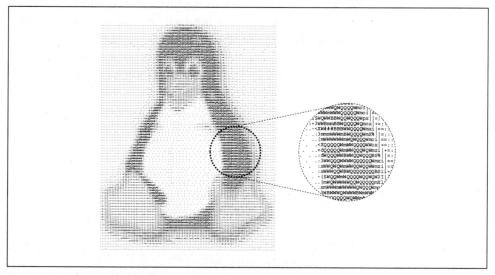

Figure 3-1. The AA-lib library may be used to render ASCII art, such as this image of "Tux," the Linux penguin

The Codes Library: A Free Compression Library

Author: David Chatenay
URL: *http://sunsite.unc.edu/pub/Linux/libs/graphics*
Platforms: Linux, SunOS, Solaris, Irix
License: GPL

The Codes Library contains functions written in C that implement several compression algorithms that you may incorporate into your application code to compress and decompress files. The library supports:

- Huffman encoding
- Adaptative Huffman encoding

- LZW-like encoding (Lempel Ziv Welch)

- LZSS-like encoding (Lempel Ziv Storer Szymanski)

- Functions to compute 16- and 32-bit error correction CRC values

The FreeType Project: A Free TrueType Font Engine

Authors: David Turner, Robert Wilhelm, and Werner Lemberg
URL: *http://www.freetype.org*
Platforms: Most
License: Open (consult documentation)

The FreeType Project set out to create a free font engine for TrueType fonts. A font engine is a program that loads font files and provides access to information about the individual characters (or glyphs) in the font. A font engine must also provide routines for rendering the glyphs of a font. In its current form, the Free-Type Project exists as a low-level font engine (or font driver) that provides a number of routines for loading TrueType fonts and rendering individual glyphs. It has also defined an API that makes it easy to implement higher-level font rendering features such as kerning, justification, rotated text, glyph caching, etc. The developers are hoping that the 2.0 release of the FreeType engine provides all of the features of a high-level rendering library.

Some features of note are:

- Support for TTF (TrueType files) and TTC (TrueType Collections)

- A management system for keeping track of multiple open fonts or sizes

- Smoothing of diagonals and curves

- Support for multiple character-mapping schemes

- A TrueType bytecode interpreter

The VFlib library (used by the Gimp) uses the FreeType library to support True-Type fonts.

gd: A GIF Manipulation Library

Author: Thomas Boutell
URL: *http://www.boutell.com/gd/*
Platforms: Most
License: Open (consult documentation)

gd is a graphics library written in C for manipulating GIF format files. It is designed as a fast, compact group of functions that may be used for creating graphics for the Web. In addition to the ability to read GIF files, gd has some (limited) drawing and painting capability, with routines for drawing lines, arcs, and polygons, cutting and pasting between images, filling contiguous areas with color, and superimposing text on images. It does not have advanced image manipulation functions such as filters or transforms, and the color palette mechanisms are fairly primitive. gd is not intended as an all-purpose image manipulation library (ImageMagick fills that niche nicely, however). It is a very popular library for web graphics programmers looking for a "quick and dirty" solution (though it's really not at all dirty).

gd has been ported to Perl and may be accessed with the GD module written by Lincoln Stein. This module is described in detail in Chapter 4, *On-the-Fly Graphics with GD*. The GD module actually uses a modified version of the gd 1.1 library, which has been optimized for use with Perl. The latest version of the GD module may be found on CPAN, or at *http://stein.cshl.org/WWW/software/GD/GD.html*.

Beginning with Version 1.3, gd is distributed with non-LZW–based GIF compression code that is based on a Run Length Encoding algorithm but is still compatible with LZW GIF decoders. This results in slightly larger files, but avoids the crippling patent problems associated with LZW-based GIF libraries.

Ghostscript: A Free PostScript Interpreter

> Author: Aladdin Enterprises
> URL: *http://www.cs.wisc.edu/~ghost/*
> Platforms: Most
> License: Aladdin Ghostscript Free Public License, GPL (see below)

Ghostscript is a package of software tools that provides an interpreter for Post-Script and Portable Document Format (PDF) files, converters between PostScript and PDF file formats, and a library of abstract functions for implementing primitive PostScript operations in C. Ghostscript may be used to render (or rasterize) Postscript files for viewing on a screen or for printing on printers that do not have a built-in PostScript interpreter.

The licensing situation for Ghostscript is perhaps a bit more complex than for other graphics libraries. The Aladdin Ghostscript distribution is covered by the Aladdin Ghostscript General Public License, which allows for free non-commercial distribution. There is also a GNU version of Ghostscript that is covered by the GNU General Public License, but it generally lags behind the Aladdin distribution by a version or so. The GNU Public License allows the software to be incorporated into commercial or non-commercial packages, provided that the end product conforms to the other requirements of the GPL. Ghostscript may also be licensed for commercial applications (such as an embedded PostScript interpreter within a printer) by contacting Aladdin. Note that you should really consult the licensing terms if you are planning on redistributing or reusing code from Ghostscript.

Ghostscript is used by ImageMagick to generate PostScript and PDF files, and is also used in Chapter 11, *Paperless Office? Not in Our Lives: Printing and the Web*, to render the output of the PostScript Perl modules developed therein.

GIFLIB and libungif

> Authors: Gershon Elber, Eric S. Raymond, and Toshio Kuratomi
> URL: *http://sagan.earthspace.net/~esr/giflib/* (GIFLIB) or
>   *http://prtr-13.ucsc.edu/~badger/software/libungif.shtml* (libungif)
> Platforms: Unix, DOS
> License: Berkeley Standard Distribution

GIFLIB is a library of C routines for dealing with GIF-formatted files that comes with a bunch of utility programs for performing common image manipulation tasks. These utilities are:

- *gif2bgi*, *gif2epsn*, *gif2herc*, *gif2iris*, and *gif2ps*: Utilities for displaying and printing GIFs on a number of devices

- *gif2rgb*, *gif2rle*, *gif2x11*, *raw2gif*, *rgb2gif*, and *rle2gif*: Conversion utilities between GIF and RGB, Utah Raster Toolkit, X11 pixmaps, raw 8-bit and 24-bit files

- *gifasm*, *gifovly*: Utilities for assembling multiple GIFs into a single multi-image GIF, or making a single GIF from a multi-image GIF

- *gifclip*, *gifflip*, *gifrotat*: Utilities for cropping, flipping, or rotating a GIF

- *gifhisto*: Utility for printing a histogram describing how often each color in the palette occurs

- *giftext*: Utility for printing a report of all the pertinent information about a GIF

- *gifclrmp*: A tool for editing GIF color maps

- *gifinter*: A tool for interlacing (or de-interlacing) a GIF

- Several "test pattern" generators

Unfortunately, the GIFLIB library is no longer actively developed (though it is maintained at its current version by Eric Raymond) due to the patent problems with LZW. The utility of GIFLIB inspired Toshio Kuratomi to branch off another library, ungiflib, which uses an uncompressed GIF storage method much like the later versions of the GD library.

ImageMagick: An All-Purpose Image Manipulation Library

Author: John Cristy
URL: *http://www.wizards.dupont.com/cristy/*
Platforms: Most (X11 required for display utilities)
License: Open (consult documentation)

The ImageMagick distribution provides a high-quality set of image manipulation functions, a standard API for interacting with graphics files, and a set of handy utilities for converting between formats and displaying images on X11 consoles.

ImageMagick's API acts as an interface to multiple graphics libraries. Most of the image manipulation routines are handled by the core ImageMagick library, but most of the reading and writing capability requires support libraries. ImageMagick uses the IJG's JPEG library for reading and writing JPEGs, Ghostscript for reading and writing PostScript and PDF files, libpng for PNG support, etc. This is transparent to the programmer, however; images of any format are read via the same ImageMagick *Read()* function and written with the *Write()* function.

ImageMagick supports over 80 file formats, including all of the formats of interest to web authors. See Chapter 5, *Industrial-Strength Graphics Scripting with PerlMagick*, for a list of most of the supported file formats.

ImageMagick includes several useful utilities:

- *convert*: A command-line utility that allows easy batch converting of graphics files between any of the supported formats

- *display* and *animate*: A program that will display an image (or, in the case of *animate*, a multi-image file) on any X11 system

- *import*: A screenshot utility that will save any X11 window as a graphics file

- *identify*: A tool that will parse an image file and print a report on its characteristics

ImageMagick also has a interface to the Perl and Python scripting languages. The Perl interface to ImageMagick (PerlMagick) is described in depth in Chapter 5.

The IPG's JPEG Library

Authors: Tom Lane, Philip Gladstone, Jim Boucher, Lee Crocker, Julian Minguillon, Luis Ortiz, George Phillips, Davide Rossi, Guido Vollbeding, Ge' Weijers, and other members of the Independent JPEG Group
URL: *http://www.ijg.org/*
Platforms: Intel x86, Unix
License: Open (consult documentation)

The Independent JPEG Group's JPEG libraries consist of a collection of C routines that are intended to be re-used in other applications. The libraries include utilities for implementing JPEG compression and decompression, as well as utilities for manipulating JPEG-encoded and JFIF files. The libraries provide support for baseline JPEG, extended-sequential, and progressive JPEG encoding methods. Though the JPEG standard provides for an arithmetic coding process, the IJG's libraries support only Huffman encoding.

The utilities and sample applications in the libjpeg package include:

- *cjpeg* and *djpeg*: Programs that convert between JPEG and other image file formats

- *jpegtran*: A utility that will allow you to perform a lossless conversion between JPEGs

- *rdjpgcom* and *wrjpgcom*: Programs that allow textual comments to be inserted in JFIF files

- Color quantization modules that may be used to render JPEGs on devices with color mapped displays

See Chapter 1, *Image File Formats*, for an in-depth description of JPEG encoding.

NetPBM

Authors: Jef Poskanzer, Greg Bothe, Jr., and the NetPBM team
URL: *ftp://ftp.x.org/contrib/utilities/netpbm-1mar1994.p1.tar.gz*
Platform: Unix
License: Open (consult documentation)

NetPBM is a set of utilities based on the popular PbmPlus package for reading and writing a wide variety of image formats and performing various image manipulation routines. The NetPBM package is similar in scope to the ImageMagick package, but while new releases of ImageMagick have been made on a regular basis since its inception, NetPBM has not been updated in quite a while. There are still a number of software packages that use NetPBM for graphics capability (the *html2ps* utility, for example), though most have migrated to the ImageMagick library. Greg Roelofs[*] is going to be taking the project over, however, which should lend NetPBM another burst of energy.

---

[*] A member of the PNG Working Group and author of *PNG: The Definitive Guide* (O'Reilly, 1999).

photopc

> Author: Eugene Crosser
> URL: *http://www.average.org/digicam/*
> Platform: Linux
> License: Open (consult documentation)

*photopc** is a collection of drivers and tools for allowing Linux systems to interface with some digital cameras, specifically those based on the Fujitsu chipset. This is a popular chipset used by Agfa, Epson, Olympus, Sanyo, and Nikon; you can follow the URL above for a current list of supported cameras. These cameras store the digital picture as a compressed JPEG and communicate with the computer through the serial port. The software implements the protocol that the cameras use to communicate with the computer and allow you to retrieve particular images from the camera; it also provides access to some of the control features of the cameras such as erasing frames. It is a handy tool if you have a digital camera and a Linux system, because most of the software that is shipped with the cameras is written for only Win32 or MacOS. After using both, I found that the command-line tools (there is also a Tcl/Tk GUI) provided with photopc were much quicker to use to download images from the camera than the GUI-driven software provided with my camera, which spent a good deal of time downloading and displaying previews that I often didn't need. Try it and judge for yourself.

libpng: PNG Image Format Support Library

> Authors: Guy Eric Schalnat, Andreas Dilger, Glenn Randers-Pehrson, and the PNG Group
> URL: *http://www.cdrom.com/pub/png/*
> Platform: Most
> License: Open (consult documentation)

The first official release of the PNG library was made in March of 1998, although libpng had been extensively used and tested for several years before that. The 1.0 release indicates that the API for the library has settled down to a stable set of routines. The libpng library is intended as a supplement to the PNG specification that will make it easier to implement PNG support for a wide range of systems and applications.

The libpng library requires the zlib compression library, which it uses to implement the Deflate compression method. The PNG file format is described in detail in Chapter 1.

---

* The author originally wrote the software for an Epson PhotoPC 500 camera.

VFlib: A Font Rasterizer

Author: Hirotsugu Kakugawa
URL: *http://www.se.hiroshima-u.ac.jp/~kakugawa/VFlib/*
Platforms: GNU-Linux, FreeBSD, Solaris, SunOS
License: Open (consult documentation)

VFlib is a C library and an API that provides access to the bitmaps of fonts of various formats, including:

- TrueType and Type 1

- The Syotai Kurabu and JG font formats for Japanese Kanji

- The X Window PCF and BDF formats

- PK, GF, VF, and TFM formats (TeX)

The VFlib library will allow a program to access font information via a unified programming interface rather than having to re-implement support for every particular font file format. Opening a font is abstracted to a call to the *VF_OpenFont1()* function, and a bitmap may be created by calling *VF_GetBitmap1()* function with the appropriate arguments.

VFlib is used by the GNU Image Manipulation Program for rasterizing fonts for use in images.

zlib: A Free Compression Library

Authors: Jean-loup Gailly and Mark Adler
URL: *http://www.cdrom.com/pub/infozip/zlib/*
Platforms: SunOS, Solaris, Linux
License: Open (consult documentation)

zlib (which is different than the Linux zlibc compression library) is an all-purpose set of C routines for efficiently compressing and decompressing files. The compression method used by zlib is the LZ77 (deflate) method, which is the same as that used by the gzip compression utility. This is no coincidence, since library author Jean-loup Gailly and Peter Deutsch, co-author of the zlib specification, are also the principal authors of gzip.

zlib is becoming an increasingly popular tool for compression. One application of note is in the libpng library, which uses zlib for implementing compression of PNG images. (Actually, zlib was specifically designed for use by PNG.) The library typically achieves compression ratios of between 2:1 and 5:1 for real-world data, though it has a theoretical maximum compression ratio of over 1000:1.

zlib also has interfaces for Perl, Python, Tcl, and Java (the Perl interface may be found on CPAN).

References

The Comprehensive Perl Archive Network (CPAN):

http://www.cpan.org

The GIF Controversy: A Software Developer's Perspective:

http://www.cloanto.com/users/mcb/19950127giflzw.html

The Open Source Definition:

http://www.opensource.org/osd.html

The GNU General Public License:

http://www.gnu.org/copyleft/gpl.html

The BSD License:

http://www.opensource.org/bsd-license.html

Textmode Quake, a version of the popular Quake game that renders its graphics in ASCII using AA-lib:

http://webpages.mr.net/bobz/ttyquake/

II

Graphics
Programming
Tools

4

On-the-Fly Graphics with GD

The GD Perl module is a collection of methods and constants for reading, manipulating, and writing color GIF files. Although it is more limited in scope than the ImageMagick package, its size and speed make it well-suited for dynamically generating GIF graphics via CGI scripts. GD has become the *de facto* graphics manipulation module for Perl; other modules such as GIFgraph (described in Chapter 6, *Charts and Graphs with GIFgraph*) extend the GD toolkit to easily accommodate specific graphics tasks such as creating graphs and charts.

The GD Perl module is actually a port of Thomas Boutell's gd graphics library, which is a collection of C routines created for manipulating GIFs for use in web applications. Early versions of the *GD.pm* module simply provided an interface to the gd library, but now GD has its own library that is optimized for use with Perl. This module was ported by Lincoln D. Stein, author of the CGI.pm modules.

This chapter starts with an overview and a sample CGI application that will implement a web-based "chess server" that interactively manipulates the pieces on a chess board. The remainder of the chapter is a more detailed description of the GD methods and constants, with additional information on more advanced topics such as using GD's polygon manipulations functions.

GD Jumpstart

Scripts that use the GD module to create graphics generally have five parts, which perform the following functions: importing the GD package, creating the image, allocating colors in the image colormap, drawing on or manipulating the image,

and writing the image to a file, pipe, or web browser. After you've installed the
GD module, just follow these five steps:

1. First you must import the GD methods into your script's namespace with the
   use function. The command **use GD** will give you access to all of the methods and constants of the GD::Image, GD::Font, and GD::Polygon classes:

   GD::Image
   > The Image class provides the means for reading, storing, and writing
   > image data. It also implements a number of methods for getting informa-
   > tion about and manipulating images.

   GD::Font
   > The Font class implements a number of methods that store and provide
   > information about fonts used for rendering text on images. Each of the
   > fonts are effectively hard-coded; they are described as a number of bit-
   > map matrices (similar to XBM files) that must be compiled as part of the
   > source during installation on your system. GD provides a limited number
   > of fonts; the GD::Font class exists to make it easier to expand font sup-
   > port in the future.

   GD::Polygon
   > The Polygon class implements a number of methods for managing and
   > manipulating polygons. A polygon object is a simple list of three or more
   > vertices that define a two-dimensional shape.

2. Create a new image. To make a new image, you can create a new, empty
   image object of a given width and height, or you can read an image from a
   file. To create an empty image, use the *new* method of the Image class, as in:

   ```
   # Create a new, empty 50 x 50 pixel image
   $image = new GD::Image(50, 50) || die "Couldn't create image";
   ```

   All image creation methods will return **undef** on failure. If the method succeeds, it will return a data structure containing the decoded GIF data for the
   image and store it in the given scalar value. This scalar can only contain one
   image at a time.

   GD supports three stored file formats: GIF, XBM (black and white X-bitmaps),
   and GD files. A GD format file is a file that has been written to a file using the
   gd() method. To read in the image data from a file, use *newFromGif()*,
   newFrmXbom(), or *newFromGd()*, depending on the format of the stored file.
   Each of these methods takes a filehandle as an argument, so you must open
   the file before you read the image data from it:

   ```
   # Read an image from a GIF file
   open (GIFFILE, "beatniks.gif") || die "Couldn't open file!";
   $image = newFromGif GD::Image(\*GIFFILE) || die "Couldn't read GIF data!";
   close GIFFILE;
   ```

```
# Read an image from an XBM file
open (XBMFILE, "ginsburg.xbm") || die "Couldn't open file!";
$image = newFromXbm GD::Image(\*XBMFILE) || die "Couldn't read XBM data!";
close XBMFILE;

# Read an image from a GD file
open (GDFILE, "ferlinghetti.gd") || die "Couldn't open file!";
$image = newFromGd GD::Image(\*GDFILE) || die "Couldn't read GD data!";
close GDFILE;
```

You are now ready to manipulate the image or write it to another file or to STDOUT.

3. If you are going to be doing any drawing or manipulation of the image, you will need to get information about the colors available in the image. GD images support a maximum of 256 colors which are stored in the image's color table. You may need to add new colors to an image's color table, or you may need to get color indices of existing colors. Use the *colorAllocate()* method with a list of decimal red, green, and blue values to add a new color to the color table. This method returns the index of the color in the color table, which you should store for use with drawing methods requiring a color index:

```
$red = $image->colorAllocate(255, 0, 0);
$grey2 = $image->colorAllocate(51, 51, 51);
```

Use *colorNearest()* and *colorExact()* to determine the color index of a color already in the color table. Use *colorsTotal()* to find out how many colors are currently allocated.

4. To draw on an image, use one of the graphics primitives. For example, to draw a 100×100 rectangle with purple lines in the upper left-hand corner of an image, use:

```
$purple = $image->colorAllocate(255, 0, 255);
$image->rectangle(0, 0, 100, 100, $purple);
```

It is possible to use any of the drawing primitives with specially defined brushes by specifying the *gdBrushed* constant instead of a color. You can also fill areas with a tiled pattern with the *gdTiled* constant.

GD provides a special class, GD::Polygon, for managing information about polygons. First create a new polygon object with *new()*, add points to it with the *addPt()* method, then draw it to an image with the *polygon()* drawing primitive. To draw the same filled purple rectangle above as a polygon, use:

```
# Create a new polygon object
my $polygon = new GD::Polygon;

# Add each of the polygon's vertices
$polygon->addPt(0,0);
$polygon->addPt(0,100);
```

```
$polygon->addPt(100,100);
$polygon->addPt(100,0);

# Allocate the color purple in the image.
# Note that if this is the first color allocated in $image,
# it will become the background color.
#
$purple = $image->colorAllocate(255, 0, 255);

# Now draw the polygon in purple on the image
$image->polygon($polygon, $purple);
```

5. When you are finished manipulating the image, you can write it to a file or to STDOUT. To write to a file, you must first open the file for writing with the *open* command. If you are working on a platform that makes a distinction between text and binary files (such as Windows 95/NT), be sure that you are writing in binary mode by calling the *binmode()* method first. To write the data as a GIF file, call the *gif()* method which returns the image data in the GIF format:

```
open OUTFILE, ">output.gif";      # Open the file for writing
binmode OUTFILE;                  # Make sure we're in binary mode
print OUTFILE $image->gif;        # Print GIF data to the file
close OUTFILE;
```

You can also write to a GD format file with the *gd()* method. Note that you can read from XBM files but you cannot write to them; you'll need an external utility if (for some reason) you want to do that. Also note that you cannot use GD manipulation routines directly on data generated by a *gif()* or *gd()* method call; all method calls should be made on the original GD::Image object.

GD images can also be handed off to other packages such as PerlMagick or GIFgraph for additional manipulation. See Chapter 6 for this discussion.

Sample Application: A Chess Board Simulator

This example implements a very crude (but workable) means for two people to play chess on the Web, using the GD module to do the actual graphical machinations involved in drawing the chess board.

The interface to the chess program is a web page that has the image of a board at the top and three forms at the bottom. The first form is for submitting a move, the second is for starting a new game, and the third is for reloading the board between moves to see if an opponent has moved. The moves are entered through the use of <SELECT> input fields, which makes for a slightly clunky interface but simplifies the example for the purposes of this chapter, as we do not have to check for valid input from the user. The interface web page is shown in Figure 4-1.

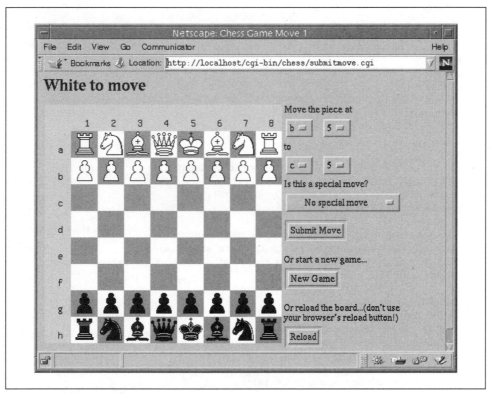

Figure 4-1. The HTML page resulting from a "new game" command

Note that this is just an example of using GD to manipulate graphics and really shouldn't be used as a chess-playing script. The chess server uses GD's image manipulation methods to create a new board from images of the individual chess pieces, and to move the pieces around on the board. It is the same as if you were sitting across the board from your opponent in a real-life game of chess; nothing is physically preventing you from making an illegal move. Our chess server does not implement an intelligent chess engine. The purpose here is not to demonstrate the inner workings of Deep Blue, but to show how to use GD in a practical application. However, it is still a working chess program; it's just probably more accurate to call it a chess board "simulator."

The *submitmove.cgi* script creates the HTML page that is the user interface. In turn, it calls the *drawboard.cgi* script that actually creates the image data and sends it to the web browser. This script uses an external file called *currentgame.txt* that contains information about who (white or black) is currently moving, the move number, and a list containing the history of moves. Note that in an actual production

script, you should explicitly unlink this file before writing to it. Here is the code
for *submitmove.cgi*:

```perl
#!/usr/bin/perl -w
#
# submitmove.cgi
# Create the web page that acts as an interface to the chess board simulator.
#
use GD;
use CGI;
use Fcntl qw(:DEFAULT :flock);          # for file locking constants
use strict;

# Initialize variables
#
my ($tile, $image, @fillcolors, $startfill, $endfill);
my ($tilew, $tileh) = (40, 40);
my ($width, $height) = ($tilew*9, $tileh*9);
my ($movenum, $tomove, @history);

# Now get the parameters passed into the script.
# Use the CGI module to parse the CGI form submmission.
# If this script was called as a result of a newboard or refresh action,
# these should all be empty.
#
my $query = new CGI;
my $action = $query->param('action');
my $startrow = $query->param('startrow');
my $startcol = $query->param('startcol');
my $endrow = $query->param('endrow');
my $endcol = $query->param('endcol');
my $special = $query->param('special');
```

At this point in the execution of the script we need to read in the state of the current game in progress. There are three possible actions, depending on how the
script was called:

- Creating a new board. In this case, just reset the state of the game.

- Making a move. If someone has made a move, the script should increment the
  move and toggle the player.

- Refreshing the screen. Because the page has a very short expiration period, it
  will not be in the user's cache when the user wants to reload the page. In this
  case, the script should not modify the current state. Note that because of the
  way this script is written, the browser's Reload button should not be used to
  check on an opponent's move. Instead, a link has been incorporated into the
  web page that will reload the page and keep its current state. Implementing
  the script so that the Reload button works correctly can be done, but it is even
  more cumbersome and beyond the scope of this example.

Continuing with the code:

```perl
if ($action eq "newboard") {
    # Starting a new game, so reset the move number to 1
    # and white should move first
    #
    ($movenum, $tomove) = (1, 'White');

} else {
    # If we get here we are either refreshing the screen, or making a move.
    # In either case we will need to parse the game file to determine the
    # current state.
    # The current state of the game is stored in a game file called
    # currentgame.txt. Open the game file and retrieve the current game
    # state.
    #
    open GAME, 'currentgame.txt';
    flock GAME, LOCK_EX;              # place an exclusive lock on the file
    while (<GAME>) {
        if (/^move number=(.+)$/) {
            $movenum = $1;            # the number of the current move
        } elsif (/^to move=(.+)$/) {
            $tomove = $1;             # white or black
        } else {
            push @history, $_;        # a history of moves
        }
    }
    close GAME;         # closes and unlocks the file
    if ($action eq "move") {
        # If this script was called because a move was made,
        # we should increment the move number
        #
        ++$movenum;

        # We should also toggle the current player
        #
        if ($tomove eq "White") {
            $tomove = "Black";
        } else {
            $tomove = "White";
        }

        # And add the current move to the history queue
        #
        push @history, "$startrow$startcol to $endrow$endcol\n";
    }
}

# Let's write our current state back to the game file,
# or create a game file if we're starting a new game...
#
open GAME, '>currentgame.txt';
flock GAME, LOCK_EX;                 # place an exclusive lock on the file
print GAME "move number=$movenum\n";
```

```
print GAME "to move=$tomove\n";
print GAME join '', @history;
close GAME;
```

The remainder of the script prints the HTML for the web page. The image of the board is an <IMG> tag that calls the *drawboard.cgi* script with a number of parameters. The parameters will all be empty unless a move has been made. The *drawboard.cgi* script understands this and will interpret the parameters accordingly.

One other item of note is the "special move" input field on the first form. In chess most moves involve only one piece (except in the case of a capture, which our program deals with by simply writing one piece over another). However, there are a few moves that require that two pieces be moved within a single turn. These cases are king- and queen-side castling and the promotion of pawns to queens. Because there are only three cases, we will implement them as special cases within the *drawboard.cgi* script. The castling moves make the assumption that the move indicated by the player is the movement of the king, and the pawn promotion assumes that the pawn is actually in a position to be promoted to a queen. The values of "O-O" for king-side castling and "O-O-O" for queen-side castling is borrowed from Portable Game Notation (PGN), a popular form for annotating chess games.

```
# Let the CGI module print the header info.
# The expire parameter tells the browser to remove this script
# from its cache after 1 second to ensure that we are generating new
# output with each invocation. We could also use a no-cache pagma.
#
print $query->header(-type    => 'text/html',
                     -expires =>'-1s',
                    );

print $query->start_html(-title => "Chess Game Move $movenum");

print "<H1>$tomove to move</H1>";

# Call the drawboard.cgi script to generate the image stream for
# the current chessboard. Pass in the current action (new, move, or
# refresh) and let the script determine which action to take.
# Note the use of the width and height parameters to the img tag...
# this allows the browser to draw the page before it has all the
# image data in hand.
#
print "<img width=$width height=$height ";
print "src=\"drawboard.cgi?action=$action&";
print "tilew=$tilew&tileh=$tileh&";

# The following fields will be blank if the action
# is 'new' or 'refresh'...
#
print "startrow=$startrow&startcol=$startcol&";
print "endrow=$endrow&endcol=$endcol&special=$special\" ALIGN=left>";
```

```
# Now print the forms at the bottom of the page
#
print <<EOF;
<FORM METHOD=POST ACTION="submitmove.cgi">
<INPUT TYPE=hidden NAME=action VALUE=move>
Move the piece at<BR>
<SELECT NAME="startrow">
<OPTION>a</OPTION><OPTION>b</OPTION><OPTION>c</OPTION><OPTION>d</OPTION>
<OPTION>e</OPTION><OPTION>f</OPTION><OPTION>g</OPTION><OPTION>h</OPTION>
</SELECT>
<SELECT NAME="startcol">
<OPTION>1</OPTION><OPTION>2</OPTION><OPTION>3</OPTION><OPTION>4</OPTION>
<OPTION>5</OPTION><OPTION>6</OPTION><OPTION>7</OPTION><OPTION>8</OPTION>
</SELECT><BR>
to<BR>
<SELECT NAME="endrow">
<OPTION>a</OPTION><OPTION>b</OPTION><OPTION>c</OPTION><OPTION>d</OPTION>
<OPTION>e</OPTION><OPTION>f</OPTION><OPTION>g</OPTION><OPTION>h</OPTION>
</SELECT>
<SELECT NAME="endcol">
<OPTION>1</OPTION><OPTION>2</OPTION><OPTION>3</OPTION><OPTION>4</OPTION>
<OPTION>5</OPTION><OPTION>6</OPTION><OPTION>7</OPTION><OPTION>8</OPTION>
</SELECT><br>
Is this a special move?<BR>
<SELECT NAME="special">
<OPTION>No special move</OPTION>
<OPTION VALUE="O-O">King side castle</OPTION>
<OPTION VALUE="O-O-O">Queen side castle</OPTION>
<OPTION VALUE="PQ">Promote Pawn to Queen</OPTION>
</SELECT><BR>

<INPUT TYPE="submit" VALUE="Submit Move"><br>
</FORM>

<FORM METHOD=POST ACTION="submitmove.cgi">
<INPUT TYPE=hidden NAME=action VALUE=newboard>
Or start a new game... <BR>
<INPUT TYPE="submit" VALUE="New Game"><br>
</FORM>

<FORM METHOD=POST ACTION="submitmove.cgi">
<INPUT TYPE=hidden NAME=action VALUE=refresh>
Or reload the board...(don't use <BR>
your browser's reload button!)<BR>
<INPUT TYPE="submit" VALUE="Reload"><br>
</FORM>
</BODY>
</HTML>
EOF
# End of submitmove.cgi
```

The *drawboard.cgi* script is called whenever the board needs to be drawn. It is passed a number of parameters by *submitmove.cgi*; the action indicates how the board is to be drawn (draw a new board, move a piece, or simply refresh the current board), *tilew* and *tileh* give the dimensions in pixels of each square on the board (to make it easy to change the size of the board), and the starting and ending row and columns are the values entered on the corresponding fields on the web page. If the action is *refresh* or *newboard*, these fields will be empty.

This script stores the current board in an external GIF file called *currentboard.gif.* Here is the code for *drawboard.cgi:*

```perl
#!/usr/bin/perl -w
#
# drawboard.cgi
# Dynamically create the image of a chess board.
#
use GD;
use CGI;
use Fcntl qw(:DEFAULT :flock);        # for file locking constants
use strict;

# Set up some variables
#
my ($image, @fillcolors, $startfill, $endfill);

# Set up a translation hash for changing row letters to numbers
#
my $i = 1;
my %rownums = map {$_ => $i++} ('a'..'h');

# Get the move passed from submitmove.cgi
#
my $query = new CGI;
my $action = $query->param('action');
my $tilew = $query->param('tilew');
my $tileh = $query->param('tileh');
my $startrow =$rownums { $query->param('startrow') };
my $startcol = $query->param('startcol');
my $endrow = $rownums { $query->param('endrow') };
my $endcol = $query->param('endcol');
my $special = $query->param('special');
```

If the current action is *newboard,* create a new chess board. This script also uses twelve small GIF files, each containing the image of a single unique chess piece. These files should have two-letter names, the first letter being the color of the piece and the second being the first letter of the piece (i.e., *br.gif* for the black rook, *wk.gif* for the white king, *wn.gif* for the white knight, etc.). These images are shown in Figure 4-2. The pieces are black and white on an off-white background; the black squares of the chess board are actually a purplish color, and the white squares are an off-white.

```perl
if ($action eq "newboard") {
    $image = new GD::Image($tilew*9, $tileh*9);

    # The background is set to the first allocated color.
    # In this case, 80% gray
```

Figure 4-2. The 12 chess piece tiles used to create a new chessboard, stored as separate GIF files. The files are (left to right) br.gif, bn.gif, bb.gif, bq.gif, bk.gif, bp.gif, wr.gif, wn.gif, wb.gif, wq.gif, wk.gif, and wp.gif.

```
#
$image->colorAllocate(204, 204, 204);
my $black = $image->colorAllocate(0, 0, 0);

# Now allocate the colors for our squares
#
@fillcolors = (
                $image->colorAllocate(255, 255, 204),   # (0) Off-white
                $image->colorAllocate(204, 102, 204),   # (1) Purple
              );

# Label the rows with letters and the columns with numbers
#
foreach (1..8) {
   $image->string(gdLargeFont,
            int($tilew/2),
         int(($_+.5)*$tileh),
         chr(96+$_), $black);
   $image->string(gdLargeFont,
            int(($_+.5)*$tilew),
         int($tileh/2),
         $_, $black);
}

# Draw a large rectangle for the light squares
#
$image->filledRectangle($tilew,$tileh,
                        $tilew*9, $tileh*9,
                        $fillcolors[0] );

# Draw the middle four rows of dark squares of the board
#
foreach my $y (3, 5) {
    foreach my $x (1, 3, 5, 7) {
        $image->filledRectangle($x*$tilew,$y*$tileh,
                                ($x+1)*$tilew-1, ($y+1)*$tileh-1,
                                $fillcolors[1] );
        $image->filledRectangle(($x+1)*$tilew,($y+1)*$tileh,
                                ($x+2)*$tilew-1, ($y+2)*$tileh-1,
                                $fillcolors[1] );
    }
}
```

```
# Finally, add the pieces to the board. The pieces are stored
# in external gif files labelled 'wp' for white pawn, 'bn' for
# black knight, etc. Each piece will be drawn with its
# corresponding square color.
#
place ('wr', 1, (1, 8));
place ('wn', 1, (2, 7));
place ('wb', 1, (3, 6));
place ('wq', 1, 4);
place ('wk', 1, 5);
place ('wp', 2, (1, 2, 3, 4, 5, 6, 7, 8));
place ('br', 8, (1, 8));
place ('bn', 8, (2, 7));
place ('bb', 8, (3, 6));
place ('bq', 8, 4);
place ('bk', 8, 5);
place ('bp', 7, (1, 2, 3, 4, 5, 6, 7, 8));
```

In the second case, a move may have been made. First check the special cases, then move the piece from one square to another with the *move()* subroutine.

```
} else {
    open BOARD, "currentboard.gif";
    $image = newFromGif GD::Image(\*BOARD);
    close BOARD;
    @fillcolors = (
                    $image->colorExact(255, 255, 204),   # (0) Off-white
                    $image->colorExact(204, 102, 204),   # (1) Purple
                  );

    if ($action eq "move") {
        # First parse $special to see if we have a special move
        #
    if ($special =~ /O-O-O/) {
        # O-O-O = Queen side castle
        # We're assuming that the actual move is the movement
        # of the king...we just have to move the castle.
        #
        move($startrow, 1, $startrow, 4);
    }
    elsif ($special =~ /O-O/) {
        # O-O = King side castle
        #
        move($startrow, 8, $startrow, 6);
    }
    elsif ($special =~ /PQ/) {
        # Promote Pawn to Queen
        # We must trust that the current piece is a pawn,
        # replacing it at the current spot with a queen
        # before it is moved later. We are also assuming
        # that the move is valid; we use the end row value to
        # determine whether the piece should be black or white.
        #
        place('bq', $startrow, $startcol) if ($endrow ==  1);
```

```
            place('wq', $startrow, $startcol) if ($endrow == 8);
        }

        # Now move the piece in question
        #
        move($startrow, $startcol, $endrow, $endcol);
    }
}
```

Now print out the graphic:

```
# Write out the current board to currentboard.gif
my $gifdata = $image->gif;
open OUTFILE, ">currentboard.gif";
flock OUTFILE, LOCK_EX;                    # place an exclusive lock on the file
binmode OUTFILE;
print OUTFILE $gifdata;
close OUTFILE;

# Let CGI module print the header info
#
print $query->header(-type => 'image/gif',
                     -expires => '-1s'
                     );
binmode (STDOUT);
print $gifdata;
```

Three subroutines are used by the *drawboard.cgi* script. The first is the *place()* subroutine called to place each piece in the board when a new board is being created. The *tilecolor()* subroutine is called to determine the color of the square based on its row and column values. Because the same piece may be placed in multiple columns within the same row (as in the row of pawns, for example), *place()* will take as parameters a piece, a row, and a list of columns in which to place the piece.

```
sub place {
    # The first two parameters are the two-letter name of the piece and
    # the row in which to place it. The piece can be placed in multiple
    # columns, so the remainder is a list of columns...
    #
    my ($piece, $y) = (shift @_, shift @_);

    open TILEFILE, $piece.".gif";
    my $tile = newFromGif GD::Image(\*TILEFILE);
    $tile->transparent($tile->getPixel(0,0));

    foreach my $x (@_) {
        # First draw the appropriate square color
        #
        $image->filledRectangle($x*$tilew,$y*$tileh,
                                ($x+1)*$tilew-1, ($y+1)*$tileh-1,
                                $fillcolors[tilecolor($x, $y)] );
        # Then copy the piece to the square
        #
```

```
        $image->copyResized($tile, $x * $tilew, $y * $tileh,
                            0, 0, $tilew, $tileh, 40,40);
    }
    close TILEFILE;
}
```

The *tilecolor()* subroutine determines the color of a square. The algorithm is simple; if the sum of the row and column is odd, the square is white.

```
sub tilecolor {
    # This routine takes a row and a column as a parameter
    # and returns 0 if that square is white, 1 if black
    #
    return abs((($_[0] + $_[1]) % 2)-1);
}
```

Finally, the *move()* subroutine actually moves a piece from one square to another using GD's *copy()* method. It doesn't check whether the piece is actually in the square indicated by the *startrow* and *startcol* variables, so it can possibly "move" an empty square to another square.

```
sub move {
    # Parameters to move are in the order: startrow, startcol, endrow, endcol
    #
    my ($srow, $scol, $erow, $ecol) = @_;
    my ($startx, $endx) = ($scol * $tilew, $ecol * $tilew);
    my ($starty, $endy) = ($srow * $tileh, $erow * $tileh);

    my $startfill = $fillcolors[tilecolor($srow, $scol)];
    my $endfill = $fillcolors[tilecolor($erow, $ecol)];

    $image->fill($startx+1, $starty+1, $endfill);
    $image->copy($image, $endx, $endy,
                $startx, $starty,
                $tilew, $tileh );
    $image->filledRectangle($startx, $starty,
                            $startx+$tilew-1, $starty+$tileh-1,
                            $startfill);
}
```

Figure 4-3 shows the board after several moves have been made.

The GD.pm Distribution

The GD module is available on every platform on which Perl is available. Several versions of Perl come with GD as a standard part of the Perl distribution, such as the Gurusamy Sarathy Win32 port and the Macintosh port, which has GD precompiled in the MacPerl application. Installation methods vary from platform to

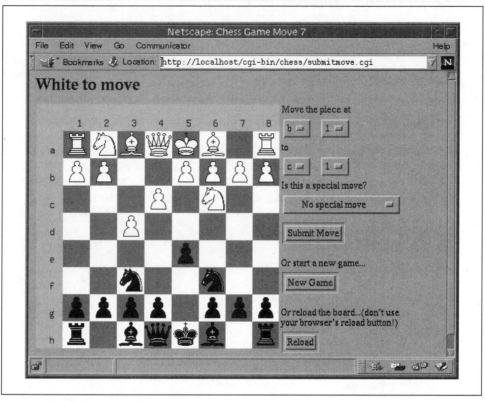

Figure 4-3. The board at the beginning of Move 4, Round 3 in the 1997 Kasparov/Deep Blue rematch

platform, but if you've ever successfully installed a Perl module on your system, you shouldn't have a problem installing GD. Refer to the README that comes with the package for platform-specific information.

To download the latest version of GD, check CPAN first via *http://www.perl.com*. The latest version of GD.pm should also be available at *http://stein.cshl.org/WWW/software/GD/GD.html*. Thomas Boutell's original C-language version of the libgd library can be found at *http://www.boutell.com/gd/gd.html*.

The copyright to the GD.pm interface is held by Lincoln D. Stein, and it is distributed under similar terms as Perl itself; it is free for any purpose, provided the statement of copyright remains attached to it. The gd C library on which GD is based is covered by a separate copyright held by the Quest Protein Database Center, Cold Spring Harbor Labs, and Thomas Boutell. See the "copying" file that comes with the standard GD distribution for more specific copyright information.

GD Objects and Methods by Category

GD provides all of the objects and methods listed in Table 4-1.

Table 4-1. GD's Object Definitions and Methods, Arranged by Category of Use

Category	Method
GD Objects	GD::Image, GD::Font, GD::Polygon
GD::Image object creation and saving methods	new(), newFromGif(), newFromXbm(), newFromGd(), gif(), gd()
GD::Image color control methods	colorAllocate(), colorDeallocate(), colorClosest(), colorExact(), colorsTotal(), getPixel(), rgb(), setBrush(), setPixel(), setStyle(), setTile(), transparent()
GD::Image drawing methods	line(), dashedLine(), rectangle(), filledRectangle(), polygon(), filledPolygon(), arc(), fill(), fillToBorder()
GD::Image drawing constants	gdBrushed, gdStyled, gdTiled, gdTransparent
GD::Image copying commands	copy(), copyResized()
GD::Image character and string drawing	string(), stringUp(), char(), charUp()
GD::Image attribute control	interlaced(), getBounds()
GD::Polygon object manipulation methods	new(), getPt(), setPt(), toPt(), length(), vertices(), bounds(), offset(), map(), scale(), transform()
GD::Font constants	gdSmallFont, gdLargeFont, gdMediumBoldFont, gdTinyFont, gdGiantFont
GD::Font information methods	width(), height()

Image Reading and Writing Methods

GD was designed specifically to handle files in the GIF format. Additional methods are available to read X Bitmap files and read and write files in its own uncompressed GD file format. All image reading and writing happens through the use of *filehandles*. This allows for a great deal of flexibility in managing the flow of image data. It is simple to write an image to a file, STDOUT, or to pipe image data between processes.

The following methods are available from the GD::Image class for reading and writing images:

new() — *create an empty image object*

```
GD::Image::new(width, height)
```

The *new()* method will return an empty image object of class GD::Image. If the width and height parameters for the starting dimensions of the image are not provided, a default value of 64×64 is used instead. If the method fails, usually when

you run out of memory, it returns undef. In this case you should signal an error
with *die():*

```
my $image = new GD::Image(25, 25) ||
        die "Can't create empty image! Probably out of memory...";
```

newFromGif() — *create a new image from a GIF file*

```
GD::Image::newFromGif(filehandle)
```

The *newFromGif()* method will read data from a GIF file. This method requires
that the *filehandle* parameter be a handle to a previously opened file. This gives
you a bit of flexibility with the option of reading the GIF data from a file or (on
Unix systems) from a previously opened pipe. The method will automatically read
the data in binary mode but you must explicitly close the filehandle when you are
through with it.

If the method succeeds, it will return a binary data stream representing the image
data. If it fails (usually if the data is not actually a valid GIF file), it returns **undef**,
in which case you should signal an error with *die()*. For example:

```
open (GIFFILE, "burroughs.gif") ||
    die "Couldn't open file!";
my $image = newFromGif GD::Image(\*GIFFILE) ||
    die "Not a valid GIF file!";
close GIFFILE;
```

As a side note on Perl syntax, the generally approved method for passing a filehandle to a function is as a reference to a "typeglob," as in:

```
somefunction(\*filehandle)
```

Passing the filehandle as a reference is preferable to passing it as a bare typeglob
in that the former method will not complain if the *use strict* or *use strict refs* pragmas are in effect.[*]

newFromXbm() — *create a new image from an X Bitmap file*

```
GD::Image::newFromXbm(filehandle)
```

The *newFromXbm()* method allows you to read from a black and white X Bitmap
file. Note that pixmaps (XPMs) are not supported, nor can you write back out to
an XBM. This method is used in the same manner as *newFromGif()*:

```
open (XBMFILE, "corso.xbm") ||
    die "Couldn't open file!"";
my $image = newFromXbm GD::Image(\*XBMFILE) ||
    die "Not a valid GD file!";
close XBMFILE;
```

---

[*] A typeglob is simply an abstract internal Perl type that was used to pass filehandles by reference before
Perl had real references. The "strict" pragma is a compiler directive that affects how sloppily Perl will let
you write your code.

newFromGd() — *create a new image from a GD file*

GD::Image::newFromGd(*filehandle*)

The *newFromGd()* method reads in image data from a file in the same manner as the previous two methods. A GD-formatted file is a special file format that was created by GD author Tom Boutell as a means of quickly saving data to disk. It is an uncompressed storage format with little overhead in the actual reading and writing of the data stream, but the image files that are created can be quite large. The GD storage format should only be used internally by your script; its lack of image compression makes it unsuitable as a permanent storage format.

An example of opening a GD file:

```
open (GDFILE, "kerouac.gd") ||
    die "Couldn't open file!";
my $image = newFromGd GD::Image(\*GDFILE) ||
    die "Not a valid GD file!";
close GDFILE;
```

gif() — *return the image in GIF format*

GD::Image::gif

The *gif()* method will convert an image into the GIF format and return it. If your platform makes a distinction between text files and binary files, make sure that you are writing in binary mode by calling *binmode()* first. You can then write the image to the previously opened file:

```
open OUTFILE, ">beatniks.gif";        # Open the file for writing
binmode OUTFILE;                      # Make sure we're in binary mode
print OUTFILE $image->gif;            # Print GIF data to the file
close OUTFILE;
```

On Unix systems, you can pipe the image data to an image viewer, such as xv or the display utility that comes with ImageMagick:

```
open (DISPLAY, "| display ") ||       # Of course, you must have already
    die "Couldn't display image!";    # installed display on your system
binmode DISPLAY;
print DISPLAY $gif_data->gif;         # Pipe GIF data to image viewer
close DISPLAY;                        # Close the pipe
```

gd() — *return the image in GD format*

GD::Image::gd

This method returns the image in the GD uncompressed storage format. It can be used for writing to a file in the same way as the *gif()* method:

```
open OUTFILE, ">neatniks.gd";         # Open the file for writing
binmode OUTFILE;                      # Make sure we're in binary mode
print OUTFILE $image->gd;             # Print GD data to the file
close OUTFILE;
```

Color Manipulation Methods

Colors are stored within GIF files as indices to a table of no more than 256 colors. GD provides a number of functions for retrieving information about an image's color table, and for manipulating entries in the table. In addition there are several "special" color constants imported into your script's namespace that are used to implement different shaped brushes and line styles. These methods and constants are:

colorAllocate() — *allocate a color in the color table*

GD::Image::colorAllocate(*red, green, blue*)

The *colorAllocate()* function is an object method that takes three decimal integers in the range 0...255 for the three color channels and allocates a space in the image's color table. The method returns the index of the color in the color table if successful, or -1 if it fails. The first color that is allocated with this method becomes the background color for the image.

colorAllocate() does not check to see if the color is already in the colormap; it is possible to have the same color allocated multiple times within a colormap. Another quirk is that GD will always keep the number of entries in the colormap to a multiple of two. Thus if eight colors are currently in a colormap and you allocate a ninth, the colormap will be expanded to include 16 colors, the ninth of which is the color you just allocated and the remainder of which are random colors. You cannot allocate more than 256 colors in an image. In this case you must first use *colorDeallocate()* to remove indices from the color table before adding new ones.

If you are going to be using the color later in your script, you should store the returned index value. For example:

```
$blue = $image->colorAllocate(0, 0, 255);
```

colorDeallocate() — *remove a color from the color table*

GD::Image::colorDeallocate(*colorindex*)

The *colorDeallocate()* method makes the color referred to by the *colorindex* parameter available for reallocation with the *colorAllocate()* method. The colorindex must be an index in the color table that was returned by one of the other color manipulation methods. Note that the color will not actually be removed from the colormap until another color is allocated. The number of colors in the colormap will not be reduced by this method.

colorClosest() — *find the closest matching color*

`GD::Image::colorClosest(red, green, blue)`

This method returns the color table index of the color that best matches the color specified by the given red, green, and blue values, or a -1 if the table has no colors allocated.

colorExact() — *find an exact match for a given color*

`GD::Image::colorExact(red, green, blue)`

The *colorExact()* method returns the color table index of a color that matches the color specified by the given red, green, and blue values. It returns a -1 if the color is not in the image's color table.

```
$DodgerBlue = $image->colorExact(30,144,255);
print "DodgerBlue is in the color table.\n" if $DodgerBlue >= 0;
```

colorsTotal() — *total number of allocated colors*

`GD::Image::colorsTotal()`

This method returns the number of colors that are allocated in the color table of an image.

getPixel() — *get color index of a given pixel*

`GD::Image::getPixel(x,y)`

The *getPixel()* method returns the color table index of the color at the specified pixel. As with all functions that return a color index, you can use the *rgb()* method to convert the index to a list of the integer red, green, and blue values.

rgb() — *get the red, green, and blue values for an index*

`GD::Image::rgb(colorindex)`

The *rgb()* method returns a list with the red, green, and blue values that correspond to the color to which the color index parameter refers. It can be used this way:

```
($red, $green, $blue) = $image->rgb($someindex);
```

transparent() — *make a color transparent*

`GD::Image::transparent(colorindex)`

The *transparent()* method makes any pixels of color *colorindex* in an image transparent. Only one color may be transparent at a time; a second call to *transparent()* will override the first call, and will return pixels that were previously transparent to their original color. To turn off transparency in an image, give *colorindex* a value of -1. To find the index of the transparent color in an image, call *transparent()* without a parameter. To make the color that is closest to white in an image transparent, try:

```
$mostestwhitest = $image->colorClosest(255,255,255);
$image->transparent($whitest);
```

This function can be used with *setBrush()* to create irregularly shaped brushes. See the *setBrush()* method for an example of this.

setBrush() — *assign a brush to an image*

GD::Image::setBrush(*image*)

The drawing commands available through GD can be called with either a solid color or with a special brush that is accessed via the *gdBrushed* constant. This brush is simply another image that must be created or read in from another GIF file. The *setBrush()* method assigns a particular image as the current brush for drawing within another image. To draw with a brush follow these five steps:

1. Create a new image object for the brush, or read the brush from a GIF file. Here we will create a new square 20×20 pixel brush:

   ```
   my $brush = new GD::Image(20, 20);
   ```

2. If you are creating a new brush with the GD drawing commands, allocate a color for the brush and draw the brush shape. In this case, the brush is a red circle:

   ```
   my $red = $brush->allocateColor(255, 0, 0);
   $brush->arc(10, 10, 20, 20, 0, 360, $red);
   ```

3. If you are creating an irregularly shaped brush, set the background color of the brush with the *transparent()* method so that the brush does not overwrite its own path:

   ```
   my $white = $brush->allocateColor(255, 255, 255);
   $brush->transparent($white);
   ```

4. Assign the brush to the image you want to draw on:

   ```
   $image->setBrush($brush);
   ```

5. Call a drawing command with *gdBrushed* as the `color` parameter to use the brush:

   ```
   $image->line(0, 0, 50, 50, gdBrushed);
   ```

setStyle() — *assign a line style to an image*

GD::Image::setStyle(*@colorindices*)

Dotted and dashed lines can be drawn using the GD drawing commands with the *gdStyled* line style instead of the *colorindex* parameter. The *setStyle()* method defines a line style for an image. Follow these steps to create a styled line:

1. Allocate the colors you wish to use in the line style, or get their color indices with the *colorExact()* method:

```
$blue = $image->colorAllocate(0, 0, 255);     # allocate blue
$red = $image->colorAllocate(255, 0, 0);      # allocate red
```

2. Create a list of color indices. Each element of the list represents one pixel in a sequence that will be repeated over the length of the drawn line. To indicate a blank space in a dashed line, use the *gdTransparent* constant instead of a color index. If a color index has already been marked as transparent for the image, it will also be transparent in the drawn line. To indicate a blue and red dashed line that repeats blue for two pixels, red for three pixels, and then a two-pixel break, use the following for the color list:

```
@linestyle = ($blue, $blue, $red, $red, $red, gdTransparent, gdTransparent);
```

3. Assign the style to the image:

```
$image->setStyle(@linestyle);
```

4. Draw with a drawing method and the *gdStyled* special color. If the *gdStyled-Brushed* constant is used, the brush pattern will be drawn for those pixels that are not set to *gdTransparent*. To draw a dashed rectangle, use:

```
$image->rectangle(0, 0, 100, 100, gdStyled);
```

Use *setStyle()* when you need to draw a line or a shape with an arbitrary dotted or dashed line; see also the *dashedLine()* method.

setPixel() — *set a pixel to a color*

```
GD::Image::setPixel(x, y, colorindex)
```

The *setPixel()* method will set the color of a given pixel to the color referred to by the *colorindex*. Use a brush associated with the image (*gdBrushed* or *gdStyled-Brushed*) to "stamp" the shape of the brush onto the image at the given center point.

setTile() — *assign a tile pattern for use with an image*

```
GD::Image::setTile(image)
```

Use the *setTile()* method to assign an image as a tile pattern for use when drawing filled shapes within an image. First call *setTile()* with an image object, then draw using the *gdTiled* special color constant instead of the drawing command's color parameter:

```
# Read in a pattern from a GIF file
open INFILE, "wallpaper.gif";
my $wallpaper = newFromGif GD::Image('INFILE');

$ Set $wallpaper as the current tilable pattern
$image->setTile($wallpaper);
```

```
# Draw a 100x100 rectangle tiled with the wallpaper pattern
$image->filledRectangle(0, 0, 100, 100, gdTiled);
```

Image Drawing and Manipulation Methods

For all of the drawing methods, the coordinate system is defined with (0, 0) as the upper-left corner of the image and the x and y values increasing down and to the right. In general, when a method takes a color index as a parameter, you should pass the index of a color previously allocated with one of the methods described in the "Color Manipulation Methods" section, or use one of the special color constants.

Two methods are provided for copying rectangular regions between images. When copying between images with different color tables, the table of the destination image is filled with as many unique colors from the source image as can fit, and the rest are intelligently matched to colors already in the destination image if the table becomes full.

The following is an alphabetical list of the drawing and manipulation methods:

arc() — *draw an arc, ellipse, or circle*

`GD::Image::arc(x, y, width, height, start, end, colorindex)`

The *arc()* method allows you to draw arcs, circles, and ellipses on an image, centered at the coordinate given by *x* and *y*. The *height* parameter indicates the maximum diameter of the on the y axis and the *width* parameter is the maximum diameter on the x axis. For a circle, the height and width would both be equal to the diameter of the circle; you can vary either value to produce ellipses of various shapes. The start and end parameters are the starting and ending angles (in degrees) that the arc should sweep through. These angles are measured from the x axis and increase in the clockwise direction, with 0 degrees at 3 o'clock, 90 degrees at 6 o'clock, and so on. To draw a circle centered at (100, 100) with a radius of 25 pixels, for example, you would use:

```
$image->arc(100, 100, 50, 50, 0, 360, $red);
```

To draw the right half of an ellipse, use:

```
$image->arc(100, 100, 100, 50, 270, 90, $red);
```

The *colorindex* parameter may be a color index or any of the special colors *gdBrushed*, *gdStyled*, or *gdStyledBrushed*.

copy() — *copy a region from one image to another*

`GD::Image::copy(srcImage, destX, destY, srcX, srcY, width, height)`

The *copy()* method will copy all pixels with the *width × height* region starting at the coordinate *srcX, srcY* of the image *srcImage* to a similarly sized region of the destination image at *destX, destY.* The source and destination images may be the same, if you wish to copy from one part of an image to another part of the same image, but the source and destination regions should not overlap.

copyResized() — *copy a sizeable region from one image to another*

```
GD::Image::copyResized(srcImage, destX, destY, srcX, srcY,
                       destWidth, destHeight, srcWidth, srcHeight)
```

The *copyResized()* method will copy a region from one image to another, with the option to scale the image region to fit the target region. The following code will copy a region from `$image2` to `$image1` and shrink it by 50% to fit:

```
# create the image objects
$image1 = new GD::Image(20, 20);
$image2 = new GD::Image(200, 200);

# This assumes we draw or read in something to copy
# ...

# copy the upper left quadrant of $image2 to $image and scale it
$image1->copyResized($image2, 0, 0, 0, 0, 20, 20, 100, 100);
```

dashedLine() — *draw a dashed line*

```
GD::Image::dashedLine(x1, y1, x2, y2, colorindex)
```

The *dashedLine()* method is a simplified way of drawing dashed lines using a standard 4-pixel dash. To create more complicated or varied dashed lines, use the *setStyle()* method and `gdStyled` constant. The *colorindex* parameter can be a color index or `gdBrushed` to draw a dashed line with the current brush.

fill() — *floodfill an area with a color*

```
GD::Image::fill(x, y, colorindex)
```

The *fill()* method will fill an area with a given color. The area to fill is defined by all those pixels neighboring the pixel at *x, y* that are of the same color as the pixel and are connected by pixels of the same color. The operation is exactly the same as the paint bucket tool in paint programs. The color can be either a color index or the `gdTiled` special color if you want to fill the area with a tiled pattern. The *fill()* method can be used to draw filled shapes with different colored borders, as in:

```
# Draw a green-filled circle with a red border
$image->arc(100, 100, 50, 50, 0, 360, $red);
$image->fill(100, 100, $green);
```

filledPolygon() — *draw previously defined polygon filled with a color*

```
GD::Image::filledPolygon(polygon, colorindex)
```

The *filledPolygon()* method is used the same way you use the *polygon()* method, except that the area defined by the polygon is filled with the given color. To draw a filled polygon with the lines stroked in a different color, use *polygon()* with the *fill()* method or draw a second non-filled polygon on top of the filled polygon. The *colorindex* may be either:

A color index
> The polygon will be filled with the specified color. If the color has been marked as transparent, the pixels will become transparent.

gdTiled
> The polygon will be filled with the pattern previously assigned as the current tile pattern with *setTile()*. If the polygon is larger than the tile pattern, the tile pattern is repeated to fill the polygon.

filledRectangle() — *draw a rectangle filled with a color*

```
GD::Image::filledRectangle(x1, y1, x2, y2, colorindex)
```

The *filledRectangle()* method draws a rectangle with its upper left corner at *x1, y1* and its lower right corner *at x2, y2.* and filled with the color indicated by *colorindex.* The *colorindex* parameter can be either:

A color index
> The rectangle will be filled with the specified color. If the color has been marked as transparent, the pixels will become transparent. Note that no mechanism is provided for stroking the border of the rectangle with a different color than the fill color. To do this you must draw a second rectangle on top of the filled rectangle with the desired border color, or use the *fill()* method.

gdTiled
> The rectangle will be filled with the pattern previously assigned as the current tile pattern with *setTile()*. If the rectangle is larger than the tile pattern, the tile pattern is repeated to fill the rectangle.

fillToBorder() — *flood-fill an area bounded by a given color*

```
GD::Image::fillToBorder(x, y, bordercolor, colorindex)
```

The *fillToBorder()* method operates in the same way as the *fill()* method, except that it will fill the area defined as all pixels neighboring the pixel at *x, y* and bordered by the color given by *bordercolor.* This can be useful when dealing with images with shapes that are filled with dithered colors, or areas where all the pixels are not of exactly the same color.

getBounds() — *get the width and height of an image*

```
GD::Image::getBounds()
```

The *getBounds()* method returns a list containing the width and height of the image in pixels. For example:

```
my ($width, $height) = $image->getBounds();
```

interlaced() — *make an image interlaced*

```
GD::Image::interlaced([True | False])
```

The *interlaced()* method will indicate that the image is to be saved in an interlaced format when it is eventually written. Calling *interlaced()* without a parameter will query whether the image is currently interlaced or not.

line() — *draw a line*

```
GD::Image::line(x1, y1, x2, y2, colorindex)
```

The *line()* method draws a single, pixel-wide line from *x1, y1* to *x2, y2*. The color parameter can be any of the following:

A color index
> The line will be drawn in the specified color. If the color has been marked as transparent, the pixels on the line will become transparent.

gdBrushed
> The line will be drawn using the current brush shape, set with *setBrush()*. To create variable width lines, use a brush of the desired thickness.

gdStyled
> The line will be drawn with dashes defined by a previous call to *setStyled()*.

gdStyledBrushed
> The line will be drawn with the current brush but only for those pixels that are not set to *gdTransparent* within the current *gdStyled* color list.

polygon() — *draw a previously created polygon shape*

```
GD::Image::polygon(polygon, colorindex)
```

This is a drawing method that will allow you to draw a polygon defined by a GD::Polygon object onto an image. You must first create a polygon object and define its points with the *addPt()* method; a polygon must have at least three points, the first and last of which will be automatically connected when it is drawn to the image. To create a four-sided red parallelogram, for example, use:

```
my $red = $image->colorAllocate(255, 0, 0);   # Allocate a color index for red
my $parallelogram = new GD::Polygon;          # Create the polygon object
$parallelogram->addPt(20, 20);                # Add the four vertices
$parallelogram->addPt(0, 100);
$parallelogram->addPt(100, 100);
$parallelogram->addPt(120, 20);
$image->polygon($parallelogram, $red);        # Draw the polygon on the image
```

To draw a filled polygon, use this method followed by a call to *fill()*, or use the *filledPolygon()* method. The *colorindex* parameter specifies the color or style of the line of the polygon, and can be one of the following:

A color index

> The lines of the polygon will be drawn in the specified color. If the color has been marked as transparent, the pixels will become transparent.

gdBrushed

> The lines of the polygon will be drawn using the current brush shape, set with *setBrush()*. To create rectangles with sides thicker than one pixel, use a brush of the desired thickness.

gdStyled

> The lines of the polygon will be drawn with dashes defined by a previous call to *setStyled()*.

gdStyledBrushed

> The lines of the polygon will be drawn with the current brush but only for those pixels that are not set to *gdTransparent* within the current *gdStyled* color list.

rectangle() — *draw a rectangle*

```
GD::Image::rectangle(x1, y1, x2, y2, colorindex)
```

The *rectangle()* method draws a rectangle with its upper left corner at *x1, y1* and its lower right corner at *x2, y2*. The *colorindex* parameter can be one of the following:

A color index

> The lines of the rectangle will be drawn in the specified color. If the color has been marked as transparent, the pixels will become transparent.

gdBrushed

> The lines of the rectangle will be drawn using the current brush shape, set with *setBrush()*. To create rectangles with sides thicker than one pixel, use a brush of the desired thickness.

gdStyled

> The lines of the rectangle will be drawn with dashes defined by a previous call to *setStyled()*.

gdStyledBrushed

> The lines of the rectangle will be drawn with the current brush but only for those pixels that are not set to *gdTransparent* within the current *gdStyled* color list.

string() — *draw a text string on an image*

```
GD::Image::string(font, x, y, string, color)
```

The *string()* method draws the string onto the image with the upper left corner of the text box starting at the coordinate *x, y*. The font must be one of the six GD fonts: *gdTinyFont, gdSmallFont, gdMediumBoldFont, gdLargeFont,* or *gdGiantFont.*

To draw a string with quotes in it, escape the quotes with a backslash (\). Because of its limited font support, GD does not interpret escaped linefeeds (or other special characters) the way that ImageMagick does. Multiple lines of text must be drawn as separate strings, with the space between lines computed using the GD::Font::height object method. You may want to consider using ImageMagick for creating text-intensive graphics anyway, as its font support is more robust than GD's font support.

An example:

```
$image->string(gdTinyFont,10, 10,"A way a lone a last a loved a long the",
$red);
```

stringUp() — *draw a text string vertically*

`GD::Image::stringUp(`*font, x, y, string, color*`)`

The *stringUp()* method will draw a string rotated 90 degrees counter-clockwise, with the lower left corner of the text block at the coordinate *x, y*. The *stringUp()* method has no corresponding *stringDown()* method. It is really only useful for applications such as labeling axes on a graph. Use the PerlMagick package if you need greater control over the positioning of your text.

Font Methods

GD provides some limited support for using different fonts when drawing text on images. Strings may be drawn horizontally or rotated 90 degrees vertically. Because of the way that fonts are implemented, there is currently no support for other angles of text rotation, which would require the use of an external rendering engine such as Ghostscript or the FreeType package. The Unix version of GD also comes with the program *bdftogd* (written by Jan Pazdziora) that will allow you to convert fonts from the Unix bdf format to a format that can be included with GD on compilation. Other programs are available for converting TrueType and PostScript fonts to bdf format.

The five built-in fonts are imported into your script's namespace as the global variables *gdGiantFont, gdLargeFont, gdMediumBoldFont, gdSmallFont,* and *gdTinyFont* (see Figure 4-4). They are all monospaced fonts with 256 characters in their character sets. The dimensions of each can be determined with the GD::Font::width and GD::Font::height object methods, or by consulting Table 4-2.

Table 4-2. The Dimensions of the Five Standard GD Fonts

Font name	Width (pixels)	Height (pixels)
gdTinyFont	5	8
gdSmallFont	6	12
gdMediumBoldFont	7	13

Table 4-2. The Dimensions of the Five Standard GD Fonts (continued)

Font name	Width (pixels)	Height (pixels)
gdLargeFont	8	16
gdGiantFont	9	15

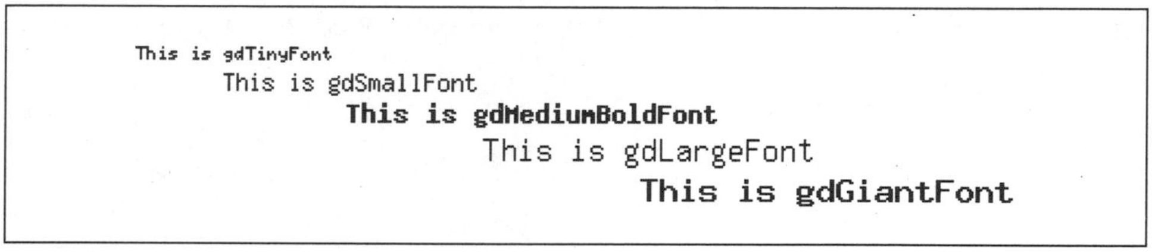

```
            This is gdTinyFont
         This is gdSmallFont
                  This is gdMediumBoldFont
                       This is gdLargeFont
                          This is gdGiantFont
```

Figure 4-4. The fonts available from GD

The GD::Font object is not currently all that useful; it is implemented primarily as a means for future expansion of the way that GD deals with fonts. However, there are a few methods for getting information about a font, described below.

nchars() — *return the number of characters in a font*
GD::Font::nchars

This method returns the number of characters in the font. All of the standard GD fonts have 256 characters in their character sets. This function is provided for future expandability.

offset() — *return the first ASCII value of a font*
GD::Font::offset

This method returns the ASCII value of the first character in the font. All of the GD fonts have an offset of 0.

width(), height() — *get the width and height in pixels*
GD::Font::width, GD::Font::height

These methods return the width and height of the font, in pixels. For example, the following will return 5 and 8:

```
($width, $height) = (gdTinyFont->width, gdTinyFont->height);
```

Polygon Methods

The GD package includes a number of polygon manipulation routines that were not part of the original GD library, just to make life a little easier. All coordinate points are defined with (0, 0) being the upper left corner of the image and (*image_width, image_height*) being the lower right corner of the image.

The following example shows how you could use the GD::Polygon class to implement a simple graphing program. The script takes any number of data sets (i.e., a
list of *y* values representing a point on the graph) and writes out a multicolored
graph with the area underneath each graph filled in with a different color (see
Figure 4-5). The script is meant as a simple practical example of using polygons;
note how the area and color of each polygon is managed with associative arrays,
and how the polygons are sorted so that they can be plotted in a sensible order:

```perl
#!/usr/bin/perl -w
#
# A polygon example that draws simple graphs.
#
use strict;
use GD;
my @polygons;                    # contains a polygon for each data set

my $max_x = 5;                   # The number of items in a data set
my $max_y = 100;                 # The maximum y value
my $x_space = 40;                # Pixels between x values
my $width = $max_x * $x_space;   # The width of the image in pixels

# An array containing three data sets
#
my @data = ( [ 70, 85, 55, 45, 50 ] ,
             [ 25, 33, 22, 5, 40 ],
             [ 50, 67, 32, 24, 77 ]);

# Now generate a polygon for each data set by calling the
# createDataSet() function. This funciton will return a
# polygon object and the area of the bounding box of the polygon.
#
my %areas;
my ($poly, $area);
foreach my $dataset (@data) {
    ($poly, $area) = createDataSet($dataset);
    push @polygons, $poly;
    $areas{$poly} = $area;
}

# Now create an image and allocate white as the background color
#
my $image = new GD::Image($width-$x_space, $max_y);
my $white = $image->colorAllocate(255, 255, 255);

# Now sort the polygons in order of decreasing area. We will
# plot the graphs with the greatest bounding area first, on the
# assumption that this will minimize the effect of one data set
# being obscured by another, since they will be drawn as filled polygons.
# Note that sorting by the bounding box alone does not guarantee
# that the graphs will be plotted in the right order, but
# it will work for most well-behaved data sets.
#
```

```perl
@polygons = reverse(sort { $areas{$a} <=> $areas{$b}; } @polygons);

# Now draw each polygon. First allocate a random color (note that this
# could be white or the same as another color).
#
my %color;              # keep track of the color index of each polygon
foreach my $poly (@polygons) {
    $color{$poly} = $image->colorAllocate(rand(255), rand(255), rand(255));
    $image->filledPolygon($poly, $color{$poly});
}

# Now go back and stroke each polygon with its color, in case it
# is obscured behind another polygon
#
map {
    $image->polygon($_, $color{$_});
    } @polygons;

open O, ">graphout.gif";     # open a file
binmode O;
print O $image->gif;         # write the image as a GIF
close O;

sub createDataSet {
    # Take a reference to an array as an argument and return a
    # polygon object and the area of the polygon's bounding box.
    #
    my $dataset = shift;
    my $x = 0;
    my $poly = new GD::Polygon;
    foreach my $y (@$dataset) {
        # translate from origin at upper left corner to
        # origin at lower left corner
        #
        $poly->addPt($x, $max_y - $y);
        $x += $x_space;
    }

    # Close the polygon by adding the following points...
    #
    $poly->addPt($width, $max_y);
    $poly->addPt(0, $max_y);
    my ($l, $r, $t, $b) = $poly->bounds;
    return ($poly, ($r-$l)*($b-$t));
}
```

Figure 4-5. A simple area graph using polygons drawn by the example script

In Chapter 6, we will look at the GIFgraph Perl module that accepts similar data sets but has a wide array of configurable options and graph output types.

addPt() — *add a vertex to a polygon object*

GD::Polygon::addPt(*x, y*)

This method adds a new vertex to a polygon object. Polygons must have at least three points and must be constructed one point at a time.

The GD::Polygon object stores all of the points in the polygon, but it is also often useful to store the points separately as a string of coordinate pairs separated by whitespace. This format is easily written to or read from a file, and it is also consistent with the syntax that many web servers use to implement image maps. It is also a more concise and flexible way of constructing polygons than stringing together long series of *addPt()* method calls. It is simple to extract the points and construct a polygon from the string:

```
# Create a new polygon object
#
my $polywolly = new GD::Polygon;

# Store the vertices of the polygon in a string consisting of
# x, y coordinate pairs separated by an arbitrary amount of whitespace
#
my $polyPoints = "0,0 10,10 30,10 20,0";

# The loop should iterate over each x,y pair
#
foreach (split /\s+/, $polyPoints) {
    $polywolly->addPt(split /,/, $_); # Split each pair into a two-value list
}

# Now draw the polygon in a (previously allocated) red color
#
$image->polygon($polywolly,$red);
```

Of course, in some cases, you will be creating a polygon dynamically, and won't necessarily know all of the vertices at once. It still may be valuable to have a portable string representation of the polygon after the fact. See the *vertices()* method description for an example of constructing a string of vertices from an existing polygon.

bounds() — *get the bounding rectangle of a polygon*

GD::Polygon::bounds

This method returns a list of values that describe the smallest rectangle that completely encloses the polygon. The return values are in a list of the form (*left, top, right, bottom*), where *left* is the x coordinate of the left side of the rectangle, *top* is the y value of the top, *right* is the x value of the right side, and *bottom* is the y value of the bottom. The following lines will draw a red box around a previously defined polygon:

```
my  @boundingBox = $poly->bounds;              # $poly is a polygon object
$image->rectangle(@boundingBox, red);
```

delete() — *remove a vertex of a polygon*
GD::Polygon:delete(*index*)

This method deletes the vertex at the given index and decrements the index of those vertices after the deleted vertex. The *delete()* method returns a list containing the coordinates of the deleted point.

getPt() — *get a vertex of a polygon*
GD::Polygon::getPt(*index*)

This method will return a list with the *x, y* coordinate of the given point of a polygon object. The first point added to a polygon has an index of 0, the second has an index of 1, and so on. If a point is removed from somewhere in the middle of the list with *deletePt()*, all points added after the removed point will have their indices decremented by 1. The method returns **undef** if the point does not exist.

```
# Retrieve the fourth point to be added to the polygon
my ($x, $y) = $polywolly->getPt(3);
```

length() — *get the number of vertices in a polygon*
GD::Polygon::length

This method returns the total number of vertices in a polygon.

map() — *move and resize a polygon*
GD::Polygon::map(*srcLeft, srcTop, srcRight, srcBottom,*
                destLeft, destTop, destRight, destBottom)

This method will scale an existing polygon to fit a region, changing the values of all of the vertices within the polygon. The first four parameters define the bounding box of the source area and the last four define the bounding box of the destination area.

offset() — *move all vertices of a polygon by the same amount*
GD::Polygon::offset(*dx, dy*)

This method will move every vertex in a polygon *dx* pixels horizontally and *dy* pixels vertically.

scale() — *scale a polygon*
GD::Polygon::scale(*hFactor, vFactor*)

The *scale()* method will shrink or enlarge a polygon by the given horizontal and vertical factors. Use a fractional factor to shrink a polygon and a positive one to enlarge it. The factor should be in multiples of the current size; for example, `$poly->scale(2, 2)` will enlarge the polygon proportionately by 200% and `$poly->scale(.5, .5)` will shrink it by half.

setPt() — *move an existing vertex of a polygon*

```
GD::Polygon::setPt(index, x, y)
```

This method allows you to change the coordinates of a particular point that has already been added to a polygon object. The method will return a warning message if the point with the given index does not exist.

toPt() — *define a polygon's vertices using relative coordinates*

```
GD::Polygon::toPt(dx, dy)
```

This method will allow you to specify the points of a polygon relative to a starting point, just like Logo-type turtle graphics. Use *addPt()* to define the first point in the polygon, then subsequent calls to *toPt()* will create new points by adding the *dx* and *dy* parameters to the x and y values of the previous point. Note that the polygon object still stores only the absolute values of the coordinates, so *getPt()* will return the same value as if you had added the point with *addPt()*.

To draw a parallelogram whose vertices are at (10, 10), (20, 20), (30, 20), and (20, 10), use:

```
my $parallelogram = new GD::Polygon;      # create a new polygon
$parallelogram->addPt(10, 10);            # add the first point
$poly->toPt(10, 10);                       # add (20, 20)
$poly->toPt(10, 0);                        # add (30, 20)
$poly->toPt(-10, -10);                     # add (20, 10)
$image->polygon($parallelogram, $black);  # draw the polygon in black
```

transform() — *transform a polygon*

```
GD::Polygon::transform(scaleX, rotateX, scaleY, rotateY, x, y)
```

This method will apply a transformation matrix to each vertex in a polygon. A transformation matrix is a way of mapping one coordinate system into another; the *transform()* method provides a means for managing multiple coordinate spaces while creating images. Each polygon can be defined in terms of its own coordinate space, for example, and then later mapped to that of the final image.

The *transform()* method takes the following as parameters (note their order, listed earlier):

scaleX, scaleY

The horizontal and vertical scaling factors within the current coordinate system (i.e., before rotations or offsets). These factors are expressed in multiples of the current polygon size, so a scale factor of 4 indicates a 400% increase in size. Use a fractional value to reduce the size.

rotateX, rotateY

The rotation factor, in degrees, to be applied to each vertex.

x, y

The horizontal and vertical offset that should be applied to each vertex.

vertices() — *get all the vertices in a polygon*

`GD::Polygon::vertices()`

This method returns all the vertices as a list. Thus, for a list of returned vertices called *@vertices,* `$vertices[0][0]` refers to the x value of the first point, and `$vertices[1][1]` refers to the y value of the second point. You may want to convert this list into a portable string of x, y pairs separated by white space as in the *addPt()* example:

```
# Save a list of vertices as a string
#
my (@vertices, $polyPoints);

# Get the list of vertices as a two dimensional array
#
@vertices = $polywolly->vertices();

# Iterate over each coordinate pair
#
foreach (@vertices) {
    # Delimit each x, y pair with a comma and each point with a single space
    #
    $polyPoints .= join(join ",", @$_)." ";
}

print "Here's all the points in polywolly: $polyPoints\n";
```

5

Industrial-Strength Graphics Scripting with PerlMagick

PerlMagick is an object-oriented Perl interface to the ImageMagick image manipulation libraries. It is probably more accurate to call it the Image::Magick Perl module. It is a more robust collection of tools than GD. In addition to GIF it can read and write many file formats including PNG, JPEG, PDF, EPS, and Photo CD. In fact, PerlMagick is a graphics acronym goldmine with over 60 different file formats supported. Unlike GD, ImageMagick provides methods for creating animated GIFs dynamically. It can be used effectively in CGI applications, but its real strength is as an offline workhorse for the batch conversion and manipulation of images. This chapter will illustrate both uses and provide a complete overview of the functions available within PerlMagick.

Some PerlMagick applications that are particularly useful when programming for the Web include:

- Creation of animated GIFs

- Creation of composite images from a sequence

- Easy reduction or thumbnailing of images (see also Chapter 10, *Web Graphics Cookbook*)

- Setting transparent colors

- Color reduction and optimization for various browsers

- Conversion between 60+ formats (e.g., Photo CD to JPEG, PDF to GIF, GIF to PNG)

- Special effects and addition of text to images

- Gamma-correction of images for color-sensitive web applications

PerlMagick is used in a number of chapter in this book. See especially Chapter 9, *Moving Pictures: Programming GIF Animation*, and Chapter 10 for some elaborate working examples using PerlMagick.

Learn PerlMagick in 21 Seconds

All of the PerlMagick methods and attributes are defined by the Image::Magick module. To make these methods and attributes available within the name space of your script, include this module with Perl's *use* function:

```
use Image::Magick;
```

You can then use the *new* constructor to create an image object that is capable of reading, manipulating, and writing images:

```
$image = Image::Magick->new;   # $image is a new image object
```

Once you are finished with an image object, you should destroy it to conserve memory resources. Do this with *undef*:

```
undef $image;                  # destroy an image object
```

You can also "empty" all of the images from an object and keep the object around for further use with:

```
undef @$image;                 # delete all images from an object
undef $image->[2];             # delete only the third image from a sequence
```

Here is a quick example script that exhibits most of the functionality of the Image::Magick module:

```
#/usr/bin/perl -w

use strict;
use Image::Magick;

# $image will be our image object and $status will be the return value
# that we can check for a successful operation
#
my($image, $status);

# Instantiate a new image object
#
$image = Image::Magick->new;

# Read in every image in the image subdirectory whose name starts
# with 'dog' and ends with a .gif extension...
# These will be the frames in an animated sequence, presumably of a dog...
#
$status = $image->Read('images/dog*.gif');
warn "$status" if "$status";
```

```
$image->Transparent('#FFFFFF');              # Set white to transparent
$image->Zoom('50%');                         # Scale the whole sequence

# Use the 216 web-safe color cube
#
$cube = Image::Magick->new;
$status = $cube->Read('NETSCAPE:');
warn "$status" if "$status";
$image->Map($cube);

# Write the whole sequence out as an animated gif file
#
$status = $image->Set(loop=>0,               # loop forever
                    dispose=>2);             # revert to background 'twixt frames
$status = $image->Write("gif:webdog.gif");
warn "$status" if "$status";

# Neatly dispose of our object
#
undef $image;
```

The ImageMagick Distribution and PerlMagick

ImageMagick was written by John Cristy and has been constantly developed and revised for several years. Newly modified versions are sometimes available every few weeks on the ftp site (see the "Where to Find It" section later in this chapter). As of this writing the current version of ImageMagick is 4.1.x, with minor version numbers incremented once every few months. PerlMagick is currently at version 1.4x. The copyright to ImageMagick and PerlMagick is held by E.I. du Pont de Nemours and Company, who graciously allow the packages to be distributed (and redistributed) for free. As of ImageMagick 4.0, PerlMagick comes with the standard distribution.

Tables 5-1 through 5-3 show the various file formats supported by ImageMagick. Most of these formats are not directly viewable on the Web, though external viewers that may be launched from a web browser are available for many of the formats. ImageMagick can be used to convert these other files to a format viewable on a browser, or to create thumbnails that link to a downloadable version of the full image. See Chapter 10 for scripts to convert and maintain groups of images in multiple formats.

ImageMagick Supported File Formats

Table 5-1. Supported File Formats for Web Publishing

Extension	Description	Multi-Image Files?
GIF, GIF87, GIF89a	8-bit color GraphDics Interchange Format	✓
JPEG	Joint Photographic Experts Group's compressed 24-bit color JFIF format	
MPEG, M2V	Motion Picture Experts Group file interchange format	✓
NETSCAPE	Netscape 216 color cube	
PDF	Portable Document Format	✓
PNG	Portable Network Graphics	
MNG	Multiple Network Graphics	✓

Table 5-2. ImageMagick Internal Formats

Extension	Description	Multi-Image Files?
CMYK	Raw cyan, magenta, yellow, and black bytes	✓
GRADATION	A gradual shading of one color into another (see *Read()*)	
GRANITE	Granite texture	
GRAY	Raw gray bytes	✓
LABEL	Text annotation	
MAP	Red, green, and blue colormap bytes followed by the image colormap indexes	
MATTE	Raw matte bytes	
MONO	Bi-level bitmap in least-significant-byte (LSB) first order	✓
MIFF	Magick image file format	
NULL	NULL image	
PLASMA	Plasma fractal image (see *Read()* method)	
RGB	Raw red, green, and blue bytes	✓
RGBA	Raw red, green, blue, and matte bytes	✓
TEXT	Raw text file—read only	✓
TILE	Tile image (see *Read()* method)	
VID	Visual image directory	✓
X	Select an image from or display image to X server screen	
XC	Constant image of X server color	

Table 5-3. Other ImageMagick-Supported Formats

Extension	Description	Multi-Image Files?
AVS	AVS X image file	✓
BIE	Joint Bi-level Image Experts Group interchange format	
BMP, BMP24	Microsoft Windows 8-bit and 24-bit bitmap image file	✓
CGM	Computer Graphics Metafile	
DCX	ZSoft IBM PC multi-page Paintbrush file	✓
DIB	Microsoft Windows bitmap image file	
EPS, EPS2, EPSF, EPSI	Adobe Encapsulated PostScript file, Level I and II	
FAX	Group 3 fax image	✓
FIG	The fig image format	
FITS	Flexible Image Transport System	
FPX	FlashPix Format	
HDF	Hierarchical Data Format	✓
JBIG	Joint Bi-level Image Experts Group interchange format	✓
MTV	MTV Raytracing image format	✓
PBM, PGM, PPM, PNM	Portable bitmap format	✓
PCD	Photo CD	
PCL	Page Control Language	
PCX	ZSoft IBM PC Paintbrush file	
PICT	Apple Macintosh QuickDraw/PICT file	
PS, PS2	Adobe PostScript file, Level II PostScript file	✓
PSD	Adobe Photoshop bitmap file	
RAD	Radiance image format	
RLA	Alias/Wavefront image file—read only	
RLE	Utah Run length encoded image file—read only	
SGI	Irix RGB image file	✓
SUN	SUN Rasterfile	✓
TGA	Truevision Targa image file	✓
TIFF, TIFF24	Tagged Image File Format, 24-bit TIFF	✓
TTF	TrueType font file	
UIL	X-Motif UIL table	
UYVY	16bit/pixel interleaved YUV	✓
VIFF	Khoros Visualization image file	
XBM	X11 bitmap file (black and white)	
XPM	X Windows system pixmap file (color)	
XWD	X windows system window dump file (color)	
YUV	Digital video (CCIR601)	✓

Where to Find It

The official web page for ImageMagick is *http://www.wizards.dupont.com/cristy/ ImageMagick.html* and the PerlMagick page is at *http://www.wizards.dupont.com/ cristy/www/perl.html*. PerlMagick is also available via CPAN at *http://www.perl.com/ CPAN-local/modules/by-module/Image/*. Several ftp mirrors for the source and pre-compiled binaries are available at *http://www.wizards.dupont.com/cristy/www/ archives.html*.

The ImageMagick mailing list is more friendly than most when it comes to asking for help. You can subscribe by sending the message "subscribe magick" in the body (not the subject) of an email to *majordomo@wizards.dupont.com*. The mailing list is archived periodically at *ftp://ftp.wizards.dupont.com/pub/ImageMagick/ mailing-list/*.

System Requirements

The ImageMagick Libraries will compile and run on the following platforms:

* Virtually any Unix system
* Linux
* Windows NT/95
* Macintosh
* VMS

An ImageMagick installation requires between 3MB and 12MB of disk space, depending on the platform, and you will need 80MB of virtual RAM (32MB of which should be real RAM) to work effectively. If you are using ImageMagick to dynamically generate web graphics, you should probably have at least 128MB of real RAM free to handle multiple simultaneous requests. Because ImageMagick was designed as a robust and versatile package, it does have additional overhead that a specialized package like GD does not have. Keep this in mind when determining the best solutions for your image serving problems.

Of course, you'll also need Perl. It is a good idea to upgrade to one of the more recent versions of Perl for better performance. Versions of Perl prior to release 5.004_4 have memory leak problems that become painfully apparent when dealing with many image objects.

ImageMagick also requires a number of freely available graphics libraries (to be installed before compilation) in order to support certain graphics formats. Many of these libraries are bundled together as the ImageMagick Plug-in Library, compiled as shared and static libraries for Linux. You can ftp the bundle from *ftp:// sunsite.unc.edu*. The Windows NT distribution comes packaged with the latest source for many of these libraries. Table 5-4 shows the primary plug-ins of interest.

Table 5-4. Graphics Libraries Required for Web File Formats

Formats	Program/Libraries Required	Source
JPEG	Independent JPEG Group libraries	*ftp://ftp.uu.net/graphics/jpeg/*
MPEG	*mpeg2decode* and *mpeg2encode*	*ftp://ftp.mpeg.org/pub/mpeg/mssg/mpeg2vidcodec_ v12.tar.gz*
PNG	Libpng, zlib	*ftp://ftp.uu.net/graphics/png/src,* *ftp://ftp.cdrom.com/pub/infozip/zlib/*
PS, EPS, EPSF, PDF	Aladdin Ghostscript	*http://www.cs.wisc.edu/~ghost/*
TIFF	Sam Leffler's TIFF software	*ftp://sgi.com/graphics/tiff/*
TrueType	FreeType	*ftp://ftp.physiol.med.tu-muenchen.de/ pub/freetype/ freetype-1.0.tar.gz*

Installing PerlMagick and the ImageMagick Libraries

If you have any experience with building and installing software from source, you should have no problems installing ImageMagick. For those who don't like to get their hands dirty (or who don't have the proper tools), pre-compiled binaries are available for the following platforms:

- Linux (RPM)
- Windows NT/95
- Solaris 2.5/2.6 (Sparc and i86PC)
- SunOS 4.1.4
- SGI Irix 6.2
- HP-UX
- AIX
- Macintosh

Installing on *nix

If you are installing from the source distribution you have two options for creating the "Makefiles" needed to compile ImageMagick. The first is GNU *configure* and the second is *imake*. I recommend using *configure* as it is a bit easier, will work on most systems, and will automatically configure and install the PerlMagick package. Some people have claimed that building the Makefile for use with shared libraries is more reliable with *imake*, but most users shouldn't have a problem with configure. If you have problems, refer to the installation instructions distributed with ImageMagick for information on using *imake* to build your Makefile.

Also, you need root access to install this software using the described methods, or you can use the **–prefix** options with *configure* to install it in a place for which you have permissions.

First uncompress and untar the package, then change to the directory that is created:

```
gunzip ImageMagick-4.1.x.tar.gz
tar -xvf ImageMagick-4.1.x.tar
cd ImageMagick
```

To compile and install ImageMagick with the default configuration, simply type:

```
./configure
make
make install
```

You should also follow this with a:

```
make check
```

which will run a test suite that will verify that everything is working properly.

Before you do this, however, you may want to change a few of the default settings if you are planning to create images for the Web. Because of the legal issues involved with the patented LZW compression scheme used in GIF files, support for LZW is turned off in the default distribution. The authors did this quite intentionally to help encourage a migration from GIF to PNG usage and so that ImageMagick may be bundled with other packages without hassle. If you want to create GIF images for the web, you probably should manually enable LZW support with the **--enable-lzw** configure option so your files don't swell to an unusable size. In addition, the **--enable-perl** option will allow you to automatically build PerlMagick along with ImageMagick. With this in mind, the suggested installation commands are:

```
./configure --enable-lzw=yes --with-perl=yes
make
make install
```

Table 5-5 provides a list of all the *configure* flags and their default and suggested settings.

Table 5-5. Configure Flags and Default and Suggested Settings

Option	Description	Default	Suggested
--enable-shared=	Build shared libraries.	No	Yes
--enable-static=	Build static libraries.	Yes	No
--enable-lzw=	Enable support for LZW compression. If this package is not enabled, your GIF, PostScript Level II, and PDF files will be uncompressed and unsuitable for use in web applications.	No	Yes

Table 5-5. Configure Flags and Default and Suggested Settings (continued)

Option	Description	Default	Suggested
--enable-16bit-pixel=	Enable 16-bit pixels. The default is 8-bit pixels (24-bit color) which is all that is needed for web-based graphics.	No	No
--with-perl=	Enable build/install of PerlMagick. If this option is not enabled you will have to manually build the code in the Perl-Magick subdirectory.	Yes	Yes
--with-bzlib=	Enable Bzlib support.	Yes	a
--with-dps=	Enable Display PostScript support.	Yes	a
--with-fpx=	Enable FlashPIX support.	Yes	a
--with-hdf=	Enable HDF support.	Yes	a
--with-jbig=	Enable JBIG support.	Yes	a
--with-jpeg=	Enable JPEG support.	Yes	a
--with-png=	Enable PNG support.	Yes	a
--with-tiff=	Enable TIFF support.	Yes	a
--with-ttf=	Enable TrueType font support.	Yes	a
--with-zlib=	Enable Zlib support.	Yes	a
--with-x=	Use the X Window System. If this option is set to no, ImageMagick will be built using the X11 stubs library and the X-based utility applications will not work.	Yes	Yes
--prefix=	Default installation path.	*/usr/local*	*/usr/local*
--x-includes=	Path to X include files.	b	b
--x-libraries=	Path to X library files.	b	b

a If a package is enabled but the required support libraries are not properly installed, the package will not be included in the build. If you later add these libraries, you will have to recompile. You should really never need to set any of these options unless there is a problem during the build due to an outdated or conflicting support library.
b *Configure* should automatically find your X11 *include* and *lib* directories. If it has problems for some reason, you can specify the paths with these flags.

Installing on Windows NT

The NT version of ImageMagick is distributed as a collection of MetroWerks Codewarrior Professional projects (files with a *.mcp* extension) and as a Visual C++ workspace (*ImageMagick.dsw*). The standard distribution is packaged with pre-compiled versions of the libraries and utilities so it isn't necessary to install from source. These binaries should also work under Windows 95. The main distribution also contains the source for the JBIG, JPEG, PNG, TIFF, TTF, and ZLIB support libraries.

To install PerlMagick, create the Makefile by running the *Makefile.nt* script, then use *nmake* to compile and install it. You will need to copy the libraries *IMagick.dll* and *X11.dll* from the NT ImageMagick directory to an appropriate path where Perl can find them or include them in the same directory as your script.

Image::Magick Attributes and Methods by Category

Image::Magick acts as a transparent interface for manipulating a wide range of image file formats. Most of these formats have certain attributes in common, though they may each implement them differently. GIF and PNG both support interlacing, for example, but have different interlacing schemes and different formats for indicating how a file is interlaced. Image::Magick allows you to set the interlacing mode for any file format with the `interlace` attribute. Image::Magick provides access to a wide range of file attributes, which are listed later in this chapter.

Image::Magick also provides many image manipulation methods that can read different formats, apply special effects filters, perform intelligent color quantization, and perform several other applications.

Most of the attributes listed can be both read and written. Those marked with an asterisk (*) are read-only (that is, they may only be used with the *Get()* method, and may not be used with the *Set()* method as described). For the methods, you can also use the name of any method with the word "Image" appended to it as an alias. For example, *ReadImage()* is an alias for *Read()* and *SharpenImage()* is an alias for *Sharpen()*.

Attributes

File

> *base_filename*, class*, comment, compress, file, filename, filesize*, format, interlace, label, magick, matte*, packetsize*, packets*, signature*, size, type*, verbose*

Image quality and color reduction

> *colors, colorspace, dither, monochrome, quality, treedepth*

Colors and transparency

> *background, bordercolor, gamma*, mattecolor, mean, normalized_max*, normalized_mean*, pixel*, texture, total_colors*

Sizing and geometry

> *base_columns*, base_rows*, columns*, density, depth*, filter, geometry, height*, montage*, page, rows*, size, units*, width*, x_resolution*, y_resolution*

Animation and sequences

> *adjoin, dispose, delay, iterations, loop*

Text and graphics

> *font, pen, pointsize*

Color management

> *blue_primary, green_primary, red_primary, rendering_intent, white_point*

Pixel access

> *colormap[i], pixel[x,y]*

Methods

File information, reading, writing

> *Animate(), Clone(), Comment(), Condense(), Display(), Label(), Read(), Signature(), Write()*

Getting and setting attributes

> *Get(), Set()*

Special effects and filters

> *AddNoise(), Average(), Blur(), Charcoal(), Contrast(), Despeckle(), Edge(), Emboss(), Enhance(), Implode(), OilPaint(), Raise(), ReduceNoise(), Shade(), Sharpen(), Solarize(), Swirl(), Texture(), Wave()*

Colors

> *Colorize(), CycleColormap(), Equalize(), Gamma(), Map(), Modulate(), Negate(), Normalize(), Opaque(), Quantize(), QueryColor(), Segment(), Threshold(), Transparent()*

Text and graphics

> *Annotate(), Draw()*

Sizing, framing, positioning

> *Border(), Box(), Chop(), Composite(), Crop(), Flip(), Flop(), Frame(), Magnify(), Minify(), Montage(), Roll(), Rotate(), Sample(), Scale(), Shear(), Spread(), Trim(), Zoom()*

Convenience functions

> *Mogrify(), MogrifyRegion(), Ping(), Transform()*

Reading and Writing Images

The *Read()* and *Write()* methods allow you to get images into or out of an image object. Internally, images are stored in a flexible abstract data structure that may be written to any of the many different supported file formats (shown in Table 5-1). The default write format is in the MIFF format (Magick Image File Format) which is created specifically for storing ImageMagick image data. If you are interested in the full specifications for the MIFF format, they are available on the CD-ROM that comes with *The Encyclopedia of Graphics File Formats* (O'Reilly, 1996).

While writing, you can set any of the attributes described in the "Attributes" section by sending it as a parameter to *Write()*. For example:

```
$image->Write(filename=>'xc:white', compress=>'Zip');
```

If you are using an X Server, you can display an image directly from Perl. The *Display()* and *Animate()* methods may be used to send it directly to the display or animate programs described at the end of this chapter.

Read() — *read one or more image files*

```
$image->Read(list)
```

The *Read()* method reads an image or an image sequence from the specified files (of any supported format) or reads in a new "blank" image with a background color. When an image is read, its file format is determined by its magic number, which is the first field in the image header. To force a specific image format, use the name of the format followed by a colon before the filename string. Filenames ending with a *.gz* or *.Z* extension (on a Unix system) will be first decompressed using uncompress or gunzip. The list can be a list of strings in any of the following forms:

```
$image->Read('gif:foo.gif')             # Read a single GIF file into $image
$image->Read('foo.gif', 'gumbar.jpg');  # Read two images into $image object
                                        # guessing the file format
                                        # from their magic numbers
$image->Read('*.gif');                  # Read all of the .gif files in the
                                        # current directory into $image

open(IMAGE, "image.gif");               # Open the file for reading
binmode IMAGE;                          # Make sure we're in binary mode
$image->Read(file=>\*IMAGE);            # Read from open Perl filehandle
```

Certain file formats allow more than one image to be contained in the same file (see Table 5-1). Each image in a sequence still may be accessed individually. For example, to set the transparent color of only the first image in a sequence to white, use:

```
$image->[0]->Transparent('#FFFFFF');
```

You can also read in specific "subimages" of a multi-resolution file format such as Photo CD or MPEG. Accessing subimages can be done with the following syntax:

```
$image->Read('pcd:image1.pcd[3]');            # Read the fourth subimage
$image->Read('mpeg:image2.mpg[20-40,70-80]');  # Read the given ranges
```

ImageMagick supports a number of custom file formats that add colors or special effects to a background. They are the *gradation, plasma, granite* (see Figure 5-1), and *tile* formats:

```
$image->Read('gradation:white-black');   # gradation gives a gradual transition
                                         # from one shade to another.
$image->Read('gradation:#FFFFFF-#000000'); # the desired shading is the
                                         # filename
$image->Read('plasma:yellow-green');     # a 'plasma fractal' pattern
$image->Read('plasma:fractal');          # A base color may be specified or
                                         # use 'fractal' for a random value

$image->Read('granite:');                # starts with a granite texture

$image->Read('tile:images/beatniks.gif');  # tile image with a texture or
                                         # file
```

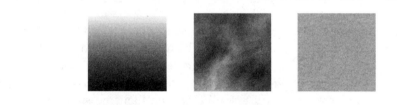

Figure 5-1. The built-in gradation, plasma, and granite "template" file formats

To create a new image with a given background color suitable for use as a blank canvas, try:

```
# Set a color for the background
# Note that xc is the file format type, in this case an X color
$background = 'xc:#grey80';              # grey80 = light grey = #CCCCCC

# Read background image color
$status = $image->Read(filename=>$background);
```

You should always check the return values of a read or write method call. If there is a problem during a read, the method will continue reading and will return an error message for each file that it could not read. You can check for a read failure with the following code:

```
$status = $image->Read('good.file', 'nonexistent.file');

# get the error number
$status =~ /(\d+)/;
```

```
$error_number = $1;

# Now print a suitable message
warn "Got error $error_number" if "$status";
```

Write() — *write one or more image files*

Write() allows you to write the data for a single image or a sequence to a file or standard output. When using PerlMagick in CGI applications, you must use a hyphen (-) as the filename to write to standard output. Calling *Write()* without a specified filename will write to the file indicated by the image's filename attribute. If there is a writing problem, *Write()* returns the number of images successfully written. Error checking may be done as for the *Read()* operation described earlier.

If you have read a sequence of images into an Image::Magick object, you can write out the entire sequence as a single file if your output format supports multiple images, or you can write individual scenes from the sequence.

Some examples:

```
$button->Write('jpeg:button.jpg'); # write to button.jpg as a JPEG

$image->Write('gif:-');            # No this isn't a smiley with half
                                   # a moustache; the - means write to STDOUT

$image->Write(file=>IMAGE);        # Write to an open Perl filehandle

$images->[0]->Write('foobar.gif'); # write only the first image in a sequence

$image->Read('foo.gif');           # If this is the only read...
$image->Write();                   # ...this will write to foo.gif
```

Instead of writing your image to a file, you can instead display it to any X11 screen. Use *Display()* to display one image at a time to the screen and *Animate()* to display an image sequence.

Getting and Setting Image::Magick Attributes

Many of the image manipulation functions—as well as *Read()* and *Write()*—allow you to set various attributes, or you can use *Set()* to do it directly, as in:

```
$image->Set(loop=>100);
$image->[$x]->Set(dither=>1);
```

Use *Get()* to get an attribute:

```
($w, $h, $d) = $q->Get('columns', 'rows', 'depth');
$colors = $q->[2]->Get('colors');
```

Ping() allows you to get certain information about an image's size without actually loading the image into memory. The functions *GetAttribute()* and *SetAttribute()* are aliases for *Get()* and *Set()* and may be used interchangeably.

adjoin — *join images into a single multi-image file*

```
$image->Set(adjoin=>{1,0})
$image->Get('adjoin')
```

Certain file formats accept multiples images within a single file. If *adjoin* is 1 and the image is a multi-image format, multiple reads to the same image object will join the images into a single file. Set adjoin to 0 if you do not want the images output to a single file.

background — *image background color*

```
$image->Set(background=>string)
$image->Get('background')
```

This attribute sets (or gets) the background color of an image. Remember that for a GIF multi-image sequence, every image is sized by default to the size of the largest image; the background color fills the remaining space.

base_columns — *base image width*

```
$image->Get('base_columns')
```

This attribute returns an integer that is the width of the image before any transformations have been performed on the image.

base_filename — *base image filename*

```
$image->Get('base_filename')
```

This attribute returns a string that is the image's original filename.

base_rows — *base image height*

```
$image->Get('base_filename')
```

This attribute returns an integer that is the height of the image before any transformations have been performed on the image.

blue_primary — *chromaticity blue primary point*

```
$image->Set(blue_primary=>x_value,y_value)
$image->Get('blue_primary');
```

This attribute returns the chromaticity blue primary point. This is a color management option.

bordercolor — *image border color*

```
$image->Set(bordercolor=>string)
$image->Get('bordercolor')
```

The **bordercolor** attribute is used in functions such as *Rotate()* and *Shear()* where an image is transformed and "empty" background spaces are created that should be distinct from the background color.

class — *image class*

```
$image->Get('class')
```

A **Direct** class image is a continuous tone image and is stored as a sequence of red-green-blue intensity values. A **Pseudo** class image is an image with a color-map, where the image is stored as a map of colors and a sequence of indexes into the map.

colormap[*i*] — *red, green, and blue component of colormap entry*

```
$image->set('colormap[i]'=>'black')
($red, $green, $blue) = $image->Get('colormap[i]')
```

This attribute sets or returns the color name (e.g., red) or hex value (e.g., #ccc) at position *i*.

colors — *preferred number of colors*

```
$image->Set(colors=>integer)
$image->Get('colors')
```

The **colors** attribute allows you to specify the maximum number of colors that an image will have after the *Quantize()* method is called. If an image has fewer unique colors, any duplicate or unused colors will be removed from the color-map. The **colorspace** and **dither** attributes also affect the results of reducing the number of colors in an image. The default colorspace for color reduction is RGB; you may get better results by first changing the colorspace to YUV or YIQ. The following example illustrates a way to preserve the transparency of an image when reducing the number of colors by first transforming the image to the Transparent colorspace:

```perl
#!/usr/bin/perl

use Image::Magick;

my $image = Image::Magick->new;
$image->Read('dog.gif');
$image->Transparent('#FFFFFF');

# Reduce to three colors, one of which is the transparent
#
$image->Quantize(colorspace=>'Transparent', colors=>3);
$x = $image->Display();
undef $image;
```

If you want to make the image black and white, set the number of colors to 2 and the colorspace to `Gray`. You can also set the `dither` attribute if you want black and white dithered approximations of colors.

See also the descriptions for `colorspace` and `dither`.

colorspace — *type of colorspace*

```
$image->Set(colorspace=>string)
$image->Get('colorspace')
```

Color reduction takes place in the RGB colorspace by default, but in certain cases you may get better results with a different colorspace. *string* corresponds to one of several color models. The values we are interested in are:

- `RGB`: red, green, blue
- `Gray` (not "Grey"): grayscale
- `Transparent`: RGB with retained transparent colors (if any)
- `YIQ`: a color model used by NTSC
- `YUV`: Luminance, Chrominance used by MPEG
- `YCbCr`: a variant of `YUV` that gives good results with skin tones
- `CMYK`: Cyan, Magenta, Yellow, Black

The `colorspace` attribute must be followed by a *Quantize()* method call for the change to take effect. The attribute may also be set directly from the *Quantize()* call, as in:

```
$image->Quantize(colorspace=>'Gray');
```

columns — *image width*

```
$image->Get('columns')
```

Returns the width (integer number of pixel columns) of the image.

comment — *image comment*

```
$image->Set(comment=>string);
$image->Get('comment')
```

Set or return the image comment.

compress — *type of compression*

```
$image->Set(compress=>string)
$image->Get('compress')
```

The default compression for an image is based on its original format; you can specify a compression type with the `compress` attribute. The value of *string* can be one of the following:

None	LZW
BZip	Runlength
JPEG	Zip

If you indicate a compression type that is incompatible with the output file type, it will simply be set to the original default value (e.g., a GIF file will ignore a *compress* attribute set to JPEG, or a PNG will ignore a *compress* attribute of Zip).

delay — *set GIF interframe delay*

```
$image->Set(delay=>{0..65535})
$image->Get('delay')
```

The delay option may be used to regulate the playback speed of an animated GIF. This integer is the number of hundredths of a second that should pass before displaying the next image in a sequence. The default is 0, which indicates that the animation should play as fast as possible. In this case, actual speed can vary from system to system so it is best to either specify a delay that looks good or be sure to test the results on a range of platforms. The maximum delay is 65535 (almost 11 minutes).

density — *image resolution*

```
$image->Set(density=>300x300)
$image->Get('density')
```

Use this attribute to set the vertical and horizontal resolution of an image. It is most useful when reading a PostScript document. The default is 72 dots-per-inch. Increase this to 144, for example, to render the PostScript to a larger sized image.

depth — *bit depth*

```
$image->Get('depth')
```

Returns the bit depth of the image, either 8 or 16.

dispose — *set GIF disposal method*

```
$image->Set(dispose=>{0,1,2,3})
$image->Get('dispose')
```

The dispose attribute sets the GIF disposal method that indicates how an image is refreshed when flipping between scenes in a sequence. You may set it to an integer between 0 and 3 that corresponds to one of the following methods:

0 None specified

1 Do not dispose

2 Restore to background color

3 Restore to previous scene

The default disposal method is 0. Disposal methods are discussed in greater detail in the section on GIF animation in Chapter 9.

dither — *apply dithering to image*

```
$image->Set(dither=>{1,0})
$image->Get('dither')
```

Most web browsers will automatically dither an image whose colors do not exactly match those in its colormap. The `dither` attribute allows you to apply Floyd/ Steinberg error diffusion, which may help smooth out the contours produced when sharply reducing colors. Note that dithering will only take effect if the image is color-quantized, which happens in one of two ways:

1. Explicitly, when you set the `color` attribute to the desired number of colors and use the *Quantize()* method to reduce the number of colors in the image.

2. Implicitly, when an image is converted from a file format that allows many colors to one that allows fewer (converting a JPEG to a GIF, for example).

file — *Perl filehandle*

```
$image->Set(file=>HANDLE)
```

The *Read()* and *Write()* methods can accept an already opened Perl filehandle. If so, the image is read or written directly from or to the specified filehandle.

filename — *filename of image*

```
$image->Set(filename=>string)
$image->Get('filename')
```

The default filename is the name of the file (or color) from which the image was read. When the *Write()* method is called without a parameter it uses the image's `filename` attribute as the target file. For example:

```
$image->Read('gum.gif');
$image->Set(filename=>'gum2.gif');
$image->Write();
```

writes to the file *gum2.gif* just like:

```
$image->Read('gum.gif');
$image->Write('gum2.gif');
```

except that in the second case, the `$image` object retains the original filename. If `$image` is a sequence of images, the default is the filename of the first image in the sequence, and changing it changes the filename for the entire sequence.

filesize — *size of file in bytes*

```
$image->Get('filesize')
```

The number of bytes that the image takes up on disk.

filter — *image resize filter*

```
$image->Set(filter=>string)
$image->Get('filter')
```

The `filter` attribute allows you to specify the filtering scheme used by the *Zoom()* or *Transform()* method when resizing an image. The value of `string` can be:

Point	Hamming	Catrom
Box	Blackman	Mitchell
Triangle	Gaussian	Lanczos
Hermite	Quadratic	Bessel
Hanning	Cubic	Sinc

The default value is `Mitchell`. In general, the Mitchell filter gives the best results and the Box filter is the fastest.

font — *text font*

```
$image->Set(font=>string)
$image->Get('font')
```

The text annotation methods *Annotate()* and *Draw()* require a `font`. This can be a fully-qualified X11 font (-*-helvetica-medium-r-*-*-12-*-*-*-*-iso8859-*), True-Type (@TimesRoman.ttf), or PostScript (Helvetica) font name. PerlMagick requires access to an X11 server, FreeType library, and Ghostscript to render X11, True-Type, and PostScript fonts respectively.

format — *image file format*

```
$image->Set(format=>string)
$image->Get('format')
```

The image `format` can be any of those supported by ImageMagick (listed in Table 5-1). Remember that some image formats require additional libraries and programs to be readable and writeable. Refer to the "Installing PerlMagick and the ImageMagick Libraries" section for information about external libraries. The `magick` attribute is an alias for format.

gamma — *image gamma*

```
$image->Set(gamma=>float);
$image->Get('gamma')
```

Set or return the image `gamma` value. Unlike method *Gamma()* that actually applies the gamma value to the image pixels, here we just set the value. This is useful if the correct gamma is already known about a particular image.

geometry — *shortcut for specifying width and height*

```
$image->Set(geometry=>string)
$image->Get('geometry')
```

The **geometry** attribute is a convenience name that allows you to specify the width and height, or a region of an image with an offset in a single string. For example:

```
geometry=>'640x800'
```

is equivalent to:

```
width=>640, height=>800
```

To refer to a 20×20 region of pixels starting at coordinate (100, 150), use:

```
geometry=>'20x20+100+150'
```

green_primary — *chromaticity green primary point*

```
$image->Set(green_primary=>x_value,y_value)
$image->Get('green_primary')
```

This attribute returns the chromaticity green primary point. This is a color management option.

height — *image height*

```
$image->Get('height')
```

Returns the height (integer number of pixel rows) of the image.

interlace — *type of interlacing scheme*

```
$image->Set(interlace=>string)
$image->Get('interlace')
```

The **interlace** attribute allows you to specify the interlacing scheme used by a GIF or Progressive JPEG file. The default value is **None**. The value of *string* can be:

> **None**
> **Line**: scanline interlacing
> **Plane**: plane interlacing

See Chapter 1 for a description of interlacing.

iterations — *add loop extension*

```
$image->Set(iterations=>integer)
$image->Get('iterations')
```

The **iterations** attribute is an alias for the **loop** attribute. The default is 1.

loop — *add loop extension*

```
$image->Set(loop=>integer)
$image->Get('loop')
```

The `loop` attribute adds the Netscape looping extension to an image sequence. Assigning a value of 0 to `loop` causes the animation sequence to loop continuously. A value other than 0 results in the animation being played for the specified number of times before stopping. The default value is 1.

magick — *image file format*

```
$image->Set(magick=>string)
$image->Get('magick')
```

The `magick` attribute is an alias for `format`, described earlier.

matte — *transparency boolean*

```
$image->Get('matte')
```

The `matte` attribute is 1 if an image has transparent colors defined.

mean — *mean error per pixel*

```
$image->Get('mean')
```

This value reflects the mean error per pixel introduced when reducing the number of colors in an image with method *Quantize()*. The mean error gives one measure of how well the color reduction algorithm performed and how close the color reduced image is to the original.

normalized_mean — *normalized mean error per pixel*

```
$image->Get('normalized_mean')
```

This value reflects the normalized mean error per pixel introduced when reducing the number of colors in an image with method *Quantize()*. The normalized mean error gives one measure of how well the color-reduction algorithm performed and how close the color-reduced image is to the original.

normalized_max — *normalized maximum error per pixel*

```
$image->Get('normalized_max')
```

This value reflects the normalized maximum error per pixel introduced when reducing the number of colors in an image with method *Quantize()*. The normalized maximum error gives one measure of how well the color reduction algorithm performed and how close the color-reduced image is to the original.

packetsize — *size of each packet of image data*

```
$image->Get('packetsize')
```

The `packetsize` attribute is the number of bytes in each run length-encoded packet of image data.

packets — *number of run length-encoded packets*

`$image->Get('packets')`

The `packets` attribute is the number of run length-encoded packets in the image.

page — *preferred size and location of the image canvas*

`$image->Set(page=>string)`
`$image->Get('page')`

Page declares the image canvas size and location. Typically this is only useful for the PostScript, text, and GIF formats. The value of *string* can be:

Letter	Executive	B5
Tabloid	A3	Folio
Ledger	A4	Quarto
Legal	A5	10x14
Statement	B4	

or a geometry (612×792). The default value is `Letter`.

pen — *annotation color*

`$image->Set(pen=>color)`
`$image->Get('pen')`

Methods *Annotate()* and *Draw()* require a pen color. The pen color specifies the color of the text or drawn object.

pixel — *color of a pixel*

`$image->Set('pixel[x,y]'=>color);`
`$image->Get('pixel[x,y]')`

The `pixel` attribute returns the red, green, blue, and opacity value (or colormap index for colormapped images) at the given coordinate as four decimal numbers separated by commas. For example, if an image has a white pixel at 20, 50:

```
@pixel = split /,/, $image->Get('pixel[20,50]');
print "Red: $pixel[0]\n",
      "Green: $pixel[1]\n",
      "Blue: $pixel[2]\n",
      "Opacity: $pixel[3]\n";
```

will print the following:

```
Red: 255
Green: 255
Blue: 255
Opacity: 0
```

If you want to change a group of pixels, use the *Draw()* method with the color primitive.

Color Hex Code and Name Conversion

When a color is returned by a *GetAttribute()* call, the returned value is a string of four integers separated by commas representing the red, green, blue, and opacity values of the image. Unfortunately, this string must be converted to a hex value string if it is to be used with other PerlMagick functions or within the HTML code of a web page. It is fairly simple to write a Perl subroutine that will do the decimal-to-hex conversion using Perl's *sprintf* function:

```
sub HexColor {
    my ($number, $hex);
    # Take only the first 3 decimal values in a comma-delimited string
    # as the Red, Green, Blue input
    (shift @_) =~ /^(\d+),(\d+),(\d+)/;
    foreach $number ($1, $2, $3) {
        $hex .= sprintf("%02X", $number);
    }
    return "#".$hex;
}
```

You can easily compute the hex string that corresponds to a color name by calling the *QueryColor()* method before calling *HexColor*. For example:

```
$hexstring = HexColor(Image::Magick->QueryColor('LemonChiffon1'));
```

returns **#FFFACD**. Appendix B provides a table of valid color names and their corresponding hex pairs.

---

pointsize — *pointsize of a font*

```
$image->Set(pointsize=>integer)
$image->Get('pen')
```

The **pointsize** attribute determines how large to draw a PostScript or TrueType font with the *Annotate()* or *Draw()* methods.

quality — *compression level*

```
$image->Set(quality=>{0..100})
$image->Get('quality')
```

The **quality** attribute sets the JPEG, MIFF, or PNG compression level. The range is 0 (worst) to 100 (best). The default is 75.

red_primary — *chromaticity red primary point*

```
$image->Set(red_primary=>x_value,y_value)
$image->Get('red_primary')
```

This attribute returns the chromaticity red primary point. This is a color management option.

rendering_intent — *(indicate intended rendering model)*

```
$image->Set(rendering_intent=>{Undefined, Saturation, Perceptual, Absolute,
    Relative})
$image->Get('rendering_intent')
```

This is a color management option.

rows — *image height*

```
$image->Get('rows')
```

Returns the height (integer number of pixel rows) of the image.

signature — *MD5 public key signature*

```
$image->Get('signature')
```

Retrieves the MD5 public key signature associated with the image, if any.

size — *width and height of a raw image*

```
$image->Set(size=>geometry)
$image->Get('size')
```

Use the `size` attribute before reading in an image from a raw data file format such as RGB, GRAY, TEXT, or CMYK. Images in the Photo CD format are stored at several different resolutions, so choose one of the following before reading the image:

> 192×128
> 384×256
> 768×512
> 1536×1024
> 3072×2048

texture — *name of texture to tile*

```
$image->Set(texture=>string)
```

The `texture` attribute assigns a filename of a texture to be tiled onto the image background. See Chapter 8, *Image Maps*, for sources of stock textures and tileable patterns.

total_colors — *number of unique colors*

```
$image->Get('total_color')
```

Use this attribute to get the total number of unique colors in an image. The returned value for a colormapped image is the number of colors in the image colormap.

type — *image type*

```
$image->Get('type')
```

The image type may be any of the following:

```
bilevel
grayscale
palette
true color
true color with transparency
color separation
```

units — *units of resolution*

```
$image->Get('units')
```

Returns the units in which the image's resolution are defined. Values may be:

```
Undefined
pixels/inch
pixels/centimeter
```

white_point — *chromaticity white point*

```
$image->Set(white_point->x_value,y_value)
$image->Get('white_point')
```

This attribute returns the chromaticity white point. This is a color management option.

width — *image width*

```
$image->Get('width')
```

Returns the width (integer number of pixel columns) of the image.

x_resolution — *horizontal resolution*

```
$image->Get('x_resolution')
```

Returns the *x* resolution of the image in the units defined by the *units* attribute.

y_resolution — *vertical resolution*

```
$image->Get('y_resolution')
```

Returns the *y* resolution of the image in the units defined by the *units* attribute.

Manipulating Images

ImageMagick provides a suite of methods for manipulating images. Many of the functions take image attributes as parameters which optionally may be given values by the *Set()* method. You can optionally add the word "Image" to most of the method calls (e.g., *AnnotateImage()* is the same as *Annotate()*). If a method takes only one parameter, you do not have to explicitly pass the parameter name. Some examples of image manipulation method calls are:

```
$q->Crop(geometry=>'100x100+10+20');
$q->[$x]->Frame('100x200');
```

In general, the **geometry** parameter is a shortcut for defining a region and an off-set within an image; for example, **geometry=>'640x800+10+10'** is equivalent to **width=>640, height=>800, x=>10, y=>10**.

The syntax for the method descriptions assume that the **$image** object has been instantiated with a call to **Image::Magick->new** and has had some sort of image data read into it with a call to the *Read()* function.

Some methods return a new image (*Average()* or *Clone()*, for example). The text will specify these methods as such, and the description for the syntax of the method call will be in the form **$result=Method()**. All other methods will operate directly on the image that called them and will return a status code indicating the success or failure of the call.

AddNoise() — *add noise to an image*

```
$image->AddNoise(noise=>string)
```

This function adds random noise to the image, where *string* specifies one of the following types:

```
gaussian          laplacian

multiplicative    poisson

impulse           uniform
```

Annotate() — *annotate an image with text*

```
$image->Annotate(font=>string,
                 box=>color,
                 pen=>colorname,
                 geometry=>geometry,
                 text=>{string, @filename},
                 align=>{Left, Center, Right},
                 x=>integer,
                 y=>integer,
                 pointsize=>integer,
                 server=>string)
```

Annotate() allows you to add text to an image, as shown in Figure 5-2. The text may be represented as a string or as data from a file if the string has an amper-sand (@) as the first character. If the text is larger than the current image size when rendered at the given point size, it will be truncated to fit within the dimensions of the image.

Figure 5-2. $image->Annotate(font => 'CenturySchL-Roma', pointsize => 24, pen => 'red', text =>"here\nkitty\nkitty", align => 'Center', y => 20);

The font can be a fully qualified X11 font (-*-helvetica-medium-r-*-*-12-*-*-*-*-*-iso8859-*), TrueType (@TimesRoman.ttf), or PostScript (Helvetica) font name. Perl-Magick requires access to an X11 server, FreeType library, and Ghostscript to render X11, TrueType, and PostScript fonts, respectively.

PerlMagick contacts an X server to obtain the specified font if the name begins with a dash (-). Use the standard form for X server fonts. Wildcards may be used instead of individual field values, as long as you provide enough information for the font server to understand which font you're looking for, as in `-*-lucida-medium-r-*-*-24-*-*-*-*-*-*-*`. In this case, the point size of the font is specified within the string. You can also use a scalable PostScript font. To find out if you have scalable fonts installed on your Unix system, type `xlsfonts -fn '*-0-0-0-0-*'`. This will return a list of all the scalable fonts available to you. Specify the point size within the font string. Finally, most X11 font aliases are accepted. X-based systems use the *fonts.alias* file to define shorter aliases for the longer form of font names. On Windows-based systems, you may simply use the name of the font family and weight.

Note that the x and y coordinates actually define the upper left corner of the bounding box of the text, not the baseline. This can become a problem when positioning text above another image or beside text of different point sizes, because we do not have direct access to the metrics of a font from ImageMagick. The same problem crops up when we need to determine whether a given length of text will fit within the dimensions of a given image, because we cannot access the widths of individual characters within the font. You can, however, determine the overall width and height of a text string:

```
$image->Read('LABEL:How big am I');
($text_width, $text_height) = $image->Get('width', 'height');
```

Append() — *append a set of images*

```
$result = $image->Append()
```

The *Append()* method takes a set of images and appends them to each other. Each image in the set must have the same width or the same height (or both). The result is a single image with each image in the sequence side-by-side if all heights are equal or stacked on top of each other if all widths are equal.

Average() — *average the colors of a set of images*

```
$result = $image->Average()
```

The *Average()* method averages the color values in a set of images and returns a new image.

Blur() — *blur the image*

```
$image->Blur(factor=>{0.0-99.9})
```

Blurs an image. **Factor** is a percentage value from 0 (least blurry) to 99.9 (blurriest).

Border() — *frame the image with a border*

```
$image->Border(geometry=>geometry,
               width=>integer,
               height=>integer,
               color=colorname)
```

This method surrounds the image with a border of **color** or with the color indicated by the **bordercolor** attribute, if no color is explicitly given. After the transformation, the image will be 2*width pixels wider and 2*height pixels taller.

Charcoal() — *special effect filter*

```
$image->(factor=>percentage)
```

A special effect filter that simulates a charcoal drawing.

Chop() — *remove a portion of an image*

```
$image->(geometry=>geometry,
         width=>integer,
         height=>integer,
         x=>integer,
         y=>integer)
```

Chop() will remove a portion of an image starting at the offset x, y, as shown in Figure 5-3. The columns x through x+width and the rows y through y+height will be chopped. If width and height are not specified, they are assumed to be the maximum width and height of the image. **Geometry** may be used as a shortcut for width and height. Figures 5-3 and 5-4 compare *Crop()* with *Chop()*.

Figure 5-3. $image->Chop('30x30+90+25')

Clone() — *create a new copy of an image*

```
$result = $image->Clone()
```

The *Clone()* method copies a set of images and returns the copy as a new image object. For example,

```
$image2 = $image->Clone();
```

will copy all of the images from $image into $image2. PerlMagick transparently creates a linked list from an image sequence. If two locations in the sequence point to the same object, the linked list goes into an infinite loop and your script will run forever until interrupted.

Instead of:

```
push(@$images, $image);
push(@$images, $image);    # warning duplicate object
```

use cloning to prevent an infinite loop:

```
push(@$images, $image);
$clone = $image->Clone();
push(@$images, $clone);    # same image but different object
```

Comment() — *add a comment to an image*

```
$image->Comment(string)
```

Add a comment to an image. Optionally you can include any of the following bits of information about the image in the string by embedding the appropriate special characters:

%b for the image file size in bytes

%d for the directory in which the image resides

%e for the extension of the image file

%f for the filename of the image

%h for the image height

%m for the image file format

%s for the scene number of the image

%t for the filename of the image file without the extension

%w for the image width

For example:

```
$image->Comment("%m:%f %wx%h"' );
```

creates a comment for the image with the string `beatniks:GIF 318x265` if
`$image` is a 318×265 image that was read from a file titled *beatniks.gif.*

Composite() — *add one image to another*

```
$image->Composite(compose=>{Over, In, Out, Atop, Xor, Plus, Minus, Add,
                            Subtract, Difference, Bumpmap, Replace,
                            MatteReplace, Mask, Blend, Displace},
                   image=>image-object,
                   geometry=>geometry,
                   x=>integer,
                   y=>integer,
                   gravity=>{NorthWest, North, NorthEast, West, Center,
                             East, SouthWest, South, SouthEast}
```

By default, *Composite()* will simply replace those pixels in the given area of the
`composite` image with those pixels of `image`. The `compose` parameter allows you
to modify the behavior of this function with the following options:

Over
  Return the union of `image` and `composite` with `composite` obscuring `image`
  in the overlap.

In
  Return the `composite` cut by the shape of `image`.

Out
  Return `image` cut by the shape of the `composite`.

Atop
  Return `image` with `composite` obscuring `image` where the shapes overlap.

Xor
  Return those parts of `composite` and `image` that are outside the region of
  overlap between the two.

Plus
  Add the values of the individual channels of `composite` and `image`, setting
  overflows to 255.

Minus
  Subtract the values of the individual channels of `image` from `composite`, setting underflows to 0.

Add

Add the values of the individual channels of `composite` and `image`, applying `mod` 256 to overflows. This compose option is reversible.

Subtract

Subtract the values of the individual channels of `image` from `composite`, applying `mod` 256 to underflows. This compose option is reversible.

Difference

Return the absolute value of `image` subtracted from `composite`—useful for comparing two similar images.

Bumpmap

Return `image` with a shading filter applied using `composite` as a mask.

Replace

Return `image` replaced with `composite`.

Displace

Return `image` with a displacement filter applied using `composite` as a mask.

The x and y parameters give the position to overlay the object and gravity specifies the preferred placement of images within a larger image.

The *Composite()* method will be used in Chapter 10 to create several "layout manager" routines that will help us piece several images together for use as menus, banner ads, and image maps. Many of the parameters described for *Composite()* are also used for the *Montage()* routine, which is a specialized variant of *Composite()* for assembling images into multi-row composites with borders and backgrounds.

Contrast() — *enhance or reduce the image contrast*

```
$image->Contrast(sharpen=>{1, 0})
```

Contrast() enhances the intensity differences between the lighter and darker elements of the image. Setting the sharpen parameter to 1 will enhance the image and setting it to 0 will reduce the image contrast.

Crop() — *crop an image*

```
$image->Crop(geometry=>geometry,
             width=>integer,
             height=>integer,
             x=>integer,
             y=>integer)
```

Crop() will extract a width by height portion of the image starting at the offset *x,y*, as shown in Figure 5-4. The `geometry` parameter is just shorthand for width and height. To crop a 100×100 region starting at 20, 20, use `Crop('100x100+20+20')`. Invoking *Crop()* with the parameter 0x0 will crop off excess "border color" from your image, where the border color is intelligently inferred by PerlMagick. Figures 5-3 and 5-4 compare *Crop()* with *Chop()*.

Figure 5-4. $image->Crop('30x30+90+25')

CycleColormap() — *displace colormap*

```
$image->CycleColormap(amount=>integer)
```

CycleColormap() shifts an image's colormap by a given number of positions. This is very useful for making spacey psychedelic effects, among other applications.

Despeckle() — *filter speckles*

```
$image->Despeckle()
```

Despeckle() reduces the number of noisy extra pixels in large areas of continuous color.

Draw() — *annotate an image with graphic primitives*

```
$image->Draw(primitive=>{Point, Line, Rectangle, FillRectangle, Circle,
                    FillCircle, Polygon, FillPolygon, Color, Matte,
                    Text, Image, @filename},
          points=>string,
          method={Point, Replace, Floodfill, Reset},
          pen=>color,
          linewidth=>integer
          server=>servername)
```

The *Draw()* method allows you to draw anywhere on an image with one of many graphics primitives. An example is shown in Figure 5-5. The `points` parameter indicates the position to start drawing and must be a string of one or more coordinates, depending on the primitive being used. A coordinate string can look like any of these:

```
"3,5"                   # a single point
"10,10 20,20"           # two coordinates for a line, rectangle or circle
"40,40 80,80 50,80 90,40"  # four points for a polygon
```

Choose one of the following primitive types:

`Point`
> Draws a point at the single specified coordinate.

Color

Use `Color` to change the color of a pixel or area of pixels. This primitive takes a single coordinate for `points`, a color for `pen`, and one of the following methods:

— `Point`: Re-colors the pixel with the pen color

— `Replace`: Re-colors any pixel that matches the color of the pixel at given coordinate with the pen color

— `Floodfill`: Re-colors any pixel that matches the color of the pixel and is a neighbor of the given coordinate. This can be thought of as the Paint-bucket method.

— `Reset`: Re-colors all the pixels in the image with the pen color

Figure 5-5. $image->Draw(primitive => 'Color', points => '55,50', method =>'Floodfill', pen => 'black')

Matte

Use the `Matte` primitive to make a pixel or area of pixels transparent. `Matte` takes a single coordinate for `points` and one of the following methods:

— `Point`: Makes the given pixel transparent

— `Replace`: Makes any pixel that matches the color of the pixel at the given coordinate transparent

— `Floodfill`: Makes any pixel that matches the color of the pixel and is a neighbor of the pixel transparent

— `Reset`: Makes all pixels in the image transparent

Text

Use the `Text` primitive to place text on an image at a given coordinate, similar to the *Annotate()* method. The text to be drawn is appended to the coordinate string given in the `points` parameter. If the string has embedded spaces or newline characters, enclose it in double quotes within the string:

```
'100,100 Yowza!'                    # a string without embedded spaces
'100,100 "Yowza yowza yowza!"'      # a string with embedded spaces
```

Optionally you can include any of the following bits of information about the image in the string by embedding the appropriate special characters:

%b for the image file size in bytes

%d for the directory in which the image resides

%e for the extension of the image file

%f for the filename of the image

%h for the image height

%m for the image file format

%s for the scene number of the image

%t for the filename of the image file without the extension

%w for the image width

For example:

```
$image->Draw(primitive=>'Text', points=>'50,50 "%m:%f %wx%h"' );
```

annotates the image with the string `"beatniks:GIF 318x265"` if `$image` is a 318×265 image that was read from a file titled *beatniks.gif*.

If the first character of the string is @, the text is read from a file titled by the remaining characters in the string.

Image

> The `Image` drawing primitive is similar in functionality to the *Composite()* method in that it allows you to overlay one image on another at a given coordinate. *Composite()* offers greater control over how the two images are composed.

Line

> The `Line` primitive draws a line between two given coordinates with the specified **pen** color and line width.

Rectangle

> The `Rectangle` primitive draws a rectangle between the given upper left and lower right coordinates with the specified **pen** color and line width.

Circle

> The `Circle` primitive uses the first coordinate to define its center and the second coordinate to define a point on the outer edge of the circle. For example, to draw a circle centered at 100,100 that extends to 150,150 use:

```
# draw a circle of radius 50 centered at 100,100
$image->Draw(primitive=>'Circle',
             points=>'100,100 150,150',
             linewidth=>10);
```

Polygon

Use the `Polygon` primitive to draw a polygon with the given coordinates as vertices, as shown in Figure 5-6. A line of given width and color is drawn between the three or more coordinates provided. The last point is automatically connected to the first point to create a closed shape.

Figure 5-6. $image->Draw(primitive => 'Polygon', points => '10,30 30,75 100,80 80,40', linewidth => 2, pen => 'blue')

@filename

If the first character of the primitive string is @, a sequence of text or graphics primitives are read from a file whose name is the remainder of the string. For example:

```
$image->Draw(primitive=>'Circle',
            points=>'100,100 150,150 100,100 120,120 100,100 110,110');
```

is the same as:

```
Draw(primitive=>'@circles.txt');
```

where *circles.txt* is a file in the same directory that contains the following primitives:

```
Circle 100,100 150,150
Circle 100,100 120,120
Circle 100,100 110,110
```

Edge() — *detect edges within an image*

`$image->Edge(factor=>`*percentage*`)`

Edge() will find the edges in an image. The `factor` parameter is a percentage (0.0–99.9%) corresponding to the amount of enhancement.

Emboss() — *emboss the image*

`$image->Emboss()`

Emboss() applies a filter to the image which transforms the image into a grayscale with a three-dimensional effect similar to that created by an embossing die.

Enhance() — *filter a noisy image*

```
$image->Enhance()
```

Enhance() applies a digital filter that will improve the quality of a noisy image.

Equalize() — *equalization*

```
$image->Equalize()
```

This function performs a histogram equalization on the image.

Flip() — *reflect an image vertically*

```
$image->Flip()
```

Flip() creates a vertical mirror image by reflecting the scanlines around the central x axis.

Flop() — *reflect an image horizontally*

```
$image->Flop()
```

Flop() creates a horizontal mirror image by reflecting the scanlines around the central y axis.

Frame() — *surround the image with a border*

```
$image->Frame(geometry=>geometry,
              width=>integer,
              height=>integer,
              inner=>integer,
              outer=>integer,
              color=>string)
```

Frame() adds a simulated three-dimensional border around the image, as shown in Figure 5-7. `Width` and `height` specify the line width of the vertical and horizontal sides of the frame, respectively (`geometry` may be used as a shortcut for `width` and `height`). The `inner` and `outer` parameters indicate the line width of the inner and outer "shadows" of the frame; a wider shadow gives the effect of a deeper frame. The width and height must both be larger than the sum of the `inner` and `outer` values if the method is to work properly.

Figure 5-7. $image->Frame(geometry => '10x10', inner => 3, outer => 3)

Note that the width and height of the frame are added to the dimensions of the image. To create a frame that maintains the original dimensions of the image, crop the image before applying the frame:

```
# Make a frame that hugs the inside border of an image,
# retaining its dimensions

my ($w, $h) = $image->Get('columns', 'rows');

# First crop the image
$image->Crop(width=>$w-20,          # width and height indicate the area
             height=>$h-20,         # to be cropped
             x=>10,                 # x and y indicate the offset
             y=>10);

# Now add the Frame
$image->Frame(width=>10,            # here width and height are the line widths
              height=>10,           # of the vertical and horizontal borders
              inner=>3,
              outer=>3,
              color=>'#FF0022');    # a reddish sort of color
```

Gamma() — *gamma-correct the image*

```
$image->Gamma(gamma=>float,
              red=>float,
              green=>float,
              blue=>float)
```

The *Gamma()* method may be used to gamma-correct an image for applications in which exact color matching is critical. The same image viewed on different platforms will have perceptual differences in the way the image's intensities are represented on the screen. To improve color reproduction, an image should be gamma-corrected for various platforms. You may specify individual gamma levels for the red, green, and blue channels, or you can adjust all three with the *gamma* parameter. Values should be in the range of 0.8 to 2.3. For example:

```
# Gamma correct an image for viewing on a Macintosh
$image->Gamma(gamma=>1.8);

# Set the gamma correction for the individual channels
$image->Gamma(red=>1.8, green=>2.2, blue=>1.9);
```

Gamma() can also be used to eliminate channels from an image by giving that channel a gamma value of 0. For more information about gamma correction, look at Charles Poynton's "Frequently Asked Questions About Gamma" at *http:// www.inforamp.net/~poynton/notes/colour_and_gamma/GammaFAQ.html.*

Implode() — *apply an implosion/explosion filter*

`$image->Implode(factor=>percentage)`

Implode() applies a special effects filter to the image where **factor** is a percentage indicating the amount of implosion. Use a negative percentage for an explosion effect. A 60% implosion effect is shown in Figure 5-8.

Figure 5-8. $image->Implode('60%')

Layer() — *extract a layer*

`$image->Layer(layer=>{Red, Green, Blue, Matte})`

An image is generally made up of three or four layers: typically red, green, blue, and pixels with an optional opacity layer for transparency. Use this method to extract a particular layer from an image.

Label() — *add a label to an image*

`$image->Label(string)`

Add a label to an image. Optionally, you can include any of the following bits of information about the image in the string by embedding the appropriate special characters:

%b for the image file size in bytes

%d for the directory in which the image resides

%e for the extension of the image file

%f for the filename of the image

%h for the image height

%m for the image file format

%s for the scene number of the image

%t for the filename of the image file without the extension

%w for the image width

For example:

```
$image->Label("%m:%f %wx%h"' );
```

creates a label for the image with the string beatniks:GIF 318x265 if $image is a 318×265 image that was read from a file titled *beatniks.gif.*

Magnify() — *scale the image to twice its size*
```
$image->Magnify()
```

Magnify() is a convenience function that will scale an image proportionally to twice its size. See also *Minify()*.

Map() — *choose a set of colors from another image*
```
$image->Map(image=>image-object,
            dither=>{1, 0})
```

Map() will change the colormap of the image to that of the image given as a parameter. This may be used to "synchronize" the colormaps of different images, or used with the special "Netscape" template format to convert an image's colormap to the 216-color web safe palette:

```
$websafe = Image::Magick->new;
$status = $websafe->Read('NETSCAPE:');
$image->Map(image=>$websafe, dither=1);      # dither to 216-color cube
```

Minify() — *scale the image to half its size*
```
$image->Minify()
```

Minify() is a convenience function that will scale an image proportionally to half its size. See also *Magnify()*.

Modulate() — *adjust the brightness, saturation, and hue*
```
$image->Modulate(brightness=>percentage,
                 saturation=>percentage,
                 hue=>percentage)
```

Modulate() lets you control the brightness, saturation, and hue of an image. Each parameter is in the form of a percentage of the current value for that parameter. For example, to decrease brightness by 10% and increase saturation by 50%, use:

```
$image->Modulate(brightness=>-10, saturation=>50);
```

Mogrify() — *alternative method calling scheme*
```
$image->Mogrify(method_name,
                parameter_list)
```

The *Mogrify()* method is a convenience function that allows you to call any image manipulation method by giving it a method name as a string and a list of parameters to pass to the method. The following calls have the same result:

```
$image->Implode(factor=>50);
$image->Mogrify('Implode', factor=>50);
```

MogrifyRegion() — *perform Mogrify() on a region*

```
$image->Mogrify(region_geometry,
                method_name,
                parameter_list)
```

MogrifyRegion() will apply the *Mogrify()* method to the region of the image referred to by the geometry string. For example, if you wish to apply the *OilPaint()* filter to a 50×50 portion of the image starting at 10,10, you could use:

```
$image->MogrifyRegion('50x50+10+10', 'OilPaint', radius=>5);
```

Montage() — *create a formatted composite image*

```
$image->Montage(background=>color,
                borderwidth=>integer,
                compose=>{Over, In, Out, Atop, Xor, Plus, Minus, Add, Subtract,
                        Difference, Bumpmap, Replace, MatteReplace, Mask,
                        Blend, Displace},
                filename=>string,
                filter =>{Point, Box, Triangle, Hermite, Hanning, Hamming,
                        Blackman, Gaussian, Quadratic, Cubic, Catrom,
                        Mitchell, Lanczos, Bessel, Sinc},
                font=>string,
                foreground=>color,
                frame=>geometry,
                geometry=>geometry,
                gravity=>{NorthWest, North, NorthEast, West, Center, East,
                        SouthWest, South, SouthEast},
                label=>string
                mode=>{Frame, Unframe, Concatenate}
                pen=>color,
                pointsize=>integer
                shadow=>{1, 0}
                texture=>string,
                tile=>geometry,
                title=>string,
                transparent=>color)
```

The *Montage()* method is a layout manager that lets you composite several images into a single image suitable for use as a visual index of thumbnails or as an image map for a variety of applications. *Montage()* allows a good deal of control of the placement and framing of the images within the composite. To create a montage, first read all of the images to be included into an Image::Magick object, and then apply the *Montage()* function with the appropriate parameters. *Montage()* will automatically scale the images to the appropriate size and compose them into a single image (or into more than one image if the number of images exceeds the number of rows and columns specified by the tile parameter). Most of the parameters sent to *Montage()* are the same as those described in the attributes section. The compose parameter offers the same overlay options as in the *Composite()* function.

See Chapter 10 for some example scripts using *Montage()* to manage thumbnails.

The parameters specific to *Montage()* include:

`filename`
> Name the montage with this string.

`filter`
> This parameter has the same options available as the `filter` attribute described previously. It controls the filtering method applied when an image is scaled to fit a tile. The default is `Mitchell`, which also provides the best results in most cases.

`foreground`
> Provide a color name for the montage foreground.

`frame`
> Surround the image with a frame of line width and height specified as `width × height`.

`geometry`
> Give the geometry of the maximum tile and border size for each tile. The default maximum tile size is 120×120.

`gravity`
> Specify one of the eight points of the compass as the preferred layout position for a tile.

`label`
> Assign this string as a label for an image.

`mode`
> Provide one of three framing options for thumbnails: `Frame`, `Unframe`, `Concatenate`. The default value is `Frame`, which enables all of the scaling and framing parameters. Setting `mode` to `Unframe` will cause the images to be montaged without frames, and `Concatenate` will cause them to be composed into a single image with each of the subimages added at their original size.

`shadow`
> If 1, add a shadow beneath the tile.

`texture`
> Apply a tileable texture to the image background.

`tile`
> Give the number of tiles per row and column as a geometry string: `rows × columns`. The default is 5×4. If the number of tiles exceeds this maximum, more than one composite image is created.

`title`
> Give this title to the montage.

`transparent`
> Make this color transparent.

Use the **directory** attribute to get a list of all the filenames of the images in a montage.

If you are creating a montage from a group of thumbnail images, it is generally a good idea to create the thumbnails in advance with *Scale()* or *Zoom()* and hand them over to the *Montage()* function to avoid memory problems.

Negate() — *apply color inversion*

`$image->Negate(gray=>{1, 0})`

Negate() flips each bit of every color in the colormap of the image, effectively negating the intensities of the three color channels, as shown in Figure 5-9. If the optional gray parameter is set to 1, only the grayscale pixels are inverted.

Figure 5-9. $image->Negate()

Normalize() — *enhance image contrast*

`$image->Normalize()`

The *Normalize()* method enhances the contrast of a color image by adjusting its colormap such that it spans the entire range of colors available.

OilPaint() — *special effect filter*

`$image->OilPaint(radius=>integer)`

OilPaint() applies a special effect filter that simulates an oil painting by replacing each pixel in a circular region specified by the radius parameter with the most frequent color occurring in that region.

Opaque() — *globally change a color*

```
$image->Opaque(color=>color,
               pen=>color)
```

Opaque() changes the entry corresponding to the color parameter in the image's colormap to the **pen** color. To change all the white pixels in an image to red, for example, use:

```
# Change all white pixels to red
$image->Opaque(color=>'white', pen=>'red');
```

Ping() — *obtain information about an image without reading it*

```
Image::Magick->Ping(filename=>string)
```

Ping() is a convenience function that returns information about a file without having to read the image into memory. It returns the width, height, file size in bytes, and the file format of the image. For multi-image files, only the information for the first image in the sequence is returned.

Quantize() — *set the maximum number of colors in an image*

```
$image->Quantize(colors=>integer,
                 colorspace=>{RGB, Gray, Transparent, OHTA, XYZ, YCbCr,
                              YCC, YIQ, YPbPr, YUV, CMYK},
                 treedepth=>integer,
                 dither=>{1, 0})
```

The *Quantize()* method sets the maximum number of colors in an image. If the specified number of colors is less than the number of colors in the image, the size of the colormap is intelligently reduced to the new number. Setting the **dither** attribute will cause the image to be dithered to more accurately represent colors. See the descriptions of the **colors**, **colorspace**, and **dither** attributes in the earlier section "Getting and Setting Image::Magick Attributes."

QueryColor() — *return numerical values corresponding to color name*

```
$image->QueryColor(list)
```

The *QueryColor()* function accepts one or more color names and returns their respective red, green, and blue color values as a comma-delimited string:

```
($red, $green, $blue) = split /,/, $image->QueryColor('PeachPuff'));
```

See Appendix B for a table of valid color names.

Raise() — *lighten or darken edges to create a 3-D effect*

```
$image->Raise(geometry=>geometry,
              width=>integer,
              height=>integer)
```

Raise() will create a three-dimensional button-like effect by lightening and darkening the edges of the image, as shown in Figure 5-10.

Figure 5-10. $image->Raise('10x10')

ReduceNoise() — *smooth an image*

```
$image->ReduceNoise()
```

The *ReduceNoise()* method smooths the contours of an image while still preserving edge information. The algorithm works by analyzing 3×3 blocks of the image for "noisy" pixels and replacing these pixels with the best match in its surrounding 3×3 block. Use *AddNoise()* to add noise to an image.

Roll() — *offset and roll over an image*

```
$image->Roll(geometry=>geometry,
            x=>integer,
            y=>integer)
```

Roll() will offset an image on the x or y axis by the given amount and roll the part that is offset to the other side of the image that has been emptied, as in Figure 5-11. In Chapter 10, we will use the *Roll()* method to automatically create seamless tiled background patterns by "rolling" the edges into the center of the image and smoothing them over with other functions.

Figure 5-11. $image->Roll(x => 50, y => 25)

Rotate() — *rotate an image*

```
$image->Rotate(degrees=>float,
              crop=>{1, 0},
              sharpen=>{1, 0})
```

Rotate() will rotate an image around the x axis by the number of degrees specified by the **degrees** parameter (0 to 360). The empty space created around the resulting parallelogram are filled in with the color defined by the `bordercolor` attribute. If the `crop` parameter is 1, the image will be cropped to the image's original size. You may also specify whether jagged edges created by the transformation should be filtered with the `sharpen` parameter.

You may want to set the `bordercolor` to the background color of the image before calling *Rotate()*, so that the end result has a consistent background color. You can then crop the excess background with the *Trim()* method:

```
# Let's set bordercolor first
$image->Set(bordercolor=>'#FFFFFF');          # we've got a white background

# Do the rotation
$image->Rotate(degrees=>60, crop=>0, sharpen=>1);

# Now trim the excess background
$image->Trim();
```

Sample() — *sample an image to given dimensions*

```
$image->Scale(geometry=>geometry,
              width=>integer,
              height=>integer)
```

Sample() scales an image to the given dimensions with pixel sampling. Unlike other scaling methods, this method does not introduce any additional colors into the scaled image.

Scale() — *scale an image to given dimensions*

```
$image->Scale(geometry=>geometry,
              width=>integer,
              height=>integer)
```

Scale() will change the size of an image to the given dimensions. The dimensions may be specified either as absolute pixel sizes:

```
$image->Scale('300x300');        # scales the image to 300 pixels by 300 pixels
```

or by percentages for proportional scaling:

```
$image->Scale('300%x300%');    # makes the image three times larger
$image->Scale('300%');          # same thing
```

Use the *Transform()* method to scale an image and automatically apply an intelligent sharpening filter that will give better results than *Scale()* in most cases.

Segment() — *segment an image*

```
$image->Segment(colorspace=>{ RGB, Gray, Transparent, OHTA, XYZ, YCbCr, YCC, YIQ,
                     YPbPr, YUV, CMYK YPbPr, YUV, CMYK },
        cluster=>float,
        smooth=>float)
```

Segment() segments an image by analyzing the histograms of the color components and identifying units that are homogeneous.

Shade() — *shade the image with light source*

```
$image->Shade(geometry=>geometry,
        azimuth=>integer,
        elevation=>float,
        color=>{1, 0})
```

Shade(), as shown in Figure 5-12, creates an effect similar to that of *Emboss()* in that it gives the edges of the image a three-dimensional look and lights it with a distant light source (in fact, *Emboss()* is a special enhanced case of the *Shade()* function). You may control the light source with the `azimuth` and `elevation` parameters; `azimuth` is measured in degrees off the x axis and `elevation` is measured in "virtual pixels" on the (also virtual) z axis. The geometry parameter may be specified as a shortcut for `azimuth`×`elevation`.

Figure 5-12. $image->Shade(azimuth => 60, elevation => 50, color => 0)

Sharpen() — *sharpen an image*

```
$image->Sharpen(factor=>percentage)
```

Sharpen() enhances an image where `factor` is a percentage (0% to 99.9%) indicating the degree of sharpness.

Shear() — *shear an image*

```
$image->Shear(geometry=>geometry,
        x=>float,
        y=>float,
        crop=>{1, 0})
```

Shear() will transform an image by shearing it along the x or y axis. The *x* and *y* parameters specify the number of degrees (-179.9 to 179.9) that the image is to be sheared along that respective axis. The empty space created around the resulting parallelogram is filled with the color defined by the `bordercolor` attribute. If the `crop` parameter is 1, the image will be cropped to the image's original size.

Signature() — *generate an MD5 signature*

`$image->Signature()`

Signature() generates an MD5 public key signature and stores it with the header information for the MIFF image format. The signature can later be used to verify the data integrity of the image. Two images with the same signature are identical.

Solarize() — *apply solarization special effect*

`$image->Solarize(factor=>percentage)`

Solarize() applies a special effect to the image, similar to the effect achieved in a photo darkroom by selectively exposing areas of photo sensitive paper to light (as in the work of Man Ray, for example). The `factor` attribute is a percentage (0% to 99.9%) indicating the extent of solarization.

Spread() — *randomly displace pixels*

`$image->Spread(amount=>integer)`

Spread() will randomly displace pixels within a block defined by the `amount` parameter, as shown in Figure 5-13.

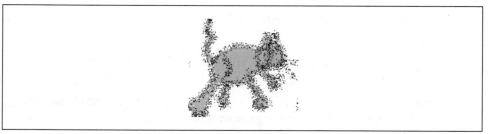

Figure 5-13. $image->Spread(amount => 5)

Swirl() — *swirl pixels around image center*

`$image->Swirl(degrees=>float)`

The *Swirl()* method swirls the pixels around the center of the image, where the *degrees* parameter indicates the sweep of the arc through which each pixel is moved; a higher degree means a more distorted image. Figure 5-14 shows a 180° swirl.

Texture() — *tile a texture on image background*

`$image->Texture(filename=>string)`

Texture() reads an image file and applies it in a tiled pattern as a "texture" to the background of the image, as shown in Figure 5-15.

Figure 5-14. $image->Swirl (degrees=>180)

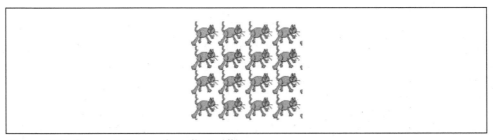

Figure 5-15. $image->Texture('smallcat.gif')

Threshold() — *divide pixels based on intensity values*

```
$image->Threshold(threshold=>integer)
```

Threshold() changes the value of individual pixels based on the intensity of each pixel. There are two cases:

1. If the intensity of a pixel is of greater intensity than the `threshold` parameter, the pixel is set to the value of the maximum intensity in the image.

1. If the intensity of a pixel is of less intensity than the `threshold` parameter, the pixel is set to the value of the minimum intensity in the image.

The resulting image is a high-contrast, two-color image in the RGB colorspace. The effects of this method within different colorspaces may vary.

Transform() — *scale or crop an image*

```
$image->Transform(crop=>geometry,
             geometry=>geometry)
```

Transform() is a convenience method that crops or scales an image to the specified dimensions with automatic sharpening. You can express the `geometry` parameter as a percentage string:

```
$image->Transform(geometry=>'50%');       # Scale proportionally to half its
                                          # size
$image->Transform(geometry=>'50%x25%');   # Scale 50% horizontally,
                                          # 25% vertically
$image->Transform(geometry=>'160x160>');  # scale so one dimension is
                                          # exactly 160 pixels
```

Transparent() — *make color transparent*

```
$image->Transparent(color=>color)
```

The *Transparent()* method makes all pixels of the given color transparent within the image. To make only certain areas of color transparent, use the `Matte` primitive with the *Draw()* function. If you write the image to a file format that does not support transparency, the original color will be written without the transparency information.

Note that each image in the sequence can be assigned a different transparency color. To make white the transparent color for the first image and black the transparent color for the second, use:

```
$image->[0]->Transparent('#FFFFFF');# Make white transparent for first image
$image->[1]->Transparent('#000000');# Make black transparent for second image
```

Multiple colors can be made transparent with:

```
$image->Transparent('#FFFFFF');  # Make white transparent for entire sequence
$image->Transparent('#000000');  # Make black transparent for sequence
```

Trim() — *remove background color from edges of image*

```
$image->Trim()
```

Trim() crops a rectangular box around the image to remove edges that are the background color.

Wave() — *special effects filter*

```
$image->Wave(geometry=>geometry,
             amplitude=>float,
             wavelength=>float)
```

The *Wave()* filter creates a "ripple" effect in the image, as shown in Figure 5-16, by shifting the pixels vertically along a sine wave whose amplitude and wavelength is specified by the given parameters.

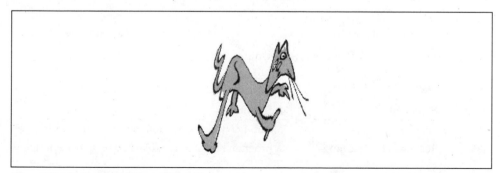

Figure 5-16. $image->Wave('20x10')

Zoom() — *scale an image with a filter*

```
$image->Zoom(geometry=>geometry,
          width=>integer,
          height=>integer,
          filter=>{ Point, Box, Triangle, Hermite, Hanning, Hamming, Blackman,
                    Gaussian, Quadratic, Cubic, Catrom, Mitchell, Lanczos,
                    Bessel, Sinc})
```

Zoom() scales an image to the specified dimensions and applies one of the given filters for a higher quality result when enlarging images than that given by the *Scale()* method.

How to Tell When Something Has Gone Wrong

Whenever most of the routines from the Image::Magick module are called, their return values are undefined if the operation was successful. This allows a very simple check for success:

```
$status = $image->Transparent('#FFFFFF');
warn "$status" if "$status";                    # print the error message, if any
```

If an error occurs, the method will return an error string that consists of a numeric status code in the range of 0 to 410 and an error message. An error code less than 400 is a warning that something happened that was probably not what you expected to happen, and errors greater than or equal to 400 indicate an unrecoverable error that should probably cause a *die()* condition, as in the following:

```
$status = $image->Read('beatniks.gif');
$status =~ /(\d+)/;
die "Got an Unrecoverable Error" if ($1 >= 400);
```

Some methods return an image when successful. In this case we should check to see if the resulting object is a reference to an image object:

```
$image2 = $image->Clone();
warn "$image2" if !ref($image2);                # print the error message, if any
```

See Table 5-6 for a list of errors and warning codes.

Table 5-6. Error and Warning Codes

Code	Mnemonic	Description
0	Success	Method completed without an error or warning
300	ResourceLimitWarning	A program resource is exhausted (e.g., not enough memory)
305	XServerWarning	An X resource is unavailable
310	OptionWarning	An option parameter was malformed

Table 5-6. Error and Warning Codes (continued)

Code	Mnemonic	Description
315	DelegateWarning	An ImageMagick *delegate* returned a warning
320	MissingDelegateWarning	The image type can not be read or written because the appropriate *delegate* is missing
325	CorruptImageWarning	The image file may be corrupt
330	FileOpenWarning	The image file could not be opened
400	ResourceLimitError	A program resource is exhausted, unrecoverable
405	XServerError	An X resource is unavailable, unrecoverable
410	OptionError	A command-line option was malformed, unrecoverable

Using the ImageMagick Utilities

The ImageMagick libraries come with a set of utility programs that are very handy to have around, and are just the thing for quick file conversions and image previewing. They also allow you to perform concise batch operations that would be much more time-consuming (if not impossible) with a GUI-based image manipulation program such as Photoshop or Paint Shop Pro. The four primary ImageMagick programs are *display, animate, convert,* and *identify.*

display

> The *display* program is a utility for displaying an image on a workstation connected to an X server. It also offers a graphical interface to many of the ImageMagick image manipulation functions.

animate

> The *animate* program is used for displaying a list of images as an animated sequence on a workstation connected to an X server. For example:

```
animate *.gif
```

> would display all of the GIF images in the current directory as an animated sequence.

convert

> The *convert* utility allows you to convert one image format to another. Most of the image manipulation functions may be applied during the conversion process. For instance, to convert a TIFF image of a quahog to a GIF image:

```
convert quahog.tiff gif:quahog.gif
```

> To convert all of the GIF images in the current directory into a single, infinitely looping animated GIF named *foo.gif* with a half second delay between frames, use:

```
convert -loop 0 -delay 50 *.gif foo.gif
```

To create a GIF image using only the 216 web safe colors, try:

```
convert -map netscape: alpha.gif beta.gif
```

identify

The *identify* program provides information from the header block of a graphics file. *Identify* returns the filename, width, height, the image class (whether it is colormapped), number of colors in the image, the size of the image in bytes, file format, and the number of seconds it took to read and process the image. Running identify with the **–verbose** parameter produces additional information, including the internal palette associated with the image, if it is colormapped. For example:

```
identify -verbose beatniks.gif
```

produces the output:

```
Image: beatniks.gif
class: PseudoClass
colors: 256
    0: (  0,  0,  0)  #000000  black
    1: (  1,  1,  1)  #010101  ~black
    2: (  2,  2,  2)  #020202  ~gray1
    3: (  3,  3,  3)  #030303  gray1
    4: (  4,  4,  4)  #040404  ~gray1
    ... (content cut for brevity)
    254: (254,254,254)  #fefefe  ~white
    255: (255,255,255)  #ffffff  white
matte: False
runlength packets: 15215 of 29100
geometry: 150x194
depth: 8
filesize: 9525b
interlace: None
page geometry: 150x194+0+0
format: GIF
```

import, mogrify, montage, combine

ImageMagick comes with a number of other utilities, most of which have overlapping functionality with methods available through the Image::Magick module. The *import* program captures an image from any visible window of an X client and writes it to an image file. The *mogrify* program applies any of the image manipulation routines to an image. The *montage* program duplicates the functions of the *Montage()* method and combine is very similar to the *Composite()* method.

WebMagick

WebMagick is a set of Perl scripts for automating the creation of elaborate collections of images and HTML pages for use on the Web. *WebMagick* is also an excellent example of an ImageMagick application written using the PerlMagick interface. It was written by Bob Friesenhahn and is available at *http:// www.cyberramp.net/~bfriesen/webmagick/index.html.*

See also the ImageMagick Studio at *http://www.sympatico.org/cristy/ MogrifyMagick/* (Figure 5-17).

Figure 5-17. The ImageMagick Studio web site provides a web-based interface to many ImageMagick functions

6

Charts and Graphs with GIFgraph

GIFgraph is a Perl module that expands on the capabilities of GD by offering a number of methods for creating graphs and charts. For quite a while, almost all of the financial graphs or web server load graphs seen on the Web were generated by GIFgraph. Now, as more money gets pumped into the back end of many web sites, companies are spending tens of thousands of dollars on customized proprietary graphing and charting packages that in some cases don't really go that much farther than the freely redistributable GIFgraph module.

In this chapter we'll implement a web biorhythms server, provide a reference to the GIFgraph methods and attributes controlling the various types of graph layouts, show how the Data::Xtab module can be used to make it easier to get real-world data into a format suitable for use with GIFgraph, and go through an example of "passing off" a GIFgraph graph to another image manipulation package such as GD.

The GIFgraph package was written by Martien Verbruggen, and is available on CPAN. It should run on any operating system that runs Perl and the GD module, which it uses for all of its drawing and file primitives. Since not all ports of GD behave correctly (for example, some older ports on Win32), be sure that you have a proper version of Perl (such as Gurusamy Sarathy's Win32 port) and GD 1.15 or higher.

Let's Make Some Graphs!

Constructing graphs with GIFgraph can be broken down into three phases. First you will need to gather the data, parse it, and organize it in a form that you can pass to the graph drawing routines. Then you will set the attributes of the graph so that it will come out the way you want it, and draw it with the *plot()* or *plot_to_gif()* method. The data for the graph must be in a very particular form before you plot the graph. It must be assigned to an array, where the first element of the array is an anonymous list of the x axis values, and any subsequent elements are different data sets to be plotted against the y axis. A sample data array would look like this:

```
@data = ( # First the time span
          [ qw(1992 1993 1994 1995 1996 1997 1998) ],

          # Data set 1 = 1000s of people in Peoria
          [ 5, 10, 8, 13, 16, 24, 32],

          # Data set 2 = 1000s of people in Santa Fe
          [6.5, 9.2, 14.2, 12.8, 22, 31.7, 3] );
```

GIFgraph implements six different types of graphs: lines, bars, points, lines and points, area, and pie (see Figures 6-3 through 6-8). A new GIFgraph object may be created with the *use* function, and then calling the *new* method associated with the graph type in question. For example, to create a new graph that connects all of the data points with different colored lines, start with:

```
use GIFgraph::lines;
$somegraph = new GIFgraph::lines( );
```

Each graph type has many attributes that may be used to control the format, color, and content of the graph. Use the *set()* method to configure your graph:

```
$somegraph->set(
              title         => "America's love affair with cheese",
              x_label       => 'Time',
              y_label       => 'People (thousands)',
              y_max_value   => 50,
              y_tick_number => 5
        );
```

Finally, draw the graph with the *plot()* method, which will create a graph and return the GIF data, or the *plot_to_gif()* method, which will create the graph, open a file, and write the graph to the file in GIF format:

```
$somegraph->plot_to_gif( "cheesegraph.gif", \@data );
```

Are you "into" biorhythms? As an example of using GIFgraph (and not as an endorsement of the validity of biorhythmic orgone radiation), we'll start this chapter with a Web Biorhythm Server. The general idea of biorhythms is that cyclic processes in nature (seasonal changes, and particularly the changing phases of the moon) are reflected in the processes of the human body. Although they have no real basis in scientific study, these cyclic patterns have entertained the imaginations of many people for many years. You can get your biorhythm read by coin-operated machines at many rest stops on America's highways.

Here's how the Biorhythm Server works: first a user will enter her birth date, and a range of dates for the biorhythm report. These are submitted via a CGI script to a Perl script that will create a graph for the three primary biorhythm patterns: physical, emotional, and intellectual. These three patterns will unfold as sine waves starting from the date of birth, with periods of 23 days for the physical cycle, 28 days for the emotional cycle, and 33 days for the intellectual cycles. These numbers are just how the biorhythmic cycles are defined; don't ask me exactly why because it's a mystery of nature.

The biorhythm page is composed of two separate Perl scripts that implement the CGI interface: *biopage.cgi* and *bio.cgi*. The *biopage.cgi* script builds the HTML page (including the form used to enter the data for the script) and passes on data to the *bio.cgi* script, which uses the GIFgraph module to create a biorhythm chart from the data and sends it to the browser as a GIF image data stream. The *biopage.cgi* script is accessed for the first time without any data fields with the URL *http://www.yoururl.com/cgi-bin/biopage.cgi*. The HTML page that is output from this script is shown in Figure 6-1.

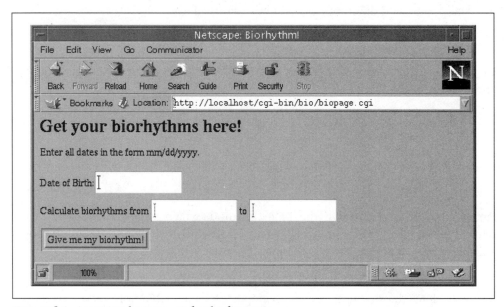

Figure 6-1. Accessing biopage.cgi for the first time

When a user enters data into the form fields and hits the Submit button, the *biopage.cgi* script is called again with the new data. Assuming the user has entered valid data, it will create a new HTML page with an embedded `<IMG>` tag that will call the *bio.cgi* script to generate the graph. The output of this script is shown in Figure 6-2.

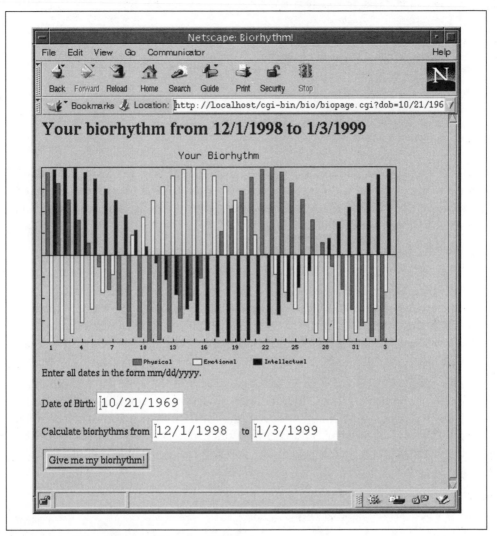

Figure 6-2. Calling biopage.cgi with valid data

The following is the code for *biopage.cgi*. Of course, to run this as a CGI application it must be in the appropriate place for the web server you are running and its permissions must be set so that the web server may execute it.

```
#!/usr/local/bin/perl
#
# biopage.cgi
# Generate the html 'wrapper' page for biorhythm graphing example.
#
use CGI;

# First get the parameters passed into the script
```

```
# Use the CGI module to parse the CGI form submission.
#
my $query = new CGI;
my $dob = $query->param('dob');
my $start = $query->param('start');
my $end = $query->param('end');

# Print the header and beginning html for the result page.
#
print $query->header(-type => 'text/html');
print $query->start_html(-title => "Biorhythm!");
```

Using this script to produce a "wrapper" result page for the image gives us a chance to check the data for errors and print a useful HTML message if something goes wrong. In a more robust version of this script, there are three situations that could cause an error that should be checked:

1. No data has been passed from the form, in which case an image should not be generated.

2. The date is not in the proper form. We are requiring a strict MM/DD/YYYY date representation, to eliminate possible Y2K problems and simplify the parsing of the date. Most of the date manipulation modules accessible via CPAN allow alternate date representations, so it should be easy to add that at a later date.

3. The range of dates is too large. Selecting a large number of dates shouldn't do anything particularly bad, but the size of the final graph is hard-coded at 500×300 pixels. Since the output is in the form of a bar graph, with three bars per day and each bar requiring 3 horizontal pixels to be a distinctly colored bar, a range of days greater than 60 or so will create illegible output.

```
if ($dob && $start && $end) {

    # In this case we have data passed in from the form.
    # Add error checking here...

    # Output the html for the image tag. This will pass the data on to
    # the bio.cgi script to generate the image data.
    #
    print "<H1>Your biorhythm from $start to $end</H1>";
    print "<IMG WIDTH=500 HEIGHT=300 ";
    print "SRC=\"bio.cgi?dob=$dob&";
    print "start=$start&end=$end\"> <BR>";

} else {

    # In this case, no data has been passed to the script; this may
    # be because this is the first invocation of the script or
    # blank fields were submitted. We can just print an appropriate
    # headline...
    #
```

```
        print "<H1>Get your biorhythms here!</H1>"
}

# Now print the html form at the bottom of the page.
# You could let the CGI module do this, but this uses a 'here' document
#
print "Enter all dates in the form mm/dd/yyyy. <BR>";
print "<FORM METHOD=POST ACTION=\"biopage.cgi?";
print "dob=$dob&start=$start&end=$end\">";

print <<EOF;
Date of Birth:<INPUT TYPE=text NAME=dob SIZE=10 VALUE=$dob><br>
Calculate biorhythms from
<INPUT TYPE=text NAME=start SIZE=10 VALUE=$start>
to
<INPUT TYPE=text NAME=end SIZE=10 VALUE=$end><br>

<INPUT TYPE="submit" VALUE="Give me my biorhythm!"><br>

</FORM>
</BODY>
</HTML>

EOF
```

The *bio.cgi* script is the one that actually does the graphical grunt work. It uses the GIFgraph::bars module to plot the bar graph and the Date::DateCalc module to perform the required date calculations. Date::DateCalc must be installed on the system running the script. Because it requires an external C library, I have placed all of the date manipulation functions in separate subroutines so that you can easily replace these date manipulation functions with whatever you have locally if Date::DateCalc cannot be installed.

Here is the code for *bio.cgi*:

```
#!/usr/local/bin/perl
#
# bio.cgi
# Dynamically generate a biorhythm bar graph from data passed in from
# a form from the web page generated by biopage.cgi. The data passed to
# this script is the date of birth, the start date, and the end date.
#
use GIFgraph::bars;
use Date::Calc(qw(Delta_Days Add_Delta_Days));
use CGI;

# We will need a decent value of pi in the calculate subroutine;
# We can do a quick approximation using the atan2 function which returns
# the arctangent of y/x for -pi to pi. Since the atan of 1 is 45
# degrees (or pi / 4 radians), we can use:
#
my $pi = atan2(1,1) * 4;
```

```perl
# Get the date of birth, start date, and end date parameters
# that were passed from the form
#
my $query = new CGI;
my $dob = $query->param('dob');
my $start = $query->param('start');
my $end = $query->param('end');

# Calculate the number of days between the start and end date
# using our own 'wrapper' datediff function...
#
my $days = datediff(parsedate($start),
                    parsedate($end));

# Calculate the number of days between date of birth and the start date
#
my $dobdiff = datediff(parsedate($dob),
                       parsedate($start));

# The xvalues list contains all of the numbers of the days within the
# start to end range. Use the daterange funtion described below to
# return all the days between two dates. This handles situations where
# the range spans a month or year border.
#
my @xvalues = daterange(parsedate($start));

# Now we can calculate the biorythmic graphs for the given range.
# The first parameter to calculate is the period of the sine wave,
# the second is the starting offset value for x, and the third is the
# number of days in the range of dates.
# pvalues = the 'physical' data set
# evalues = the 'emotional' data set
# ivalues = the 'intellectual' data set
#
my @pvalues = calculate(23, $dobdiff % 23, $days);
my @evalues = calculate(28, $dobdiff % 28, $days);
my @ivalues = calculate(33, $dobdiff % 33, $days);

# Organize the data in a form that we can pass to a plotting routine...
#
my @data = (\@xvalues,
            \@pvalues,
            \@evalues,
            \@ivalues,
           );

# The 'legend' is the set of labels for the various data sets
#
my @legend = ('Physical', 'Emotional', 'Intellectual');

# Create a new bar graph
#
my $graph = new GIFgraph::bars(500,300);
```

```
# Set the attributes for the graph
#
$graph->set(x_label             => '',     # No labels
            y_label             => '',
            title               => 'Your Biorhythm',

            # The y values are representing non-quantitative 'good' and 'bad'
            # values so we won't plot numerical values on the y axis
            #
            y_plot_values       => 0,
            y_max_value         => 1,         # sine range is -1 to 1
            y_min_value         => -1,
            y_tick_number       => 8,
            long_ticks          => 0,         # use short ticks on axes
            x_label_skip        => 3,         # print every third x label

            # Since we are using a bar graph, we want the x axis labels along
            # the bottom edge of the graph so it doesn't get messy...
            #
            zero_axis           => 0,
            zero_axis_only      => 0,
        );

# Add the legend to the graph
#
$graph->set_legend(@legend);

# Draw the graph and write it to STDOUT
#
print STDOUT $query->header(-type => 'image/gif');
binmode STDOUT;                       # switch to binary mode, if you have to
print STDOUT $graph->plot(\@data );
```

Four helper routines are called by the *bio.cgi* script: *calculate, parsedate, datediff,* and *daterange.* The *calculate* subroutine actually does the trigonometric calculations and returns a complete data set, ready for graphing. Specifically, it takes the period of the sine wave (defined as the somewhat arbitrary 23, 28, and 33 days for the emotional, physical, and intellectual cycles, respectively), and an initial "offset." Because the sine function starts at y=0 for the user's date of birth and continues oscillating through its cycle as time advances, the function will have a certain starting value at the starting date of the range. The offset value is the number of days that the function has progressed into its cycle at the date indicated by *$start.* It can be calculated by finding the difference between the start date and the date of birth, dividing by the period, and taking the remainder.

The *calculate* routine returns a list containing the y values for the given range of dates, which may be passed off to the graphing routines. Here is the code:

```
sub calculate {

    # This routine will calculate the biorhythm y values for a given number
    # of days. The parameters are the period of the sine wave,
```

```perl
    # and the initial offset.
    #
    my ($period, $offset) = @_;
    my ($y, $count, @returnlist);

    foreach $count (0..$days) {

        # We can express the desired x value in degrees by multiplying
        # the count (plus the previously computed offset) by 360 and
        # dividing by the period of the sine wave.
        # Since the sin function expects a parameter in radians,
        # convert to radians by multiplying by $pi/180.
        # this simplifies to:
        #
        $y = sin((($count+$offset)/$period) * 2 * $pi);
        push @returnlist, $y;
    }


    return @returnlist;
}
```

The three date manipulation functions are:

```perl
sub parsedate {

    # Parse the month, day, and year from a given date string.
    # In this case, the string is represented as a forward slash-
    # delimited string of numbers. This routine could be replaced
    # with a more robust parsing routine, if that's something
    # that you're interested in...
    #
    $_[0] =~ /(.+)\/(.+)\/(.+)/;
    return ($1, $2, $3);
}


sub datediff {

    # This routine will calculate the difference between two dates.
    # It is in a separate routine so that it can be easily changed
    # with whatever date modules are installed locally.
    # In this case, we're using the Date::Calc module.
    # The Delta_Days function takes arguments in the form  yy, mm, dd.
    # We are passing the two date parameters as mm1,dd1,yy1,mm2,dd2,yy2.
    #
    return Date::Calc::Delta_Days($_[2],$_[0],$_[1],
                                  $_[5],$_[3],$_[4]);
}


sub daterange {

    # This routine takes a starting date in the form mm, yy, dd
    # and an offset number of days and returns a list
    # of all the days between date and the date that is offset days
    # away. In this case we use the Date::Calc module's Add_Delta_days
    # function, using only the day field returned by the function.
    #
```

```
    my (@returnlist, $yy, $mm, $dd);

    foreach my $day (0..$days) {

        # Add_Delta_Days takes a yy, mm, dd date and an offset.
        # It returns the new date as a yy, mm, dd list
        #
        ($yy, $mm, $dd) = Date::Calc::Add_Delta_Days($_[2],
                                                      $_[0],
                                                      $_[1],
                                                      $day);
        push @returnlist, "$dd";
    }
    return @returnlist;
}
```

You should have a workable biorhythm server at this point. Though I am not generally a technophobe, I think it would be very sad if they ever replaced the coin-operated biorhythm machine at the Vince Lombardi rest area on Rt. 95 in New Jersey with an Internet kiosk running this script.

GIFgraph Reference

Table 6-1 lists the methods and attributes provided by GIFgraph.

Table 6-1. Methods and Attributes by Category

Category	Method
GIFgraph classes	GIFgraph::lines, GIFgraph::bars, GIFgraph::points, GIFgraph::linespoints, GIFgraph::area, GIFgraph::pie, GIFGraph::colour
Methods that apply to all graph classes	*new()*, *set_text_clr()*, *set_title_font()*, *plot()*, *plot_to_gif()*, *set()*
Methods for pie charts	*set_label_font()*, *set_value_font()*
Methods for charts with axes	*set_x_axis_font ()*, *set_x_label_font ()*, *set_y_axis_font ()*, *set_y_label_font ()*
Methods for legends	*set_legend()*, *set_legend_font()*
Methods for dealing with GIFgraph colors	*_rgb*, *_hue*, *_luminance*, *colour_list*, *read_rgb*, *sorted_colour_list*
Attributes for all graphs	accentclr, axislabelclr, b_margin, bgclr, dclrs, fgclr, gifx, gify, interlaced, l_margin, label-clr, logo, logo_position, logo_resize, r_margin, t_margin, textclr, transparent
Attributes for bars, lines, points, line-spoints, and area charts	axis_space, box_axis, long_ticks, overwrite, tick_length, two_axes, x_label_skip, x_plot_values, x_ticks, y_label_skip, y_min_value, y_max_value, y_plot_values, y_tick_number, zero_axis, zero_axis_only

Table 6-1. Methods and Attributes by Category (continued)

Category	Method
Attributes for graphs with lines	`line_types, line_type_scale, line_width`
Attributes for graphs with points	`markers, marker_size`
Attributes for legends	`legend_marker_width, legend_marker_height, legend_placement, legend_spacing, lg_cols`
Attributes for pie graphs	`d, pie_height, start_angle`

GIFgraph Methods

This section details the GIFgraph methods.

new() — *create a new graph object*

```
new GIFgraph::bars(width, height)
new GIFgraph::lines(width, height)
new GIFgraph::points(width, height)
new GIFgraph::linespoints(width, height)
new GIFgraph::area(width, height)
new GIFgraph::pie(width, height)
```

The *new()* method creates a new graph object. The *width* and *height* parameters are optional; if they are not set, the graph is created with a default width of 400 pixels and height of 300 pixels. GIFgraph implements six different kinds of graphs:

GIFgraph::bars

A graph where the data is represented as colored bars (Figure 6-3).

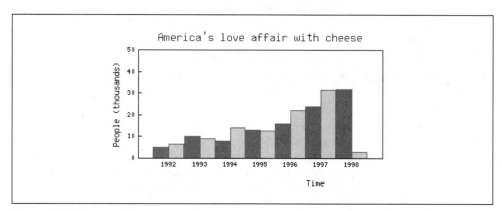

Figure 6-3. A bars graph

GIFgraph::lines

A graph with lines connecting the data points (Figure 6-4). Use a linespoints graph to plot the data points as well as the lines.

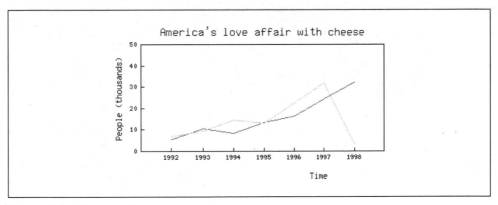

Figure 6-4. A lines graph

GIFgraph::points

A graph with only the data points plotted (Figure 6-5).

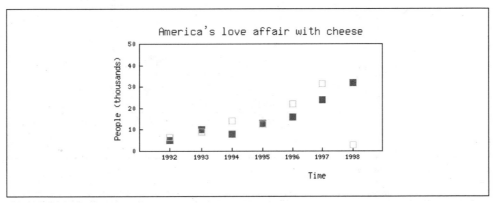

Figure 6-5. A points graph

GIFgraph::linespoints

A graph with lines connecting visible data points (Figure 6-6).

GIFgraph::area

A graph with lines connecting the data points and the area under the line filled with a color (Figure 6-7).

GIFgraph::pie

A graph where points in the data set are represented as slices of a pie (Figure 6-8).

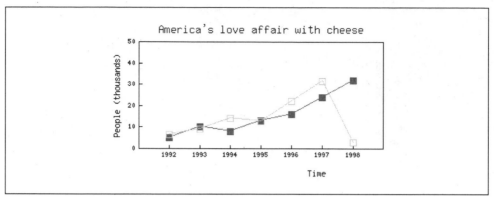

Figure 6-6. A linespoints graph

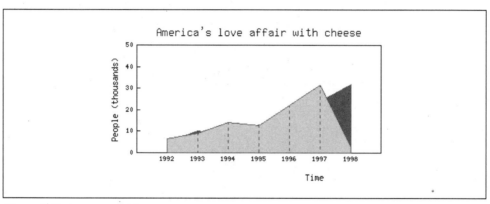

Figure 6-7. An area graph

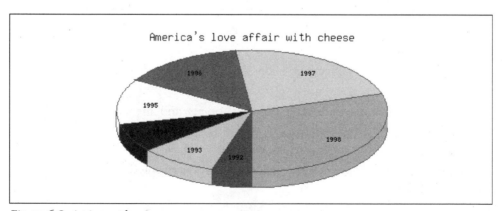

Figure 6-8. A pie graph

set_text_clr — *set the color to be used for drawing text*

`GIFgraph::set_text_clr(colorname)`

This method will set the color to be used for all of the text within a graph. The *colorname* must be a valid GIFgraph color name (see "Colors in GIFgraph"). You can also specify the colors of individual elements of a graph separately with the *set()* method and the attributes `textclr`, `labelclr`, and `axislabelclr`.

Here is an example:

```
$somegraph->set_text_clr( 'dgreen' );          # dgreen is the same as #007F00
```

set_title_font() — *set font for graph title*

`GIFgraph::set_title_font(fontname)`

This method sets which of the five GD fonts used to title the graph. The *font-name* parameter should be one of: `gdSmallFont`, `gdLargeFont`, `gdMediumBoldFont`, `gdTinyFont`, or `gdGiantFont`. The default font is `gdLargeFont`. Note that in order to use these fonts you must import the GD module first with the command `use GD`.

plot() — *generate a GIF from data*

`GIFgraph::plot(\@data)`

The *plot()* method will take a data set, plot it according to the type of graph object and the values of the attributes that have been set, and return a scalar containing the GIF data. This function is used most often for plotting a graphic to STDOUT in CGI applications. Note that the data set is passed as a list of references to arrays; the first array in the list represents the values for the x axis, and each array after that represents a different set of y values to be plotted. For example, the following data will generate a graph with the month names on the x axis and two sets of numbers plotted against the y axis:

```
@data = (
         [ qw(JAN FEB MAR APR MAY JUN JUL AUG SEP OCT NOV DEC) ],
         [ 5,   8,   24,   32,  12,  18,  11,  21,   22,  9,   29,   16 ],
         [ 6.5, 12.8, 31.7,  3,   9,  15,  14.8, 21.2,  7,  9.9, 10,  7.2 ]
         );
$graph->plot(\@data);
```

If the arrays are not set up correctly (if, for example, the arrays are not all the same length), Perl will complain with a "length misfit" error. The data sets may be padded with undef values if the values are not to be plotted.

plot_to_gif() — *generate a GIF from data and write to a file*

```
GIFgraph::plot_to_gif(filename, \@data)
```

This method performs the same operation as *plot()*, but writes it to the file indicated by the *filename* string; this is simply a convenience routine that allows you to bypass the opening of a filehandle. For example:

```
$graph->plot_to_gif('graphout.gif', \@data);
```

set() — *change the attributes of a graph object*

```
GIFgraph::set(attribute1 => value1, attribute2 => value2 ...)
```

The *set()* method allows you to change the values of one or more attributes of a graph object. The attribute definitions should be passed as key=>value pairs. For example, to change the point size of the line width of a graph with lines, use:

```
$linegraph->set( line_width => 4 );
```

Many of the attributes are only applicable to certain types of graphs. For example, a pie chart will have different attributes than a chart with axes,. These attributes are explained in detail in the "Attributes of GIFgraph Objects" section.

set_label_font, set_value_font — *set fonts for pie graphs*

```
GIFgraph::set_label_font(fontname)
GIFgraph::set_value_font(fontname)
```

These methods may only be applied to pie charts. They allow you to set the font to be used to label the slices of a pie graph. Valid fontnames are gdSmallFont, gdLargeFont, gdMediumBoldFont, gdTinyFont, and gdGiantFont.

set_x_label_font, set_y_label_font, set_x_axis_font, set_y_axis_font — *set fonts for graph elements*

```
GIFgraph::set_x_label_font(fontname)
GIFgraph::set_y_label_font(fontname)
GIFgraph::set_x_axis_font(fontname)
GIFgraph::set_y_axis_font(fontname)
```

These methods may only be used on graphs with axes (any graph but a pie chart). They allow you to set the font used to label the x and y axes and the font that is used to label the individual values on each axis. Valid fontnames are gdSmallFont, gdLargeFont, gdMediumBoldFont, gdTinyFont, and gdGiantFont. The default font for the labels is gdSmallFont and for the axis values it is gdTinyFont. Note that in order to use these fonts you must import the GD module first with the command use GD.

set_legend() — *set the strings for the graph's legend*

```
GIFgraph::set_legend(@legend_keys)
```

A legend is a key that appears along the bottom or right side of a graph that gives a label for the color of each data set. If the *set_legend()* method is used to assign a list of legend strings to a graph, it will appear centered under the x axis of the graph. The elements of the *@legend_keys* list correspond to the individual data sets described in the list sent to the *plot()* routine. Undefined or empty legend keys will be skipped.

set_legend_font() — *Set the font for legend text*

```
GIFgraph::set_legend_font(fontname)
```

This method sets the font for the legend text. The *fontname* parameter can be any valid GD font name; the default is gdTinyFont. You must import the GD module first with the command use GD.

Attributes of GIFgraph Objects

GIFgraph has several attributes that you can set to control the layout, color, and labels on your graph. Some of these attributes are applicable only to certain types of graphs. For example, the pie_height attribute should only be set for graphs of type GIFgraph::pie. These attributes are relegated to their own sections. Those attributes shared by all graphs are:

```
t_margin=>integer
b_margin=>integer
l_margin=>integer
r_margin=>integer
```

These attributes allow you to set the top, bottom, left, and right margins, respectively. The margin is defined as the blank space between the bounding box of the graph and the edge of the GIF graphic. The default margins are 0 pixels.

```
logo=>filename
logo_position=>{'LL', 'LR', 'UL', or 'UR'}
logo_resize=>scalefactor
```

You may associate a logo (a separate GIF file) for inclusion in the corner of a graph. This logo can be positioned and resized within the graph by setting the logo_position and logo_resize attributes. The value of logo_position indicates one of the four corners of the graph with "LL," "LR," "UL," or "UR" corresponding to the lower/upper left/right corners. The default position is "LR" (lower right corner). The logo_resize attribute should be expressed in multiples of the original logo size, i.e., 2 for 200%, .5 for 50%. For example, the following lines will include the file *mylogo.gif,* shrink it by 50%, and include it in the upper right corner of a previously defined graph named *$graph*:

```
$graph->set(logo=>'mylogo.gif',logo_resize=>.5,logo_position=> 'UR');
transparent=>{1, 0}
```

If the `transparent` attribute is set to 1, the background color (set with the `bgclr` attribute) will be marked as transparent. The default value for transparent is 1.

`interlaced=>{1, 0}`

The *interlaced* attribute allows you to indicate whether the graph is stored as an interlaced GIF. The default value is 1.

`bgclr=>`*colorname*
`fgclr=>`*colorname*
`textclr=>`*colorname*
`labelclr=>`*colorname*
`axislabelclr=>`*colorname*
`accentclr=>`*colorname*

These attributes set the background, foreground, text, label, axis label, and accent colors, respectively. The *colorname* should be a valid GIFgraph color name (see "Colors in GIFgraph").

`dclrs=>\`*@colornames*

The `dclrs` (data colors) attribute controls the colors for the bars, lines, markers, or pie slices. The attribute should be given a reference to an array containing the desired set of color names. The first line/point/bar/pie slice (depending on the particular type of graph) will be the color of the first element in the array, the second will be the color of the second element, and so on. For example, if you set `dclrs` to the following array of color names:

```
$graph->set(dclrs => ['green', 'red', 'blue')]);
```

The first data set will be green, the next red, the third will be blue, the fourth will be green, the fifth red, and so on. The default value is: `[ qw(1red 1green 1blue 1yellow 1purple cyan 1orange) ]`.

Attributes for graphs with axes

`long_ticks=>{1, 0}`
`tick_length=>`*integer*

If the `long_ticks` attribute is 1, the graph's ticks will all be the same length as the axes, creating a grid across the graph. (A tick is the position where a value is labeled on an axis.) If `long_ticks` is 0, the ticks will be as many pixels long as the value of the `tick_length` attribute. The default values are `long_ticks=0` and `tick_length=4`.

`x_ticks=>{1, 0}`

If `x_ticks` is set to 0, the ticks on the x axis will not be drawn. The default value is 1.

`y_tick_number=>`*integer*

This attribute controls the number of ticks to be plotted on the y axis. Thus the increment between ticks will be (`y_max_value` – `y_min_value`) / `y_tick_number`. The default value for `y_tick_number` is 5.

`x_label_skip=>`*integer*
`y_label_skip=>`*integer*

If `x_label_skip` is set to an integer greater than 1, only those ticks numbered as multiples of `x_label_skip` will be labeled on the graph. For example, a value of 2 causes only every second tick to be labeled, 5 means every fifth should be labeled, etc. The same holds true for `y_label_skip`. The default values for both attributes are 1.

`x_plot_values=>{1, 0}`
`y_plot_values=>{1, 0}`

If either of these attributes is set to 0, the values on the given axis will not be printed. The tick marks will still be plotted. The default value for both attributes is 1.

`box_axis=>{1, 0}`

If this attribute is 1, the axes are drawn as a box rather than as two lines. The default is 1.

`two_axes=>{1, 0}`

If you have two data sets that you wish to plot against two axes on the same graph, you can set the `two_axes` attribute to 1. The first data set will be plotted against an axis to the left and the second set will be plotted against the axis to the right. The default value is 0.

`zero_axis=>{1, 0}`
`zero_axis_only=>{1, 0}`

If `zero_axis` is set to 1, an axis will always be drawn at the `y=0` line. If `zero_axis_only` is 1, the zero axis will be the only axis that is drawn and all x axis values will be plotted on this axis. If both attributes are 0, all x values will be plotted along the bottom border of the graph. The default values for both attributes are 1.

`y_max_value=>`*float,* `y1_max_value=>`*float,* `y2_max_value=>`*float*
`y_min_value=>`*float,* `y1_min_value=>`*float,* `y2_min_value=>`*float*

These values control the maximum and minimum values to be plotted on the y axis of a graph. Setting a value of `y_min_value` that is greater than the smallest value in the data set, or a value of `y_max_value` that is less than the greatest value within the data set, will result in an error. For bar and area graphs, the range of points defined by these attributes must include 0. If it does not, the values will be extended to include 0.

When plotting two data sets on two separate axes, use `y1_min_value` and `y1_max_value` to define the range of the left axis and `y2_min_value` and `y2_max_value` to define the range of the right axis.

The default values are the minimum and maximum values of the data sets.

`axis_space=>`*integer*

This attribute controls the amount of space (in pixels) to be left between each axis and its corresponding text. The default value is 4 pixels.

`overwrite=>{0..2}`

The `overwrite` attribute controls the appearance of bar graphs with multiple data sets. The attribute may be set to one of the following values:

0   Bars of different data sets will be drawn next to each other.

1   Bars of different sets will be drawn in front of each other.

2   Bars of different sets will be drawn on top of each other, to show a cumulative effect.

The default value is 0.

Attributes for graphs with lines

`line_types=>\@`*typelist*

This attribute lets you specify the styles of lines with which each data set should be plotted on the graph. The list of line types is a reference to an array of integers. The default value is 1, which means that all data sets will be plotted as solid lines. You can also choose from the following types:

1   Solid line

2   Dashed line

3   Dotted line

4   Dot-dashed line

To indicate that the first data set should be plotted as a dashed line, the second as a solid line, and the third as a dot-dashed line, set `line_types` with:

```
$graph->set(line_types => [2, 1, 4]);
```

`line_type_scale=>`*integer*

This attribute controls the length of the dashes in the dashed line types. The default value is 6 pixels.

`line_width=>`*integer*

This attribute controls the width of the lines in the graph. The default value is 1 pixel.

Attributes for graphs with points

`markers=>\@markerlist`

The **markers** attribute controls the order and styling of the point markers used to plot points in graphs of type **points** or **linespoints**. The attribute is set with a reference to an array of integers that correspond to the following marker types:

1 Filled square

2 Open square

3 Horizontal cross

4 Diagonal cross

5 Filled diamond

6 Open diamond

7 Filled circle

8 Open circle

The default value is $(1,2,3,4,5,6,7,8)$, which means that the first set of data points are plotted with filled squares, the second with open squares, and so on.

`marker_size=>integer`

This attribute controls the size of the point markers. The default value is 4 pixels.

Attributes for legends (axes-type graphs only)

`legend_placement=>{ 'BL'| 'BC' | 'BR' | 'RT'' | 'RC'' | 'RB' }`

This attribute controls placement of the legend within the graph image. The value is supplied as a two-letter string, where the first letter is placement (a "B" or an "R" for bottom or right, respectively) and the second is the alignment ("L," "R," "C," "T," or "B" for left, right, center, top, or bottom). The default value is "BC" for center aligned on the bottom of the graph. The legend will automatically wrap, depending on its placement.

`legend_spacing=>integer`

This attribute specifies the number of pixels in the blank margin around the legend. The default value is 4 pixels.

`legend_marker_width=>integer`
`legend_marker_height=>integer`

These attributes control the height and width of a legend marker in pixels. The default values are 12 for width and 8 for height.

`lg_cols=>`*integer*

> This attribute allows you to force a legend at the bottom of a graph into a specified number of columns. The default value is intelligently computed when the legend is plotted.

Attributes for pie graphs

`d=>{1, 0}`

> If the `d` attribute of a pie graph is set to 1, it is drawn with a three-dimensional look, with the "thickness" of the pie chart taken from the `pie_height` attribute. The default value for pie charts is 1.

`pie_height=>`*float*

> This attribute sets the height of the graph if it is a three-dimensional pie graph (i.e., if `d` is set to 1). The default for `pie_height` is 10% of the height of the total GIF image.

`start_angle=>`*degrees*

> This attribute gives the angle at which the first slice of a pie chart is plotted. The default starting angle is 0 degrees, which corresponds to 6 o'clock.

Colors in GIFgraph

All GIFgraph color routines taking *colorname* as a parameter expect a string with the name of a valid color. GIFgraph comes bundled with the GIFgraph::colour[*] package that provides some methods for organizing and manipulating *colorname* strings. GIFgraph has 29 predefined *colorname* strings (see Table 6-2); you can define additional strings in an external file by using the *read_rgb()* method.

Table 6-2. Predefined GIFgraph Color Names and Numerical Representations

Color Name String	Red	Green	Blue	Hex Representation
white	255	255	255	#FFFFFF
lyellow	255	255	0	#FFFF00
gold	255	215	0	#FFD700
cyan	0	255	255	#00FFFF
pink	255	183	193	#FFB7C1
lgray	191	191	191	#BFBFBF
lorange	255	183	0	#FFB700
lbrown	210	180	140	#D2B48C

---

[*] GIFgraph's author, Martien Verbruggen, lives in Australia, hence the Australian spelling of "colour." Note that the GIFgraph methods that deal with colors (*set_text_clr()*, for example) have abbreviated the word to alleviate the need for multiple method names mucking up everyone's namespace.

Table 6-2. Predefined GIFgraph Color Names and Numerical Representations (continued)

Color Name String	Red	Green	Blue	Hex Representation
lgreen	0	255	0	#00FF00
yellow	191	191	0	#BFBF00
orange	255	127	0	#FF7F00
dpink	255	105	180	#FF69B4
green	0	191	0	#00BF00
marine	127	127	255	#7F7FFF
gray	127	127	127	#7F7F7F
dyellow	127	127	0	#7F7F00
dgreen	0	127	0	#007F00
lpurple	255	0	255	#FF00FF
dbrown	165	42	42	#A52A2A
dgray	63	63	63	#3F3F3F
purple	191	0	191	#BF00BF
lred	255	0	0	#FF0000
red	191	0	0	#BF0000
dpurple	127	0	127	#7F007F
dred	127	0	0	#7F0000
lblue	0	0	255	#0000FF
blue	0	0	191	#0000BF
dblue	0	0	127	#00007F
black	0	0	0	#000000

Calling the *use* method with the *:colours* tags will import the *_rgb()*, *_hue()*, and *_luminance()* functions. The *:lists* tag will import only *colour_list()* and *sorted_colour_list()*, and the *:files* tag will import the *read_rgb()* function.

The various methods, in alphabetical order, are:

colour_list — *return all valid color names*

```
GIFgraph::colour::colour_list( [number] )
```

The *colour_list* method will return a list of strings of valid color names known to GIFgraph. The number of strings returned is specified with the optional number parameter; if no number is specified, all the defined names are returned. The default list is the list of 29 colors listed in Table 6-2.

hue — *return hue of a color*

```
GIFgraph::colour::_hue(R, G, B)
```

This method will return the hue of a color represented by the given RGB list. The hue is represented as a floating point number in the range 0 to 1, where 0 is black and 1 is white. For example:

```
use GIFgraph::colour qw(:colours);
print _hue(51, 51, 51);                  # This is actually 20% grey
```

will give us a value of .2 for output.

luminance — *return luminance for a color name*

```
GIFgraph::colour::_luminance(R, G, B)
```

This method will return the luminance of a color represented by the given RGB list. The luminance is represented as a floating point number in the range 0 to 1, where 0 is black and 1 is white. For example:

```
use GIFgraph::colour qw(:colours);
print _luminance(255, 105, 180);         # This is a dark pink
```

will give us a value of .558091470588235. You probably will never need to know a color's luminance to this degree of precision, but it's there if you need it.

read_rgb — *read in color names from a file*

```
GIFgraph::colour::read_rgb(filename)
```

This method will allow you to use color names other than those that are pre-defined for GIFgraph. You must first specify the new colors in a text file in the format of the *rgb.txt* file that is used to define colors in the X Window system. Each color is represented as a line in the file, with the red, green, and blue values followed by the color name string. Each field is separated by whitespace. For example, a file named *newcolors.txt* that defines the three colors SlateBlue, SeaGreen, and PeachPuff would look like:

```
106 90 205 SlateBlue
46 139 87 SeaGreen
255 218 185 PeachPuff
```

and could be used in a GIFgraph script with the addition of the following lines:

```
use GIFgraph::colour qw(:files);
read_rgb('newcolors.txt');
```

rgb — *return RGB values for a color name*

```
GIFgraph::colour::_rgb(colorname)
```

Returns a list of the red, green, and blue values, in decimal, for a given color name string.

sorted_colour_list — *return color names sorted by luminance*

`GIFgraph::colour::sorted_colour_list(`*number*`)`

The *sorted_colour_list()* method will return a list of strings of valid color names known to GIFgraph, sorted in order of decreasing luminance. The number of strings returned is specified with the optional *number* parameter; if no number is specified, all the defined names are returned. The default return value is the list of 29 colors listed in Table 6-2, sorted by luminance.

Creating Data Sets with Data::Xtab

When you are working with real-world data from normalized tables or from database engines, you will find that the data will often require a good deal of manipulation to get it into a well-formed GIFgraph data set format. The Data::Xtab module, available on CPAN, was written by Brian Jepson as a tool for making this sort of raw data easier to graph. It will "cross-tabulate" data from one form into another that is easy for GIFgraph to digest.

Take as an example the case of creating a graph based on the contents of an access log for a proxy server. Let's say that there are three computers on a network that all share the same proxy server for access to the Internet. For each HTTP request, an entry is made in a log file called *proxy-log*. The format for each entry in the log in this example is the same format as that of the httpd-cern proxy server:

```
host - - [day/month/year:hour:minute:second zone]
"GET url version" status bytes
```

Or, looking at a few lines of the actual log file:

```
burroughs.as220.org - - [07/Feb/1998:23:35:06 +0500]
    "GET http://flatzilla.as220.org/images/spacer.gif HTTP/1.0" 200 61
snuggles.as220.org - - [07/Feb/1998:00:45:38 +0500]
    "GET http://flatzilla.as220.org/images/image.gif HTTP/1.0" 200 1624
snuggles.as220.org - - [08/Feb/1998:00:45:39 +0500]
    "GET http://flatzilla.as220.org/images/single.gif HTTP/1.0" 200 1499
gumbo.as220.org - - [08/Feb/1998:01:12:12 +0500]
    "GET http://flatzilla.as220.org/images/beatniks.gif HTTP/1.0" 200 1744
burroughs.as220.org - - [08/Feb/1998:01:12:16 +0500]
    "GET http://www.jodi.org/index.html HTTP/1.0" 200 8666
burroughs.as220.org - - [08/Feb/1998:01:46:31 +0500]
    "GET http://somesite.edu/subgenius/picture.gif HTTP/1.0" 200 1831
burroughs.as220.org - - [08/Feb/1998:02:46:32 +0500]
    "GET http://somesite.edu/smt.html HTTP/1.0" 200 16870
gumbo.as220.org - - [08/Feb/1998:03:22:50 +0500]
    "GET http://somesite.edu/smt.html HTTP/1.0" 200 8655
gumbo.as220.org - - [08/Feb/1998:03:22:50 +0500]
    "GET http://somesite.edu/smt.png HTTP/1.0" 200 2560
snuggles.as220.org - - [08/Feb/1998:03:24:33 +0500]
    "GET http://www.smt.com/home.html HTTP/1.0" 200 2345
    ...
```

Let's say that we want to create a graph that shows the relative load on the proxy server over the course of the day by plotting the time of day versus the number of bytes requested per hour. Thus, the x axis will be time (0:00 to 23:59), the y axis will be total bytes transferred (in Kbytes), and each computer on the network will be represented as a separate data set. Extracting the pertinent information and putting it into a tabular form (for the log file described above), we get Table 6-3.

Table 6-3. Pertinent Data Extracted from Proxy Log File

Host address	Hour of Day	KBytes Transferred
burroughs.as220.org	23	0.061
snuggles.as220.org	0	1.624
snuggles.as220.org	0	1.499
gumbo.as220.org	1	1.744
burroughs.as220.org	1	8.666
burroughs.as220.org	1	1.831
burroughs.as220.org	2	16.870
gumbo.as220.org	3	8.655
gumbo.as220.org	3	2.560
snuggles.as220.org	3	2.345

Data in a table of this form is a perfect candidate for the Data::Xtab module. Xtab will analyze the data by setting up a series of hash tables, and then it will pivot the data to create a new table of n rows, where n is the number of unique data sets present in the starting data. In this case, the resulting table will have three columns, one for each of the computers *burroughs, snuggles,* and *gumbo.* The columns of the pivoted table will correspond to each of the elements of the x labels; in this case, the hours of the day. Xtab can generate the x labels, or you can explicitly provide them as a parameter (which is the recommended method). Furthermore, values that end up in the same row and column are added together to produce Table 6-4.

Table 6-4. Pivoted Data Table Returned from Data::Xtab Module

Host Address	Kb at 23:00	Kb at 0:00	Kb at 1:00	Kb at 2:00	Kb at 3:00
burroughs.as220.org	0.061	0	10.497	16.870	0
snuggles.as220.org	0	3.123	0	0	2.345
gumbo.as220.org	0	0	1.744	0	11.215

The data is almost in a form suitable for passing off to the GIFgraph *plot()* method. One thing to keep in mind is that Xtab adds a "total" data set to the end of the output table whose columns contain a summation of the table's columns. If you do not want this data set in your graph, use the *pop()* function to remove it from the end of the list before plotting.

The following code implements the above example, yielding the output shown in Figure 6-9.

```perl
#!/usr/local/bin/perl
#
# proxygraph.pl
# Create a graph illustrating the load on a proxy server by analyzing its
# log.
#
use strict;
use Data::Xtab;
use GIFgraph::bars;           # a bar graph is appropriate for this type of data

my @data = parse_log('proxy-log');

# The outputcols parameter lists the labels and the order for the x axis
# values
#
my @outputcols = (0..23);
my $xtab = new Data::Xtab(\@data, \@outputcols);

my @graph_data = $xtab->graph_data;
pop @graph_data;   # Remove the row of totals
my $proxygraph = new GIFgraph::bars(500,200);

$proxygraph->set( 'x_label' => 'Hour of Day',
                  'y_label' => 'Kb requested',
                  'title' => 'Total Load by Hour',
                  'y_max_value' => 8000,
                  'y_min_value' => 0,
                  'y_tick_number' => 5,
                  'y_label_skip' => 2 );

print $proxygraph->plot_to_gif('proxyload.gif', \@graph_data );

sub parse_log {
    # Parse a log file given a filename;
    # returned table is in the form of Table 6-3.
    #
    my $filename = shift @_;
    my @returnvalue;
    my ($host, $hour, $bytes);

    open INFILE, $filename || die "Couldn't open $filename!";
    while (<INFILE>) {
        # The format of log file is same as httpd-cern format.
        # This regular expression will extract the hostname,
        # the hour, and the number of bytes from one entry...
        #
        $_ = /^(.+?)\s.+?:(..):.+?\s(\d+?)$/;
```

```
        # Coerce the hour and bytes into number scalars.
        # Also convert the bytes into kilobytes.
        #
        ($host, $hour, $bytes) = ($1, $2+0, $3/1000);

        # There may be cases where certain fields don't exist; ignore them
        #
        if ($host && $hour && $bytes) {
            push @returnvalue, [ $host, $hour, $bytes ];
        }
    }
    return @returnvalue;
}
```

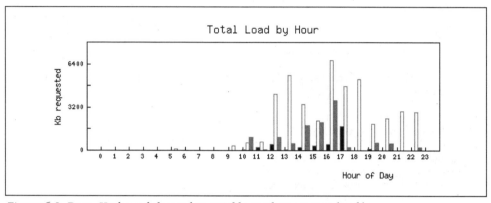

Figure 6-9. Data::Xtab module used to quickly analyze a proxy log file

Passing GIFgraph Graphs to GD Objects

GIFgraph uses the GD module's drawing primitives internally for drawing its graphs. Unfortunately there are no explicitly exported methods for interfacing GIFgraph objects with other GD objects. However, it is easy to pass a GIFgraph drawing to a GD object for further manipulation. This section will expand on the biorhythm example from the beginning of the chapter by merging the graph with another GIF image that will act as a frame for the graph.

For our purposes, the *biopage.cgi* script can still be used to generate the HTML page that drives the example. The *bio.cgi* script that generates the graph image will have to be replaced with the following script, whose output is shown in Figure 6-10:

```
#!/usr/local/bin/perl
#
# bio.cgi (modified)
# This script demonstrates how to pass a graph drawn with GIFgraph to an
# image created with the GD module.
#
use strict;
```

```perl
use GD;
use GIFgraph::bars;
use Date::Calc;
use CGI;

my $query = new CGI;

# Retrieve the parameters passed in from the form
#
my ($dob, $start, $end) =( $query->param('dob'),
                           $query->param('start'),
                           $query->param('end')
                    );

# The following section is the same as the bio.cgi script from the
# beginning of the chapter (without the comments)
#
my $pi = atan2(1,1) * 4;
my $days = datediff(parsedate($start),
                    parsedate($end));
my $dobdiff = datediff(parsedate($dob),
                       parsedate($start));
my @xvalues = daterange(parsedate($start));
my @pvalues = calculate(23, $dobdiff % 23, $days);
my @evalues = calculate(28, $dobdiff % 28, $days);
my @ivalues = calculate(33, $dobdiff % 33, $days);
my @data = (
        \@xvalues,
        \@pvalues,
        \@evalues,
        \@ivalues,
        );
my @legend = ('Physical', 'Emotional', 'Intellectual');
my $graph = new GIFgraph::bars(370, 190);
$graph->set(
            x_label             => '',
            y_label             => '',
            title               => '',
            y_plot_values       => 0,
            y_max_value         => 1,
            y_min_value         => -1,
            y_tick_number       => 8,
            long_ticks          => 0,
            y_label_skip        => 2,
            x_label_skip        => 3,
            zero_axis           => 0,
            zero_axis_only      => 0,
        );

$graph->set_legend(@legend);
```

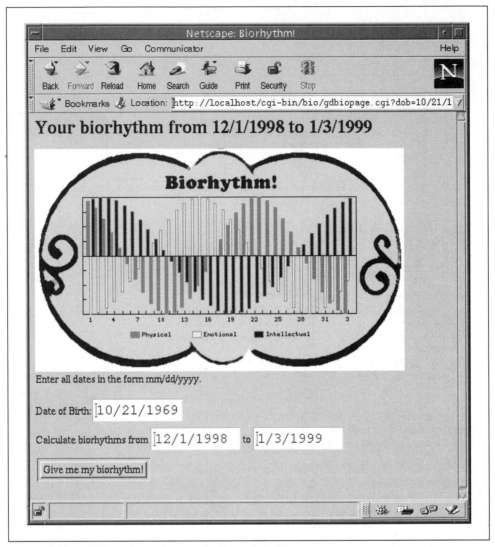

Figure 6-10. A GIFgraph graph passed off to a GD object

The big switcheroo happens at this point. Because GD does all of its reading and writing through the use of filehandles, we must present our GIFgraph image on a filehandle. The transfer between packages is done in three steps:

1. Open a filehandle for reading and writing.

2. Rewind the filehandle with the seek function.

3. Read the data on the filehandle into a GD object.

This can be coded as:

```
open GRAPH,"+>temp.gif";                # Open a r/w filehandle
print GRAPH $graph->plot(\@data );      # Plot the graph to the filehandle
seek GRAPH, 0, 0;                       # Rewind the filehandle to beginning
my $gdgraph = newFromGif GD::Image(\*GRAPH);  # Read into GD object
close GRAPH;
```

The remainder of the script will read in a previously created image to use as a border for the biorhythm graph, merge the two images with GD's *copy()* method, and print the final composite image as a GIF to the web browser using GD's *gif()* method:

```
# Create a new image object for our final image,
# from the bfile background.gif, which is a previously created image
# (500x300) that will make a nice border for the graph.
#
open BKGRND, "background.gif";
my $image = newFromGif GD::Image(\*BKGRND);
close BKGRND;

# Allocate white as the first (background) color in the final image
#
$image->colorAllocate(255,255,255);

# Copy the graph into the center of the background
#
$image->copy($gdgraph,65,65,0,0,370,190);

# Send the image data to the web browser
#
print STDOUT $query->header(-type=>'image/gif',
                            -expires=>'+1s' );
binmode STDOUT;
print STDOUT $image->gif();
```

The *calculate, parsedate, datediff,* and *daterange* subroutines used for the date manipulation functions are the same as those for the *bio.cgi* example at the beginning of the chapter.

7

Web Graphics with the Gimp

The GNU Image Manipulation Program (Gimp) has been around since 1995. The Gimp story was begun by two University of California at Berkeley students named Spencer Kimball and Peter Mattis, who started writing a "Photoshop-like" program for an undergraduate class in computer science. Over the course of the next year they crafted the program into a smart, expandable image manipulation system. The first public release was version 0.54, at which point they invited others to contribute. A couple of years and several thousand lines of code contributed by people all over the world later, Gimp 1.0 was released. It is a remarkably slick and stable platform for creating computer graphics, particularly graphics intended for use on the Web.

The Gimp has received a lot of positive press as a "Linux thing." That is, as a shining example of the power of the open source development model. The pieces of the core Gimp distribution (as well as the majority of the plug-ins) are covered by the GNU Public License. It has also moved beyond its origins on the Linux platform; there are versions for other Unix platforms, as well as ports for an OS/2 version of Gimp (URL) and a limited Win32 port. It is probably more accurate to call the Gimp a success story for the free software movement as a whole.

Right off the bat I'm going to say that this chapter is not intended as a manual for the Gimp. There is a fine 500+ page "open document" manual available called the *Gimp Users Manual* (GUM), written by Karin and Olof Kylander of Frozenriver Systems (see the "References" section at the end of this chapter). This chapter is geared toward those who don't necessarily start by reading the manual, and who want to start using the Gimp for making web graphics and creating plug-ins with Perl for advanced web graphics applications. The chapter starts with a quick tour of the Gimp by stepping through the process of creating an animated "electronic marble," then talks about some of the Gimp features that are particularly suited to web graphics creation, and ends with a description of the Perl-Gimp interface that allows you to write powerful image manipulation scripts with Perl.

You may also find some of the Gimp information in the appendices helpful. Appendix A is an overview of the interface and functions of Gimp Version 1.0. Appendix B is a reference to the core set of procedures that may be accessed by Perl scripts using the Gimp module.

Quick Gimp

If you have ever used Adobe Photoshop or other image manipulation software, you will be immediately familiar with the layering metaphor used by the Gimp. If you have never used another image manipulation package, you will become quickly accustomed to the idea—the Gimp is a friendly place to start.

As a quick introduction to the concepts and features of the Gimp, let's go through the steps to construct an animated "electronic marble" that you can add to your electronic marble collection and trade with your friends. The final result is shown in Figure 7-1.

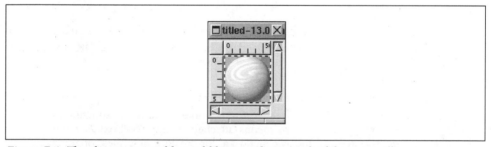

Figure 7-1. The electronic marble could become the pet rock of the new millennium

Step 1. Open a New Document and Create a Background

I probably should have started with Step 0, which is starting the Gimp. To start the program, simply type `gimp` at the command line. If everything is installed properly, you will see a splash screen and a progress bar listing the various steps of the startup process. Startup is usually very quick, but it can get bogged down if you have many brushes or patterns installed. The Toolbox will appear (and a helpful tip of the day from Wilbur the Gimp) when the program is loaded (see Figure 7-2).

To start a new document, select *File → New*. The New Image window allows you to select the starting width and height of the image, whether the image should be

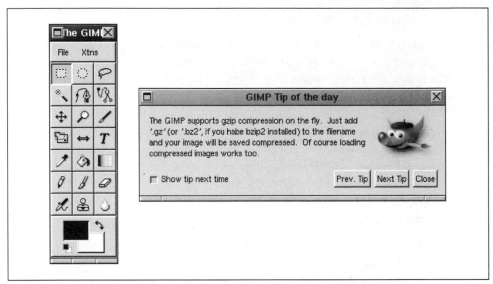

Figure 7-2. The Toolbox and an optional Tip of the Day are the first windows to appear. The Tip of the Day database, which contains the answers to many of the most frequently asked questions, is browsable via the File menu.

RGB or Grayscale, and the background color of the image. Our marble will be 120×120 RGB pixels, with a background color of white. Select OK and a new image window will appear.

 This is probably a good time to make a note about menu structure in the Gimp. There are two menus attached to the Toolbox: *File* and *Xtns*. The items in the *File* menu are for creating new files, opening existing files, editing preferences, etc. The *Xtns* menu contains extensions such as the Procedural Database Browser and scripts that generate new images. Once an image window is open, there is a menu associated with the image that may be accessed by holding down the right mouse button. This menu provides options that will be applied only to the image contained in that window. In this example, menu items will refer to the image menu (and not the tool box menu) unless specifically stated otherwise. On the Gimp mailing lists and text-based documentation, menu items are generally referred to in the form *MenuName → Item → SubItem*, which would refer to the menu option *SubItem* that is the hierarchical child of *Item* in the *MenuName* menu. This convention will be used in this chapter also.

Step 2. Apply a Radial Gradient

To get started, we need to create a radial-filled pattern on the background layer. The tool for this job is the Gradient Tool. Double-clicking on any of the 21 tools in the Toolbox will bring up a window that allows you to control the options for that tool. Double-click on the Gradient Tool to bring up the Gradient Options dialog box. To create a radial gradient pattern, we will use most of the default gradient settings, and change the Gradient option from Linear to Radial.

 The Gimp has multiple levels of Undo (and Redo). The Undo and Redo commands may be found under the *Edit* menu. You can specify the number of Undo levels in the *File → Preferences* dialog.

The Blend attribute determines the starting and ending colors of the gradient, which may be set by adjusting the foreground and background colors in the Toolbox. These colors may be specified in one of four ways:

- Double-click on the appropriate square in the Toolbox. This will bring up the Color Picker dialog box, where you can pick a color on a color wheel or specify numbers for each of the hue, saturation, value, and RGB channels.

- Call up the Palettes dialog box under the *Dialogs* menu. The Palettes dialog allows you to choose among dozens of predefined groups of colors.

- Use the Color Picker tool (the eyedropper icon). The Color Picker will allow you to select the color of a pixel in any open image window.

- With the desired colors and the Gradient Tool selected, click on the image somewhere near the center and drag the pointer to the edge of the window, and you will end up with something like Figure 7-3.

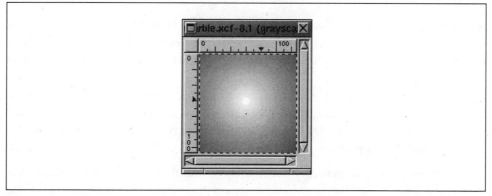

Figure 7-3. The marble after Step 2

Step 3. Create a New Layer

The next step is to make the pattern a little more complex by overlaying another gradient on top of the background. To do this you must first create a new layer. Select *Dialogs → Layers & Channels*. This dialog, shown in Figure 7-4, displays a cross-section of all of the layers in your document, and provides mechanisms for moving layers forward and backward, controlling the opacity and the mode in which the layers are combined, and specifying which layers are visible and which are not. The Layers dialog provides several other options, such as the ability to modify each of the individual channels of the image, but these advanced topics are beyond the scope of this chapter.

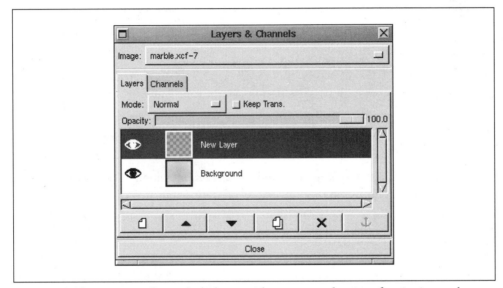

Figure 7-4. The Layers & Channels dialog provides many mechanisms for viewing and manipulating the layers in an image

Along the bottom of the Layers dialog box are six buttons. The leftmost button (which is marked with a document icon) will add a new layer to the image. Click this button now and you will see a new layer appear in the Layers window. You can specify the background color for the new layer the same way that you specified the background color for the document. For this layer, you should select the Transparent option (the default value). In the Gimp, the transparent color is indicated in the image window by a gray checkerboard pattern if there are no opaque pixels behind the transparent pixels.

The new layer will automatically become the currently selected layer. One of the most confusing things for image manipulation beginners is keeping track of the current working layer. It is a good idea to keep the Layers & Channels window open, especially when working on complex images with many layers. If you find yourself using a tool on a selection and you aren't getting the results you anticipated, make sure that you have selected the correct working layer before you do anything else.

Step 4. Apply a Custom Gradient with Transparency

Now we can apply a second gradient, this time a Custom gradient that is provided by the Gradient Editor tool. First select *Dialogs → Gradient Editor*. This will bring up the window shown in Figure 7-5.

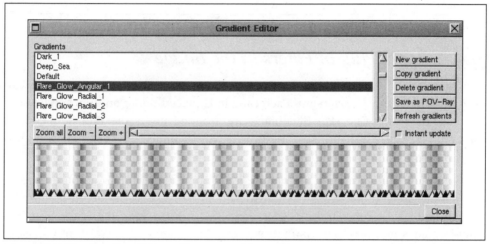

Figure 7-5. The Gradient Editor allows you to choose from over 60 custom gradient effects, or to modify them and create your own

After a little searching, it looks as if the *Flare_Glow_Angular_1* gradient might do a nice job. Scroll through the window and select this gradient, then double-click on the gradient tool in the Toolbox again. For the second layer, we will set the Blend attribute to *Custom (from editor),* which will tell the tool to use the gradient that has been selected with the Gradient Editor. Then change the Gradient attribute to *Conical (symmetric)* and click and drag the gradient in the image window. The gradient has transparency in it, so you should see the radial gradient from the background showing through as in Figure 7-6.

Step 5. Merge the Layers

Looking ahead to step 6, we will be applying some filters to the image. However, we want to apply the filters to the image as a whole, not to separate layers. To combine the two layers into a single layer, use the *Layers → Merge Visible Layers* option. This will combine any layers that have an eyeball next to them in the Layers & Channels window (the visible layers) into a single layer.

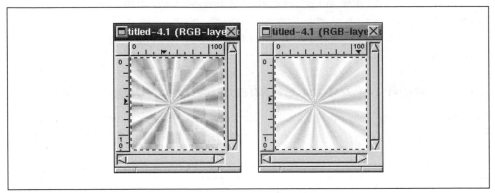

Figure 7-6. A custom gradient with transparency overlaid on the background pattern

Step 6. Apply Plug-In Filters to the Image

The Gimp's robust collection of plug-ins for filtering and manipulating images can be found under the *Filters* menu. Each plug-in is placed under an appropriate sub-heading. All of the Gaussian Blur filters are grouped under the Blur subheading, for example. The Whirl and Pinch filter will create a similar effect to that of a glass artist whirling the glass for a marble.

In Step 7 we will map the image to a sphere to create the final marble image. If you simply use the image we have created thus far, you will notice a line where the left and right sides join together imperfectly. This is where the Make Seamless plug-in comes into play. This plug-in will take an image and make it into a seam-less pattern, suitable for tiling on a plane or, in this case, mapping to a sphere. The resulting images after the Whirl and Pinch and Make Seamless filters have been applied are shown in Figure 7-7.

Step 7. Apply an Animation Script

The penultimate step in making the electronic marble is mapping it to a sphere and animating it so that it looks like it rotates. The Gimp comes with a script that does just such a thing, and it is available under the *Script-Fu → Animators → Spinning Globe* menu. The Spinning Globe script is written in the Gimp's Scheme-based Script-Fu scripting language, and it simply strings a bunch of other com-mands together to get a desired effect. The Spinning Globe script will create a user-definable number of layers (frames in the animation) and will map the source image to a sphere on each layer to give the illusion of a spinning globe. All you have to do is select the script, hit the OK button, and watch it go! The result is shown in Figure 7-8.

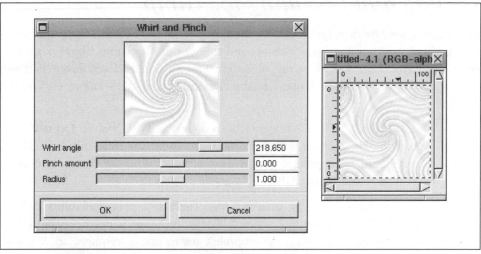

Figure 7-7. The marble after applying Whirl and Pinch (left) and Make Seamless (right)

Figure 7-8. The Gimp comes with several scripts that automate specific animation procedures, such as the Spinning Globe script, shown here with the Film filter applied

The scripting capability of the Gimp is one of its more impressive features. The last section in this chapter goes into much more about scripting using the Gimp-Perl extension that lets you write Gimp scripts in Perl for use as extensions, plug-ins, or even standalone image manipulation scripts.

Step 8. Save the Marble as an Animated GIF

Saving the image as an animated GIF is simple. First convert the image to Indexed mode, which will color-quantize the image to 256 or fewer colors, then select *File → Save As* and provide a name with a *.gif* extension. The Gimp will automatically know to save it as a GIF and, after asking you a few more questions about GIF comments and interlacing, your file will be saved to disk in the GIF89a format. At this point you have a nice little electronic marble to add to your collection.

Getting and Installing the Gimp

There are a number of ways of getting the Gimp. The main ftp site is *ftp.gimp.org*, which also lists 20 or so mirror sites around the world. The Gimp home page is at *http://www.gimp.org*. A wide array of online information and resources is available, a sampling of which is listed in the "References" section at the end of the chapter.

To reiterate, the Gimp is free software covered by the GNU Public License. You can download the program and libraries and use them for free, but you should read and understand the license if you plan on redistributing the Gimp or re-using any of the code covered by the GPL.

The Gimp installs easily on most Unix systems. There is a port available for OS/2, as well as a limited port for Win32 systems. The Win32 port is not necessarily part of the mission of the core Gimp development team, and it requires an X server and a number of supporting DLLs to operate. It does work, nonetheless, and you can find out how to get it working by visiting the URL listed in the "References" section. A true Win32 port would first require a port of the underlying GTK toolkit, which is underway.

The easiest way to get the Gimp—if you are running Linux or Solaris—is to grab a binary image from the *binaries* subdirectory of the main ftp site. These are available as Debian packages, RPM packages, and a dynamically linked precompiled binary for Solaris 2.5.1 and above. If you are running a different Unix, or if you just like compiling things yourself, you can get the source and compile it with a standard configure/make procedure.

There are a number of requirements for a successful Gimp installation:

- You will need the GTK libraries. GTK (see the sidebar "GTK: The Gimp Toolkit") is the stylish widget set that the Gimp uses for its GUI. You must install GTK before you install the Gimp. The latest stable version of the GTK toolkit should always be available at *ftp://ftp.gimp.org/pub/gtk*, or you can go directly to the GTK home page at *http://www.gtk.org*.

- You may need supporting libraries to support specific file formats such as JPEG, TIFF, or PNG. See Chapter 3, *A Litany of Libraries*, for a discussion of various image code libraries.

- To use Debian or RPM binary images, you must have the libc6 (sometimes called glibc version 2) installed on your system. This C library is a standard part of new Linux distributions, but older systems should be upgraded, or you will have to compile the code from source.

- There are two optional collections of add-ons available with the standard distribution: *gimp-data-extras* and *gimp-plugins-unstable*. The first contains a number of gradients, patterns, and brushes that may be used with the Gimp. The second consists of a number of plug-ins from the registry that are either in development, or are not-quite-ready-for-prime-time. They may not all work perfectly, but there's some nice work in there. Most of these plug-ins can be retrieved individually from the *registry.gimp.org* site as well.

- There are additional requirements for using Perl, Python, or Java as your scripting language of choice. The requirements for the Perl scripting interface are described later in the chapter.

All you have to do to install from source is:

1. Install GTK, if you haven't already.

2. Install support libraries (JPEG, PNG, TIFF, etc.) if needed.

3. Enter the Gimp source directory and run the configure shell script by typing `./configure`

4. Type `make`

5. Type `make install`

6. Install the gimp-data-extras, if desired.

That's all there is to it! If you have problems, someone else has probably already encountered them and reported them to the mailing list. Check there first. (The mailing list archives are referenced at the end of the chapter.) Most installation problems occur when upgrading the Gimp without cleanly uninstalling the previous version. By following the instructions explicitly, most people should not have problems installing the program.

There's actually one more way to acquire the Gimp. A commercial venture called Wilberworks, Inc. sells CDs containing the whole works for a reasonable price. Wilberworks is a company formed by Scott Goehring, one of the Gimp developers, that has contributed to the Gimp development effort by hiring programmers to work on certain parts of the project, and by providing another distribution channel for free software. The Gimp is also provided with most modern Linux distributions such as Red Hat and Debian.

GTK: The Gimp Toolkit

GTK stands for the Gimp Toolkit. It is an object-oriented API for graphical user interfaces built on the X Window system. Though it started as a widget set for the Gimp, it is now used in several different Open Source projects, most notably the GNOME desktop project (*www.gnome.org*). GTK is covered by the GNU Public License and has bindings for many programming languages, including Perl.

The GTK home page is at *http://www.gtk.org*.

Using the Gimp for Day-to-Day Web Projects

The Gimp does not have many of the features needed by a professional service bureau for doing sophisticated graphics destined for print media. Not with Version 1.0, anyway. It is not a Photoshop-killer, nor is it necessarily the one tool best suited for all image manipulation tasks. But when it comes to creating web graphics (or any image meant to be viewed on the screen, for that matter), it can be considered the most important tool in your toolbox.

Image Formats

Because of the Gimp's plug-in architecture, support for many image file formats has always been available. It is also relatively easy to contribute new plug-ins as new formats come along. File format handlers are registered in the Procedural Database as two entries: a load procedure and a save procedure. For example, there are the *file_gif_load* and *file_gif_save* procedures that handle the loading and saving of all GIF format images.

The Gimp supports each of the major web graphics formats very well. Each of the formats (GIF, JPEG, and PNG) deserve a few comments, however.

GIF

Probably the number one most frequently asked question on the Gimp mailing lists is "Why can't I save such-and-such a file as a GIF?" The answer is usually, "You can't save an RGB image directly in the GIF format; convert it to Indexed mode." The *Indexed* menu option in the *Image* menu will allow you to convert the image to Indexed mode. In Indexed mode, each pixel in the image is represented as an index to a color in a palette that is saved with the image. Contrast this with RGB mode, where each pixel in the image is represented as a list of numbers representing the red, green, and blue values of the color. The Gimp can treat grayscale images as indexed images with a palette of 256 levels of gray, so you can also save grayscale images directly to GIF files.

Converting an image with multiple layers to Indexed mode will create a single global palette for the entire image sequence. The Gimp does not support local palettes. This is sort of a tricky thing, since whether local palettes are used or not is really in the details of the particular file format. Local palettes in a multi-image GIF may be implemented by saving each layer as a separate file (with its own palette) and piecing them together later with ImageMagick's *convert* utility.

The Indexed Color Conversion dialog box offers four options:

Generate optimal palette

This option is equivalent to Adobe Photoshop's Adaptive palette; it creates a palette with the specified number of colors. Remember that GIFs can contain at most 256 colors in a single palette. The Gimp will give you a warning message when you change an image with alpha channels or multiple layers to Indexed mode, recommending that you choose no more than 255 colors if the image is intended as a transparent or animated GIF. This allows a palette entry for the transparent index.

Use WWW-optimized palette

This option will use the 216-color web safe palette and will dither the image if the dither options are set and the colors in the image do not exactly match those of the palette. If the dither options are not set, the colors will be mapped to their nearest equivalent in the web safe palette.

Use custom palette

The Gimp comes with several dozen custom palettes, which may be selected with this option.

Use black and white (1-bit) palette

This option, with the dither option selected, is the best way to convert a color image to a black and white bitmap. It is the equivalent of Photoshop's Bitmap image mode.

Once an image is converted to Indexed mode, you can look at and edit the palette with the Indexed Color Palette dialog box available under the *Dialogs* menu option (Figure 7-9). Changes made to the palette are applied to the image when the dialog is closed.

There is one last bit of information to keep in mind when creating GIF files. If you don't want a multi-layer image saved as a multi-image file, you must first combine the layers into a single layer. This can be done in one of several ways:

Flatten Image

The Flatten Image command will combine all layers marked as visible in the Layers dialog box into a single layer. All layers that are not visible will be

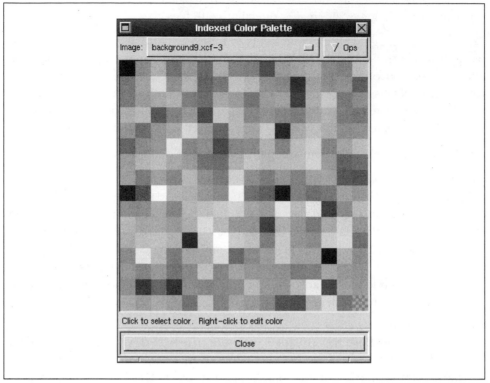

Figure 7-9. The Indexed Color Palette dialog box allows you to view and edit the palette of an image in Indexed color mode

discarded, so be careful when using this option. If you save the image as a GIF after flattening it, you will only get a single-image GIF.

Merge Visible Layers

Use the Merge Visible Layers command (in the *Layers* menu) to combine the layers marked as visible into a single composite layer and retain any other layers. Layers that are not visible will remain as separate layers, and will appear as separate frames in a multi-image file if the image is saved as a GIF.

The Semi-Flatten Plug-in

The Semi-Flatten Plug-in provides a more robust way of combining layers that contain alpha channels for use as transparent GIFs. Its usage is discussed next in the "Transparency in the Gimp" section.

JPEG

You can save files as JPEG files if you have installed the Gimp with JPEG support. Because Gimp uses the standard IJG JPEG libraries (described in Chapter 3), you will have to have them installed on your system. If you are using one of the binary distributions of the Gimp (a Debian or RPM package), the JPEG and PNG libraries should come bundled with the package. If you are installing from source, the libraries are available at *ftp://ftp.gimp.org/pub/gimp/libs.*

The most important thing to remember when working on JPEGs with the Gimp is to save the original image as a separate file, preferably saved in the XCF format (Gimp's internal format that preserves information about layers and channels and such). This is because each time you decode a JPEG document, edit, and re-encode it, you lose information. JPEG must be thought of as a delivery or archival format and not as a working format. Saving images in the XCF format and exporting images as JPEG allows you to have both delivery and modifiable working versions of your image.

JPEGs may be saved at a range of quality levels. As you would expect, a higher quality level indicates a better image and a larger file, while lower quality ratings indicate a higher compression ratio and a loss of image quality. In the Gimp, the default quality setting is .75 on a scale of 0 to 1, which for most purposes is the maximal compression level with no appreciable loss of image quality. You can, however, adjust the quality level to suit your needs in the Save as JPEG dialog box (Figure 7-10).

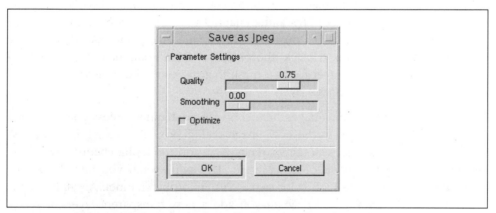

Figure 7-10. The Save As JPEG dialog box allows you to adjust the quality settings for the resulting file

PNG

To get PNG support, you must have installed the PNG libraries (described in Chapter 3) at the time you compile the Gimp. If you use a precompiled binary you should not have to worry about it.

When you save an image as a PNG file, you are presented with the PNG Options dialog box that will prompt you for a compression level (0 = none and 9 = maximum) and interlacing options (see Figure 7-11).

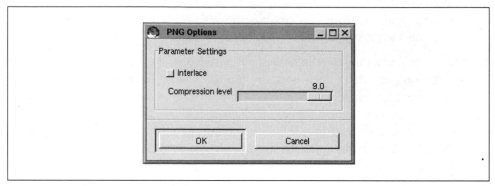

Figure 7-11. The Save As PNG dialog box at present offers only Interlacing and Compression options

Even though the PNG format supports a 16-bit alpha channel, you should save your PNG files with a single transparent color until web browsers support the full PNG standard.

Transparency in the Gimp

The Gimp deals with transparency by allowing an alpha channel to be included with each layer of an image. This alpha channel (or *alpha mask*) can be thought of as a grayscale layer that sits on top of the image layer, but instead of having pixels ranging from white to black, the pixels go from completely transparent to completely opaque. This layer forms a mask that indicates the transparency of the pixels on the underlying image layer.

When you first open a new image, there is no alpha channel, unless you opted for a transparent background in the new image dialog box. The very important first step in creating an image with transparency is to add the alpha channel by selecting the *Alpha → Add Alpha Channel* menu. This will switch you into the RGBA color space, which is the RGB color space with an alpha channel. An alpha channel will be automatically added when you add a new transparent layer, or when you apply a filter that requires transparency.

Once you have an alpha channel, you can use the eraser tool to "paint" an alpha mask. Use the Opacity setting in the Brush Selection dialog and the Incremental option in the Eraser Tool Option dialog to create gradations of transparency. You can also use the Cut or Clear options from the *Edit* menu to make selections transparent. The vignette in Figure 7-12 was created by using the eraser tool to create a transparent "frame," which was then plopped on top of the photograph.

An often-asked question is, "How do you fill an area with a transparent color?" The method that affords you the most control is the *<Image> → Select → By Color...*

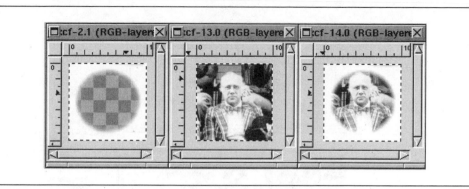

Figure 7-12. Once an image has an alpha channel, the eraser tool may be used to add transparency to parts of the image

tool. This tool will create a selection area consisting of all of the pixels of a given color in an image. Simply use this tool to select the color you wish to be transparent, then select *<Image> → Edit → Clear,* which will make the selected area transparent if there are no layers beneath the selection (if there are, they will show through the selection). Figure 7-13 shows the Select By Color dialog being used on a typical web graphic logo.

Perhaps the second most asked question is, "How do I make my anti-aliased text look nice when it's on a transparent background?" Anti-aliased text on a transparent background does not work very well without a bit of tweaking. What generally happens is that the edges become dithered when the image is saved in Indexed mode, leaving a "halo" of color if the text was created against a different background than that of the final web page. Not using anti-aliasing results in text that looks choppy and flat. Web designers have come up with several methods for working around the problem of only having one transparency index; the Gimp has a special plug-in that provides an easy solution to this problem. It is the Semi-Flatten plug-in found under the *<Image> → Filters → Colors* menu.

There are essentially two ways of dealing with the problem of anti-aliased text or shapes on a transparent background:

- The first method is to compose the image directly against the desired background color. If you have multiple layers with transparency, merge them into a single layer with Merge Visible Layers when you are ready to save the image. Next, remove the alpha channel with Flatten. Now use Select By Color to select the color you wish to make transparent (or use the Magic Wand tool to select an area). Put the alpha channel back in the image with *<Image> → Image → Alpha → Add Alpha Channel,* then clear the selected area, making it transparent. Convert to Indexed mode and save.

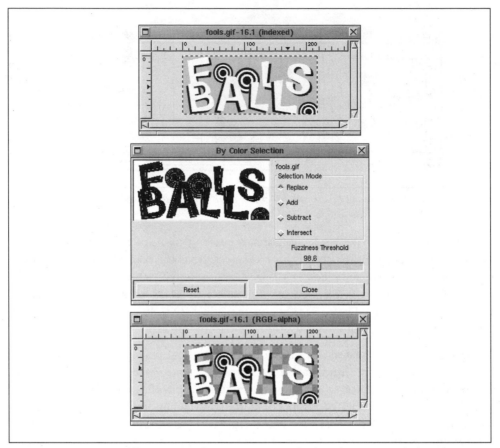

Figure 7-13. You can fill an area with a transparent color by selecting it with the Select By Color tool and clearing it with Clear or Cut

- The second method uses the Semi-Flatten plug-in. First compose the image on a transparent background. When you are ready to save, merge the layers into a single layer with Merge Visible Layers. You still need to know (approximately) the color of the background on which the image will eventually appear; select this color as the background color in the Toolbox. Then select *Filters → Colors → Semi-Flatten* and the plug-in will merge the semi-transparent pixels with the current background color. Set the background color in the Toolbox to the background color against which the text will be displayed on the web page. Apply the *Semi-Flatten* filter, which will flatten all semi-transparent pixels, and leave the completely transparent pixels the way they are. Convert to Indexed mode and save.

The Semi-Flatten plug-in will intelligently merge all of the pixels that are not completely transparent and give them new values that keep the desired look. The

Flatten plug-in, incidentally, removes the alpha channel from an image. Semi-Flatten affords us an option that removes all of the semi-opaqueness (leaving the 100% transparent pixels as they are) but keeps the look of the image with the alpha channel. Once an image going on the Web has been semi-flattened, it can be changed to Indexed mode (if you are saving it as a GIF), or you can just save it (if you are saving as a non-indexed PNG).

Figure 7-14 shows anti-aliased text that has been semi-flattened so that it can retain its original look with only one transparent color.

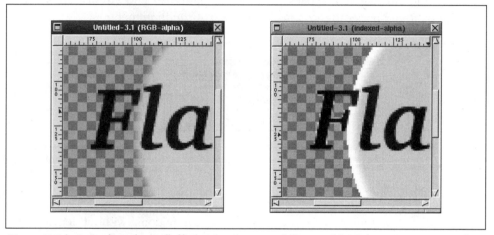

Figure 7-14. Anti-aliased text (left) that has been semi-flattened (right) retains its original look with only one transparent color

You may want to check out the Webify plug-in, a script written in Perl by Marc Lehmann. Webify automates common actions performed to prepare simple transparent images for the Web. It can flatten an image, make the background transparent, convert it to Indexed mode, and autocrop it. It is also a good example of writing scripts in Perl, which we shall talk about shortly.

Using the Gimp for GIF Animation

Although it was not necessarily designed as an animation system, the Gimp has several features that make it a handy tool for making simple flipbook GIF animations. Each layer may be thought of as a separate frame in the animation, with the background as the starting frame (Frame 0). When a multi-layer Gimp image is saved as a GIF, it will be automatically saved as a multi-image animated GIF89a file. Note that if you are creating a regular single-frame GIF and forget to merge the layers into a single image with *Layers → Merge Visible Layers* before saving, you may accidentally end up with an animated GIF.

The looping and global delay values may be set in the Save As GIF dialog. You may set the disposal method or delay rate for each of the individual frames by typing the values into the name field of the particular layer in the Layers & Channels dialog. Double-clicking on a layer will bring up the Edit Layer Attributes dialog (see Figure 7-15) which gives access to these attributes. The label should be in the following form (where "combine" is the disposal method in this case):

```
Frame 10 (100ms) (combine)
```

Three tools that come with the standard distribution are invaluable for animation. They are the Animation Playback, Animation Optimize, and Animation Unoptimize filters, found under the *<Image>→ Filter→ Animation* menu.

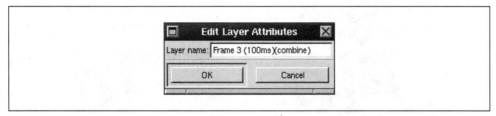

Figure 7-15. Specify the delay time and the disposal method in the Edit Layer Attributes dialog

Animation Playback

The Playback tool allows you to preview animations without leaving the Gimp. It brings up a dialog box (Figure 7-16) that will play the animation in a preview window and allow you to start, stop, rewind, and step through the sequence.

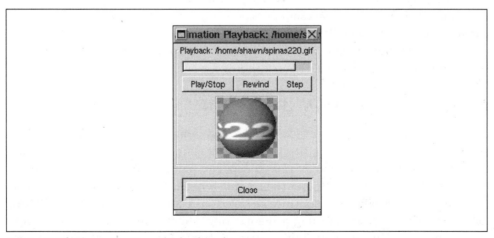

Figure 7-16. The Animation Playback tool

Animation Optimize

This plug-in will create the smallest possible GIF file by removing all redundant pixels between frames. If a pixel does not change between two frames, this plug-in will make the pixel in the second frame (and each frame thereafter for which it does not change color) transparent. This should be applied as the final step before saving the images, because it would be kind of difficult to work with after it is optimized, as you can see in Figure 7-17.

Animation Unoptimize

This plug-in performs the reverse operation of the Animation Optimize plug-in, restoring the original, unoptimized image.

Figure 7-17. The Animation Optimize tool will create a smaller GIF file by removing redundant pixels

Gimp 1.0 comes with several Script-Fu animation scripts that act as macros for automatically creating an animated sequence:

Blend

The Blend animator requires at least three source images (one on each layer) and will create a nice fading transition between scenes that can be very dramatic (see Figure 7-18).

Color Cycling

The Color Cycling script repeatedly applies the Alien Map filter for a far out effect.

Rippling

This animator creates a rippling effect by applying various filters. This could be useful to get the effect of a flag rippling with the wind.

Spinning Globe

The Spinning Globe animator was used at the beginning of this chapter to create the electronic marble. It repeatedly maps the image onto a sphere with the *<Image>→ Filters → Map → Map Object* filter until it looks like, you guessed it, a spinning globe.

One last Script-Fu animator of note is the MergeAnim script written by Raphael Quinet (*http://www.gamers.org/~quinet/gimp/merge/*). This very handy script will allow you to overlay an animation with transparency on a background image by

Figure 7-18. The Blend animator script will create dramatic fades between three or more layers

repeatedly merging the background with each of the individual frames. It can be an excellent work saver.

Scripting the Gimp in Perl

The Gimp-Perl package, written by Marc Lehmann, allows you to write Gimp plug-in scripts in Perl. The Gimp actually has its own internal scripting language called Script-Fu that allows you to access internal procedures and plug-ins and create high-level scripts. Script-Fu is based on the Scheme programming language. All of the scripts that come bundled with the Gimp are Script-Fu scripts. Scripts and plug-ins written in Perl are sometimes referred to as Perl-Fu scripts.[*] The remainder of this chapter is going to be focused on writing plug-ins with Perl rather than in Script-Fu for two reasons:

- Perl is a much more robust scripting language and has many "hooks" to the world outside the Gimp that are very useful when creating plug-ins that are meant to be integrated into web applications.

- Because Script-Fu was the first scripting engine to be distributed with the Gimp, it is documented in other places; see the Gimp Users Manual at *http:// manual.gimp.org* if you are interested in Script-Fu tutorials.

If you want to write plug-ins that are meant to be usable by anyone with a copy of the Gimp, you may want to consider writing it in Script-Fu, since the Script-Fu interpreter is the "official" script interpreter distributed with the Gimp (at least, the

---

[*] The vocabulary of the Gimp may be confusing at first. A plug-in is typically a Gimp extension that has been written in C. A script generally refers to a Script-Fu macro. Script-Fu is actually a language based on Scheme; some people may refer to it as Scheme but that isn't technically accurate, though it is pretty much true. Some people call scripts Script-Fus. A Perl script may be referred to as a plug-in or a script; we will call them plug-ins for the very practical reason that they belong in the plug-in directory. I guess Perl-Fu should technically refer to scripts written with the Gimp::Fu module, but I think it is fair to use Perl-Fu to refer to Gimp-Perl scripting in general.

only one as of Version 1.0).* Also, the Gimp-Perl interface must be installed separately, and is pretty complex. Not too complex, though, and with that complexity comes power. The focus on Script-Fu may change in the future, however. There is even a Script-Fu-to-Perl converter available (the *scm2perl* script that comes with the Gimp-Perl distribution) to help along the migration from Scheme-based to Perl-based scripting.

The Perl-Fu package (as we shall call the Gimp-Perl interface) is available on CPAN. It comes with a number of modules:

Gimp

The Gimp module is the primary interface to the Gimp. It provides a number of procedures that facilitate communication between a script and the program, and defines a number of constants that may be used to make scripts more readable. It is possible to write scripts using only the Gimp module, which would have to follow the interface defined for writing plug-ins in C, and there is a difference between scripts run from the command line and those run as a plug-in. The only reason to write a script using solely the Gimp module is that the Gimp module makes it slightly easier to write command-line only scripts (such as the example in the sidebar "gimptool: A Utility for Installing Plug-ins" that extracts information from the Procedural Database) because there is no need to provide all of the information needed to register the script with the Gimp. In general it is better to write scripts using the Gimp::Fu module, which simplifies much of the work your script needs to do.

Gimp::Fu

Gimp::Fu provides a simplified framework for writing plug-in scripts with the Gimp module. It may be run from the command line (Gimp::Fu will start up a connection with the Gimp if one is not already running) or as a plug-in (i.e., from one of the Gimp's menus) without additional code. Gimp::Fu also provides a GTK dialog box for scripts that runs interactively, and a method for sending default parameter values to a script. The amount of information you need to provide the Gimp about the script is also reduced to just the essentials. It also provides a few additional data types, such as PF_FONT, PF_TOG-GLE, and PF_SLIDER. And if that's not enough, scripts written with Gimp::Fu will be more portable with future versions of the Gimp.

Gimp::Data

This module allows you to store and retrieve plug-in data within the main Gimp application so that you can preserve state between invocations of your script using a hash rather than procedure calls.

---

* Gimp-Perl is gaining headway, however. There is already a separate repository at the Gimp Plug-in Registry for Gimp-Perl scripts.

Gimp::PDL

> The Gimp::PDL module allows the use of Perl Data Language objects ("piddles") to manipulate tiles and pixel regions. The PDL module is a separate module (available on CPAN) that may be used for quickly manipulating large arrays of data. PDL makes Perl a viable platform for implementing complex image manipulation routines which require fast access to large amounts of pixel data.

There are also two packages of documentation of interest: Gimp::Pixel, an introduction to operating on the raw pixels of an image, and Gimp::OO, a guide to writing object-oriented Gimp scripts.

There's a lot behind this Gimp-Perl interaction, much more than we can cover in this chapter. Here we will deal primarily with the Gimp and Gimp::Fu modules and the fundamentals in writing a Gimp plug-in as it may be applied to common web tasks. To reiterate, the Gimp module provides access to all of the Gimp procedures and constants, and the Gimp::Fu module provides us with access to an abstract template for script writing.

Every Gimp script written in Perl will have a similar structure. The script itself consists of a function call to the *Gimp::Fu::register* method, and a function that will be invoked when the plug-in is called from the command line, from a Gimp menu selection, or from another plug-in.

A plug-in must be installed with the gimptool (see sidebar) before it may be used from a Gimp menu. It will appear as a menu item in either the *Toolbox* or *Image* menus. Its position in the menu hierarchy depends on how it was registered (we will see in a moment how to register a script).

Before we move on to describe the structure of a Gimp plug-in, you should make sure you have installed the Gimp-Perl package and its various dependencies.

Installing the Perl-Fu Modules

To install and use the Perl-Fu package, you must acquire and install several other packages. Besides the basic requirements of the Gimp and the GTK toolkit, you will need:

Gtk-Perl

> A Perl interface that enables Perl scripts to call GTK widgets. You can find it on CPAN or at *ftp://ftp.gimp.org/pub/gtk/perl/*. For all you developers using the Perl-Tk interface, this module is something worth investigating as a general purpose GUI toolkit for Perl.

gimptool: A Utility for Installing Plug-ins

The *gimptool* utility is a little tool that comes with the Gimp distribution that helps you build plug-ins from source and install plug-ins and scripts. It is a shell script and resides in the same directory as the gimp executable, typically */usr/local/bin/*. It is generally a good idea to use *gimptool* to install plug-ins rather than doing it manually.

The *gimptool* accepts the following options:

`--version`
> Prints the version number of the Gimp that is currently installed.

`--build plug-in-source.c`
> Typically, the source code for a plug-in is distributed as a single file containing the C code for the plug-in. This option will compile and link a plug-in, given a filename. With any of the options that build a plug-in, you may use the `--cflags` option to print a list of all of the compiler flags needed to compile the plug-in, or the `--libs` option to print a list of the linker flags needed.

`--install plug-in-source.c`
> This option is used by a user to install a personal copy of a plug-in. It will compile and link a plug-in, given a filename. It will also install the plug-in in the user's personal Gimp plug-in directory (*~/.gimp/plug-ins/*).

`--install-admin plug-in-source.c`
> This option is used by the system administrator to install a plug-in for use by all users of the machine. It will compile, link, and install `plug-in-source.c` into the system-wide Gimp plug-in directory (typically */usr/local/lib/gimp/1.0/plug-ins*).

`--install-bin plug-in-name`
> This option will install a pre-compiled plug-in or a plug-in written in Perl into the user's personal Gimp plug-in directory.

`--install-admin-bin plug-in`
> This option will install a pre-compiled or Perl plug-in into the system-wide Gimp plug-in directory.

`--install-script script.scm`
> This option will install a Script-Fu script (*script.scm*) into the user's personal Gimp script directory (*~/.gimp/scripts*).

`--install-admin-script script.scm`
> This option will install Script-Fu script into the system-wide Gimp script directory (typically */usr/local/share/gimp/scripts*).

PDL

> The Perl Data Language, which is a module that allows you to easily and quickly manipulate a large amount of pixel data. PDL is needed to use the Gimp::PDL module. Note that PDL is optional; it only needs to be installed if you are going to be using it, and you can always install it later. It may be found via CPAN. You will need version 1.9906 or higher.

Perl Version 5.005 or greater

> This version of Perl comes with some built-in functions that Gimp-Perl requires, such as Data::Dumper (which allows you to display Perl data structures, and was available as an external module prior to of Perl 5.005). I also had several problems with earlier versions of Perl and Gimp-Perl which magically disappeared when I upgraded Perl.

These modules should be installed prior to an attempted installation of Perl-Fu. On Unix you should be able to install the Perl-Fu package by doing the following:

```
perl Makefile.PL
make
make test
make install
```

This will also install the example plug-in scripts and the Perl Server. For the non-Unix ports, consult the documentation provided with the distribution.

Anatomy of a Plug-In

Each Gimp user has a personal Gimp directory in his home directory called *~/.gimp*. This directory contains personal plug-in and script directories, and preference settings in the *gimprc* file. When the Gimp starts up, it loads its plug-ins from two places: from the personal plug-ins directory of the user who launched the Gimp, and from the system-wide plug-in directory (which for Version 1.0 is typically */usr/local/lib/gimp/1.0/plug-ins*).

The Gimp will assume that every file in these directories is a plug-in that is meant to be loaded at runtime. A plug-in may be written in any language. If it is written in C, it must be built and installed with the *gimptool* utility so that a binary image sits in the plug-in directory. If the plug-in is written in Perl, the script itself is also installed in the appropriate plug-in directory with the *gimptool*. The following command will install the Perl script in the user's personal plug-in directory and set the proper permissions:

```
gimptool --install-bin plug-in.pl
```

When the Gimp launches, it will make sure that the script is parseable and has all of the information that it expects, then it will execute the *register* method (if it is written using Gimp::Fu). The *exit main* function call will then return control to the

Gimp, which will finish its startup sequence. If there is a problem at any step along the way and your script crashes, you will get an error message saying:

```
wire_read: unexpected EOF (plug-in crashed?)
```

If this happens while the Gimp is starting up, it may give you a helpful error message. Generally the problem is in the format of your *register* method (assuming that your script is syntactically correct), so you should be sure that it fits the format in the following example. If it happens during runtime, it is a problem with the logic of your script. It is a good idea to test the syntax of your script before you install the plug-in with Perl's –c switch.

At this point we are probably overdue for an example that puts all this stuff together. The following example is a plug-in that appears under the *<Image>* → *Web Graphics* menu (which it creates if you don't have one yet). When selected, the plug-in will allow you to preview exactly how the image would look as a tileable background in a web browser by saving a temporary HTML page and a temporary GIF in your local Gimp temp directory, then launching the web browser of your choice with that page as the URL to load.

```perl
#!/usr/bin/perl
#
# Test As Background
# A plug-in for the Gimp, written in Perl.
#
use Gimp qw(:auto );          # import constants and such
use Gimp::Fu;
Gimp::set_trace(TRACE_ALL);   # Enable trace output

register(
        "test_background",                                    # Name
        "Test an image as a background in a web browser.",    # Blurb
        "Test an image as a background in a web browser.
         Requires an Indexed color image",                   # Help
        "SPW",                                                # Author
        "(c) 1999 SPW",                                       # Copyright
        "1999-02-20",                                         # Date
        "<Image>/Web Graphics/Test As Background",            # Menu path
        "INDEXED*",                                           # Images accepted
        [],       # A list of parameters; we don't need any for this example...
     \&test_background   # a reference to the function that does all the work
     );

sub test_background {
    # The plug-in subroutine.
    #
    my ($img, $drawable) = @_;       # access parameters

    # Grab the location of the Gimp's temporary user directory with the
    # Gimp's gimp_temp_name function so that we can create two files called
    # backtest.gif and backtest.html there.
    #
```

```
     my $filename = gimp_temp_name('');
     $filename =~ s/^(.*)\/(.*)$/$1\/backtest/g;

     # Save the file as a GIF; this will fail if it is not Indexed
     #
     file_gif_save(RUN_NONINTERACTIVE, $img, $drawable,
                   "$filename.gif",
                   "$filename.gif",
                   0, 0, 0, 0);

     # Print a temporary html page using the saved GIF as the background
     #
     open O, ">$filename.html";
     print O "<HTML><HEAD>";
     print O "<META HTTP-EQUIV=\"expires\" CONTENT=\"0\"></HEAD>";
     print O "<BODY BACKGROUND=\"$filename.gif\">";
     print O "This is how the image would look as a background pattern.";
     print O "</BODY></HTML>";

     # Now pass it off to your favorite web browser
     #
     my $url = "file:$filename.html";
     extension_web_browser(1, $url, 0);
     return ();           # Always return something...
}

exit main;               # Hand over control to the gimp...
```

You will notice that there are really only two sections to this script; the call to
register, and the plug-in function.

The register method

Gimp::Fu's *register* method allows your plug-in to register itself in the Gimp's Procedural Database (PDB). When a plug-in is selected from one of the Gimp's
menus, it looks at the PDB to determine which function should be called. For a
plug-in written in Perl, this means that it will call whatever subroutine you have
provided as an argument. This function takes a list of eleven parameters that
describes the script and registers it with the Gimp PDB. The parameters are:

Name

A string that is the name of the script as it should appear in the Procedural
Database. To keep the internal procedural namespace somewhat organized, it
is good practice to prepend *perl_fu* to the name of the function. If the name
doesn't start with *perl_fu* (as in the background tester), the Gimp::Fu module
will add it for you, unless you prefix the name field with a single plus sign
(+). This way, all Gimp-Perl plug-ins will be grouped together by the PDB
Browser.

Blurb

A string that will be displayed in the PDB under the entry for this script.

Help

A string containing a more in-depth description of what the script does.

Author

A string containing the names of the authors.

Copyright

A string containing the copyright information for the script or plug-in.

Date

The date that the script was written.

Menu Path

At the top level, the Gimp has two menu structures to which the script may be added: one under the Toolbox, and one that pops up when the right mouse button is pressed on an image.

The *Menu Path* field is a string that provides two pieces of information. First, it tells the Gimp where to place the script in the menu hierarchy. Secondly, it tells the Gimp how the script is going to be used and what sort of parameters it should expect. In general, if the script is associated with the Toolbox, it will not be operating on a currently open image, and will be generating a new image. If it is associated with the *Image* menu, then the script will always be sent the image (PF_IMAGE) and the drawable (PF_DRAWABLE) as parameters on which the script should function. The actual image and drawable will be those of the window where the plug-in call originated.

To assign a script called My Script to the Toolbox, use the string:

```
<Toolbox>/Xtns/Web Graphics/My Script
```

You can create a new top-level menu item (and distort your toolbox) with:

```
<Toolbox>/Stupid Perl Tricks/My Script
```

To assign the script to the Image menu, use:

```
<Image>/Web Graphics/My Script
```

A quick suggestion about menu organization: several Script-Fu scripts are included under a Script-Fu menu item. In general, there is no need to keep plug-ins written in Perl separate from those written in Script-Fu or any other language. It is better to place the plug-in in the appropriate category (i.e., if it is a filter, place it with the rest of the filters under the *Filter* menu hierarchy).

Image Types

For scripts that operate on an image (i.e., they have been listed under the <*Image*> menu with the *Menu Path* field), you must specify the types of image that the script can handle. Seven values may be used: RGB (only RGB images), RGBA (only RGB images with an alpha channel), RGB* for either, GRAY (only grayscale images), INDEXED (only indexed color images), INDEXEDA (indexed with alpha), or * (any type of image).

A Parameter List

The parameter list is a reference to an array that describes the parameters to the script. Each parameter is in turn expressed as a reference to an array with four elements that describe the parameter:

Parameter type

A parameter may be one several data types. All of the type constants listed after the table are exported into your namespace when you include the :auto or :const import arguments in the use statement. The type constants are the standard Gimp data types, with the string *PARAM* prepended to them. Gimp::Fu provides more types, which have the string *PF_* prepended to them. They are listed in Table 7-1.

Table 7-1. Parameter Types

Parameter Types	Description
PF_INT32, PF_INT16, PF_INT8 or PARAM_INT32, PARAM_INT16, PARAM_INT8	Three flavors of integers
PF_FLOAT or PARAM_FLOAT	A floating point number
PF_STRING or PF_VALUE or PARAM_STRING	A string
PF_COLOR or PF_COLOUR or PARAM_COLOR	A color description in the form #RRGGBB or as a reference to a three-element array containing the decimal equivalents, or as an X Window color name
PF_IMAGE or PARAM_IMAGE	An image
PF_DRAWABLE or PARAM_DRAWABLE	A drawable
PF_CHANNEL or PARAM_CHANNEL	A channel
PF_LAYER or PARAM_LAYER	A layer
PF_TOGGLE or PF_BOOL	A Boolean value
PF_SLIDER	A graphical widget that provides a means of specifying values in a discrete range. Uses the "extra options" field in the parameter list to specify the minimum value, the maximum value, and the step for each discrete movement of the slider.
PF_SPINNER	The same as PF_SLIDER, but the graphical widget is a spin knob instead of a horizontal slider.
PF_FONT	A font string

Table 7-1. Parameter Types (continued)

Parameter Types	Description
PF_BRUSH, PF_PATTERN, PF_GRADIENT	A string containing the name of a brush, pattern, or gradient

Parameter name

If the script is run in interactive mode, this string will appear as a label next to the user input field.

Help string

The Help string will be listed next to the parameter in the PDB Browser. It is useful for describing the type of data that the parameter is expecting.

Default value

You can specify a default value to be used by the plug-in. If it is called in interactive mode, this value will be filled in as the default value for the parameter in the plug-in dialog box, and in non-interactive mode, this value will be used for the parameter data.

Optional extra arguments

Some data types take extra arguments (such as PF_SLIDER) as shown in the following list.

Some valid parameter list elements are:

```
[ [ PF_COLOR,    "Color",       "Text color",        [255, 0, 0]          ],
  [ PF_TOGGLE,   "Copy?",       "Work on a copy?",   1                    ],
  [ PF_DRAWABLE, "Drawable",    "The drawable"                            ],
  [ PF_STRING,   "Text",        "Some text",         "HamHam"             ],
  [ PF_SPINNER,  "Angle",       "Rotate angle",      45,    [0, 360, 5]] ],
  [ PF_SLIDER,   "Compression", "Compression Level", 7,     [0, 9, 1]  ] ]
```

If your plug-in is associated with the *<Image>* menu hierarchy, the script will be sent two additional parameters that you do not need to specify in the parameter list. These are the current image (of type PF_IMAGE) and the current drawable (of type PF_DRAWABLE). There is actually a third parameter, *run_mode,* that other plug-ins have to include, but the Gimp::Fu module handles this for you. The run mode indicates whether the plug-in should be run *interactively* (i.e., show dialog boxes which the user can use to control the script) or *non-interactively* (for command-line scripts, or scripts that do not require human input). The run mode can be accesed through the $run_mode global variable exported by the Gimp module.

Return values

The parameter list is followed by an optional list of return values, in the same format as the parameter list (but without default values). If the script returns an image, you do not need to explicitly list it here, but you do need to make

sure that your script returns the image with the *return* function. If the script
does not have any return values, this field may be left out (the Gimp::Fu module enables this).

The plug-in function

The last parameter to *register* should be either an an anonymous subroutine
that does all the work of your plug-in, or a pointer to a subroutine defined
elsewhere in the script (as in the background tester script).

The plug-in subroutine

This is the actual procedure that does whatever it is that your script is supposed to
do (in the background image tester example, it is the *test_background* function).
This procedure must be provided to the register method as a parameter, because
this is how the Gimp knows which procedure does all the work.

The parameters are retrieved via the @_ array, just like they would be for any other
Perl subroutine. The return value must be specified explicitly with the **return**
statement, or by leaving the return value as the last line of the subroutine. Here's
an example of a script that accepts a number of parameters and returns a new
image (whose output is shown in Figure 7-19). In fact, the script automates the
electronic marble example at the beginning of this chapter. It takes three parameters (the number of frames, and a start and end color for the gradient) and creates
a multi-layered image with the final "marble."

```perl
#!/usr/bin/perl -w
#
# Electronic Marble
# A plug-in for the Gimp, written in Perl, that automates
# the example at the beginning of the chapter.
#
use Gimp qw(:auto);
use Gimp::Fu;

register(
        "perl_fu_electronic_marble",                    # Name
        "Make an 'electronic marble'.",                 # Blurb
        "Creates an animated sphere that is multi-colored and looks like
         a marble.",                                    # Help
        "Shawn P. Wallace",                             # Author
        "(c) 1999 SPW",                                 # Copyright
        "1999-02-21",                                   # Date
        "<Toolbox>/Xtns/Web Graphics/Electronic Marble", # Menu path
        "*",                                            # Images accepted
        # Three parameters
        [
          [ PF_INT, "Frames", "Number of frames", 10],
          [ PF_COLOR, "Start color", "Start color for gradient", [255, 0, 0] ],
          [ PF_COLOR, "End color", "End color for gradient", [255, 255, 0] ]
        ],
        # Two return values
```

The Gimp Is a Self-Documenting System

Each procedure in the PDB has a help string, written by the author, which (the user hopes) gives a good idea about how to use the procedure. The help string will not appear in the PDB browser, but the help strings associated with each parameter will appear in the PDB browser. Nevertheless, it is an efficient means of creating a self-documenting system, because as plug-ins or scripts are added to the system, their documentation is automatically registered in the procedural database. In fact, it is very easy to use the Gimp module to create an up-to-date "manual" consisting of all of the help fields with the following standalone script, which may be called from the command line (in case you didn't realize it, this is also an example of using the Gimp module to write standalone scripts):

```perl
#!/usr/bin/perl

use Gimp qw(:auto );

# This is a standalone script only so it needs to define a net()
callback
#
sub net {
    # The net() procedure is called when the script is started by the
    # Perl network server extension, rather than being started directly
    # by the Gimp.
    #
    my ($blurb, $help, $author, $copyright, $date, $type, $args, $rvals);

    # Get the names of all the procedures from the PDB
    #
    my @procnames = gimp_procedural_db_query(qw(.* .* .* .* .* .* .*));
    shift @procnames;          # discard the number returned

    # Now iterate through the names, get the 8 info fields for each
    # and print out the name, author, and help fields
    #
    foreach my $name (@procnames) {
        ($blurb, $help, $author,
         $copyright, $date, $type,
         $args, $rvals) = gimp_procedural_db_proc_info($name);
        print "$name\n";
        print '-' x length($name);
        print "\nAuthor: $author\nWhat it does: $help\n\n";
    }
}

# Hand over control to gimp, who will call the net() callback
#
exit main;
```

—Continued—

If you have the Gimp running, just turn on the Perl Server extension by selecting it from the menu, then run the script from the command line and redirect
the output to a file with:

```
perl listhelp.pl > gimp_help.txt
```

This will generate an entry for each procedure that looks like this:

```
gimp_procedural_db_query
------------------------
Author: Spencer Kimball & Peter Mattis
What it does: this procedure queries the contents of the Procedural
Database. It is supplied with seven arguments matching procedures on
{name, blurb, help, author, copyright, date, procedure type}. This is
accomplished using regular expression matching. For instance, to find
all procedures with "jpeg" listed in the blurb, all seven arguments can
be supplied as ".*", except for the second, which can be supplied as
".*jpeg.*"...
```

Voila! An instant manual that consists of roughly 120K of documentation that
was embedded in the Procedural Database.

```
            [ [ PF_INT, "width", "Width of image" ],
              [ PF_INT, "height", "Height of image" ]
            ],
            \&make_marble
);

sub make_marble {
    # The plug-in subroutine.
    # First get the parameters passed to the procedure...
    #
    my ($frames, $start, $end) = @_;
    my $width = rand(200)+56;        # Set a random width and height
    my $height = $width;             # ...but make it square

    # Step 1: Create a new image
    #
    my $img = gimp_image_new($width, $height, 0);
    my $background = gimp_layer_new($img, $width, $height,
                                    RGB_IMAGE, "Background",
                                    100, NORMAL_MODE);

    # Note that we are using only procedural-style syntax here...
    #
    gimp_image_add_layer($background, -1);    # -1 = position = background

    # Step 2: Set the colors and apply a gradient
    #
    my $drawable = gimp_image_active_drawable($img);  # get the drawable

    # Set foreground and background colors for use by the blend tool.
    #
    gimp_palette_set_foreground($start);
```

```perl
gimp_palette_set_background($end);

# Apply a gradient with the blend tool (gradient tool). For
# a description of the parameters, see the appendix.
#
gimp_blend($img, $drawable, FG_BG_RGB, NORMAL_MODE, RADIAL,
           100, 0, 0, 0, 0, 0, int($width/2), int($height/2),
           $width, $height);

# Step 3: Add a new transparent layer
#
my $layer1 = gimp_layer_new($img, $width, $height,
                            RGB_IMAGE, "Layer 1",
                            0, NORMAL_MODE);
gimp_image_add_layer($img, $layer1, 0);     # 0 = position

# Step 4: Apply a custom gradient
#
gimp_gradients_set_active('Flare_Glow_Angular_1');
gimp_blend($img, $drawable, CUSTOM, NORMAL_MODE, CONICAL_SYMMETRIC,
           100, 0, 0, 0, 0, 0, int($width/2), int($height/2),
           $width, $height);

# Step 5: Merge the Layers into a single layer
#
my $layer = gimp_image_merge_visible_layers($img, 0);

# Step 6: Apply the whirl and pinch and make seamless filters
#
$drawable = gimp_image_active_drawable($img);
plug_in_whirl_pinch(RUN_NONINTERACTIVE, $img, $drawable, 90, 0, 1);
plug_in_make_seamless(RUN_NONINTERACTIVE, $img, $drawable);

# Step 7: Implement something like the spinning globe script
# which consists of repeated calls to the Map Object plug-in,
# one for each frame.
#
my $frame;
for (my $angle=-179; $angle <= 180; $angle += 360/$frames) {
    $frame = gimp_layer_copy($layer, 1);
    $img->add_layer($frame, 0);

    # The Map Object plug-in has a bunch of parameters;
    # these are all the default values used by the plug-in, with
    # the exception of the 'rotation angle y' parameter,
    # for which we use our current value for $angle
    #
    plug_in_map_object( RUN_NONINTERACTIVE, $img, $frame,
                        1,                   # 1 = sphere
                        .5, .5, 2,           # viewpoint x, y, z
                        .5, .5, .5,          # position x, y, z
                        1, 0, 0,             # axis 1 x, y, z
                        0, 1, 0,             # axis 2 x, y, z
                        0, $angle, 0,        # rotate angle x, y, z
                        0,                   # lightsource = point
```

```
                    [255, 255, 255],    # lightsource color
                    -.5, -.5, 2,        # light position
                    -1, -1, 1,          # light direction
                    .3, 1, .5,   0, 27, # material info
                    1,                  # antialiasing
                    1,                  # tile?
                    0,                  # create new image
                    1,                  # transparent background
                    .25                 # sphere radius
        );
    } # end of for loop

    # Now remove the original merged layer
    #
    gimp_image_remove_layer($img, $layer);

    # Then create a new display
    #
    gimp_display_new($img);

    return ($width, $height);        # Return the width and height
}

exit main;
```

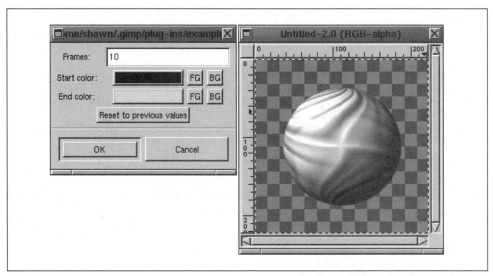

Figure 7-19. A script written with Gimp::Fu that takes a number of parameters and returns a new image

Within the plug-in subroutine you will generally call various Gimp procedures that manipulate an image. The Gimp module provides this interface to the Gimp's Procedural Database. You can use either procedural-style or object-oriented syntax for calling Gimp procedures.

```
    $img = gimp_image_new(256, 256, RGBA)     # procedural-style syntax
```

```
$img = new Image(256, 256, RGBA)          # OO-style syntax
```

Appendix C provides a reference to the standard Gimp functions available to your script for the Gimp 1.0 distribution. The appendix divides the procedures into functional categories and also provides some examples of calling the procedures in both procedural-style and OO-style syntax.

References

There are a number of fine web pages that are linked from the Gimp home page that offer tutorials, scripts, news, and links to yet more fine web pages about the Gimp. The pages of particular note are:

The Gimp News page by Zach Beane:

http://xach.dorknet.com/gimp/news/

The Automated Plug-in Registry maintained by Ingo Lütkebohle:

http://registry.gimp.org/

The Gimp Patches Page maintained by Zach Beane:

http://xach.dorknet.com/gimp/news/patch.html

GUM, the Gimp Users Manual, by Karin and Olof Kylander, an "open document" covered by their own GDPL (Graphic Documentation Project Copying License):

http://manual.gimp.org
ftp://manual.gimp.org/pub/manual/GimpUserManual-1.0.0.pdf (PDF version)
http://manual.gimp.org/ (HTML version)

Online documentation for Gimp-Perl (manpages in HTML form):

http://lehmann.home.ml.org/gimp.html

Dov Grobgeld's Gimp-Perl tutorial:

http://imagic.weizmann.ac.il/~dov/gimp/perl-tut.html

Federico Mena-Quintero's page (author of Gradient Editor):

http://www.nuclecu.unam.mx/~federico/gimp/el-the-gimp.html

The Gimp CVS site (for developers and bleeding edge scenesters only):

http://www.gimp.org/devel_cvs.html

Jürgen Erhard's Wish List, which is a list of possible future improvements to the Gimp that grows as people add them and shrinks as they get implemented:

http://members.tripod.com/~Juergen_Erhard/computers_contribute_gimp_index.html

The Gimp Bug List maintained by Scott Goehring at Wilburworks:

http://www.wilberworks.com/bugs.cgi

OS/2 Port:

http://www.netlabs.org/gimp/

Win32 Port:

http://www.geocities.com/SiliconValley/Garage/8516/gimp/gimpw32.html

Win32 Native GTK Port:

http://www.vtt.fi/tte/staff/tml/gimp/win32

If you intend to help develop the Gimp you should also check out the various Gimp IRC channels, where most of the decisions are actually made. The hostname, port, and location of each of these IRC channels existing as of this writing (culled from the Gimp home page) are:

    irc.canweb.net.net:6666 from Toronto, CA
    irc.mint.net:6666 from Maine, USA
    irc.coherent.net:6666 from Chicago, USA
    irc.eanut.org:6666 from Texas, USA
    rudolf.canberra.edu.au:6666 from Australia
    dazed.nol.net:6667 from Texas, USA
    irc.germany.gimp.org:6667 from Bielefeld, Germany
    irc.chillin.org:6667 from Florida, USA

For those of us who don't need to have our finger on the pulse of the Gimp in real-time, there's the gimp-developer mailing list, which is hosted by the University of California at Berkeley. You can subscribe to it by sending the message

    subscribe gimp-developer your-email-address

to *majordomo@scam.xcf.berkeley.edu*. The developer list is a fairly high traffic list, and is probably too much information for mere users. There is also a user-oriented list, which can be subscribed to by sending the message

    subscribe gimp-user your-email-address

to the same address.

The mailings lists are archived at:

http://www.findmail.com/listsaver/gimp-developer/
http://www.findmail.com/listsaver/gimp-user/
http://www.findmail.com/listsaver/gimp-announce/

and

http://www.levien.com/~gimp-user/current/
http://www.levien.com/~gimp-dev/current/
http://www.levien.com/~gimp-ann/current/

III

Dynamic
Graphic
Techniques

8

Image Maps

Image maps allow a web developer to associate actions with regions of an image. A user's click may activate a link to another page, run a server-side script, or launch a client-side JavaScript program. In the typical nerdy hipster parlance of the Web, these regions are known as "hot spots."

The requirements for a working image map are:

- An image that can be included as an inline image on a web page (generally this means GIF, JPEG, or PNG).

- Some means of displaying the image and finding the coordinates of the regions you want to define.

- If a client-side map, a <MAP> element in the same document that defines the regions of the image map.

- If a server-side map, a map file on the server that defines the regions of the image map in a format that the server recognizes.

- If a server-side map, an image map program that handles the resolution of the region from the coordinate clicked by the user (most web servers now come with this program preconfigured or built-in, so you probably don't have to worry about it).

The most difficult part of dealing with image maps from a programming or automation point of view is the generation of the coordinates for the regions within the image. This generally requires some intervention by the author. There are some ways of setting up a site so that certain types of image maps may be generated automatically.

Several people and companies have created tools for making it easier to designate regions within an image map. A few of these free or inexpensive tools are discussed at the end of the chapter.

Client-Side Versus Server-Side

In the beginning there was only one option for implementing clickable image maps: the image map program that ran on the NCSA web server. This configuration is now known as the server-side image map. Over the next few years the inadequacies of this approach became apparent and an alternative means of processing the image map within the user agent was proposed and popularly accepted. This approach is known as a client-side image map. The differences are as follows:

Client-side

> The "map" associated with the image is embedded within the same document as the image. When the user clicks on an image, the coordinates of the point are interpreted by the user agent and resolved by looking at the map for the image. If the point is within a region, the target URL is followed by the user agent. Many browsers also provide contextual information based on the internal map by displaying the URL associated with a region in the status bar of the browser when the mouse passes over the region.

Server-side

> The map associated with the image resides on the server in a text file that generally ends with a *.map* extension. This map file is specified in an HTML document by the **HREF** attribute of an anchor element that contains the image. When the user clicks on an image, the coordinates of the point are sent to the server as an HTTP request, and the server attempts to resolve the request by parsing the map file. If the point is within one of the defined regions, that region's URL is followed and returned to the client. With server-side maps, the browser has no idea about the region definitions and cannot give feedback to the user.

Client-side maps are preferable to server-side maps for several reasons, the most important of which is that they offer a better response time to the users actions. They are also more efficient in their use of bandwidth, and once a page is loaded, they don't necessarily require an open connection to the server. Take, for example, a server-side image map whose regions are not clearly defined. If the user requires ten clicks to successfully find the "hot spot," that results in a lot of network traffic with no results. Here's what the server log could look like for this frustrating session:

```
dyn090e.shemp.net - - [18/Apr/1998:21:24:16 -0400]
                    "GET /shawn/face.map?52,61 HTTP/1.1" 200 -
```

```
dyn090e.shemp.net - - [18/Apr/1998:21:24:18 -0400]
                        "GET /shawn/face.map?123,60 HTTP/1.1" 200 -
dyn090e.shemp.net - - [18/Apr/1998:21:24:19 -0400]
                        "GET /shawn/face.map?211,90 HTTP/1.1" 200 -
dyn090e.shemp.net - - [18/Apr/1998:21:24:20 -0400]
                        "GET /shawn/face.map?95,320 HTTP/1.1" 200 -
dyn090e.shemp.net - - [18/Apr/1998:21:24:21 -0400]
                        "GET /shawn/face.map?21,302 HTTP/1.1" 200 -
dyn090e.shemp.net - - [18/Apr/1998:21:24:22 -0400]
                        "GET /shawn/face.map?247,341 HTTP/1.1" 200 -
dyn090e.shemp.net - - [18/Apr/1998:21:24:23 -0400]
                        "GET /shawn/face.map?248,103 HTTP/1.1" 200 -
dyn090e.shemp.net - - [18/Apr/1998:21:24:25 -0400]
                        "GET /shawn/face.map?65,80 HTTP/1.1" 200 -
dyn090e.shemp.net - - [18/Apr/1998:21:24:27 -0400]
                        "GET /shawn/face.map?36,205 HTTP/1.1" 200 -
dyn090e.shemp.net - - [18/Apr/1998:21:24:31 -0400]
                        "GET /shawn/face.map?260,196 HTTP/1.1" 302 -
dyn090e.shemp.net - - [18/Apr/1998:21:24:32 -0400]
                        "GET /panicband.html HTTP/1.0" 302 -
```

Another major advantage to using client-side maps is that they allow the user agent to provide the user feedback about which regions of the image map are "hot" and which are not. This is especially important for images where the defined regions are not visually obvious.

The last important reason why you should generally choose to use client-side maps is that they provide text-based browsers the ability to interpret the options embedded in the image map description and represent them as a textual list of links.* A client-side image map rendered in Lynx, for example, will first appear as [USEMAP] (unless the image has an ALT tag specified, in which case that text will be displayed). When this link is selected, the following menu is provided, where each numbered item is a link to the appropriate URL:

```
facemap
MAP: http://www.shemp.org/index.html#facemap

    1. Ear
    2. Nose
    3. Eye
```

Having said all that nasty stuff about how awful server-side image maps are, I'll take several steps back and say that they do have their uses. If you have an image map that is meant to be used on many pages, a server side map will allow you to share a map file between many images. Or you may have a very complicated image map that would be too bulky to include as part of a document. Or you may

---

* There is actually a work-around for presenting textual representations of server-side image maps that most servers have implemented, but it is really better for the client to have the map information on hand so that it can render it however it wants.

want to generate an image map dynamically and reference it from a static HTML page. We will look at some of these applications later in the chapter.

While most browsers support client-side image maps, some older browsers do not (specifically, Netscape Navigator before Version 2.0 or Internet Explorer before Version 3.0). To accommodate those users, you may implement both client- and server-side image maps within the same tag. In this case, the user agent will use the client-side map description named *internalmap* if it is able, and failing that, it will use the server-side map described in *mapfile.map*:

```
<A HREF = "mapfile.map">
    <IMG SRC = "images/imagemap.gif" ISMAP USEMAP="#internalmap">
</A>
```

Implementing Client-Side Maps

The `USEMAP` attribute of the `<IMG>` tag indicates that the image is a client-side image map. The `USEMAP` attribute is assigned a reference to a named `<MAP>` element that exists separately within the document. Multiple images within a document may share the same region definitions by simply referring to the same `<MAP>` element. For example, the following HTML element indicates that the image called *face.gif* (shown in Figure 8-1) should be associated with the `<MAP>` element named *facemap*:

```
<!-- A Client-side image map -->
<IMG SRC="face.gif" USEMAP="#facemap">
```

Figure 8-1. An image map

The <MAP> tag

The definition for a client-side map is constructed with the `<MAP>` element. The `<MAP>` element is defined for HTML specifications after Version 2.0.

The <MAP> tag must contain a **NAME** attribute, which assigns the name that the <IMG> tag's **USEMAP** attribute will specify, as shown in the earlier example. The <MAP> tag requires a start tag and a closing tag. The content of the <MAP> element can be a number of **AREA** elements which define the regions. Defining the regions with a list of **AREA** elements would look like this:

```
<MAP NAME="facemap">
    <AREA SHAPE=rect COORDS="252,168, 273,246"
        HREF="http://www.shemp.org/panicband.html" ALT="Ear">
    <AREA SHAPE=poly COORDS="141,166, 125,236, 193,232, 164,162"
        HREF="http://www.shemp.org/frodus.html" ALT="Nose">
    <AREA SHAPE=circle COORDS="100,180,30"
        HREF="http://www.shemp.org/as220.html" ALT="Eye">
</MAP>
```

If regions defined within the same <MAP> element overlap with each other, the region that is defined first will be the one that takes precedence. This definition can be used effectively to produce complicated clickable areas with the simple shape primitives available with the **AREA** element. For example, to produce a clickable 20×20 circle, surrounded by a "dead region" of 20 pixels, which in turn is surrounded by another 20-pixel–wide clickable concentric ring, use the following ordering of **AREA** statements (whose regions are pictured in Figure 8-2):

```
<IMG SRC="circles.gif" USEMAP="#circles">
<MAP NAME="circles">
    <AREA SHAPE=circle
        COORDS="75,75,20"
        HREF="inner.html">
    <AREA SHAPE=circle
        COORDS="75,75,40"
        NOHREF >
    <AREA SHAPE=circle
        COORDS="75,75,60"
        HREF="outer.html">
</MAP>
```

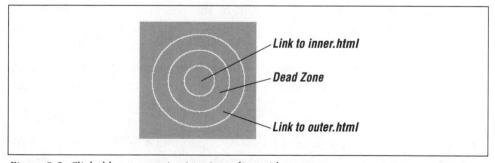

Figure 8-2. Clickable concentric rings in a client-side map

The <AREA> tag

The <AREA> tag defines a region of a client-side image map. It consists of a lone start tag and one or more of the following attributes:

SHAPE

> The SHAPE attribute defines the shape of the clickable region. Acceptable values are:
>
> — default: The entire image
>
> — rect: A rectangular region
>
> — circle: A circular region
>
> — poly: A polygonal region

COORDS

> The COORDS attribute is a comma-delimited list of coordinates that define the edges of the region. The coordinate system is based on (0, 0) being the upper left corner of the image. The number and order of coordinates depends on the shape of the region:
>
> — default: No coordinates are specified.
>
> — rect: A rectangular region needs two coordinates, the upper left and lower right corners.
>
> — circle: A circular region needs one coordinate and a value for the radius of the circle, in pixels.
>
> — poly: For a polygonal region the coordinates should be a list of three or more points that define the vertices of the polygon. It is assumed that the side of the polygon between the last and first points are joined. A polygon can have at most 100 vertices.

HREF

> The HREF attribute specifies the URL of the resource or link that will be requested when the user clicks on this region.

NOHREF

> The NOHREF is a Boolean attribute that specifies that the region has no action associated with it. It can be used to "knock out" area regions defined by other AREA tags within the same <MAP> element.

ALT

> The ALT attribute provides a short description that may be used by the browser to provide contextual information about the clickable areas, or may be used by browsers that are not equipped to deal with images.

ONFOCUS

> This attribute may be used to assign a JavaScript event handler script to the region that will be called whenever the mouse is over that region.

ONBLUR

> This attribute can be used in a similar way as the ONFOCUS attribute, but it is activated when the region of the image map loses the focus.

Server-Side Maps

The ISMAP Boolean attribute in an <IMG> tag indicates that the image should be treated as a server-side image map. The <IMG> element should be enclosed in a hyperlink that points to the map file on the server to be used by the image:

```
<!-- A Server-side image map -->
<A HREF = "face.map">
    <IMG SRC = "images/facemenu.gif" ISMAP>
</A>
```

When the user clicks on a point in the image, its coordinates are sent to the server by appending a question mark and the x and y coordinates to the URL given in the HREF attribute. Text-based user agents will always send a (0, 0) coordinate when the link is selected. In the above example, the server would get the following HTTP request when a user clicks on the point at (65, 80):

```
GET /face.map?65,80 HTTP/1.1
```

 In general, it is a good practice to specify the complete URL for each of the actions in the map file. Relative path names (such as *../foo.html*) will be interpreted by the web server as *relative to the location of the map file*. This could lead to confusion, so just use the whole URL.

The map file resides on the server and provides a description of the various regions within the image map, in much the same way as the area statements of a client-side map. There are a few different formats for server-side map files. The most popular is the original NCSA format (used by Apache, WebStar, WebSite, etc.), which describes the regions as in the following example:

```
# NCSA-style image map file = face.map

# The Right Ear: upper left and lower left points of a rectangle
rect http://www.shemp.org/example/panicband.html  252,168 273,246

# The Nose: a polygon described by four points
poly http://www.shemp.org/example/frodus.html  141,166 125,236 193,232
164,162
```

```
# The Right Eye: A circle with a center point and a radius
circle http://www.shemp.org/example/as220.html   100,180 30
```

The older, deprecated format for map files is the CERN format, which orders the coordinates and URL slightly differently:

```
circ    (306,204) 7          http://www.shemp.org/example/foobar.html
rect    (324,131) (353,261)  http://www.shemp.org/example/bargum.html
circ    (103,279) 43         http://www.shemp.org/example/foogum.html
```

 A note about scaled image maps: if an image is scaled by the web browser with the WIDTH and HEIGHT attributes (by specifying dimensions larger or smaller than that of the source image), and the image is used as an image map, the clickable regions of the map are *not* scaled along with the image. Each of the clickable regions are defined as points within the frame of the image and have no relation to the content of the image. This should be obvious, but is still worth noting.

An Alternative: Image Buttons with the <INPUT> Tag

The HTML form element can also be used to simulate a clickable image map. If an INPUT field of a form is given the type image, the field will be rendered as an inline image which, when clicked, will perform the action given in the ACTION field of the form enclosing it. This type of element is generally called an Image Button. An example of an Image Button that calls a script called *processclick.cgi* is:

```
<FORM ACTION="http://www.shemp.net/cgi-bin/processclick.cgi">
    <INPUT TYPE="image"  NAME="img"  SRC="menu.gif">
    <INPUT TYPE="hidden" NAME="dept"  SRC="hardware">
</FORM>
```

When the action specified by the form is a script, the script is sent the x and y coordinates that the user clicked and the other information contained in the form. This is why the Image Button is useful; scripts called from regular image maps have direct access to the clicked coordinates, but cannot be sent additional input. The x and y values for this example would be passed as parameters named *img.x* and *img.y*, like this:

```
http://www.shemp.net/cgi-bin/
processclick.cgi?img.x=189&img.y=122&dept=hardware
```

This example could be useful in that the same menu image and CGI script could be used for different departments, and the script could handle the context, rather than having a separate CGI script for each department's image map.

As another example, the following CGI script will allow the user to click on the Image Button and, using the GD module, will flood-fill the area indicated by the user's click with the color specified by the user, as seen in Figure 8-3. Here's the HTML for the page:

```html
<!--An example of an Image Button within an INPUT field -->
<HTML>
<BODY>
<FORM ACTION="cgi-bin/floodfill.cgi">
    <INPUT TYPE="image" NAME="image1" SRC="face.gif">
    <INPUT TYPE="hidden" NAME="name" VALUE="face.gif">
    <SELECT NAME="color">
        <OPTION VALUE="255,0,0">Red</OPTION>
        <OPTION VALUE="0,255,0">Green</OPTION>
        <OPTION VALUE="0,0,255">Blue</OPTION>
    </SELECT>
</FORM>
</BODY>
</HTML>
```

And here's the code, which needs to be set up as a CGI script with all the proper permissions and such:

```perl
#!/usr/local/bin/perl

# floodfill.cgi
# A CGI script that will fill a region that is specified
# by an Image Button from the floodfill.html page.
#
use strict;
use CGI;
use GD;

# Get the parameters:
#  1. x and y coordinates of click
#  2. The name of the image file (passed from hidden field)
#  3. The color with which to fill the region
#
my $query = new CGI;
my $x = $query->param('image1.x');
my $y = $query->param('image1.y');
my $imagename = $query->param('name');
my @color = split /,/, $query->param('color');
my $fillcolor;                       # The fillcolor is the index in the colormap

# Open the image and read it in as a GIF
#
open(INFILE, "$imagename") || die "Couldn't open file.";
my $image = newFromGif GD::Image(\*INFILE);
close INFILE;

# If the color map is full, substitute the nearest color,
# otherwise allocate the color.
#
```

```
if ($image->colorsTotal() == 256) {
    $fillcolor = $image->colorClosest(@color);
} else {
    $fillcolor = $image->colorAllocate(@color);
}

$image->fill($x, $y, $fillcolor);          # fill the region
print $query->header(-type => 'image/gif');  # print the header
binmode(STDOUT);
print $image->gif;                          # send the image
```

The INPUT tag essentially provides the same interface as a server-side image map, but it requires that you implement the translation of the clicked coordinate into a meaningful form. It can be used in applications where the few shape-defining primitives of the image map are not robust enough to describe a very complicated shape. The Perl CGI::ImageMap module provides some routines for dealing with this implementation, and for emulating the behavior of regular image maps.

Image Map Tools

There are basically two ways of specifying the coordinates of the regions within an image map. The first is the "brute force" or "map hacker" method of using an image display program such as *xv*, Paint Shop Pro, or *display* to bring up the image in a window and manually picking out the points that define the shapes. The second method is with a WYSIWYG image map editor.

Most of the commercial image editing packages aimed at web developers (such as Adobe ImageReady and Macromedia Fireworks) offer built-in tools for making image map regions fairly painless. Some web server packages also come with image map tools. The following is a collection of tools that are either freeware or shareware; ftp addresses are provided when available.

Map Hacker Tools for Generating Coordinates

These tools offer the ability to manually pick out coordinates for use in image maps:

xv

> *xv* is a useful all-purpose interactive image manipulation program written by John Bradley for the X Window System. It offers the ability to quickly manipulate many image file formats, and provides a nice interface for common tasks such as cropping, sizing, and manipulating the color tables of images. It can be used to find coordinates for defining image map regions by clicking the mouse inside the image window and drawing a selection rectangle, which can be fine-tuned with handles. The info window will display the size and position of the rectangular region. Individual points of a polygon or a circle must

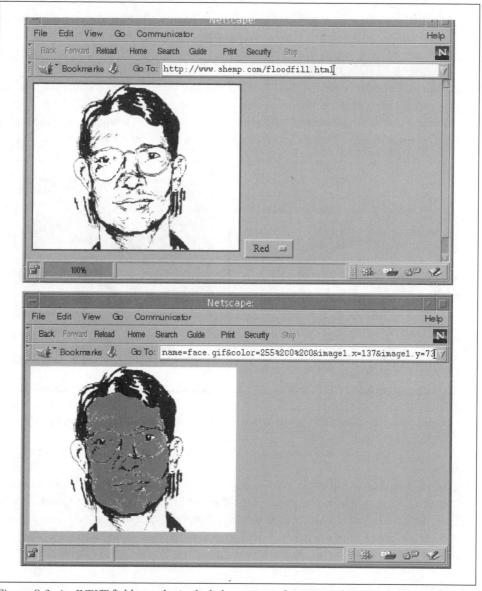

Figure 8-3. An INPUT field may be included as a part of an HTML form element as an alternative clickable image map method. These two screenshots show the image before (top) and after (bottom) the form was submitted by clicking on the forehead in the image.

be picked out individually. Version 2.x was free (Version 3.0 and later are shareware). Version 2.0 of *xv* is available from *ftp://ftp.x.org/R5contrib/* and Version 3.0 may be had at *ftp://ftp.cis.upenn.edu/pub/xv/*.

display

> The *display* program comes with the ImageMagick distribution (see Chapter 5,
> *Industrial-Strength Graphics Scripting with PerlMagick*) and will display a
> wide range of graphics file formats on any client connected to an X server. It
> provides a graphical interface to many of the ImageMagick manipulation func-
> tions and acts very nicely as a tool for quickly determining the coordinates of
> an image map region. Figure 8-4 shows the information provided by *display*
> when an area of an image is selected. It is available from the ImageMagick
> home page at *http://www.wizards.dupont.com/cristy/ImageMagick.html*.

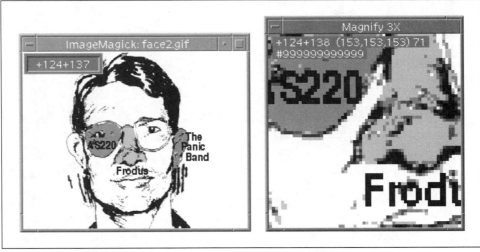

*Figure 8-4. ImageMagick's display utility may be used (on X-based platforms) to gather
coordinates for image map files*

Gimp

> As of this writing there is not a Gimp plug-in that will automatically generate
> an image map file in the manner of the WYSIWYG tools. The Gimp can be
> used in a similar way as *xv* or *display*, however, and I'm sure someone will
> write a plug-in at some point. Check *http://registry.gimp.org* for Gimp plug-ins.
> See Chapter 7, *Web Graphics with the Gimp*, for more on the Gimp.

WYSIWYG Map Editing Tools

There are several commercial packages that have built-in support for image maps,
such as Adobe Fireworks or most WYSIWYG HTML authoring programs. There are
also several free utilities that do just as good a job:

MapEdit

> MapEdit is an image map editor written in Java, which means it should be
> pretty much platform-independent. It allows you to define regions within an

image with several drawing tools. It is primarily intended for creating client-side maps, but it will also export NCSA style server-side map files. MapEdit will prompt you for an HTML file in which the image map is referenced and will change the file directly. If there are multiple image maps within a file it will provide a selection list. When an image is selected and a region is defined, the program will prompt you for the information to be added to that region's AREA tag. MapEdit is available at *http://www.boutell.com/mapedit/.*

Client-Side Image Map Editor (CSIME)

CSIME is another Java-based editor for creating client-side image maps. It is platform-independent (if you can run Java) and free. You can get it at *http://web.wwa.com/~myc/csime/.*

Map This

Map This is a free image map utility for Windows. It also creates server-side (NCSA or CERN) or client-side map files. Map This is available at *http://galadriel.ecaetc.ohio-state.edu/tc/mt/.*

Translating Server-Side Image Maps to Client-Side Format

The NCSA server-side image map format can be a convenient way of storing the information about an image map's region because it is a very simple format stored in a portable text file. It is also good form to offer a server-side version of an image map script as a backup to the client-side map. You may find it helpful to have a script that will translate a server-side map file into a client-side format for these reasons or because you are "modernizing" legacy image maps.

The following script will take an NCSA-format server-side map file as an argument and print it to the command line for cutting and pasting into an HTML document (or for inclusion in a larger HTML formatting project). It handles two special cases that crop up when dealing with older-format server-side image maps:

1. Circular regions were sometimes described by two (x, y) coordinates—a center point and a point on the outer edge of the circle—rather than the client-side syntax of center point and the radius.

2. If the default region is listed first in a client-side map it will mask the definitions of other regions. This script will move default region descriptions to the end of the map element.

The translation script, called *servertoclient.pl,* is called with the name of a server-side map file as a parameter. Here is the code:

```
#!/usr/local/bin/perl -w

# servertoclient.pl
```

```perl
# Converts NCSA-format image map files to client-side format
#
use strict;

my $servermap = $ARGV[0];
my $validshape = "default|rect|circle|poly";
my (@lines, @endlines, $shape, $url, @coords, $coordstring);
my $count = 0;

# We might need these, if there are circles defined with four values
#
my ($x1, $y1, $x2, $y2, $radius);

# The file is read in first and stored in a list of lines
# so that we can move any default regions at the top of the file
#
if ($servermap) {
    open(INFILE, $servermap) || die "Can't open file $servermap...\n";
    while (<INFILE>) {
        if ($_ =~ /^default/) {
            push @endlines, $_;
        } else {
            push @lines, $_;
        }
    }
    push @lines, @endlines;    # tack on any default definitions
    close INFILE;
} else {
    die "Please specify a server-side image map file...\n";
}

print "<IMG SRC=\"**image name goes here**\" USEMAP=\"#$servermap\">\n";
print "<MAP NAME=\"$servermap\">\n";

foreach my $line (@lines) {
    $count++;
    if ( ($line =~ /^#/) || ($line eq "\n") ) {
        # A comment or blank line; do nothing
    } else {
        # The format of the map file is:
        # SHAPE (arbitrary whitespace) URL (WS) COORD1 (WS) COORD2...
        # Where the coordinates may be separated by commas or by
        # arbitrary whitespace. This regex should do the job.
        #
        ($shape, $url, @coords) = split /\s+?/, $line;
        if ($shape =~ m/$validshape/o) {
            # The coords list may still contain x,y chunks;
            # split the coordinates into a discrete list
            #
            @coords = map {split ','} @coords;

            # Check to see if it is an old circle definition;
            # two x,y coordinates means it is...
            #
```

```
            if (($shape=~/circle/) && (@coords == 4)) {
                ($x1, $y1, $x2, $y2) = @coords;

                # Good ol' pythagorean theorem
                #
                $radius = int(sqrt(abs($x2-$x1)**2 + abs($y2-$y1)**2));
                @coords = ($x1, $y1, $radius);
            }
            # In a client-side definition, all coordinates are
            # separated by commas...
            #
            $coordstring = join ",", @coords;
            print "<AREA SHAPE=$shape\n";
            print "      COORDS=\"$coordstring\"\n";
            print "      HREF=\"$url\">\n";
        }
    }
}
print "</MAP>\n";
```

Image Maps on the Fly: A Clickable "Wander" Engine

As an interesting example of generating clickable image maps on the fly, let's create a web page that will be driven by what we'll call a *wander engine*. The web page will allow the user to wander through a landscape by clicking on directional links, and the changing landscape will appear as a dynamically generated image (see Figure 8-5). Each landscape area will be called a room. Each room can contain objects that will be overlaid on the background by the CGI script that dynamically creates the image (the background used in this example is pictured in Figure 8-6 and the three objects are in Figure 8-7). The composite image will be an image map where each of the objects can be clicked on to perform some action.

Figure 8-5. The wander engine allows the user to navigate a landscape with objects by clicking on navigational links or on the objects themselves

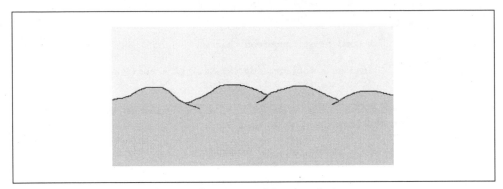

Figure 8-6. The background image for room 3 of the "wander"

Figure 8-7. The image files for objects 2, 3, 4, and 6 in the example

All of the information about a room is contained in the *rooms.db* database. For this example, the database will be implemented using Shishir Gundavaram's Sprite module (available from CPAN), which uses SQL queries to access the data and stores the data as simple text files. The fields in the *rooms.db* database are:

- The room number
- The filename of the background image
- A description of the room
- The rooms numbers to the north, south, east, and west
- A list of the objects in the room

Here is the *rooms.db* file that we will be using for this example:

```
Room::Background::Description::North::South::East::West::Objects
1::images/room1.gif::You are standing on a hillside.::2::3::4::5::2,3,4,6
2::images/room2.gif::You are in a maze of twisty wormholes,
                all alike.::6::7::8::9::5
```

The information for each of the objects is stored in the *objects.db* database. The fields in the object database are:

- The object number

- The filename of the image file for the object

- A descriptive name for the object

- The x and y values for the coordinate that specifies the placement of the upper left corner of the image

- The URL of the action associated with the image

The object database would look something like this:

```
Object::File::Name::X::Y::URL
1::images/foogum.gif::some gum::50::50::http://www.shemp.org/eat.cgi?item=1
2::images/worm.gif::a sad worm::28::98::http://www.shemp.org/wormhole.cgi
3::images/tree.gif::a lumpy tree::100::15::http://www.shemp.org/tree.html
4::images/flowers.gif::a patch of flowers::275::20::http://www.shemp.org/
f.html
5::images/bargum.gif::some bargum::70::100::http://www.shemp.org/bargum.cgi
6::images/apple.gif::a juicy apple::185::120::http://www.shemp.org/
eat.cgi?item=6
```

The CGI script that generates the web page is called *wander.cgi*. It is called by passing it a room number as a parameter, as in the URL *http://shemp.net/cgi-bin/rooms.cgi?room=1*. This script does a number of things:

1. Retrieves the information about the current room and the objects in that room from the room and object databases.

2. Sorts the objects in order of increasing area. This is so that when we add the **AREA** elements to the **<MAP>** element, the smallest images will be added first and will get precedence over the larger images. Also, when the image is created, the object images must be added in the reverse order, so that the larger objects are added first and the smaller objects added later.

3. Prints the HTML for the resulting page. This page includes a description for a client-side image map (a **<MAP>** element) that is generated by the data retrieved from the object database, and an **<IMG>** element that calls the *drawroom.cgi* script to dynamically create the image of the room. The background image and the objects (if any) are passed to the *drawroom.cgi* script in the following form:

```
<IMG SRC="drawroom.cgi?background=backgroundname,0,0
                &object1=object1name,x,y
                &object2=...">
```

The navigation links and description for the room are also appended after the image. Here is the code for *wander.cgi:*

```perl
#!/usr/local/bin/perl -w
use strict;
use CGI;
use Image::Size;
use Sprite;          # The Sprite module is used to manage the databases

my ($number, $background, $description,
    $north, $south, $east, $west, $objectlist);
my (%file, %name, %x, %y, %width, %height, %area, %url);

# Retrieve the parameters passed in via name value pairs
#
my $query = new CGI;
my $room = $query->param('room');

# Get relevant info from the room database with the Sprite module.
# Sprite allows you to use SQL queries with simple flat text files.
#
my $db = new Sprite;
$db->set_delimiter('Read',   '::');

# Sprite may need to know your operating system; valid strings are:
# Unix, Win95, Windows95, MSDOS, NT, WinNT, OS2, VMS, or MacOS.
$db->set_os('Unix');


# Print the header for the HTML page...do it here so that error
# messages can be sent to the browser...
#
print $query->header(-type=>'text/html');

print <<EndHead;
<HTML>
<HEAD>
<TITLE>Wander Room #$room</TITLE>
</HEAD>

<BODY>
EndHead

# Query the room database (rooms.db) and select all of the columns of
# data for the room in question.
#
my @data = $db->sql (<<EndSQLQuery);
        select * from rooms.db
        where (Room = "$room")
EndSQLQuery

# The data is returned as a multi-dimensional array.
# The first element gives the return status of the query.
#
```

```
if (!(shift @data)) {
   die "There was an error reading from the room database!<BR></BODY></HTML>";
}


# De-reference the return data and store it in our local room variables
#
foreach my $row (@data) {
    ($number, $background, $description,
     $north, $south, $east, $west, $objectlist) = @$row;
}


# The object list for the room is stored in the database
# as a comma-delimited list
#
my @objects = split ",", $objectlist;


# Find information about the objects in the room by querying the object
# database (objects.db)...
#
foreach my $object (@objects) {
    @data = $db->sql (<<EndSQLQuery);
        select * from objects.db
            where (Object = "$object")
EndSQLQuery

    if (!(shift @data)) {
        print "There was an error reading from the object database!<BR>";
    }

    # De-reference the object data and store it in the various
    # object info hashes
    #
    foreach my $row (@data) {
        $file{$object}     = @$row[1],
        $name{$object}     = @$row[2],
        $x{$object}        = @$row[3],
        $y{$object}        = @$row[4],
        $url{$object}      = @$row[5];
        ($width{$object}, $height{$object}) = imgsize($file{$object});
        $area{$object}     = $width{$object} * $height{$object};
    }
}


$db->close;


# Sort the objects by size first, in order of increasing area.
# The objects should be added to the image from largest to smallest.
# The objects should be listed in the MAP element from smallest to
# largest.
#
@objects = sort { $area{$a} <=> $area{$b} } @objects;


# Print the image tag that will call the image creation script
#
```

```perl
print "<IMG SRC=\"drawroom.cgi?background=$background,0,0";
my $count = 0;

foreach my $object (@objects) {
    $count++;
    print "&object$count=".$file{$object};
    print ",$x{$object},$y{$object}";
}
print "\" USEMAP=\"#Room$room\">";

# Print the room description and the navigation links
#
print <<EndHTML;
<P>$description
</P>
<A HREF="wander.cgi?room=$north">North</A> |
<A HREF="wander.cgi?room=$south">South</A> |
<A HREF="wander.cgi?room=$east">East</A> |
<A HREF="wander.cgi?room=$west">West</A>
<BR>
EndHTML

# Print the map element. Each object will be clickable and will
# have a url action associated with it.
#
print "<MAP NAME=\"Room$room\">\n";
for my $object (@objects) {
    print "<AREA HREF=\"$url{$object}\"";
    print "  SHAPE=rect";
    print "  COORDS=\"$x{$object},$y{$object},";
    print $width{$object}  + $x{$object} . ",";
    print $height{$object} + $y{$object} . "\">";
    print "There is $name{$object} here.<BR>\n";
}
print "</MAP>";
print "</BODY></HTML>";
```

The *drawroom.cgi* script uses the GD module to combine the background and objects into a single image on the fly. It is called from the image tag of the page generated by *wander.cgi* with parameters indicating the background GIF file and the individual object GIF files. Each parameter consists of a comma-delimited list of the image filename and the x, y offset of each object. The background image has a hard-coded offset of 0, 0 to keep a consistent format. The URL that would invoke the *drawroom.cgi* script would look something like:

```
<IMG SRC="drawroom.cgi?background=images/background.gif,0,0&
object1=images/frobotz3.gif,100,100&object2=images/frobotz1.gif,150,100&
object3=images/frobotz2.gif,0,0" USEMAP="#Room2">
```

The code for *drawroom.cgi* is as follows:

```
#!/usr/local/bin/perl -w
```

```
use strict;
use CGI;
use GD;

my (%filename, %x, %y);

# Get the parameters. Since there is not a fixed number of objects
# in any particular room, we must get the list of parameter names
# and iterate over the number of parameters.
#
my $query = CGI->new;
my @paramnames = $query->param;

# Each parameter consists of a comma-delimited string containing
# the filename, and x and y offset of the object.
#
foreach my $paramname (@paramnames) {
    ( $filename{$paramname},
      $x{$paramname},
      $y{$paramname} ) = split ",", $query->param($paramname);
}

open(INFILE, $filename{'background'});
my $background = newFromGif GD::Image(\*INFILE);

my ($overlay, $white);
```

One important thing to note is the order that the objects are placed onto the background image. Each of the objects was sorted by area in the *wander.cgi* script and passed into *drawroom.cgi* in order of increasing size. The largest object should be placed first, and smaller objects placed on top. This will reduce the risk of larger objects completely obscuring smaller objects in case their regions overlap. Note that this is the reverse of the order that the regions are listed in the <MAP> element.

```
# Copy the objects onto the background.
# Grep will return only the parameter names beginning with the string 'object.'
#
for (reverse (grep /^object/, @paramnames)) {
    open INFILE, $filename{$_};
    $overlay = newFromGif GD::Image(\*INFILE);

    $white = $overlay->colorClosest(255, 255, 255);
    $overlay->transparent($white);
    $background->copy($overlay, $x{$_}, $y{$_}, 0, 0, $overlay->getBounds());
}

# Print the MIME header, then the GIF data
#
print $query->header(-type => 'image/gif',
                     -expires=>'-1s');
binmode(STDOUT);
print STDOUT $background->gif;
```

9

Moving Pictures: Programming GIF Animation

This chapter will tell you how to program GIF animations. GIF animation should be thought of as flip book animation. Just as a flip book is not an appropriate format for *Fantasia,* GIF animation is not an appropriate format for long works, large images, or sequences that require many frames per second to be effective. Also, any sort of presentation that necessitates interaction with the user will require another solution based in Java, JavaScript, or some other language or plug-in. GIF animation does have strengths, however, the foremost of which include:

- *No plug-ins needed.* The user looking at your web page will not be required to have a specially configured browser or download a plug-in to view your animation.

- *Independent of server configuration.* GIF animation requires nothing fancy on the server-side either. Animations are served just like every other image because they are just regular GIF files.

- *Quick feedback for the user.* GIF animations are streaming animations and as a multimedia format are as efficient as you can get. Contrast the response time of a GIF animation with an animation done in Java and you will understand their appeal.

This chapter starts with a brief discussion of the general concepts behind GIF animation, and then presents seven common problems and solutions. The last section in the chapter details the implementation of GIFscript, a language for describing the construction of animated GIF files as an alternative to GUI-based programs such as GIFBuilder or GIF Construction Kit. As another alternative, the Gimp has some sophisticated plug-ins for creating and optimizing GIF animations. See Chapter 7, *Web Graphics with the Gimp*, for a complete discussion of the Gimp and its animation plug-ins.

Anatomy of a GIF89a Animation

Every GIF file is potentially a self-contained animation. It is a common misconception that only GIF89a files can contain multiple images; the GIF87a specification also allows for multiple images in the same file. There's actually nothing preventing web browsers from reading multi-image GIF87a files and displaying them as a series of frames in an animation. The reason that animations are implemented in the GIF89a format is that the GIF89a specification defines a number of *extension blocks* that allow information to be embedded in a file that can be used by web clients to control aspects of the animation, such as the number of times it loops or how the refresh between frames is handled. These extension blocks are either included in the file's header or they are associated with a particular image in the sequence.

There were four extension blocks introduced with the GIF89a specification. Only two of these, the *Application Extension* and the *Graphics Control Extension*, are of concern when dealing with animations. The Application Extension is a block within the file that may be used to store information to be used by a particular application. Netscape used the Application Extension Block to implement looping. This extension has been widely adopted so you could say that the loop extension is no longer "application specific," but it is an Application Extension Block nonetheless. The Graphics Extension Block contains information about the interframe delay, the disposal method used between frames, the transparency index for a scene, and the user input flag that can be used to synchronize the presentation of scenes with user interaction.

In this chapter we will use the PerlMagick module to write scripts as examples for the topics covered. Currently other GIF manipulation libraries, such as GD.pm, do not implement the inclusion of multiple images within a file, and cannot be used for animation work. ImageMagick allows multi-image files and also allows you to open MPEG documents, which enables you to create animation files with digital video editing software, save them as MPEGs, and use ImageMagick to convert them for use as GIF animations.

Looping

Netscape was the first company to define an Application Extension for specifying the number of times the browser should iterate through the sequence of images when rendering the file, which is why this extension block is sometimes referred to as the *Netscape Loop Extension*. However, it has been universally accepted as the *de facto* means of indicating the number of loops, so it is probably good practice to just refer to it as the Loop Extension. Just remember that as an Application

Extension Block, it is not part of the GIF89a specification, and support for this information is left to the client.

With PerlMagick, you can define an infinite loop by setting the `loop` attribute of an image to 0. By setting the loop attribute, you are adding an Application Extension Block to the file with the appropriate value. The default value for `loop` is 1, which means the animation should play through once and end with a still final frame. The `loop` attribute must be set for the *entire* image sequence, as in:

```
use Image::Magick;
my $image = new Image::Magick;
$image->Read(qw(scene0.gif scene1.gif scene2.gif scene3.gif));
$image->Set(loop=>0);          # Setting an infinite loop for the sequence
```

A looping extension that is associated with only a particular scene within the sequence will be ignored by the browser. That is, the following will not have the desired effect:

```
$image->[3]->Set(loop=>0);   # Won't work: an attempt to loop a particular
                             # scene
```

Disposal Methods

The *Disposal Method* is a number within the Graphics Control Extension Block that indicates how an image frame is to be disposed of when the next image in the sequence is displayed. The number is an integer between 0 and 3 that corresponds to one of the following methods:

0   No method specified

1   Do not dispose of this image before displaying next image

2   Restore the area occupied by this image to the background color before displaying the next image

3   Restore the area occupied by this image to the last image that was defined with a disposal method of 0 or 1 before displaying the next image

Figure 9-1 shows the original image of a sample animation. Figures 9-2 and 9-3 show the impact of various disposal settings.

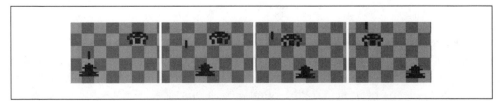

Figure 9-1. The original image file with a transparent background, appearing as a checkerboard pattern

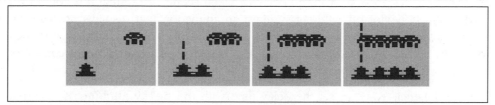

Figure 9-2. Disposal method = 0 (no method specified) or 1 (do not dispose); these methods layer the individual scenes on top of one another, creating a trail. Most browsers interpret a disposal method of 0 to mean "do not dispose."

Figure 9-3. Disposal method = 2 (restore to background); this method will replace the area taken up by the previous frame with the background color. Most browsers have not implemented a disposal method of 3 (return to previous).

The graphics control block can appear anywhere within the file, so the disposal method may be set for individual scenes within a sequence. The default setting for the disposal method of each scene is 0. To implement objects moving against a static background, use a disposal method of 3. This will refresh the area taken up by a scene with part of the last image in the sequence that was defined with a disposal method of 0 or 1 (note that this is not fully implemented in some versions of Netscape, and possibly other browsers). For example:

```
use Image::Magick;
my $image = new Image::Magick;
$image->Read(qw(scene0.gif scene1.gif scene2.gif scene3.gif));
$image->Set(disposal=>3);        # Set all scenes as 'dispose to previous'
$image->[0]->Set(disposal=>1);   # Specify the first image as the static
                                 # background
```

For the image created by this script, scenes 0 and 1 will have a disposal value of 1 (do not dispose) and scenes 2 and 3 will have a value of 2 (restore to background color).

Interframe Delay

The amount of time that the browser should wait before displaying the next image in the sequence may be defined by the *DelayTime* field of the Graphics Control Extension Block. This value is always represented in hundredths of seconds (e.g., 6,000=one minute). If the delay time is set to 0, the client should display the scenes as fast as possible, with no delay between scenes. Note that this could lead to different behavior on different systems; an animation that displays properly on your test system could run too fast on a faster system. It is generally a good idea to specify a minimum delay time so that you have the maximum level of control of the end result of your efforts.

With PerlMagick you can set the delay time with the `delay` attribute. Acceptable values are in the range 0 to 65,535, which is an upper limit of approximately 11 minutes. The delay time can be set for the sequence as a whole, or for individual scenes within a sequence:

```
use Image::Magick;
my $image = new Image::Magick;
$image->Read(qw(scene0.gif scene1.gif scene2.gif scene3.gif));
$image->Set(delay => 400);        # Set delay time to 4 sec. for every scene
$image->[2]->Set(delay => 200);   # Set delay time to 2 sec. for the third
                                  # scene
```

If the *User Input Flag* is also specified for the scene, the browser should continue to display the sequence either when the delay period is over or when input is received from the user.

Local and Global Palettes

The GIF89a specification allows you to specify a *local palette* for each individual scene in a file, or a *global palette* that defines the colors for all of the scenes in a file. Some browsers have a problem with local palettes when the palette for the next image in a sequence is loaded before the currently displayed image is disposed. This results in a flashing effect if the two scenes have significantly different local palettes.

By default, PerlMagick creates a local palette for each image in a file. To create a global color palette with PerlMagick, set the `colors` attribute of the sequence to 256 and call the *Quantize()* method to perform the color reduction (the `color` attribute can actually be set within the *Quantize()* method call). This will create the smallest necessary palette from each of the local palettes and create a single palette containing all of the colors used in the file. If the total number of colors exceeds 256, the palette is intelligently reduced to 256 by the ImageMagick color reduction routines. If there are transparent colors within the image, set the `colorspace` attribute to `Transparent` first to preserve the transparency.

Here's an example:

```
use Image::Magick;
my $image = Image::Magick->new;
$image->Read(qw(scene0.gif scene1.gif scene2.gif scene3.gif));
$image->Quantize(colorspace=>'Transparent', colors=>256);
```

Currently ImageMagick does not actually create a single global palette for the entire file. It actually creates a single palette based on the local palettes, and then replaces the individual local palettes with this global palette. This behavior may change in the future, but the end effect is the same as a single global palette.

Transparency

Each image within a GIF file may have an associated Graphics Control Block, which can mark one color index in the image's color table as transparent. When a color index is marked transparent, the web browser will simply ignore pixels with the same color index. One transparency index may be assigned per image if each image has a local palette. If an image is using the global palette, it will have the same (if any) transparent color as defined for the global palette.

Interlacing

Interlacing is set as part of the header information for the entire file. It is generally used as a means of displaying some information about an image as the image stream is being loaded. Most browsers have disabled interlaced rendering for GIF files containing more than one image. This is primarily because an animated GIF might be looped, making the interlacing scheme useless after the first time around, or because the "fade-in" effect of the interlacing may ruin the flow of the animated action. Check your browser to see if and how interlaced multi-image files are handled.

User Input

The GIF specification defines a User Input Flag as part of the Graphics Control Extension Block. If this flag is true, the client should wait for some sort of interaction from the user (a mouse click or a keyboard stroke) before showing the next scene in the sequence. You may ask why such an extension would be necessary in a world with JavaScript and Dynamic HTML. The User Input Flag actually allows you to encode a rudimentary level of interactivity directly within the document, rather than as event handlers within the display engine. It would allow you to program a file as a slide presentation, for example.

As of this writing, this extension has not been implemented in the popular web browsers. Check your browser's documentation to see if it is supported.

Seven Easy Pieces with PerlMagick

Because the PerlMagick module implements the full GIF89a specification and allows us to include multiple images in a single file, we will use it to create some useful solutions to common GIF animation problems. Two of the seven following "recipes" show examples of moving graphical elements called sprites around in an animation ("#1: Simple Sprites" and "#2: Several Simple Sprites"); two illustrate some built-in features of PerlMagick that simplify certain tasks ("#3: Applying an Effect Iteratively" and "#4: Producing a Separate File for Each Frame"); one is a utility script for breaking an image into a regular grid so that parts of it can be animated separately ("#6. Splitting an Image"); one shows a combination of image-splitting and applying an effect iteratively by allowing you to define a window through which a graphic can continuously scroll ("#5: Scrolling an Image Through a Frame"); and the last example reconstructs a split image by generating an HTML table ("#7: Reconstituting Split Images").

But first, a quick review of PerlMagick concepts. PerlMagick uses an object interface to its methods and attributes. An image object that has been instantiated with `new Image::Magick` can read in image files of many formats with the *Read()* method. An image object may be passed to another image object with the *Clone()* method. Several images can reside within the same image object. Each of these individual images are referred to as *scenes* and can be retrieved by treating the object as a reference to an array. For example:

```
$image2 = $image1->[3]->Clone();
```

In this line, the image object `$image2` will be assigned a copy of the fourth frame of `$image1`. The image or sequence of images is written to a file with the *Write()* method. If the `adjoin` attribute of the image object is set to 1 (which is the default value), the entire sequence will be written as a single multi-image file, if the specified format supports multi-image files (like GIF does). If `adjoin` is 0, each image in the sequence will be written to a separate file with the scene number appended to the name of the file (see "Producing a Separate File for Each Frame").

Another useful tool for creating animated GIFs is the *convert* program that comes with the ImageMagick distribution. It has a command line that implements all of the methods and attributes available to PerlMagick and more. It can be very useful for doing quick tasks like reversing a sequence of images:

```
convert gif:image.gif[19-0] revimage.gif
```

This call to *convert* will read in the first 20 scenes of *image.gif* in reverse and write the reversed sequence to the file *revimage.gif*. Of course, the same can be done with PerlMagick, with a bit more overhead:

```
#!/usr/local/bin/perl -w

# reverse.pl
```

```
# Reverse the sequence of scenes in an animated GIF.
#
use strict;
use Image::Magick;

my ($filename, $status, $image);

if ($filename = $ARGV[0]) {
    my $image = new Image::Magick;
    my $revimage = new Image::Magick;

    $status = $image->Read("$filename");              # Read in entire sequence
    die "Couldn't open file $filename!" if "$status";

    $revimage->Read("$filename".'['.(@$image-1).'-0]');  # Write in reverse
    $revimage->Write("$filename.reversed");
    print STDERR "Done!...\n";
} else {
    print "Please provide the name of a multi-image GIF...\n";
}
```

For a more complete discussion of the ImageMagick utility functions and PerlMagick, see Chapter 5, *Industrial-Strength Graphics Scripting with PerlMagick*.

And now, seven easy pieces.

#1: Simple Sprites

As an example of moving small graphical elements (called "sprites" from now on) around the frame of an animation, let's use the "Hello World" of GIF animation, a simple bouncing ball (shown in Figure 9-4 with its disposal method set to 1).

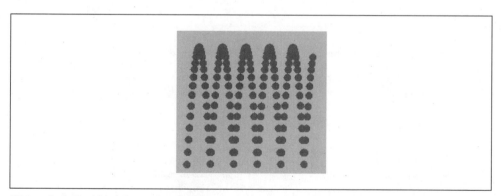

Figure 9-4. Yep, it's a bouncing ball

The first thing that sets sprite-based animation apart from simple flipbook animation is that the sprite has some sort of rule system or function governing its movement. In the case of the bouncing ball, the ball needs a function that will simulate its bouncing through space. That is, a function that will give a value of x and y

(the horizontal distance travelled and the height above some defined ground level) and given a value of *t* (time). In this case we will use a sine wave to model the trail of the ball, where each value of *x* is proportionate to *t* (the ball travels a fixed number of pixels in the *x* direction for each unit of time). If we define a value for the bounce (maximum height), the ground (the *y* row of the image off which the ball will bounce), and a length (the period of the sine wave, or the length of two bounces), we can represent this function as:

```
y = int(ground - abs((bounce * sin(x/length) * 2 * pi)))
```

The second thing that we need to know about sprite animation is that each sprite in the sequence should be placed within the frame by setting the offset of the upper left corner of the sprite. This is accomplished with PerlMagick by setting the **page** attribute to the desired coordinate. For example, to offset the second scene of a sequence so that the upper left corner is at 50, 50 relative to the rest of the sequence, use:

```
$image->[1]->Set(page =>'+50+50');
```

See Chapter 5 for a more detailed description of geometry syntax in PerlMagick.

In the following example, each sprite (ball) is added as an individual scene and the offset of the scene is set with the **page** attribute. Note that the y coordinate is actually the upper left-hand corner (the 0, 0 coordinate relative to the sprite) of the scene. Thus, the bottom of each ball is actually bouncing off of the 210th row of the image, because **$ground = 200** and the height of the sprite is 10 pixels. It really doesn't matter in this case, but you should be aware of this behavior and subtract the dimensions of the sprite if exact positioning is critical.

```
#!/usr/local/bin/perl -w

# ball.pl
# One bouncing ball; the quintessential animation example.
#
use strict;
use Image::Magick;

my $background = new Image::Magick;

my $pi = atan2(1,1) * 4;        # We'll need pi for the sine function
my $bounce = 150;               # How high to bounce in pixels
my $ground = 200;               # Pixel row number marking "ground"
my $length = 60;                # The horiz. length of 2 bounces
my $increment = 1;              # number of x to travel pixels per scene
my ($y, $imagecount) = (0, 0);

# First draw the ball
#
my $ball = new Image::Magick;
$ball->Set(size=>'10x10');
```

```
$ball->Read(filename=>'xc:white');
$ball->Draw(primitive => 'FillCircle',
            points => '5,5 8,8',
            pen => '#FF0000');          # a red ball
print STDERR "Adding balls...\n";
for (my $x = 0; $x < $length; $x += $increment) {

    # A sine function with negative values "reflected" around the
    # x axis gives a nice approximation of bouncing ball behaviour.
    # $ground is the x-axis for the sine wave (the "ground" off which
    # the ball will bounce), $bounce is the magnitude, and
    # $length is the period. (also: sin is in radians)
    #
    $y = int($ground - abs(($bounce * sin(($x/$length) * 2 * $pi))));

    # Use the page attribute to move the ball to the apprpriate coordinate
    # and set the disposal method to 'replace with background color'
    #
    $background->[$imagecount] = $ball->Clone();
    $background->[$imagecount]->Set(page    => "+$x+$y",
                                    dispose => 2);

    $imagecount++;
}


$background->Set(loop => 0);       # Make it loop infinitely
$background->Transparent('#FFFFFF');
print STDERR "Writing file...\n";
$background->Write("gif:bouncingball.gif");
print STDERR "Done!...\n"
```

Five frames from the resulting animation are shown in Figure 9-5. This example is fairly trivial, in that it only deals with a single sprite moving through a frame. The next example illustrates a means of efficiently handling several sprites with different functions describing their movement.

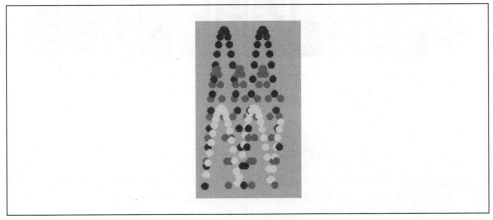

Figure 9-5. A composite image of the frames from the animation resulting from the script balls.pl

#2: Several Simple Sprites

Let's say that there were three balls in the above example: red, green, and blue. If you simply add each sprite as a separate scene, each ball will only appear in the sequence once every three frames, resulting in a flashing effect. What you need to do is compose the three sprites to a single larger sprite that represents that scene in the sequence.

There is a fairly straightforward mechanical algorithm for adding more than one sprite per scene to a sequence. It consists of five steps:

1. Create a scene with a transparent background.

2. Calculate the x and y values for each of the sprites. Also calculate the minimum x and minimum y values.

3. Add the sprites with the *Composite()* method to the scene created in step 1.

4. Crop the scene to the smallest bounding box that contains all of the sprites. Generally this is the rectangular area defined by the points (x_{min}, y_{min}) and $(x_{max}+sprite_{width}, y_{max}+sprite_{height})$.

5. Add the scene to the sequence and offset it so that the upper left corner is at (x_{min}, y_{min}) with the **page** attribute.

In the case of the three bouncing balls, the x values will be the same for each of the balls in each scene. Thus we only need to calculate the value of y_{min} to accurately place the composite sprite. Some scenes from the resulting sequence of images are shown in Figure 9-6 with a gray background added to delineate the bounding box of each scene.

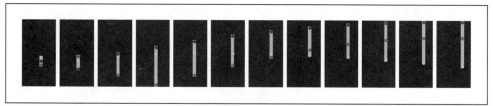

Figure 9-6. Several reduced frames from the animation, on a black background to show the bounding box of each scene

Here's the script for several simple sprites:

```
#!/usr/local/bin/perl -w

# balls.pl
# Three bouncing balls are merged into each scene of action,
# which is optimized to take as little space as possible.
#
use strict;
```

```perl
use Image::Magick;

my $imageout = new Image::Magick;     # The final output image
my $tempimage = new Image::Magick;    # Used as a temp image
my $blank = new Image::Magick;        # The blank background on which
                                      # to composite the sprites
my $balls = new Image::Magick;        # This holds the images of the sprites

# Draw three balls (red, green, blue) in three separate
# scenes of a single image file
#
my @color = ('#FF0000', '#00FF00', '#0000FF');
foreach my $ball (0..2) {
    $balls->Set(size=>'10x10');
    $balls->Read('xc:white');
    $balls->[$ball]->Draw(primitive => 'FillCircle',
                          points => '5,5 8,8',
                          pen => shift(@color));
}

my $pi = atan2(1,1) * 4;              # Calculate pi for the sine function
my @bounce = (150, 100, 200);         # How high to bounce
my @ground = (200, 200, 200);         # What row to bounce from
my @length = (60, 85, 100);           # The horiz. period of the bounces
my ($width, $height) = (256, 256);    # Max. width and height of frame
my $increment = 1;                    # number of x pixels to travel pixels per scene
my $numsprites = 3;                   # Number of sprites

# Now set up some variables needed to calculate the bounding box
# of the sprites...
#
my (@y, @ysort, $ymin);
my $imagecount = -1 ;                 # Initialize the image count

# Set the max. frame size of the combined sprites. Because of the
# way we are structuring the calculation of the sprites' positions,
# we know that the width will always be the width of the sprite.
#
$blank->Set(size=>"10x$height");
$blank->Read('xc:white');             # Read in a white background

# Now construct the scenes:
#
for (my $x=0; $x < $width; $x+=$increment) {

    # In order to find the bounding box of the sprites, we must
    # find the minimum of the y coordinates. First calculate
    # all of the y coordinates, then sort them and take the min.
    #
    foreach (0..$numsprites-1) {
        $y[$_] = int($ground[$_] -
              abs(($bounce[$_] * sin(($x/$length[$_]) * 2 * $pi))));
    }
    @ysort = sort {$a<=>$b} @y;
```

```
    $ymin = shift @ysort;

    $tempimage = $blank->Clone();      # Copy the blank image
    $imagecount++;

    # Now add each of the sprites to the single composite sprite
    #
    foreach (0..$numsprites-1) {
        $tempimage->Composite(compose=>'Over',
                              image=>$balls->[$_],
                              geometry=>"+0+".$y[$_]);
    }

    # Now crop the composite sprite to its bounding box.
    # Crop('0x0') will do this.
    #
    $tempimage->Crop('0x0');

    # Copy the cropped composite sprite to the next scene in
    # the output image
    #
    $imageout->[$imagecount] = $tempimage->Clone();

    # Set the offset of the composite sprite and set the disposal method
    #
    $imageout->[$imagecount]->Set(page=>"+$x+$ymin",
                                  dispose=>2);
    undef $tempimage;                       # Clean up temp image

}
$imageout->Transparent('#FFFFFF');      # Set the transparency for the sequence
$imageout->Set(loop=>0);                # Infinite loop
print STDERR "Writing file...\n";
$imageout->Write("gif:bouncingballs.gif");
print STDERR "Done!...\n";
```

#3: Applying an Effect Iteratively

You can use the toolbox of effects provided by PerlMagick to create animations that swirl, throb, or blur. This is done by reading in a clean copy of the original image and applying the appropriate effect to the scene. For this example, we will write a script that will apply the *Blur()* method to each scene in the animation, resulting in a sequence of images that go from blurriest to least blurry.

The way that the script is set up, the effect is applied to the entire sequence with each iteration. Thus, if we iterate *n* times, the first scene will have the effect applied *n* times, and the final scene will have it applied one time. If the opposite ordering is desired (i.e., from less blurry to more blurry), simply reverse the sequence with ImageMagick's convert utility:

```
convert effectsout.gif[19-0] effectsout.reverse.gif
```

You can then append this reversed image to the original to create a "throbbing" effect:

```
convert effectsout.gif effectsout.reverse.gif effectsout.throbbing.gif
```

Here's the script that, when applied to the image of a web access counter, creates the sequence of images in Figure 9-7.

```
#!/usr/local/bin/perl -w

# applyeffect.pl
# Create an animated GIF by repeated applying an effect to
# an image, in this case, Blur.
#
use strict;
use Image::Magick;
my $image = new Image::Magick;
my $filename = 'counter.gif';          # The file to use
my $frames = 20;                       # Number of scenes

for (0..$frames-1) {
    $image->Read("$filename");
    # Apply a blur to the entire sequence. This means that the
    # first scene will be blurred $frames times, and the last will
    # be blurred but once...
    #
    $image->Blur(100);
}
$image->Set(loop=>0);                  # Infinite loop
print STDERR "Writing file...\n";
$image->Write('gif:effectsout.gif');
print STDERR "Done!...\n";
```

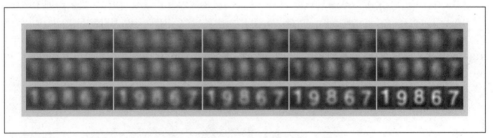

Figure 9-7. The sequence of images created by running applyeffects.pl on an image of a web access counter

#4: Producing a Separate File for Each Frame

Sometimes you may want to break up an animated GIF into separate files for each scene in the original file. This capability is built into the PerlMagick package. Actually, it can be done even more easily with the *convert* utility:

```
convert +adjoin somefile.gif
```

Or you can do it in Perl:

```
#!/usr/local/bin/perl -w

# separate.pl
# Create a separate file for each scene in an animated GIF.
#
use strict;
use Image::Magick;
my ($filename, $status, $image);
unless ($filename = $ARGV[0]) {
    die "Please provide the name of a multi-image GIF...\n";
}

my $image = new Image::Magick;
$status = $image->Read("$filename");    # Read in entire sequence
die "Couldn't open file $filename!" if "$status";

# The adjoin attribute indicates whether the sequence should
# be saved as a single file or not. Here we choose not.
#
$image->Set(adjoin=>0);
print STDERR "Writing scene files...\n";
$image->Write("$filename");
print STDERR "Done!...\n";
```

This will create a file for each scene where the name of each file is the original filename with the scene number appended. For example, if the original file was called *somefile.gif* and it consisted of five frames, the following files would be created: *somefile.gif.0, somefile.gif.1, somefile.gif.2, somefile.gif.3, somefile.gif.4*. Note that this behavior can cause problems on DOS-based machines, which will truncate the scene number. Also, you should move the extension *.gif* to the end of the string before using it on the Web, as many browsers use the extension to determine the content of the image. These problems can be accommodated by changing the `write` statement in the Perl script so that the frame number is placed at the beginning of the name, as in:

```
foreach (0..@$image-1) {
    $image->[$_]->Write("$_$filename");
}
```

#5: Scrolling an Image Through a Frame

The following script will take a single image and will create a continuous scrolling effect (right to left) through a fixed-width frame. Some frames from the resulting sequence are shown in Figure 9-8. The frame width is determined by the *$framew* variable and the smoothness of the overall effect is set with the *$increment* variable (a larger value creates choppier movement, but a smaller file size).

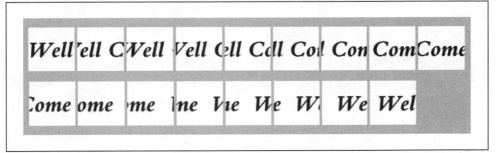

Figure 9-8. Some frames from the resulting animation of an image scrolling seamlessly through a frame

To create a seamlessly scrolling image, take a copy of the first frame's worth of rows from the original image and append them to the right of the image. The *Crop()* method is iteratively applied to this image, with the result saved as the next scene in the sequence.

```perl
#!/usr/local/bin/perl -w

# scroll.pl
# Scroll an image through a frame from right to left.
# The width of the frame is determined by $framew and
# the number of frames to produce is given by $frames
#
use strict;
use Image::Magick;

my ($filename, $status) ;
my $framew = 100;
my $frames = 10;

unless ($filename = $ARGV[0]) {
    die "Usage: perl scroll.pl filename\n";
}

my $image = new Image::Magick;        # composite source file
my $tempimage = new Image::Magick;    # used later as a temp image
my $imageout = new Image::Magick;     # final output image

$status = $image->Read("$filename");
die "$status" if "$status";
my ($width, $height) = $image->Get('width', 'height');

# The increment of each scene shift (in pixels) is given by $increment.
# A smaller increment will produce smoother action and larger files.
#
my $increment = 15;

print STDERR "Creating scenes...\n";
my $count = -1;
```

```perl
# We will use Image::Magick's Roll() and Crop() functions
# to shift the image with each frame and crop to an appropriate size.
#
my ($rollgeometry, $cropgeometry);
for (my $x=0; $x < $width; $x+=$increment) {
    # Set up the geometry strings for the next roll and crop
    #
    $rollgeometry = $framew."x$height+$x+0";
    $cropgeometry = $framew."x$height";

    # The Clone() method copies the content of $images
    # into the temporary image.
    #
    $tempimage = $image->Clone();
    $count++;
    print STDERR "Roll $rollgeometry\n";
    $tempimage->Roll("$rollgeometry");          # Roll it
    print STDERR "Cropping\n";
    $tempimage->Crop("$cropgeometry");          # Crop it


    # Now copy the area to the next frame of the output image.
    #
    $imageout->[$count] = $tempimage->Clone();
    undef $tempimage;                           # Clean up
}

$imageout->Set(loop=>0);                        # Set infinite loop
print STDERR "Writing file...\n";
$imageout->Write("gif:out.$filename");
print STDERR "Done!...\n";
```

#6. Splitting an Image

Sometimes you may want to cut up an image into smaller pieces. This could be because you wish to reconstruct the pieces of the image using a table, or because you only want to animate part of the image and delete those tiles that do not change between scenes. The following script will take an image name and the number of rows and columns into which the image will be split. For example:

```
perl split.pl someimage.gif 4 3
```

would split the image *someimage.gif* into four rows and three columns, creating twelve separate output files (if *someimage.gif* consists of a single image).

The algorithm is simple:

1. Create lists defining the horizontal and vertical cropping grids. Each element of the grid lists should be the upper left coordinate of the corresponding tile. The size of a tile should be determined by calculating the difference between an element in the list and the next element in the list. Because of rounding

errors, the last element in each list should be the width or height of the image, in case the number of tiles per row or column is not an even multiple of the dimensions of the image. For example, splitting a 257×257 pixel image into four rows and three columns would produce the following horizontal and vertical crop grid lists:

```
# Horizontal crop grid list
(0, 85, 170, 257)          # Note the extra 2 pixels in 3rd column

# Vertical crop grid list
(0, 64, 128, 192, 257)     # Note the extra pixel in the 4th row
```

2. Create each frame by traversing the cropping grid lists and cropping the source image appropriately.

This script saves each of the tiles with the (x, y) coordinate of the upper left-hand corner of the tile appended to the filename. If the original image contains multiple scenes, the scene number is also appended to the filename. Thus,

```
somefile.230.454.0
```

would be the tile in the first scene with its upper left corner at (230, 454). This makes it easy to reconstitute the entire image sequence by iterating through the tiles and adding them to the appropriate scenes with the appropriate offsets.

```perl
#!/usr/local/bin/perl -w

# split.pl
# Split all of the images within a file into segments.
# The command line parameters are the filename, number of rows,
# and number of columns.
#
use strict;
use Image::Magick;

my ($filename, $hgrid, $vgrid, $status) ;

# Check to see if the three required parameters are provided...
# $vgrid is the number of rows, $hgrid is the number of columns
#
unless (($filename = $ARGV[0]) && ($vgrid = $ARGV[1]) && ($hgrid = $ARGV[2]))
{
    die "Usage: perl split.pl filename rows columns\n";
}

my $images = new Image::Magick;           # source file
my $images2 = new Image::Magick;          # used later as a temp image
$status = $images->Read("$filename");     # file may be multi-image
die "Couldn't open file $filename!" if "$status";

my $imagecount = @$images;                # number of scenes

print STDERR "Writing scene files...\n";
```

```perl
my ($width, $height) = $images->Get('width', 'height');
my @x = (0);              # This list contains the x values of the crop grid
my @y = (0);              # This contains the y values

# Set up the horizontal crop grid.
# Because of rounding errors, not all tiles will be the same
# dimensions unless $width is a multiple of $hgrid. To make sure
# we don't lose any pixels, the last tile in the grid should
# always crop to the width of the image...
#
foreach my $count (1..$hgrid) {
    if ($count == $hgrid) {
        push @x, $width;        # crop to the edge
    } else {
        # otherwise the width of the tile should be int($width/$hgrid)
        #
        push @x, $count * int($width/$hgrid);
    }
}

# Now set up the vertical crop grid...
#
foreach my $count (1..$vgrid) {
    if ($count == $vgrid) {
        push @y, $height;
    } else {
        push @y, $count * int($height/$vgrid);
    }
}

my $geometry;             # This will be the string passed to Crop()

# The Cropping loop...
#
foreach my $ycount (0..$vgrid-1) {
    foreach my $xcount (0..$hgrid-1) {
        # The Clone() method copies the content of $images
        #
        $images2 = $images->Clone();

        # Set up the geometry string
        #
        $geometry = ($x[$xcount+1] - $x[$xcount])."x".
                    ($y[$ycount+1] - $y[$ycount]).
                    "+$x[$xcount]+$y[$ycount]";
        print STDERR "Crop $geometry\n";
        $images2->Crop("$geometry");

        # Write a file consisting of the cropped tile for
        # each scene. The filename will be in the form
        # filename.x.y.scene where x and y is the coordinate of
        # the upper left coordinate of the tile.
        #
        $images2->Set(delay=>rand(1000), loop=>0);
```

```
                        $images2->Write("gif:$x[$xcount].$y[$ycount].$filename");
            undef $images2;       # Clean up
        }
    }
    undef $images;                # Clean up
    print STDERR "Done!...\n";
```

#7: Reconstituting Split Images

One way to reconstruct the split images is by using an HTML table. You should use a table as the structural element rather than simply stringing the images together because a table may be embedded anywhere in the document and will still be laid out properly.

To automatically generate the HTML necessary to reconstruct a split image, add the following code to the *split.pl* script in place of the loop marked "Cropping loop." It will print the HTML table to STDOUT, which may be cut and pasted into a web page, or redirected to a file:

```perl
print STDERR "Paste this HTML into your document...\n";
print STDOUT "<TABLE BORDER=0 CELPADDING=0 CELLSPACING=0>";
print STDOUT "  <TR><TD>";

# The Cropping loop...
#
foreach my $ycount (0..$vgrid-1) {
    foreach my $xcount (0..$hgrid-1) {
        # The Clone() method copies the content of $images
        #
        $images2 = $images->Clone();

        # Set up the geometry string
        #
        $geometry = ($x[$xcount+1] - $x[$xcount])."x".
                    ($y[$ycount+1] - $y[$ycount]).
                    "+$x[$xcount]+$y[$ycount]";
        $images2->Crop("$geometry");

        # Write a file consisting of the cropped tile for each scene.
        #
        $images2->Set(delay=>rand(1000),    # this is for a special effect
                    loop=>0);
        $images2->Write("gif:$x[$xcount].$y[$ycount].$filename");
        print STDOUT "<IMG SRC=\"$x[$xcount].$y[$ycount].$filename\">";
        undef $images2;       # Clean up
    }
    print STDOUT "<BR>";
}
print STDOUT "</TD></TR>";
print STDOUT "</TABLE>\n";
```

If you send *split.pl* a multi-image file, the file is split into the requisite number of tiles, and each tile is itself a multi-image file. You will notice that the script above sets the delay between frames to a random pause between 0 and 10 seconds. If you recompose a multi-image file with this script, you get an interesting "video wall" effect as the different tiles are animated at different frame rates and they go in and out of phase. Figures 9-9 and 9-10 show some scenes of an example of this application.

Figure 9-9. An interesting effect may be achieved by splitting a multi-image file into tiles with different delay rates. This figure shows the three scenes in the original multi-image file

Figure 9-10. This figure shows six frames from the resulting reconstructed image, as it would be displayed in the browser

GIFscript, an Animation Scripting Language

Most of the documentation that you will find about constructing animated GIFs will start with the suggestion "First get a program like GIFBuilder or GIF Construction Set. Then you'll be ready to start making animated GIFs. . . ." These are programs that are available primarily for Windows and Macintosh machines, and they typically have a graphical user interface that will allow you to place images in a certain order and adjust the attributes of the various images in the sequence. The value of these programs is that they allow you to represent the layout of the animation file in a succinct, readable form, and they allow you to describe the layout of files in a more abstract form than what is achievable by the Perl scripts we have looked at so far. However, most of these tools still require you to assemble the scenes of the animation by hand, and they do not store the description of the sequence in a form that is separable from the actual image file. That's where GIFscript comes in.

GIFscript is actually just a syntax and an interpreter that lets you define the sequence of images in a GIF animation as a simple text file. The interpreter is a Perl script that acts as an interface to the ImageMagick routines that do all the image crunching work. We'll call the text file that describes the animation a *frame description file*.

A GIFscript frame description file consists of a number of instructions for adding images to an animation and for controlling the attributes of the images such as the interframe delay, the placement of scenes within the frame, the transparent colors, etc. An instruction may be followed by an optional list of parameters and an optional block of attributes or other instructions. A GIFscript frame description file looks like this:

```
# Set the current output file to these two files
output niceanimation.gif
       niceanimationcopy.gif

# Add an image with the add instruction
# The following block can contain attributes
add marx.gif
    {     delay 23
          page = +20+20     }

# You can add more than one image at a time
# The attributes will be set for each of them
add sartre.gif fromm.png
    {     delay=500          }

# Attributes can be of the form attribute=value or attribute value
add wfpc02.gif {     delay 1220 }

# ImageMagick routines are applied to the last image added
emboss

# The repeat instruction repeats a block of instructions
repeat 2 {
    add engels.gif { delay 100 }
    add sunset.gif { delay = 1440
                             page +100+100 }
}
```

This file is passed to the GIFscript interpreter, *gifscript.pl* (described later), like this:

```
perl gifscript.pl filename.txt
```

The valid GIFscript instructions are:

init

> The `init` instruction takes a list of attributes in the block section. It will
> ignore any tokens in the parameter list. The attributes are applied to the image
> sequence as a whole. For example, the GIFscript command:

```
init { delay=200 loop=0 }
```

> will set the interframe delay and the loop attributes for the entire image
> sequence, overriding previous values.

add

> The `add` instruction takes a list of filenames in the parameter list and an
> optional block of attributes to be set for each of the images in the parameter
> list. Each of the specified files will be added as separate scenes within the
> image sequence and the attributes will be applied to each in turn. For exam-
> ple:

```
add file1.gif file2.png file3.jpg { delay=100 dispose=1 }
```

> will read in the three images and set their `delay` and `dispose` attributes.

repeat

> The `repeat` instruction takes a number as a parameter (additional parameters
> will be ignored) and a block of GIFscript instructions. The instructions in the
> block will be executed the appropriate number of times. For example:

```
repeat 2 {
    add file1.gif file2.gif
}
```

> would be the same as writing:

```
add file1.gif file2.gif file1.gif file2.gif
```

output

> The `output` instruction takes a filename or a list of filenames as a parameter.
> If there is a block associated with the output instruction it is ignored. The
> default output filename for the final image sequence is *outfile.gif*. With the
> `output` instruction, you can redirect the output so that it is written to a differ-
> ent file or several different files. The image from that point on will be redi-
> rected to the specified files. For example:

```
output fileout.gif
```

> will change the current output file to *fileout.gif*. When the GIFscript inter-
> preter recognizes an output instruction, it checks to see if images have already
> been added to the sequence. If they have, the images are first written to the

current output file name, then the output filename is changed. In the following example:

```
add file1.gif file2.gif
output fileout.gif
add file3.gif file4.gif
```

the images *file1.gif* and *file2.gif* would be written as scene 0 and scene 1 of *outfile.gif* (the default value) and the images *file3.gif* and *file4.gif* would be written as scene 0 and scene 1 of *fileout.gif*.

Various PerlMagick method names

You can also specify a number of PerlMagick methods as GIFscript instructions. These instructions take an optional block of attributes and ignore tokens in the parameter list. The valid methods are:

AddNoise	Composite	Flop	Normalize	Shear
Annotate	Contrast	Frame	OilPaint	Signature
Average	Crop	Gamma	Opaque	Solarize
Blur	CycleColormap	Implode	Quantize	Spread
Border	Despeckle	Label	Raise	Swirl
Box	Draw	Magnify	ReduceNoise	Texture
Charcoal	Edge	Map	RollRotate	Threshold
Chop	Emboss	Minify	Scale	Transparent
Clone	Enhance	Modulate	Segment	Trim
Colorize	Equalize	Montage	Shade	Wave
Comment	Flip	Negate	Sharpen	Zoom

All of these instructions are simply executed by PerlMagick with the *Mogrify()* method. They are only applied to the current scene within the sequence, so in the following:

```
add file1.gif file2.gif file3.gif
emboss
```

only the third scene in the sequence (the image from *file3.gif*) would be embossed.

The attributes that may be set from GIFscript correspond exactly to the attributes that may be set with PerlMagick. They are:

Adjoin	Colors	delay	gamma	loop	pixel
Background	Colorspace	dispose	interlace	matte	quality
Bordercolor	Compress	dither	iterations	mattecolor	texture

The GIFscript interpreter consists of four sections:

- The main body
- The *processtokens()* subroutine
- The *parseinstruction()* subroutine
- The *extractattributes()* subroutine

The main body takes care of reading in the frame description file and extracting a list of valid tokens, which it passes on to the *processtokens()* subroutine. For example, the file shown at the beginning of this section would be translated into the following token stream (shown here delimited by ampersands):

```
output&niceanimation.gif&niceanimationcopy.gif&add&marx.gif&{&delay&23&page&+
20+20&}&add&sartre.gif&fromm.png&{&delay&500&}&add&wfpc02.gif&{&delay&1220&}&
emboss&repeat&2&{&add&engels.gif&{&delay&100&}&add&sunset.gif&{&delay&1440&pa
ge&+100+100&}&}
```

As an added feature, the code from the GIFscript frame description file that created it is added as a comment to any files that are written with PerlMagick's *Comment()* method. You can view the comment field of a GIF file with ImageMagick's *identify* program with the **-verbose** option.

The main body of the GIF script interpreter follows:

```perl
#!/usr/local/bin/perl -w

# gifscript.pl
# Implements a GIFscript interpreter. GIFscript is a portable,
# compact way of describing the layout of animated GIF files
# as regular ASCII format files.
#
use strict;
use Image::Magick;

# Take the name of the GIFscript 'frame description file' as a parameter.
#
my $filename = $ARGV[0];
my ($imagefile, @params, $params, $status, $value);
my ($line, @tokens);

# $instructions is the list of valid instructions
# Create a string of valid instructions separated by '|'
# for use in later regexes
#
my $instructions = join "|",
    qw(init add repeat output
        AddNoise Annotate Average Blur Border Box Charcoal Chop Clone Colorize
        Comment Composite Contrast Crop CycleColormap Despeckle Draw Edge
Emboss
        Enhance Equalize Flip Flop Frame Gamma Implode Label Magnify Map Minify
        Modulate Montage Negate Normalize OilPaint  Opaque Quantize Raise
```

```
            ReduceNoise RollRotate Scale Segment Shade Sharpen Shear Signature
            Solarize Spread Swirl Texture Threshold Transparent Trim Wave Zoom
            );

    # $attributes is the list of valid attributes
    #
    my $attributes = join "|",
        qw(adjoin background bordercolor colors colorspace compress delay
            dispose dither gamma interlace iterations loop matte mattecolor
            pixel quality texture
            );

    my @outfiles = qw(outfile.gif);        # Set the default filename

    # First open the frame description file
    #
    if (defined($filename)) {
        open INFILE, $filename
            || die "There was a problem opening the file $filename\n";
    } else {
        die "Please provide the name of a frame description file...\n";
    }
    my $imagecount = -1;
    my $image = new Image::Magick;

    print "\nProcessing frame description file $filename...\n";
    while (<INFILE>) {
        $line = $_;

        # First pass: remove all whitespace, blank lines, and comment lines
        #
        if ( ($line =~ /^\s*#/) | ($line eq "\n") ) {
            # A comment or blank line; do nothing
        } else {
            $line =~ s/^(\s+)//;       # Remove leading space
            $line =~ s/{/ { /g;        # add space around start brackets
            $line =~ s/}/ } /g;     # add space around end brackets
            $line =~ s/(\s+)/ /g;  # replace all whitespace with single spaces

            # Allow a equal sign surrounded by an arbitrary amount of
            # whitespace (or no whitespace) to separate an attribute
            # from a value; simply remove the '='
            #
            $line =~ s/($attributes)\s*=\s*(.+?)\b/$1 $2/g;
            push @tokens, split ' ', $line;
        }
    }

    processtokens(@tokens);      # The processtokens subroutine does all the work.

    foreach my $outfile (@outfiles) {
        print "Writing to file $outfile\n";
        $image->Write("gif:$outfile");
    }
    exit (1);
```

The *processtokens()* subroutine is called for the first time in the main body of the script, and may be called recursively if a *repeat* instruction occurs and a block of instructions has to be processed. Essentially, the routine traverses the list of tokens and, upon finding a valid instruction, processes the instruction.

```perl
sub processtokens {
    # This subroutine will take a list of tokens as a parameter
    # and parse them. Valid instructions will be processed, invalid
    # instructions will be ignored.
    #
    my @tokenlist = @_;

    # The attribute hash holds attributes to be sent to ImageMagick;
    # $token is the current token;
    # $params is the parameter list for an instruction;
    # $block is the block associated with an instruction (if any);
    # $remainder is the rest of the script that remains to be parsed.
    #
    my %attributehash;
    my ($token, $params, $block, $remainder);

    while (@tokenlist) {
        $token = shift @tokenlist;            # get the next token

        # If it is a valid instruction, process;
        # otherwise, look at the next token
        #
        if ($token =~ /^($instructions)$/) {

            # Most instructions will need the information in the
            # parameter list and the block; parse these first...
            # the parseinstruction subroutine returns references
            # to a parameter token list, the tokens in the block,
            # and the list of remaining tokens...
            #
            ($params, $block, $remainder) = parseinstruction(@tokenlist);
            @tokenlist = @$remainder;          # de-reference remainder

            # Process each instruction:
            #
            # if 'init', the attributes in the block should be applied
            # to the entire image.
            #
            if ($token eq 'init') {
                %attributehash = extractattributes(@$block);
                $image->Set(%attributehash);
                $imagecount++;
            }

            # If 'output', the image sequence compiled so far should
            # be written to the current output file(s) and the
            # output file for the remainder should be set to whatever
            # is in the parameter list...
            #
```

```perl
        elsif (($token eq 'output') && defined(@$params)) {
            if ($imagecount >= 0) {
                foreach my $outfile (@outfiles) {
                    print "Writing to file $outfile\n";
                    $image->Write("gif:$outfile");
                }
                $imagecount = -1;
                undef @$image;
            }
            @outfiles = @$params;
        }

        # If an 'add' instruction, the files in the parameter list
        # should be added to the current image sequence.
        # Also apply the attributes in the block (if any) to the
        # current image in the sequence.
        #
        elsif (($token eq 'add') && defined(@$params)) {
            %attributehash = extractattributes(@$block);
            foreach my $filename (@$params) {
                print "ADDING: $filename...\n";
                $status = $image->Read($filename);
                if ("$status") {
                    print "Couldn't add $filename!\n";
                } else {
                    $imagecount++;
                    $image->[$imagecount]->Set(%attributehash);
                }
            }
        }

        # If 'repeat', the instructions contained in the block should be
        # repeated for the number of times indicated by the first
        # parameter
        elsif ($token eq 'repeat') {
            if (defined(@$params[0])) {
                foreach (1..@$params[0]) {
                    processtokens(@$block);      # recursive
                }
            }
        }

        # Otherwise we just pass the instruction and the attributes
        # contained in the block on to the ImageMagick routines
        # with the Mogrify() method...
        else {
            %attributehash = extractattributes(@$block);
            $image->Mogrify("$token", %attributehash);
        }

    } else {
        print "Ignoring token: $token...\n";      # An invalid instruction
    }
  }
}
```

The *parseinstruction()* subroutine is called whenever a valid instruction is recognized by *processtokens()*. It takes a list of tokens as a parameter and breaks this list up into a list of parameters, a block delineated by brackets, and a list of the remaining tokens. It returns references to the parameter list, the list of tokens in the block, and the list of remaining tokens.

```perl
sub parseinstruction {
    # When an instruction is recognized, break it up into
    # an optional parameter list and an optional block. Return references
    # to the parameter list, the block of tokens list, and the remainder
    #
    my @tokenlist = @_;
    my $token;
    my (@params, @block);
    my $bracketcount = 0;          # allows nested brackets

    $token = shift @tokenlist;

    while (defined($token) &&
           ($token ne '{') &&
           !($token =~ /^($instructions)$/)) {      # stop at an instruction
        push @params, $token;
        $token = shift @tokenlist;
    }

    if (defined($token) &&
        ($token eq '{')) {
        # Start of a block
        $token = shift @tokenlist;
        $bracketcount = 1;
        while (defined($token) && $bracketcount) {
            $bracketcount-- if ($token eq '}');
            $bracketcount++ if ($token eq '{');
            push @block, $token;
            $token = shift @tokenlist;
        }
    }

    # If no block is defined, we still have the look-ahead
    # token. If it's an instruction, put it back on the list,
    # otherwise ignore it...
    #
    if (defined($token) &&
        ($token =~ /^($instructions)$/)) {
        unshift @tokenlist, $token;
    }

    # There will always be an extra } at the end of the block;
    # get rid of it...
    pop @block;
    return ([@params], [@block], [@tokenlist]);   # return references

}
```

The *extractattributes()* subroutine is called whenever an instruction is encountered that needs to look at a block of attributes. It takes a list of tokens and separates them into key value pairs, discarding invalid attributes and attributes without values. It returns a hash of key-value pairs that can be passed directly to PerlMagick's *Set()* method.

```
sub extractattributes {
    # Takes a list of tokens as a parameter, checks to see if each
    # is a valid attribute, checks that the list has a value for each
    # key, and returns the valid attributes as a key=>value hash.

    my @tokenlist = @_;
    my (%returnhash, $token, $value);

    $token = shift @tokenlist;
    while (defined($token)) {
        if ($token =~ /^($attributes)$/) {
            $value = shift @tokenlist;
            if (defined($value)) {
                $returnhash{$token} = $value;
            }
        }
        $token = shift @tokenlist;
    }
    return %returnhash;
}
```

One of the benefits of using a GIF construction system such as GIFscript is that it can act as an intermediate description language that will make automating the creation of animations easier. A program creating GIFscript frame description files doesn't even have to have the PerlMagick package and ImageMagick libraries installed since it is only creating text files.

10

Web Graphics Cookbook

Several idioms have evolved on the Web that are worth examining in depth; the phenomenon of web counters, for example, or the culture of web cams. This chapter provides some reusable examples of common web graphics applications:

- The *BrokenImage module* that enables Perl-based CGI scripts that generate graphics to present error messages to a web browser rather than a generic broken image icon.

- A *web page access counter* that will be updated every time a user views the page. Even though some people rail against counters, they are still a much asked-for feature by new web authors.

- A *JavaScript rollover* example, because rollovers are also a much requested feature, and they are too widely used to be ignored.

- A *Web Cam* how-to.

- A section on providing *ASCII ALT attributes* so that your images may be viewed in some approximation by text-only browsers.

- *Thumbnailing scripts* that will ease the tedium of making thumbnails of large groups of images.

Each recipe is broken down into three sections: a discussion of the problem, what is required for the example, and a discussion of a possible solution or implementation.

The BrokenImage Module

A web page that accesses a dynamically generated image runs the risk of displaying uninformative "broken" images if the script that generates the image fails to successfully complete its operation. The fact that an `<IMG>` element that calls a script from its SRC attribute expects a valid stream of image headers and data can make it somewhat difficult to debug tricky image generation scripts. It would be nice to be able to return an informative error message rather than that generic broken image icon.

Requirements

> CGI Perl module
> GD Perl module

Solution

It is easy to write a Perl module to generate this new kind of broken image icon. The script below may be used like any other Perl module; it is especially useful within CGI scripts that expect a valid stream of GIF image data as their output. The BrokenImage module implements two methods that return two different styles of broken images icons, *black_box()* and *icon()*. The *black_box()* method takes a string of arbitrary length and returns a GIF with the text rendered in yellow on a black box. The *icon()* method takes an error number and returns a GIF with the error number in a gray shadowed box. They may be called from a Perl script with the following code:

```
use BrokenImage;
my $error = new BrokenImage;
$error->black_box("This is the black box method, yellow on black...");
```

or:

```
use BrokenImage;
my $error = new BrokenImage;
$error->icon(9327);
```

These examples will return the GIF images in Figure 10-1. Different styles may be added to the BrokenImage module by adding subroutines to draw different kinds of images using the GD module as described in Chapter 4, *On-the-Fly Graphics with GD*.

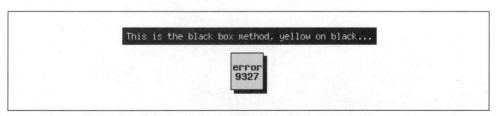

Figure 10-1. The BrokenImage module provides methods for returning meaningful error messages from a CGI script that generates images

The code for *BrokenImage.pm* is:

```perl
#!/usr/bin/perl -w
# The BrokenImage module
#
package BrokenImage;

use strict;
use CGI;          # use the CGI module to write the header
use GD;           # use GD to draw the image

sub new {
    my $proto = shift;                    # allow use as a class or object method.
    my $class = ref($proto) || $proto;    # see perltoot manpage
    return bless({}, $class);
}

# Now define some different styles of broken images for different apps.
#
sub black_box {
    # One style that is a black box with text in yellow
    # Takes a string of text as a parameter.
    #
    my $self = shift;
    my $text = shift;

    my $image = new GD::Image(6 * length($text) + 10, 20);
    my $black = $image->colorAllocate(0, 0, 0);
    my $yellow = $image->colorAllocate(255, 255, 0);
    $image->string(gdSmallFont, 5, 3, $text, $yellow);
    printImage($image);
}

sub icon {
    # An icon with an error code.
    # Takes a short string as a parameter.
    #
    my $self = shift;
    my $code = shift;

    my $image = new GD::Image(43,48);
    my $white = $image->colorAllocate(255, 255, 255);
    my $black = $image->colorAllocate(0, 0, 0);
    my $gray = $image->colorAllocate(213, 213, 213);
    $image->filledRectangle(4, 4, 42, 47, $black);
    $image->filledRectangle(0, 0, 38, 43, $gray);
    $image->rectangle(0, 0, 38, 43, $black);
    $image->string(gdMediumBoldFont,
                   3, 10, "error", $black);
    $image->string(gdMediumBoldFont,
                   int(20-3.5*length($code)), 21, $code, $black);
    printImage($image);
}
```

```
sub printImage {
    # Print the image for the requesting client.
    # Called by each style.
    #
    my $image = shift;

    my $query = new CGI;
    print $query->header(-type    => "image/gif",
                         -expires => '0s');
    print $image->gif;
}

1;    # Modules should return true
```

A Web Page Access Counter

There are a number of qualities that every good web access counter should have. The counter should be:

- *Simple*: Why make a complicated web counter?

- *Object-oriented*: Everything else is object-oriented these days, why not a counter? (Actually, the counter itself won't be object-oriented because it doesn't have to be, but it will use the Broken Image object to display error messages.)

- *Interpreted*: We'll be using Perl, so this shouldn't be a problem.

- *Robust*: It would be nice if the counter had the ability to use different sizes and styles of images for the numbers.

- *Secure*: You don't want other people using your counter on their web page (without your permission).

- *Portable*: It shouldn't be tied to a proprietary web server configuration.

- *High-performance*: The counter's going to be run every time someone hits your page, so it had better be fast.

Sorry, I got my notes mixed up; those are actually the buzzwords for Java, not for web counters. Well, we'll try to take as many into account as we can anyway. Oh, and if you think you need a counter on your web page, fine, do it. Don't let other people boss you around, although diehard bandwidth conservationists may make fun of you.

Requirements

The CGI module
The GD module
The BrokenImage module (described earlier)

Solution

The counter will use the GD module described in Chapter 4 to create the image of the numbers. It will actually just pull in precreated GIF images for each of the digits in the number and merge them into a single GIF file, which it will send back to the browser. The digit images may be one of several interchangeable styles. The style used may be indicated with a parameter passed to the CGI script. The digits used in this example will look like lottery-style ping pong balls, as in Figure 10-2.

Figure 10-2. Each of the digits used by the access counter is stored in a separate GIF file, named 1.gif through 0.gif

These files should be stored in a directory with the name of the style, in this case *lottery*. The web page using the counter can then refer to the style *lottery*, which will indicate that the counter script is to pull the digit images from the *lottery* directory.

The counter script allows for multiple counter files, which means that more than one user on a multi-user system may use the same script to maintain many discrete page counts. The count file is a simple text file that contains two fields of information: the current count and a list of all of the URLs that may use that particular count file. To start a new counter for use on the web page of a new user named Lizzie that resides on a computer in the domain *www.shemp.net*, you would create a file with a unique name (*lizzie.txt*, for example) with the following two lines in it:

```
0
www.shemp.net
```

The first line of the count file is the current count. It should be initialized to 0 or whatever starting number is desired. The second line is a list of all the URLs, or *referrers,* that may use the count file; if there is more than one URL, each URL in the list should be separated by the OR operator (a vertical bar |) and the whole list should be terminated with a newline. All the URLs should be on the same line. For example, if Lizzie had two web pages, one at *www.shemp.net/~lizzie* and one at *www.buckbuck.com/~lizzie*, and she wanted to use the same counter on both pages, she could setup the counter file like so:

```
0
www.shemp.net|www.buckbuck.com
```

This would actually allow any page from the *www.shemp.net* or *www.buckbuck.com* domains to use the counter. To limit use to a single page, use:

```
0
www.shemp.net/~lizzie/home.html|www.buckbuck.com/~lizzie/index.html
```

To allow anyone in the world to use your counter file, just leave out the referrer line.

The count file may reside anywhere on the host computer, as long as the permissions are set correctly. Because the script will have to read and write to the count file, the file should have its owner set to whatever user the web server is running under, and should have read/write permissions for that user. The popular Apache web server, for example, runs as the user nobody by default. If you are running an Apache web server that runs as user nobody on a Unix system, you could set the permissions by typing the following at the shell prompt:

```
chmod 600 count.txt
chown nobody count.txt
```

If the *counter.pl* script resides in the *cgi-bin* directory of your web server (and the counter file named *count.txt* is also in the *cgi-bin* directory), the counter can be included on a web page with an HTML tag like this:

```
<IMG SRC="cgi-bin/counter.pl?countfile=count.txt&style=lottery">
```

The counter script uses the *CGI.pm* and *GD.pm* modules, and the BrokenImage module described earlier in this chapter.

Figure 10-3 shows the counter script in action.

Figure 10-3. Who would have thought that over 30,000 people would want to visit my crummy home page?

```perl
#!/usr/bin/perl -w
# counter.pl
# A web access counter that is Simple, Interpreted, Robust, Secure, etc. etc.
#
use strict;

use CGI;                   # used for parsing params and printing headers
use GD;                    # used to create the image
use BrokenImage;           # used to create an 'error image' in case of an error
use Fcntl qw(:DEFAULT :flock);          # for file locking constants

my $query = new CGI;
my $error = new BrokenImage;

# Retrieve the parameters
#
my $countfile = $query->param('countfile');
my $referer = $query->referer() ;
my $style = $query->param('style');

# If the style parameter is not included, use the default style
#
unless (defined($style)) {
    $style = "default";
}

# If there is no referrer, allow any http request to use the counter
#
unless (defined($referer)) {
    $referer = '';
}

# Open the counter file
#
unless (open COUNT, "+<$countfile") {
    exit $error->black_box("Couldn't open file $countfile...");
}

# Read the counter file data
#
my $count = 0;
flock COUNT, LOCK_EX;          # Place an exclusive lock
$count = <COUNT>;              # The current count
my $users = <COUNT>;           # The list of valid referrers
chop($users);

# Compare the referrer URL with the list of valid
# referrers; if the referrer does not begin with the
# requisite referrer, send back an error
#
unless ($referer =~ /http:\/\/($users)(.*)/) {
    exit $error->black_box('You do not have privileges to access this
counter.');
}
```

```
# Now rewind the filehandle and write the updated count
#
$count++;
seek COUNT, 0, 0;
print COUNT "$count\n$users";
close COUNT;                    # closing releases the lock

# Now create the counter image
#
my $d;                          # A digit image
my $x = 0;                      # The current x offset for the digit
my $trans;                      # A transparent color, if any
my ($digitw, $digith) = (50, 50);  # Maximum width and height of each digit
my ($width, $height) = (0,0);   # The actual w & h of each digit
my $maxh = 0;                   # The max actual height
my @digits = split '', $count;  # A list of digits

# A temporary image
#
my $tmp = new GD::Image($digitw * @digits, $digith);

# Read each digit and composite onto $tmp
#
foreach my $digit (@digits) {
    unless (open DIGIT,"$style/$digit.gif") {
        $error->black_box("Couldn't open $style/$digit.gif.");
    }
    $d = newFromGif GD::Image(*DIGIT);
    close DIGIT;

    # Get the width & height of this digit and save the height
    # if it is the biggest height yet...
    #
    ($width, $height) = $d->getBounds();
    $maxh = $height if ($height > $maxh);

    # Since transparency is not preserved with a Copy,
    # save whether the 'background' of the digit image is transparent
    #
    $trans = (($d->transparent) && ($d->getPixel(0,0)));

    # Copy to the temporary image
    #
    $tmp->copy($d, $x, 0, 0, 0, $width, $height);
    $x+=$width;
}

# Do the equivalent of a crop, trimming off unused background.
#
my $image = new GD::Image($x, $maxh);
$image->copy($tmp, 0, 0, 0, 0, $x, $maxh);

# If the background of the original digit was transparent,
# make the final image background transparent
#
```

```
$image->transparent($image->getPixel(0,0)) if $trans;

# Print it out with an appropriate header
#
binmode STDOUT;
print $query->header(-type => "image/gif",
                     -expires=>'0s');
print $image->gif;
```

A JavaScript Rollover Menu

How do you do that trick where a button image appears to highlight itself or one image replaces itself with another when the mouse passes over it?

Requirements

A JavaScript-capable browser

Solution

Use JavaScript. A JavaScript program may be incorporated anywhere in a web page with the <SCRIPT> element, as in this simple program:

```
<HTML>
<HEAD>
<TITLE>Hello</TITLE>
</HEAD>
<BODY>
<SCRIPT LANGUAGE="JavaScript">
document.write("JavaScript says ", document.title);
</SCRIPT>
</BODY>
</HTML>
```

JavaScript allows you to dynamically access elements within the document and manipulate them, as in this example, which allows the title of the document to be used as data within the body. Combined with the onMouseOver and onMouseOut attributes of a hyperlink element, you can use this capability to dynamically change the image that is displayed based on the user's mouse movements. This is popularly known as a *rollover*. A typical application of a rollover is to highlight a selection from a menu when the mouse passes over it. Figure 10-4 shows such a menu, with two items. When the mouse is not over either of the images, the menu appears as on the left. When the mouse is passed over each item in turn, the appropriate image is highlighted, as in the center and right-hand images. We will use this example to explore JavaScript rollovers in greater depth.

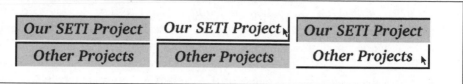

Figure 10-4. JavaScript rollovers are often used to highlight items in a menu when the mouse passes over them

There are a few things we need to know about JavaScript before continuing:

- The **onMouseOver** attribute of a hyperlink element can define a series of Java-Script routines that are to be executed whenever the mouse is moved over the contents of the link (in this case, each link will be wrapped around an image of each menu selection). These routines may be thought of as *event handlers*. The *onMouseOut* attribute defines an event handler that is called when the mouse leaves the confines of the image. Each of these handlers may be a list of valid JavaScript commands or functions defined elsewhere in the page, and must be terminated with a **return true** statement.

- JavaScript defines a number of objects that allow you to refer to and set the attributes for elements of the web page. These objects are created with the *new* method, and their attributes may be referred to with the syntax *object.attribute* (thus, *document.title* is the <TITLE> attribute of the current document in the example at the beginning of this section).

- JavaScript defines an Image object. The Image object has an attribute (**Image.src**) that allows you to read and write the URL of the source image file. This is what makes dynamic in-place image replacement possible. There are also several other read-only attributes of the Image object which correspond to the attributes defined by HTML.

The first step in creating a rollover is to cache all of the images that are to be used in the rollover within JavaScript objects. When the page is first parsed by the web browser, the browser will load all of the cached source images and hold them in off-screen JavaScript objects until they are called for. For the menu highlight example of Figure 10-4, the script would start something like this:

```
<HTML>
<BODY>
<SCRIPT>
    button1on  = new Image; button1off = new Image;
    button2on  = new Image; button2off = new Image;
    button1on.src  = "button1on.gif";
    button1off.src = "button1off.gif";
    button2on.src  = "button2on.gif";
    button2off.src = "button2off.gif";
```

This will cache four images that may later be referred to within a JavaScript script as *button1on, button1off, button2on,* and *button2off.* The next step is to define a simple JavaScript function called *swap()* that we can call from an event handler that will exchange one image with another. The first parameter to the *swap()* function is the name of the target image (as defined by the NAME attribute of the <IMG> element) and the second is the name of the cached image with which it is to be swapped:

```
    function swap(img1, img2) {
        img1.src = img2.src;
    }
</SCRIPT>

<A HREF = "link1.html"
   ONMOUSEOVER = "swap(button1, button1on); return true"
   ONMOUSEOUT  = "swap(button1, button1off); return true">
<IMG NAME = "button1" SRC = "button1off.gif" BORDER = 0>
</A> <BR>

<A HREF = "link2.html"
   ONMOUSEOVER = "swap(button2, button2on); return true"
   ONMOUSEOUT  = "swap(button2, button2off); return true">
<IMG NAME = "button2" SRC = "button1off.gif" BORDER = 0>
</A>
</BODY>
</HTML>
```

This technique may be used to swap any number of images from a single event handler. Suppose you wish to expand on the example of Figure 10-4 by adding a "banner" section that displayed an appropriate image as each of the menu selections was highlighted. This might look something like Figure 10-5.

Using the same approach as the previous example would result in a page that would look like this:

```
<HTML>
<BODY>
<SCRIPT>
    banner0 = new Image;
    banner1 = new Image;
    banner2 = new Image;
    button1on  = new Image; button1off = new Image;
    button2on  = new Image; button2off = new Image;

    banner0.src    = "banner0.gif";
    banner1.src    = "banner1.gif";
    banner2.src    = "banner2.gif";
    button1on.src  = "button1on.gif";
    button1off.src = "button1off.gif";
    button2on.src  = "button2on.gif";
    button2off.src = "button2off.gif";
```

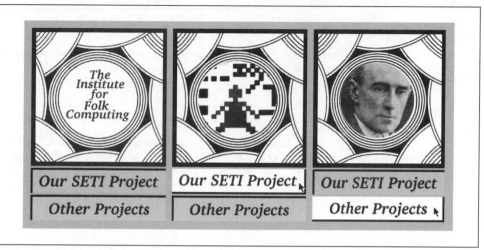

Figure 10-5. Any number of JavaScript functions may be called from a single event handler. In this case, two images are swapped for each onMouseOver and onMouseOut event.

```
            function swap(img1, img2) {
                 img1.src = img2.src;
            }
</SCRIPT>
<IMG NAME = "banner" SRC = "banner0.gif" BORDER = 0> <BR>

<A HREF = "link1.html"
    ONMOUSEOVER = "swap(banner, banner1);
                   swap(button1, button1on); return true"
    ONMOUSEOUT  = "swap(banner, banner0);
                   swap(button1, button1off); return true">

<IMG NAME = "button1" SRC = "button1off.gif" BORDER = 0>
</A><BR>

<A HREF = "link2.html"
    ONMOUSEOVER = "swap(banner, banner2);
                   swap(button2, button2on); return true"
    ONMOUSEOUT  = "swap(banner, banner0);
                   swap(button2, button2off); return true">

<IMG NAME = "button2" SRC = "button2off.gif" BORDER = 0>
</A>
</BODY>
</HTML>
```

This is clearly a lot of code to define a simple two-item menu, and with each option that is added, the code needed to implement that option would add to the clunkiness of the page. This sort of page is more difficult to maintain than a "pure HTML" page. Some might say that a more elegant solution would be to create an extensible JavaScript class that would implement rollovers and have the entire web page generated by JavaScript. I don't recommend this approach because JavaScript is far from a standard feature in web browsers (and even if it is supported, a good number of users have JavaScript turned off) and it is not necessarily easier to maintain a "pure JavaScript" page, either. It is best to keep it simple (and optional) when adding frills such as these features.

A Web Cam

You have a video camera and a computer connected to the Internet (and a web page) and your want to set up a web cam, like one of the hundreds found on sites such as *http://www.camcentral.com.*

Requirements

> A video camera
> Frame-grabbing hardware and software
> A connection to the Internet

Solution

It is perhaps prudent to ask yourself right at the offset if you really need a web cam. The resources involved are not that demanding, but really, why bother putting new images of your fish tank or computer on the Web every 10 seconds? There are a lot of dud web cams out there whose value could be argued on a conceptual art basis and not much else.

The organization I work for once set up a web cam to document a gallery opening on the Web. The opening was four hours long and the camera was trained on the refreshments table so that people could check out the web site before coming to the opening to see if there was any cheese and wine left. Seriously though, people had fun watching themselves appear on the Web every 20 seconds or so. It was not the most utilitarian application of the Web, but it was a fun addition to our web page. Because there was polenta at the opening and the polenta trays happened to be set up right in front of the camera, we called it the Polenta-Cam (see Figure 10-6).

The Polenta-Cam was actually set up on a Windows NT system, but web cams may be set up on any platform. They are particularly popular on GNU-Linux systems, probably because Linux people are a bit more playful with their hardware (and that's as far as I'll go with the sociological exploration of web cam administrators). We'll look at the possibilities on several platforms.

The Polenta-Cam used a regular consumer-grade VHS video camera to take the pictures, and an inexpensive frame-grabber called Snappy made by Play Inc.

Figure 10-6. Three different views taken by the "Polenta-Cam" web cam that was set up to document the refreshment table at a gallery opening

(*http://www.play.com*) that plugs into the parallel port on your computer. Unfortunately, Snappy does not have drivers for Linux or Macintosh systems. The Quick-Cam from Connectix (*http://www.connectix.com*) is a popular, inexpensive camera that is available for most platforms, including Linux and FreeBSD.

The Snappy frame-grabber comes with software that will capture a new image from the camera at user-specified intervals. Most frame-grabbers come with this software. There are also some free and shareware programs that will give you this capability, some of which are listed in Table 10-1. This software should control the camera and allow you to specify regular intervals at which images should be grabbed.

Table 10-1. Several Commercial and Shareware Frame-Grabber Programs

Software	Platform	URL	Cost ($ = approx $25)
Connectix QuickCam Software	Win32, Mac, Linux, FreeBSD	*http://www.crynwr.com/qcpc/*	free
EasySnap	Win32	*http://198.69.204.5/~lmo/easysnap.htm*	?
Ispy	Win32	*http://www.ispy.nl/*	$$
SiteCam	Mac	*http://www.rearden.com/*	$$$$$
Snap n Send	Win32	*http://www.snapnsend.com/*	$$$$
SpyCam	Win32	*http://www.netacc.net/~waterbry/SpyCam/SpyCam.htm*	$
StripCam	Mac	*http://www.stripcam.org/*	beta
Timed Video Grabber	Mac	*http://www.avernus.com/~allon/TVG.html*	beta
Webcam32	Win32	*http://www.kolban.com/webcam32/*	$

The frame-grabber software will snap an image at a regular interval and will write it to a file on the local computer. Getting the image to appear on the Web depends on how your computer is connected to the Internet:

- If the computer to which the web cam is connected is also your web server, simply reference the image saved by the frame-grabber within a web page.

- If you are connected to a LAN that is connected to the Internet, the most elegant solution is to mount the directory in which the web cam image resides so that it is visible to the web server. Exactly how you would do this depends on your LAN configuration, platform, and your access privileges. If you don't know how to do this, consult your system administrator.

- If you connect via a dial-up connection, you must have a program that will automatically ftp the image to the computer on which your web page resides. If you are using a dial-up connection to serve your web cam images, you should probably take a couple of steps back and question whether your web cam is worth it.

When we set up the Polenta-Cam, the web page that displayed the current image was a simple HTML page that contained information about the gallery opening. The page had an HTTP "refresh" header that would automatically reload the page every 20 seconds, which was the same interval at which the images were being saved. A refresh header is written as a META element in the HEAD section of an HTML document:

```
<HEAD>
   <META HTTP-EQUIV="Refresh" CONTENT="20">  <!-- Reload in 20 seconds -->
</HEAD>
```

A web cam can be like a tree falling in the forest; you need people to actually see your pictures for them to have any meaning. And from a user's perspective, web cams can be hit or miss. Visiting an office web cam in the middle of the night can result in a black screen that doesn't really communicate anything. Therefore it is a nice feature to create an archive of past snapshots to give people a better idea of the magnitude of your web cam project. The following Perl script may be set up to run at hourly intervals to create a web page that will contain the current web cam image and a rotating list of snapshots taken at the top of the hour for the past eight hours. The script assumes that the current web cam snapshot is named *nowimg.jpg* and that the archived images are named *image0.jpg* through *image8.jpg*.

```
#!/usr/bin/perl -w
# A Web Cam template script
# Generate a web page for framing a web cam image that contains an archive
# of the past twelve hours of snapshots.
#
use strict;
my $hour = (localtime)[2];       # get just the hour
```

```perl
$hour -= 12 if ($hour > 11);    # convert 12 to 0, 13 to 1, etc.
my @filename = qw(image0 image1 image2 image3 image4 image5
                  image6 image7 image8 image9 image10 image11);

# Copy the current web cam image to the file labelled
# with the current hour
#
open I, "nowimg.jpg";
undef $/;
my $img = <I>;
open O, ">image$hour.jpg";
binmode O;
print O $img;
close O;

# Now print the HTML page
#
open O, ">webcam.html";
print O <<EndPrint;

<HTML>
<HEAD>
<META HTTP-EQUIV="Refresh" CONTENT=20>
</HEAD>
<BODY>
<H1>Current Picture</H1>
<IMG SRC="nowimg.jpg" ALT="Current picture">
<H1>Pictures from the past 12 hours</H1>

EndPrint

for (my $h = $hour-1; $h >= 0; $h--) {
    print O qq(<IMG SRC="$filename[$h].jpg" ALT="Picture taken at
$h:00"><BR>\n);
    print O "Picture taken at $h:00<BR>\n";
}
for (my $h = 11; $h > $hour; $h--) {
    print O qq(<IMG SRC="$filename[$h].jpg" ALT="Picture taken at
$h:00"><BR>\n);
    print O "Picture taken at $h:00<BR>\n";
}
print O "</BODY>\n</HTML>";
```

ASCII ALTs

The ALT attribute of an <IMG> element is used to provide content for browsers that cannot render graphics. In general, the ALT attribute should only be used to provide useful information (see the ALT guidelines in Chapter 2, *Serving Graphics on the Web*). In other words, if you have a bunch of little red ball images as bullets on a page, the ALT text "little red ball" isn't exactly helpful. In some circumstances, however, you may have an image that you would like to have displayed on both a graphics-capable and a text-only browser. The graphical browser could simply display the image, and the text browser could use an alternative representation rendered as ASCII art. ASCII art is an esoteric pastime on Usenet and the Web. It is the art of arranging characters in the ASCII character set to simulate the shades and nuances of the pixels of an image. Of course, not all images may be rendered successfully as ASCII art. Photographs in particular are difficult to identify in ASCII art form unless they are sufficiently large. Some images translate surprisingly well, however, particularly very graphic images like logos or other graphic elements. Figure 10-7 is an example of a web page that uses ASCII art.

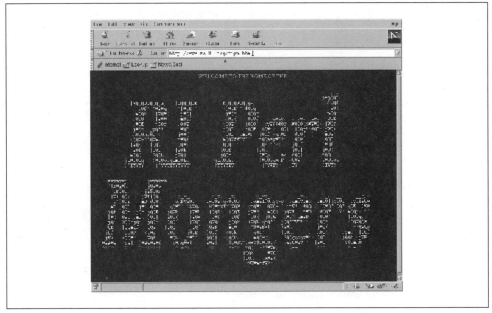

Figure 10-7. ASCII art may be used to sometimes surprising effect on the Web—and it is quick to download

Requirements

The Gimp
AA-Lib

Solution

Text-only browsers simply plop the `ALT` text into the document in place of the image. However, you cannot embed HTML within the `ALT` text string. Thus, the following HTML tag:

```
<IMG SRC="gum.gif" ALT="
AAAAAAAAAAAA
```

```
BBBBBBBBBBBB
CCCCCCCCCCCC
DDDDDDDDDDDD
">
```

would, if you viewed it from a text-only browser, produce the output:

```
AAAAAAAAAAAA BBBBBBBBBBBB CCCCCCCCCCCC DDDDDDDDDDDD
```

And if you attempted to add an HTML linefeed with `<BR>` elements to the end of each line within the `ALT` text string, you would get:

```
AAAAAAAAAAAA<BR> BBBBBBBBBBBB<BR> CCCCCCCCCCCC<BR> DDDDDDDDDDDD<BR>
```

The solution is to wrap the image element up in a `<PRE>` tag, which will maintain the exact formatting of the `ALT` text, and render it in a fixed width font (which, if you're using a text-only browser, will be the standard font anyway). The HTML code:

```
<PRE>
<IMG SRC="gum.gif" ALT="
AAAAAAAAAAAA
BBBBBBBBBBBB
CCCCCCCCCCCC
DDDDDDDDDDDD
">
</PRE>
```

Will render the desired output of:

```
AAAAAAAAAAAA
BBBBBBBBBBBB
CCCCCCCCCCCC
DDDDDDDDDDDD
```

The best way to generate ASCII art is with the Gimp, described in Chapter 7, *Web Graphics with the Gimp*. The Gimp has a plug-in that uses AA-Lib (see Chapter 3, *A Litany of Libraries*) to save an image as an ASCII art approximation. To use the plug-in, the image must be in Grayscale mode and you must select Save As from the *File* menu. Save the image with the extension *.ansi*, or choose AA from the Save Options list in the Save dialog. The AA plug-in will provide you with many options (see Figure 10-8):

Text file

This option will cause the image to be broken down into 2×2 blocks of pixels. Each of these blocks will be represented by the ASCII character that closest matches the luminance of that 2×2 block. This will result in a text file where each line has half as many characters as the image is pixels wide. The same is true for the number of lines in the file. Thus a 300×200 pixel image would be translated to a text file of 100 lines, with each line containing 150 characters.

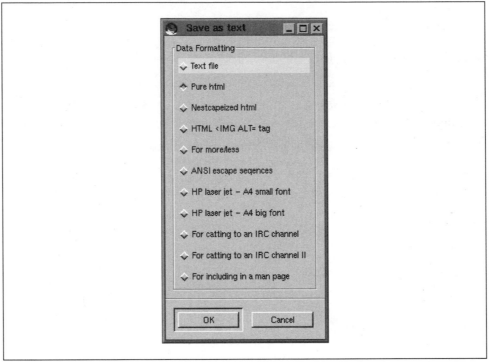

Figure 10-8. The Gimp's AA (ASCII Art) plug-in provides many options for the aspiring ASCII artist

Pure HTML

This performs the same operation as the *text file* option, but it also includes HTML code before and after the image text (the HTML, BODY, and PRE tags). Note that this option is intended for ASCII art that is to be used directly within the body of an HTML document and not necessarily within an <ALT> tag.

Netscape-specific HTML

This option will do the same as *Pure HTML* but will attempt to render the image more accurately by setting the COLOR attribute of the <FONT> tag to various grayscale levels to add depth to the rendition.

HTML <IMG ALT=> tag

This option will automatically wrap up the ASCII art object in an <IMG> element with the <ALT> attribute and <PRE> tags.

Other options

The plug-in provides several other options that are optimized for particular applications, such as:

— A document meant to be viewed with a pager such as more or less

— An ANSI escape sequence (suitable for startup screens)

— As a document to be printed on a laser printer

— As text to be sent to an IRC channel

— As text to be included in a manpage

The resulting ASCII image will always be larger than the source image. The actual "resolution" of the resulting image depends on the font that is used by the display client to render the text. There is really no means for controlling the way that the image is finally viewed. There are, however, a few rules of thumb to follow:

- The AA plug-in subsamples the source image into 2×2 blocks of pixels. Also, a standard terminal window (which most viewers using a text-only browser will be using) is 80 characters wide. Thus, your starting image should be no more than 160 pixels wide (actually 159 pixels due to rounding errors) if you want the final image to stay within the confines of the average user's screen. The typical depth of a standard default terminal window is 25 lines or so.

- The ideal font for displaying ASCII art is a square, fixed font (i.e., the width of each character in the font is the same and the width is equal to the height). A font that is anything other than square will result in an ASCII art image being displayed malproportioned (see Figure 10-9, left). In reality, there are few square fonts, though most text-only displays use fixed width fonts. A typical fixed width font has a width of 6 pixels and a height of 12 pixels. Thus, the height is twice the width, which may be accounted for by scaling the source image by 50% before saving as ASCII art (see Figure 10-9, right) to correct the aspect ratio.

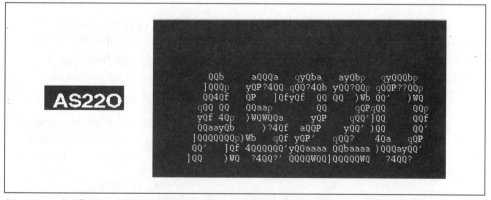

Figure 10-9. The aspect ratio of an ASCII art image will usually have to be adjusted to achieve a similar look and feel to the original image

- You will also have problems with the ASCII art image being larger than the source image. Because each ASCII character represents a 2×2 block, and each ASCII character is (for a 6×12 font anyway) 6 screen pixels wide, the ASCII image will be rendered 3 times larger than the source image. Of course, if different font sizes are used, this ratio will be different. For the case of a 6×12 font, you can get an ASCII image that is almost exactly the same size as the source image by resizing the image to 33% its size before saving. This may not be sufficient resolution to achieve legible output, however, so you should experiment.

- The AA plug-in will actually translate the inverse of the image, so that the ASCII art image must be viewed as white text on a black background in order to give an accurate representation. To reverse this effect, simply inverse the image before saving it.

These rules of thumb, along with the Gimp's AA plug-in, should get you on the road to becoming a true ASCII artist. I look forward to visiting more web pages that are "Best Viewed with Lynx"!

Thumbnailing

You have a bunch of image files (or PostScript or PDF files) for which you would like to create smaller thumbnail images.

Requirements

ImageMagick with Ghostscript support

Solution

The ImageMagick package provides for several methods of thumbnailing images. One high-level method is the Visual Image Directory virtual file format that is defined by ImageMagick. You can convert a number of image files into a Visual Image Directory with the convert utility:

```
convert 'vid:*.gif' png:imageindex.png
```

If ImageMagick is installed on your system, this command will convert every GIF format file in the current directory into a single image that contains thumbnails of all of the images and will save it as a PNG file called *imageindex.png*. The resulting image will look like Figure 10-10.

The Visual Image Directory is essentially a high-level function that uses some of the lower-level ImageMagick routines to read in a bunch of images, scale them into thumbnails, provide borders, labels, drop shadows, and a background, and write it out to the appropriate file. You can access all of these functions via the PerlMagick interface to ImageMagick (described in Chapter 5, *Industrial-Strength Graphics Scripting with PerlMagick*).

Figure 10-10. ImageMagick's Visual Image Directory format provides a quick and easy means of thumbnailing images

The Visual Image Directory has a number of default parameters. It will automatically place at most six thumbnails in a row and will tile the background with a gray granite texture, for example. If you want greater control over the layout and look of your thumbnails, you can use the *Montage()* method within a Perl script as in the following example:

```
#!/usr/bin/perl -w
# A script to create thumbnails using Montage()
#
use strict;
use Image::Magick;
my $img = new Image::Magick;
my $montage = new Image::Magick;

# Read all of the images with a .gif extension in the images subdirectory
#
my $status = $img->Read('images/*.gif');
print STDERR $status;     # will return an error message if there were
                          # problems

# Montage() returns a new image
#
$montage = $img->Montage(geometry    =>'100x100',
                         tile        =>'2x2',
                         borderwidth =>2);
$montage->Write('gif:montageout.gif');
```

This script will produce a grid of thumbnails as a single image as in Figure 10-11. The *Montage()* PerlMagick method allows you to set several attributes of the resulting image. Figure 10-12 (left) is the result of changing the *Montage()* method call in the above example with the following statement:

```
$montage = $img->Montage(geometry=>'100x100',
                         tile => '2x2',
                         background =>'#FFFFFF',
                         font =>'-adobe-times-medium-r-normal--*-*-*-*-*-*-*-*',
```

```
                    pointsize =>12,
                    label =>"%f\n%wx%h\n(%b)",
                    borderwidth => 2);
```

and Figure 10-12 (right) shows the result of changing the statement to:

```
$montage = $img->Montage(geometry    =>'100x100',
                    tile        =>'2x2',
                    title       => 'Directory: images',
                    background  =>'#FFFFFF',
                    label       => "%f",
                    mode        =>'Frame',
                    borderwidth => 2);
```

Figure 10-11. The Montage() PerlMagick function allows you to combine several images into a single thumbnail directory

The `tile` attribute to the *Montage()* method controls the number of thumbnails per row and column. If there are more thumbnails than will fit within the specified tile geometry, additional images will be added to the Image::Magick object. Setting the `adjoin` attribute of the object to 0 will cause each of these groups of thumbnails to be written to a separate file when the *Write()* method is called (see Figure 10-13).

If you have a web site that distributes documents that were also intended as printed documents, you may have an archive of PostScript or PDF files. You may want to create an index of these files with an image of the cover page serving as a link to the ftp site from which they may retrieve the original document. The following script may be run from the command line to generate just such an index. It will create an HTML document and a thumbnail image of the first page of any number of PDF files.

```
#!/usr/bin/perl
# A script that will create thumbnails of the first page
# of any number of PDF files provided on the command line, and will
# also write out a simple HTML index file.
#
```

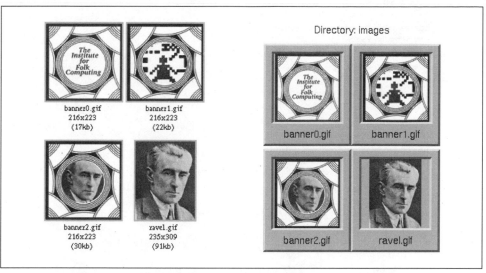

Figure 10-12. The Montage() method accepts several attributes. The font, pointsize, and label attributes may be set to customize the label beneath each thumbnail (left), the mode attribute optionally provides each thumbnail with a frame, and the title attribute may be used to provide a title (right)

Figure 10-13. If the number of thumbnails exceeds the specified number of rows and columns, they will be grouped into separate image files

```
use strict;
use Image::Magick;

# Retrieve the arguments provided on the command line
#
my @files = @ARGV;
die "You must provide a list of files.\n" unless (@files);

my $i=0;
my $img = new Image::Magick;
my $montage = new Image::Magick;

# To only read the first page from each PDF file we must append
# the string '[0]' to each of the file names
#
```

```perl
my @files2read = map { 'pdf:'.$_.'[0]' } @files;

my $status = $img->Read(@files2read);
print STDERR $status;
unless ($status) {
    # Create the thumbnails
    #
    $montage = $img->Montage(geometry=>"150x150",
                             tile=>'1x1',
                             borderwidth=>2,
                             mode=> 'Frame',
                             label=>'%f',
                            );
    # Rather than let PerlMagick name each file, we want to control
    # the naming scheme, so we'll write out each image from this loop.
    foreach my $image (@$img) {
        $montage->[$i]->Write("gif:thumb$i.gif");
        $i++;
    }
}

# Now create an index HTML file with links to each of the
# original documents and include the image of each first page
# as the content of each hyperlink.
#
open O, ">pdfindex.html";
print O "<HTML><BODY>";
$i = 0;
foreach my $file (@files) {
    print O qq(<A HREF="$file"><IMG SRC="thumb$i.gif"></A>\n);
    $i++;
}
print O "</BODY></HTML>";
```

If, for example, you had a directory called *pdfdocs* that contained the following PDF files:

```
GimpUserManual.pdf
ImageMagick.pdf
hoosick.pdf
```

you could run the script to batch process the files with the following at the command line:

```
perl pdfconvert.pl pdfdocs/*.pdf
```

This would create three image files in the directory in which the script was run called *thumb0.gif, thumb1.pdf,* and *thumb2.pdf,* and an HTML index of the documents called *pdfindex.html.* Note that this is not a CGI script; it is a batch-processing script that may be run periodically by the web site administrator. The web page that is created by the script is shown in Figure 10-14.

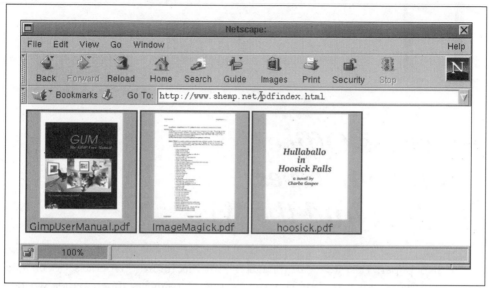

Figure 10-14. The pdfconvert.pl script creates an HTML index of a group of PDF files. An image of the first page of each PDF document serves as an ftp link to the document.

References

The Connectix Quick Cam Third Party Driver Page:

http://www.crynwr.com/qcpc/

The Genericam "webcam templates" Page:

http://occonnect.com/johnqpublic/index.html

11

Paperless Office?
Not in Our Lives:
Printing and the Web

People like paper. Despite years of talk about the future "paperless" electronic office, and the obvious environmental concerns of using as much paper we do, people still like paper. Most companies creating systems to do business electronically over the Web will run into the problem of integrating printing services with their web front end.

Adobe PostScript is the standard programming language for representing printed pages. This chapter will introduce you to PostScript, and will provide a framework for easily generating PostScript code in the form of the *PostScript* package of Perl modules. These modules may be easily integrated into a CGI application, and an example is provided in this chapter. The PostScript package includes three main modules:

- *PostScript::TextBlock.* This module provides a *text block* object to which you can add text of different fonts and sizes. The PostScript code to draw the text block with arbitrary margins at any coordinate on a page may be automatically generated.

- *PostScript::Document.* This module provides a *document* object that allows you to easily generate multipage PostScript text blocks with headers, footers, page numbers, and all.

- *PostScript::Elements.* This module provides methods for generating the PostScript code to draw primitive shapes such as lines, boxes, and circles.

The modules present an easily expandable framework for generating PostScript code from Perl. Before delving into the internals of the PostScript modules, however, we have to learn a little about PostScript. You should learn everything you need to know about PostScript in the next section.

Everything I Needed to Know About PostScript I Learned Here

PostScript is a programming language for representing two-dimensional graphics. It was one of the many innovations of the late 1970s to come out of the Xerox Palo Alto Research Center (PARC) and have a significant impact on the way people think about and use computers today. It was the brainchild of John Warnock, who used the language to research graphic arts applications of computers. In 1982, Warnock and Chuck Geschke formed Adobe Systems and the language that they developed at PARC was redesigned and packaged as PostScript.

PostScript has gone through several revisions over the course of the past 16 years, referred to as PostScript Level I, Level II, and Level III. There are several other page description formats in the PostScript family, each with its own application niche:

- *Portable Document Format* (PDF). PDF files have become a common format for the electronic distribution of documents originally created as print documents in PostScript. PDF files can be printed or viewed on a screen with a viewer such as Adobe Acrobat Reader.

- *Encapsulated PostScript* (EPS). Encapsulated PostScript is a standard format for including a PostScript page description in other page descriptions. An EPS file is simply a one-page PostScript file (representing any combination of text or graphics) that strictly follows the document structuring conventions (described later) and is self-contained to the point that it does not depend on the existence of external graphics states.

- *EPSI and EPSF.* An EPSI (Encapsulated PostScript Interchange/File Format) file is simply an EPS file that is bundled with a bitmapped preview image. An EPSF is an EPSI formatted for the Macintosh, where the PostScript code is stored in the data fork of the file and a PICT format preview image is stored in the resource fork.

- *Precision Graphics Markup Language* (PGML). PGML was proposed to the World Wide Web Consortium as a potential standard for vector graphics represented in XML for the Web. It is a joint specification of Adobe, IBM, Netscape, and Sun and uses the PostScript imaging model described in this chapter. PGML will most likely merge with the VML (Vector Markup Language) proposal into a consolidated vector graphics format. (For a comparison of PGML and VML, see *http://www.xml.com/xml/pub/98/06/vector/vmlpgml.html.*)

PostScript is a page description language. A PostScript file is simply a text file that contains the PostScript code to draw one or more pages. This file is then sent to a PostScript interpreter, which executes the program and draws the pages.

Generally, the PostScript interpreter is embedded in the output device. If you are printing to a laser printer, for example, the laser printer has a built-in a PostScript interpreter that will render the final pages. There is also the Ghostscript package, available for most operating systems, which consists of a number of PostScript rendering tools, including an interpreter and a PostScript viewer. Ghostscript is used by many of the software packages in this book (such as the Gimp and ImageMagick) for parsing and generating PostScript, EPS, and PDF files. It also comes as a standard package in most Linux distributions (see the sidebar "Getting Ghostscript").

Getting Ghostscript

Ghostscript is a free PostScript interpreter. There are actually two different versions of Ghostscript: the Aladdin Systems distribution and the GNU distribution. The distinction is in the licensing. The Aladdin Free Public License allows the free use and redistribution of the Ghostscript source code, but it does not allow the free commercial distribution of the code. The GNU distribution is covered by the GNU General Public License, which allows commercial distribution as a part of an Open Source package. The GNU distribution generally lags behind the Aladdin distribution by a version number or so (as of this writing, the current version of Aladdin Ghostscript is 5.10, whereas GNU Ghostscript is at Version 4.03). Both versions are available at the Ghostscript home page, *http://www.cs.wisc.edu/~ghost/*.

Ghostscript will run on virtually any platform. To view the PostScript examples in this chapter, you must send the code to the Ghostscript interpreter, which will then render the page. In a command-line environment, this can be done by typing at the shell prompt:

```
gs filename.ps
```

where *filename.ps* is the name of the PostScript file generated by the example. There is also a PostScript viewer with a GUI called GSView, which is also available from the main Ghostscript site.

There are several noteworthy aspects of the PostScript imaging model to discuss before we proceed to writing some scripts to generate PostScript files from the Web. We should start with the way that PostScript defines a page.

The Page

A PostScript page is defined in terms of an ideal coordinate system, with the point 0, 0 in the lower left-hand corner, and x and y values increasing up and to the right (see Figure 11-1). This coordinate system is called the *default user space,* and its definitions may be changed within a PostScript program using a number of transformation operators such as *scale, rotate,* and *translate.* The default grid unit size is 1/72 of an inch (a point), which is a convention inherited from the print industry, where the printer's point is defined as 1/72.27 inch. A point on the grid of the page may be represented using any arbitrary number. For example,

```
40.345 60.234 moveto
```

is a valid PostScript statement, and it will be rendered to the resolution of the final output device. The device may not be able to make the distinction between 40.3 and 40.345, so it will render it according to its own internal *device space*, which we do not have to worry about. PostScript's transformation operators imbue the language with a great deal of power for rendering complex page descriptions. They are, however, beyond the scope of this introduction, and are documented in the books on PostScript listed at the end of this chapter.

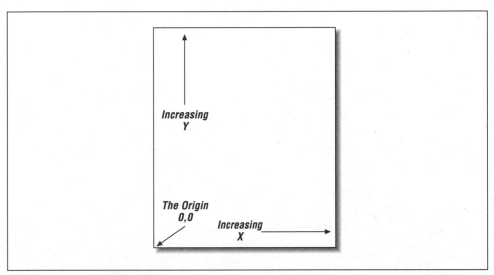

Figure 11-1. The PostScript page is defined in terms of an ideal coordinate system with its origin anchored in the lower left corner

PostScript can handle any arbitrary page size, but the sizes of interest are those corresponding to the standard paper sizes listed in Table 11-1. Note that for the "A" and "B" series of paper (whose sizes are measured in millimeters), each numbered paper type is defined by rotating the previous numbered paper type from "portrait" to "landscape" (so that the width is greater than the height) and vertically splitting the paper in two. Thus, an A0 sheet has the same area as two A1 sheets, four A2 sheets, sixteen A3 sheets, etc. This is useful when the final output is intended for a commercial printer who will print many pages on a single larger sheet that will later be folded or trimmed to the desired final page size.

Table 11-1. Standard Paper Sizes, in Points

Paper Type	Dimension in Points (Width × Height)	Paper Type	Dimension in Points (Width × Height)
Letter (8.5" × 11")	612 × 792	B0	2920 × 4127
Legal (8.5" × 14")	612 × 1008	B1	2064 × 2920
Ledger (17" × 11")	1224 × 792	B2	1460 × 2064
Tabloid (11 × 17")	792 × 1224	B3	1032 × 1460
A0	2384 × 3370	B4	729 × 1032
A1	1684 × 2384	B5	516 × 729
A2	1191 × 1684	B6	363 × 516
A3	842 × 1191	B7	258 × 363
A4	595 × 842	B8	181 × 258
A5	420 × 595	B9	127 × 181
A6	297 × 420	B10	91 × 127
A7	210 × 297	#10 Envelope	297 × 684
A8	148 × 210	C5 Envelope	461 × 648
A9	105 × 148	DL Envelope	312 × 624

A PostScript page is composed by drawing on it with the various drawing operators. When the page has been completely drawn, the *showpage* operator is called to render the page and clear the current page so that the next drawing commands will be executed on a blank page. Further drawing commands will be executed on a clean white page. For example, the following trivial program will output two separate pages (as shown in Figure 11-2):

```
/Times-Roman findfont 48 scalefont setfont
100 400 moveto
(This is Page 1) show
showpage
100 400 moveto
(This is Page 2) show
showpage
```

Some PostScript Functions

Looking at the previous example, you will notice that the parameters associated with an operator are listed before the operator rather than after the operator, as in most procedural languages such as Perl.* This is because PostScript uses an *operand stack* to hold numbers, objects, and the results of executed commands. In line 2 of the example, the integers 100 and 400 are placed on the operand stack. The

---

* PostScript is actually very much like the FORTH programming language.

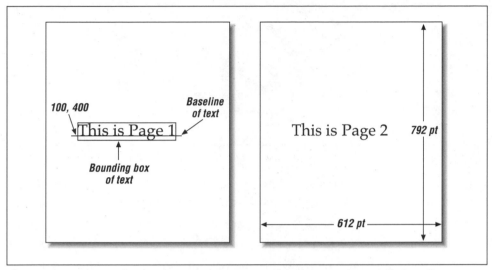

Figure 11-2. Output of a simple PostScript program that draws two pages (reduced)

moveto function then pops the two values from the top of the stack and uses them as its arguments. If the function returns a value, it is pushed on the top of the stack. In the following addition operation, the operand stack would be left with the value 4 on top:

```
2 2 add
```

PostScript is a full-blown programming language with many features and subtleties. In this chapter we will only use a simple subset of the full collection of Post-Script functions. These may be considered the core set of procedures that you will need in order to do anything useful with PostScript. These functions can be strung together to create complex drawings (see Figure 11-3):

```
100 50 moveto
100 100 lineto
50 100 50 0 180 arc
37.5 100 37.5 180 360 arc
50 100 25 0 180 arc
37.5 100 12.5 180 360 arc
.5 setgray
8 setlinewidth
stroke
showpage
```

The *moveto* function sets the current point to a coordinate value without adding to the current path. Think of the *moveto* function as lifting the pen off of the paper and placing it at a new coordinate.

The *arc* function adds the path of a counterclockwise arc to the current path. This function takes five parameters: the x and y values of the coordinate at the center

Figure 11-3. Complex paths may be created by stringing several drawing functions together

of the arc, the radius of the arc, and two angles that describe the sweep of the arc. For example, the path of a complete circle with radius 25 centered at 50, 50 would be created with:

```
50 50 25 0 360 arc
```

Note that this statement will just create the path of the arc. To actually draw the path, you must call the *stroke* function, which will draw the line on the page in the current tint and with the current line width. The tint of the line, expressed as a percentage of black, can be set with the *setgray* function. The current line width can be set with the *setlinewidth* function, where the width is expressed in points.

The *save* and *restore* functions can be used to save a path for later use. If you wish to draw a box that is filled with a 20% gray screen and stroked with a 2-pt black line, for example, you actually have to create two separate paths: one to tell the *fill* function which area to fill and one to tell the *stroke* function how to draw the line. The path for the box may be created once for the *fill*, saved, and later restored for the *stroke* operation:

```
0 0 moveto
0 100 lineto 100 100 lineto
100 0 lineto 0 0 lineto      % Draw a box
gsave                        % Save the current path
.8 setgray fill              % fill with a 20% screen (1 = white, 0 = black)
grestore                     % restore the path before stroking the lines
0 setgray 2 setlinewidth     % Now draw the outline of the box with a 2 pt line
stroke
showpage
```

PostScript files describe a set of commands for drawing arbitrary shapes on a page. Text is drawn in the same way that a line or a circle would be drawn; it is treated as a collection of paths that make up the shapes of the letterforms. These letter-form descriptions are stored in fonts. The current font may be specified within a PostScript program with the *setfont* function, which expects a font dictionary on the operand stack. A font dictionary may be loaded with the *findfont* function.

Once a font dictionary is loaded, it may be scaled to a particular size with the *scalefont* function. Typically, you would specify a font with the sequence:

```
\Times-Roman findfont   % Assuming you have the font Times-Roman on your system
12 scalefont            % set the size of the font
setfont                 % use 12 pt Times-Roman as the current font
```

The *show* function can then be used to draw a string on the page with the current font:

```
\Times-Roman findfont 12 scalefont setfont
(Yowza yowza yowza!) show
```

PostScript is generally used to create vector graphics, but it can also be used to render raster graphics with the use of the *image* function. Image inclusion in PostScript documents can be considered advanced programming territory and beyond the scope of this introduction. However, the PerlMagick module described in Chapter 5, *Industrial-Strength Graphics Scripting with PerlMagick* (which also depends on the Ghostscript interpreter) provides an easy way of reading in a raster image such as a GIF file and generating the PostScript code necessary to render the image. It will even handle color images properly. To generate a printable PostScript page that incorporates a graphic, you would first use Image::Magick to convert the graphic to an EPS file, read the file back in, then print the EPS code at an appropriate place in the PostScript output. In this case we want to use an EPS file for the graphic because an EPS file is simply a chunk of PostScript code that can be embedded in other documents because it is self-contained and does not contain a **showpage** command. An example of using Image::Magick to embed an EPS called *quahog.gif* on a page with some text:

```
#!/usr/bin/perl -w
#
# Using Image::Magick to embed a graphic (as an EPS) within
# a PostScript file
#
use Image::Magick;
my $image = Image::Magick->new;

# Read in a graphic
#
$image->Read('gif:quahog.gif');

# Set the x, y coordinate for the lower left hand corner
# of the graphic with the 'page' attribute. See chapter 5 for
# more details on Image::Magick...
#
$image->Set(page => '+100+200');

# Write out the image to a temporary EPS file, since we
# cannot transfer the EPS code directly to a scalar with Image::Magick
#
```

```
$image->Write('eps:quahog.eps');

# Open the temporary file and read in the EPS code
#
open(EPS, 'quahog.eps') or die "Couldn't open quahog.eps: $!";
undef $/;
my $eps = <EPS>;
close EPS;

# Open the output file and write out the PostScript code
# with the embedded EPS...
#
open(OUT, '>psoutput.ps') or die "Couldn't open psoutput.ps: $!";
print OUT <<EndPrint;
/Times-Roman findfont 48 scalefont setfont
100 150 moveto
(This is an EPS graphic) show
EndPrint
print OUT $eps;
print OUT "showpage\n";
close OUT;
```

The ImageMagick convert utility is also very useful when converting between graphics formats like GIF, JPEG, and PNG and PostScript formats. For example:

```
convert gif:quahog.gif ps:quahog.ps
convert gif:quahog.gif eps:quahog.eps
```

will convert the GIF file to a PostScript file and an EPS file, respectively.

The PostScript Document Structuring Conventions

PostScript is a programming language and, like most modern languages such as C or Perl, it is loose in its definition of what a "properly structured" program is. As with other languages, a poor program structure can cause a PostScript program to be unreadable by programmers and, in certain cases, cause it to be unprintable by certain rendering devices. Certain structuring conventions have been proposed by Adobe that should be followed by PostScript programs that define page descriptions. These conventions are intended to:

- Ensure that each page of the document may be rendered independently of any other page in the document

- Guarantee that the resources needed by the program will be available

- Allow the program to be handled by printer utility programs such as print spoolers and log generators

- Allow the easy generation of cover pages or trailer pages

- Allow overlays such as "draft" markings or watermarks to be optionally added to a document

- Allow the document to be easily included in other documents

- Provide the PostScript interpreter with sufficient information to render the document as efficiently as possible

- Allow better error reporting

Conformance to the Document Structuring Conventions is achieved by adding comments that identify the various parts of the document. PostScript structural comments should begin at the beginning of a line with a %% or %! and end with a newline. Note that Version 3.0 of the Document Structuring Conventions (*http:// www.adobe.com/supportservices/devrelations/PDFS/TN/5001.DSC_Spec_v3.0.pdf*) is a document of over 100 pages describing these rules in depth. The following is an overview of the conventions applicable to this chapter.

A PostScript document is divided into two main sections—the *prolog* and the *body*.

The prolog

The prolog consists of a *header* and a section for defining procedures that are to be made available to every page of the document. The header contains information about the document as a whole, such as the number of pages, title, creator, colors used, etc. The header is terminated with the `%%EndComments` comment. The prolog itself is terminated with the `%EndProlog` comment.

The %! "magic number" and version

Every PostScript program must start with the string `%!`. This string is a two-byte "magic number" that designates the file as a PostScript file. The first line should also contain a string that describes the version of the Document Structuring Conventions that is being used. For our purposes, each PostScript file we generate will start with the line:

```
%!PS-Adobe-3.0
```

Information for print spoolers

Several structural comments have been defined specifically so that print spoolers can obtain information about a document to help identify it. Some of these are:

```
%%Title:
%%Creator:
%%CreationDate:
%%For:
```

The number of pages

The document header should contain the comment `%%Pages:` followed by the number of pages in the document. If this is not known at the outset, the information can be filled in later or included at the end of the document by including the comment `%%Pages: (atend)` in the prolog, then specifying the page count in a comment at the end of the file.

Bounding box

The bounding box of the document is represented as the lower left and upper right corners of the box that describes the maximum bounds of all drawing to be done in the document. Typically, this corresponds to the page size in points (see Table 11-1). For example,

```
%%BoundingBox: 0 0 612 792
```

would indicate a document to be rendered on a Letter-sized page.

Procedural definitions

Typically the procedural definitions section contains a number of custom generic procedures generated by a specific application for drawing text and images. PageMaker, for example, will generate a standard prolog of proprietary functions and definitions that are used to render files formatted by PageMaker. Typically these prologs are copyrighted (and fairly obfuscated), so be careful about copying functions from other files' prologs!

The beginning of the procedures section is marked with a `%%BeginProlog` comment. Each procedure definition should be enclosed within a `%%BeginResource:procset` and a `%%EndResource` comment. Here is an example of a properly commented procedure definition:

```
%%BeginProlog
%%BeginResource:procset
%
% define a procedure to draw a scalable unit circle
%
/circle { 0 0 .5 0 360 } def
%%EndResource
...
%%EndProlog
```

The body

The body of a properly structured document should consist of a succession of page descriptions, with each page starting with a `%%Page:` comment. It is important that each page be *independent* of any other page in the document. This means that the code to generate the page cannot rely on the graphics state left by the previous page, that fonts loaded in the course of rendering previous pages should be reloaded, and procedures defined on other pages should be redefined or moved to the prolog section where they are available document-wide.

The code for each page description should end with a *showpage* operand, which will render the page and clear the current page to white. With these conventions in mind, a typical PostScript program might look something like this:

```
%!PS-Adobe-3.0
%%Title: Felt for Farnsworth
%%Creator: ShempMaker 5.0
```

```
%%For: Tuti Cuandohead
%%Pages: (atend)
%%BoundingBox: 0  0  612  1008
%%EndComments

%%BeginProlog
%%BeginResource:procset
% A procedure could go here
%%EndResource

% A list of procedures can follow

%%EndProlog

%%Page: 1
% Code to draw page 1
/Times-Roman findfont 48 scalefont setfont
100 400 moveto
(This is Page 1) show
showpage

%%Page: 2
% Code to draw page 2
/Times-Roman findfont 48 scalefont setfont
100 400 moveto
(This is Page 2) show
showpage

%%Page: 3
% Code to draw page 3
/Times-Roman findfont 48 scalefont setfont
100 400 moveto
(This is Page 3) show
showpage

%%Trailer
%%Pages: 3
%%EOF
```

Remember that the conventions described above are merely that subset of the Document Structuring Conventions used in this chapter. To do larger scale development work with PostScript, you should retrieve the full DSC document from *http://www.adobe.com.*

Using the PostScript Modules on the Web

As an example, let's design a web page for an online record label. The record label, Apocabilly Records, ships every purchase with a shipping invoice that until now had been created as the merchandise was shipped. Our web page will process the order, and create a PostScript shipping invoice all at once.

Converting HTML to PostScript and Vice Versa

Most web browsers will allow you to print an HTML document on a PostScript printer or to a file. (Simply select your browser's Print option, which usually provides a "to file" option.) However, the quality of the translation will vary from browser to browser, and not all browsers will translate all HTML features accurately. For those "power users" who need something better, there is html2ps, written by Jan Kärrman of Uppsala University.

The html2ps program is written in Perl and is highly configurable, allowing you to choose (if you want to) how nearly every HTML tag will be represented. It handles image inclusion, tables, and even frames. You can get it at *http://www.tdb.uu.se/~jan/html2ps.html.*

Going from PostScript to HTML is much tougher because PostScript does not require very strict document structuring in a valid PostScript program. In fact, none of the several utilities for translating PostScript to HTML that I tested are worth recommending as a general purpose solution. There are, however, some programs that will work in certain circumstances, such as the ps2html script (*ftp://bradley.bradley.edu/pub/guru/ps2html/home.html*) that was written to translate the journals of the John Hopkins University Press.

The web page will take information submitted from an HTML form and call a script called *processorder.cgi,* which will log the order in some sort of database and create the shipping invoice. The web page that the customer would see is shown in Figure 11-4. It is assumed that prior to this point, some sort of shopping cart script was used to catalog the user's selections as he navigated the site.

The HTML code for this web page would look something like the code below. Notice the FORM element with fields to retrieve the customer's name, address, city/state/zip, and the hidden text fields containing the merchandise order and the total amount of the purchase. These fields were created by our hypothetical shopping cart script and will be passed on to the *processorder.cgi* script upon submittal of the form for inclusion in the final shipping invoice.

```
<HTML>
<HEAD>
<META HTTP-EQUIV="Content-Type" CONTENT="text/html">
<TITLE>Apocabilly Records Order Form</TITLE>
</HEAD>
<BODY>

<TABLE CELLSPACING=0 BORDER=0>
<TR><TD VALIGN="TOP">
<P>
<IMG SRC="apocabilly2.gif" WIDTH=287 HEIGHT=96
```

```
            ALT="Apocabilly Records, Since 1998></P>
</TD>
<TD VALIGN="TOP">

<H1>Order Form</H1>
<H2>Order Your Favorite Apocabilly Records Here!</H2>
<P>All orders shipped within 2 working days, COD.</P>
<FORM ACTION="cgi-bin/processorder.cgi" METHOD="POST">

<P>Name:<BR>
<INPUT TYPE="text" MAXLENGTH="80" NAME="name">
<BR>

Address:<BR>
<INPUT TYPE="Address" MAXLENGTH="80" NAME="address">
<BR>
City/State/Zip:<BR>
<INPUT TYPE="text" MAXLENGTH="80" NAME="citystatezip">
</P><P>
<STRONG>Your shopping cart contains the following items:</STRONG>
</P><P>
(1) The Buck Buck Brothers sing Esperanto Love Songs @$12 <BR>
(2) The BeatLess: Meet the BeatLess @$12 <BR>
(1) Old Tyme Tin Can Banjo Tunes @$5
</P><P>

<INPUT TYPE="hidden" NAME="merchandise" VALUE="(1) The Buck Buck Brothers
sing Esperanto Love Songs @$12 \n(2) The BeatLess: Meet the BeatLess @$12 \n
(1) Old Tyme Tin Can Banjo Tunes @$5 \n">
</P><P>

<STRONG>Your total order comes to: $41</STRONG></P>
<P>
<INPUT TYPE="hidden" NAME="total" VALUE="$41">
<INPUT TYPE="submit"  VALUE="Order Now!" >
</P>
</FORM>
</TD></TR>
</TABLE>
</BODY>
</HTML>
```

When the form is submitted, the script is called, which will process the order and create a PostScript invoice on the server that can be later printed and mailed with the merchandise as a paper record of the transaction. If you were to actually implement an online ordering system, of course, you would have to deal with the various security issues involved with processing personal financial information online. This script side-steps that issue and merely prints the invoice:

```
#!/usr/local/bin/perl

use CGI;
use PostScript::TextBlock;
```

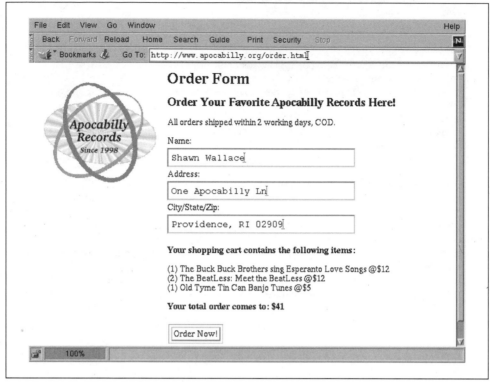

Figure 11-4. The order form for the Apocabilly Records web site will "automagically" create a PostScript invoice when an order is submitted. This invoice can be printed and mailed to the customer with the merchandise.

```
use PostScript::Elements;

# Get the parameters passed into the script
#
my $query = new CGI;
my $name = $query->param('name');
my $address = $query->param('address');
my $citystatezip = $query->param('citystatezip');
my $merchandise = $query->param('merchandise');
my $total = $query->param('total');

# Do whatever needs to be done to place an order here...
# If it is successful, continue...

print $query->header(-type => 'text/html');
print $query->start_html(-title => "Order completed!");
print "Your order has been placed. Thanks!";

# Now let's generate a PostScript invoice to complete this example...
#
my $lines = new PostScript::Elements;
```

```
# First add a 2 pt border with a 36 pt border around the page
#
$lines->addBox(points    => [36,756, 540, 720],
               linewidth => 2);

# Now draw the line dividing the title and the address section
#
$lines->addLine(points => [46,650, 566,650]);

# Finally, draw the line separating the address and order sections
#
$lines->addLine(points => [46, 550, 566,550]);

# Altogether there are five discrete blocks of text, so we will need
# five TextBlock objects...
#
my $tb  = new PostScript::TextBlock;
my $tb2 = new PostScript::TextBlock;
my $tb3 = new PostScript::TextBlock;
my $tb4 = new PostScript::TextBlock;
my $tb5 = new PostScript::TextBlock;

my $date = "10/21/2001";      # We'll hard-code the date; that's one way
                              # to avoid Y2K problems :)

# Now add the text to the various text blocks
#
$tb->addText(text => "Apocabilly Records\n",
             size => 48, leading => 56);
$tb->addText(text => "Ordered on $date\n",
             size => 24, leading => 30);

$tb2->addText(text => "SHIP TO:\n   $name\n   $address\n   $citystatezip\n",
              size => 14,
              leading => 18 );

$tb3->addText(text => "FROM:\n   Apocabilly Records\n   1249 Foo St.\n".
                      "   Hoosick Falls, NY 51209\n",
              size => 14,
          leading => 18 );

$tb4->addText(text => "YOUR ORDER:\n\n$merchandise",
              size => 16, leading => 30);

$tb5->addText(text => "TOTAL: $total",
              size => 16, leading => 30);

# Then generate the code by calling the Write() method for each object
#
my $code = $lines->Write();

# The Write() method for a TextBlock returns a list containing the
# code and the remainder that didn't fit in the specified region.
# In this example, we will discard the remainder, only taking the code
```

```
# and appending it to the code generated thus far.
#
$code .= [$tb->Write(530, 100, 46, 756)]->[0];
$code .= [$tb2->Write(260, 130, 46, 640)]->[0];
$code .= [$tb3->Write(260, 130, 306, 640)]->[0];
$code .= [$tb4->Write(530, 480, 46, 560)]->[0];
$code .= [$tb5->Write(260, 30, 306, 76)]->[0];

# Write the PostScript code to the file called invoice.ps
# in a real system, this should be a unique filename
#
open OUTFILE,">invoice.ps" or die "Couldn't open invoice.ps: $!";
print OUTFILE $code;
close OUTFILE;
```

The final output of this script is shown in Figure 11-5.

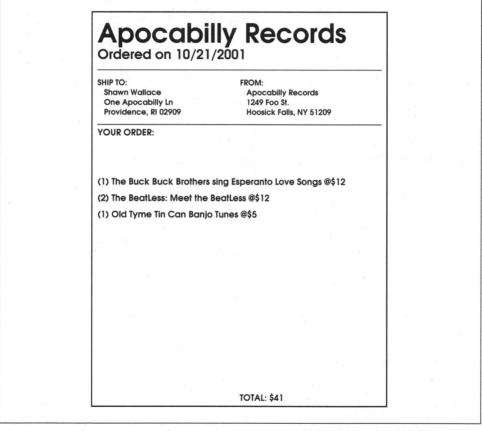

Figure 11-5. A shipping invoice for an imaginary record label, generated via a CGI script using the PostScript package

The PostScript::TextBlock Module

The TextBlock module is an object that may be used to construct a block of text in PostScript. It is meant to be a simple abstract interface for generating PostScript code from Perl scripts or CGI scripts such as the example in the previous section. For now, let's look at some simple examples of using the TextBlock module:

```
use PostScript::TextBlock;
my $tb = new PostScript::TextBlock;
$tb->addText( text => "Hullabalo in Hoosick Falls.\n",
              font => 'CenturySchL-Ital',
              size => 24,
              leading => 26
          );
$tb->addText( text => "by Charba Gaspee.\n",
              font => 'URWGothicL-Demi',
              size => 12,
              leading => 14
          );
print 'There are '.$tb->numElements.' elements in this object.';
open OUT, '>psoutput.ps' or die "Couldn't open psoutput.ps: $!";
my ($code, $remainder) = $tb->Write(572, 752, 20, 772);
print OUT $code;
```

As you can see, the TextBlock module allows the web programmer to create printable documents without any knowledge of PostScript. The PostScript code generated by this script looks like this:

```
0 setgray
0 setgray 20 746 moveto
/CenturySchL-Ital findfont
24 scalefont setfont
(Hullabalo in Hoosick Falls.) show
0 setgray 20 732 moveto
/URWGothicL-Demi findfont
12 scalefont setfont
(by Charba Gaspee.) show
```

The *TextBlock.pm* and *Metrics.pm* modules should be installed in the appropriate directory for your distribution of Perl. If you have downloaded the source from CPAN (which may actually be a newer version than that described here), the Makefile provided should install everything in the proper places. Here's the code for the PostScript::TextBlock module:

```
# TextBlock.pm
# An object that may be used to construct a block of text in PostScript
#
package PostScript::TextBlock;
use strict;
use PostScript::Metrics;

# The valid text block attribute names
#
```

```
my @paramnames = ( 'text', 'font', 'size', 'leading');

# The default attribute values
#
my %defaults = (
                text    => '',
                font    => 'CharterBT-Roman'
                size    => 12,
                leading => 16
               );
```

The *new()* method will return a new TextBlock object. A TextBlock is implemented as an anonymous list of text elements, where an element is a string of text
to be drawn in a certain font, at a certain size and leading.

```
sub new {
    # The constructor method
    #
    my $proto = shift;              # allow use as a class or object method
    my $class = ref($proto) || $proto;# see perltoot man page

    # A text block consists of a list of 'elements',
    # (not to be confused with the PostScript::Elements object)
    #
    my $self = [];

    return  bless($self,$class);
}
```

The *addText()* method will push a new text element onto the list of elements in
the TextBlock. PostScript uses parentheses to delineate a string sent to the *show()*
function so the *addText()* method must escape left and right parentheses.

```
sub addText {
    # Add an element of text to the TextBlock
    #
    my $self = shift;
    my %params = @_;
    $params{'text'} =~ s/(\(|\))/\\$1/g;      # escape parentheses

    # Use the default values if an attribute is not given
    #
    foreach (@paramnames) {
        $params{$_} = $defaults{$_} unless ($params{$_});
    }
    push @$self, { %params };
}
```

The *numElements()* method returns the number of text elements in the TextBlock.

```
sub numElements {
    # Returns the number of elements in the TextBlock
    #
```

```
        my $self = shift;
        return $#{@$self}+1;
    }
```

The *Write()* method takes four parameters: *w, h, x,* and *y,* where *w* and *h* are the width and height of the block (in points), and *x* and *y* specify the upper left corner of the TextBlock (in the PostScript coordinate system). This method returns a string containing the PostScript code that generated the block, and a TextBlock object that contains the portion that doesn't fit within the given bounds.

The algorithm for writing a TextBlock is a little circuitous:

1. An element is taken from the text block and split into words.

2. If a word is longer than the line, the word is split into characters.

3. Words are added to the line until we run out of words.

4. If there are elements left in the TextBlock and we still haven't completed a line, continue with the next element and calculate the maximum leading of the elements included in the line.

5. Once we have a completed line, see if it fits in the remaining area designated for the TextBlock. If it does, draw the line and subtract its height from the remaining available area. If it does not fit, put the elements in the line back on the TextBlock and return the code and the remainder of the TextBlock that did not fit in the area.

Note that this algorithm has a problem if a single character does not fit within the proscribed area. The solution for this case we will leave as an exercise for the reader.

```
sub Write {
    # The Write() method takes four parameters: w, h, x , and y,
    # where w and h are the width and height of the block (in points),
    # and x and y specify the upper left corner of the TextBlock (in the
    # PostScript coordinate system). This method returns a string containing
    # the PostScript code that generated the block, and a TextBlock object
    # the contains the portion that doesn't fit within the given bounds.
    #
    my $self = shift;
    my ($w, $h, $x, $y) = @_;

    my ($x1, $y1) = ($x, $y);
    my $returnval = "";
    my @remainder = ();
    my ($maxlead, $wcount, $linebuffer) = (0, 0, "");
    my ($line, $word, @words);
    my $wordwidth;
    $returnval .= "0 setgray\n";

    my $element = {};
    my $index = 0;
```

```
$element = $self->[$index];

my $maxindex = $self->numElements;
my $firstindex = 0;

ELEMENT:  while (($index < $maxindex) && ($y1 >= ($y-$h))) {
    $wcount = 0;
    ($line, $word) = (undef, undef);
    @words = ();
    $linebuffer = "";
    $maxlead = 0;
    $firstindex = $index;

    # Loop until a complete line is formed, or
    # until we run out of elements
    #
    LINE: while (($index < $maxindex) && $wcount<=$w) {
        $linebuffer .= "/$element->{font} findfont\n";
        $linebuffer .= "$element->{size} scalefont setfont\n";

        # Calculate the maximum leading on this line
        #
        $maxlead = $element->{leading} if ($element->{leading} > $maxlead);

        @words = split /( +|\t|\n)/, $element->{text};
        while (@words) {
            $word = shift @words;
            $wordwidth = PostScript::Metrics::stringwidth($word,
                                                $element->{font},
                                                $element->{size});

            # If the word is longer than the line, break by character.
            # Note that we could still have the problem of a single
            # character not fitting the width, which we will leave
            # as an exercise for the reader.
            #
            if ($wordwidth >$w) {
                unshift @words, split //, $word;
                $word = shift @words;
                $wordwidth = PostScript::Metrics::stringwidth($word,
                                                    $element->{font},
                                                    $element->{size});
            }
            $wcount += $wordwidth;

            # If we've gone over, push the word back on
            # for later processing.
            #
            if (($wcount>$w) || ($word =~ s/\n//)) {
                unshift @words, $word;
                last LINE;
            }
            $line .= $word;
        }
```

```
            $index++;
            $element = $self->[$index];
        }

        # Show the line
        #
        if (defined($line)) {
            $linebuffer .= "($line) show\n";
        }

        # Subtract the maximum leading from the current coordinate
        #
        $y1 -= $maxlead;

        # If this line doesn't fit, put the elements making up the line
        # back on for later processing...
        #
        if ($y1 < ($y-$h)) {
            for (my $i=$firstindex; $i < $maxindex; $i++) {
                push @remainder, $self->[$i];
            }
            last ELEMENT;
        } else {
            # Put any remaining words back for later processing
            #
            if ($#words) {
                $element->{text} = join '', @words;
            } else {
                $index++;
                $element = $self->[$index];
            }
            $returnval .= "0 setgray $x1 $y1 moveto\n";
            $returnval .= $linebuffer;
        }
    }
    return ($returnval, bless([@remainder], 'PostScript::TextBlock'));
}
1;      # All Perl modules should return true
```

The four methods implemented by PostScript::TextBlock are described as follows:

new() — *create a new PostScript::TextBlock object*

```
$tb = new PostScript::TextBlock
```

This method instantiates a new object of class PostScript::TextBlock.

addText() — *add a new element to a text block*

```
$tb->addText( text   => $text,
              font   => $font,
              size   => $size,
              leading=> $leading )
```

The *addText()* method will add a new text element to the TextBlock object. A "text element" can be thought of as a section of text that has the same characteristics (i.e., all the characters are the same font, size, and leading). This representation allows you to include text rendered in multiple fonts at multiple sizes within the same text block by including them as separate elements. Different alignment options have not been included in this version of the TextBlock module, but would be fairly easy to add. All text is left-aligned.

This method takes up to four attributes. If the `font`, `size`, or `leading` attributes are not provided, the default attributes for the TextBlock object are used. The attributes are:

`text`

> The `text` attribute is required, though nothing bad will happen if you leave it out. This is simply the text to be rendered in the text block. Line breaks may be inserted by including a \n newline string.

`font`

> The `font` attribute is a string indicating the name of the font to be used to render this element. The PostScript package uses an internal description of the font metrics of various fonts, which is contained in the PostScript::Metrics module. The PostScript::Metrics module supports the following fonts, which corresponds with the set of default Ghostscript fonts with have AFM files:

CenturySchL-Bold	NimbusMonL-BoldObli	URWBookmanL-DemiBoldItal
CenturySchL-BoldIta	NimbusMonL-Regu	URWBookmanL-Ligh
CenturySchL-Ital	NimbusMonL-ReguObli	URWBookmanL-LighItal
CharterBT-Bold	NimbusRomNo9L-ReguItal	URWGothicL-Book
CharterBT-BoldItalic	NimbusSanL-BoldCond	URWGothicL-BookObli
CharterBT-Italic	NimbusSanL-BoldCondItal	URWGothicL-DemiObli
CharterBT-Roman	NimbusSanL-Regu	URWPalladioL-Bold
	NimbusSanL-ReguCond	URWPalladioL-Ital
	NimbusSanL-ReguCondItal	URWPalladioL-Roma
	NimbusSanL-ReguItal	

> The font must be available to the PostScript interpreter that is used to render the page described by the program. If the interpreter cannot load the font, it will usually attempt to substitute a similar font. If a font is substituted with a font with different metrics, lines of text may overrun the right margin of the text block, because the length of a line is determined by the sum of the widths of the individual characters in the line.

Consult the documentation of your printer or PostScript interpreter to determine how to find which fonts are available to you. You can get a list of the currently fonts currently supported by PostScript::Metrics module with the following:

```
use PostScript::Metrics;
@okfonts = PostScript::Metrics->listFonts();
```

Note that just because the font is defined by PostScript::Metrics, it does not mean that it is installed on your system. You must make sure that it is installed, and that your PostScript interpreter can access it.

size

The size of the font, in points.

leading

The size of the space left for the line, from baseline to baseline.

numElements() — *return the number of elements in a block*

```
$tb->numElements()
```

Returns the number of elements in the Text Block object. An element is created each time the *addText()* method is called.

Write() — *return the PostScript code for a block*

```
$tb->Write( $width, $height, $xoffset, $yoffset )
```

The *Write()* method will generate the PostScript code that will render the text on a page when passed to a PostScript interpreter such as Ghostscript. The four parameters are expressed in points and indicate the width and height of the box within which the text should be printed, and the x and y offset of the upper left corner of this box.

Unlike all of the other tools described in this book which define the origin (0, 0) as the upper left-hand corner of the image, PostScript uses a Cartesian coordinate system. That is, the origin is at the lower left corner of the page.

Standard page sizes in points are listed earlier in Table 11-1.

The *Write()* method returns two values: a string consisting of the PostScript code (suitable for printing to a file), and a TextBlock object containing the elements (and partial elements) that did not fit within the specified area, if any. If the entire text block fits with the area, the remainder will be **undef**. The remainder can be used to lay out multiple pages and columns in a similar manner to most modern desktop publishing programs. In general, the *Write()* method should be called as

Accessing Information About Fonts

The *Write()* method uses the PostScript::Metrics module to determine the width of each character; widths vary from font to font and character to character. If you were writing a straight PostScript program, you would let the PostScript interpreter do this for you. The TextBlock module, however, also needs to know the width of each character so that it knows where to break lines and pages. The PostScript::Metrics module contains the font metrics (i.e., a list containing the width of each character in the font) for a bunch of fonts that are listed under the description of the *addText()* method. This set of metrics started with the descriptions for all of the default fonts with AFM files that came with GhostScript. To add support for a new font, you must create the array with the metrics for that font and add it to the PostScript::Metrics module. This array looks like:

```
my %fonts = (
# 95 entries for each font, corresponding to ASCII 32-126
# Each character is based on a one point font size and is expressed
# in 1/1000ths of points
#
'NimbusSanL-Regu' => [
278,    278,    355,    556,    556,    889,    667,    221,    333,    333,
389,    584,    278,    584,    278,    278,    556,    556,    556,    556,
556,    556,    556,    556,    556,    556,    278,    278,    584,    584,
584,    556,    1015,   667,    667,    722,    722,    667,    611,    778,
722,    278,    500,    667,    556,    833,    722,    778,    667,    778,
722,    667,    611,    722,    667,    944,    667,    667,    611,    278,
278,    278,    469,    556,    222,    556,    556,    500,    556,    556,
278,    556,    556,    222,    222,    500,    222,    833,    556,    556,
556,    556,    333,    500,    278,    556,    500,    722,    500,    500,
500,    334,    260,    334,    584,
],
# more font definitions here
);
```

For a font with an AFM file, the AFM file can be parsed to generate this table with Gisle Aas's Font::AFM module, available on CPAN. The table is used by the Metrics' *stringwidth* method, which calculates the total width of a string at a given font size:

```
sub stringwidth {
    my ($string, $fontname, $fontsize) = @_;
    my $returnval = 0;

    foreach my $char (unpack("C*", $string)) {
        $returnval+=$fonts{$fontname}->[$char-32];
    }
    return ($returnval*$fontsize/1000);
}
```

in the following example, which writes the PostScript code to a file called *psoutput.ps*:

```
#!/usr/bin/perl -w

use PostScript::TextBlock;
my $tb = PostScript::TextBlock->new;

$tb->addText( text => "The next sentence is false. ");
$tb->addText( text => "The previous sentence is true. ");

# Open the file for output (always check return value...)
#
open OUT, '>psoutput.ps' or die "Couldn't open psoutput.ps: $!";

# Retrieve the code and write the portion that fits the proscribed area
#
my ($code, $remainder) = $tb->Write(572, 752, 20, 772);
print OUT $code;
```

Style Sheets

It is very easy to create style sheets for a document:

```
# Define the styles
#
%body = ( font => 'URWGothicL-DemiObli', size => 12, leading => 16 );
%head1 = ( font => 'NimbusSanL-BoldCond', size => 24, leading => 36 );
%head2 = ( font => 'NimbusSanL-BoldCond', size => 18, leading => 30 );

# Use them where appropriate
#
$tb->addText(text => "Chapter 10\n", %head1);
$tb->addText(text => "Spokane Sam and His Spongepants\n", %head2);
$tb->addText(text => "It was a dark and stormy night and Spokane Sam\'s
Spongepants were thirsty...", %body);
```

Multipage Documents with PostScript::TextBlock

The TextBlock object by itself can only print on a single page. In some (perhaps many) cases you will need the capability to handle several pages worth of text, and have them all come out as a several-page PostScript document. This is why the *TextBlock::Write()* method returns the code and a TextBlock representing the text that doesn't fit in the region passed to the *Write()* method. You can use this remainder to print a text block that spans multiple pages, something like this (of course, you must add enough text to the text block first):

```
open OUT, '>psoutput.ps' or die "Couldn't open psoutput.ps: $!";
my $pages = 1;

# Create the first page
#
```

```
    my ($code, $remainder) = $tb->Write(572, 752, 20, 772);
    print OUT "%%Page:$pages\n";        # this is required by the Adobe
                                        # Document Structuring Conventions

    print OUT $code;
    print OUT "showpage\n";

    # Print the rest of the pages, if any
    #
    while ($remainder->numElements) {
        $pages++;
        print OUT "%%Page:$pages\n";
        ($code, $remainder) = $remainder->Write(572, 752, 20, 772);
        print OUT $code;
        print OUT "showpage\n";
    }
```

However, you could just use the PostScript::Document module described in the
next section and not worry about it. The Document object will handle everything
for you.

Multipage Documents with PostScript::Document

The PostScript::Document module comes with the PostScript package. It creates an
abstract interface for creating generic multiple page textual documents. You can
think of a Document object as a big text block with additional attributes and methods that allow it to span multiple pages. You can also include page numbers, and
textual headers and footers that appear on each page of the document.

The Document object is used in a similar manner to the TextBlock object to do the
following:

1. Instantiate a new document with the *new()* method and a number of optional
   parameters defining the attributes of the page.

2. Add text elements to the document with the *addText()* method.

3. Create the PostScript as a string of code with the *Write()* method.

4. Write the code to a file, and pipe or append it to other code.

A sample script using this module that reads a text file and appends a title, header,
and footer to it would look something like this:

```
#!/usr/bin/perl -w

use strict;
use PostScript::Document;
my $doc = new PostScript::Document;

$doc->addText( text => "Hullabalo in Hoosick Falls.\n",
```

```
                                 font => 'CenturySchL-Ital',
                                 size => 24,
                                 leading => 100
                            );
        $doc->addText( text => "by Charba Gaspee.\n",
                                 font => 'URWGothicL-Demi',
                                 size => 18,
                                 leading => 36
                            );
        $doc->addHeader(text => "Hullabaloo in Hoosick Falls",
                                 font => 'URWGothicL-Demi',
                                 size => 9,
                                 leading => 11
                            );
        $doc->addFooter(text => "Page ##Page",
                                 font => 'URWGothicL-Demi',
                                 size => 9,
                                 leading => 11
                            );

        # Now read in a big text file and add it
        #
        open I, "example.txt" or die "Couldn't open example.txt: $!";
        undef $/;
        my $text = <I>;
        $doc->addText( text => $text,
                                 font => 'URWGothicL-Demi',
                                 size => 14,
                                 leading => 24
                            );


        open OUT, '>psoutput.ps' or die "Couldn't open psoutput.ps: $!";
        my $code = $doc->Write();    # use defaults
        print OUT $code;
```

The PostScript::Document module will be installed when you install the PostScript
package.

```
        # Document.pm
        # This module allows for the easy construction of multi-page textual
        # reports with the PostScript::TextBlock module.
        #
        package PostScript::Document;
        use strict;
        use PostScript::TextBlock;

        # Some standard paper sizes
        #
        my @papers = qw( Letter Legal Ledger Tabloid A0 A1 A2 A3 A4 A5 A6 A7 A8
                         A9 B0 B1 B2 B3 B4 B5 B6 B7 B8 B9 Envelope10 EnvelopeC5
                         EnvelopeDL Folio Executive );
```

```
# Dimensions of standard papers
#
my %width = (  Letter => 612,       Legal => 612,
               Ledger => 1224,      Tabloid => 792,
               A0 => 2384,          A1 => 1684,
               A2 => 1191,          A3 => 842,
               A4 => 595,           A5 => 420,
               A6 => 297,           A7 => 210,
               A8 => 148,           A9 => 105,
               B0 => 2920,          B1 => 2064,
               B2 => 1460,          B3 => 1032,
               B4 => 729,           B5 => 516,
               B6 => 363,           B7 => 258,
               B8 => 181,           B9 => 127,
               B10 => 91,           Envelope10 => 297,
               EnvelopeC5 => 461,   EnvelopeDL => 312,
               Folio => 595,        Executive => 522
           );
my %height = (  Letter => 792,   Legal => 1008,
                Ledger => 792,   Tabloid => 1224,
                A0 => 3370,          A1 => 2384,
                A2 => 1684,          A3 => 1191,
                A4 => 842,           A5 => 595,
                A6 => 420,           A7 => 297,
                A8 => 210,           A9 => 148,
                B0 => 4127,          B1 => 2920,
                B2 => 2064,          B3 => 1460,
                B4 => 1032,          B5 => 729,
                B6 => 516,           B7 => 363,
                B8 => 258,           B9 => 181,
                B10 => 127,          Envelope10 => 684,
                EnvelopeC5 => 648,   EnvelopeDL => 624,
                Folio => 935,        Executive => 756
        );


# Valid attribute names
#
my @paramnames = qw( paper width height
                     rmargin lmargin tmargin bmargin );


# Default values of document attributes
#
my %defaults = (
                paper   => 'Letter',
                width   => $width{'Letter'},
                height  => $height{'Letter'},
                rmargin => 36,          # .5 inches
                lmargin => 36,
                tmargin => 36,
                bmargin => 36,
                );
```

The *new()* method constructs a new Document object, which is simply an anonymous hash containing a number of attributes describing the dimensions of the

document, a PostScript::TextBlock object representing the body of the document, and two PostScript::TextBlock objects representing the header and footer for the document. If an attribute is not provided, the default value (as defined above) will be used.

Note that this is a very simple-minded representation of a document. Most documents consist of rules, boxes, figures, and images in addition to plain text. The full-fledged version of the PostScript module would allow more complex documents to be created by representing the content of the document as a list of arbitrary PostScript::TextBlock or PostScript::Element objects, instead of a single TextBlock.

```perl
sub new {
    # The constructor method
    #
    my $proto = shift;                    # allow use as a class or object method
    my $class = ref($proto) || $proto;# see perltoot man page

    # Allow a user to specify only a paper size and set the
    # width and height accordingly
    #
    if (defined ($params{'paper'})) {
        $params{'width'} = $width{$params{'paper'}}
        if defined($width{$params{'paper'}});
        $params{'height'} = $height{$params{'paper'}}
        if defined($height{$params{'paper'}});
    }

    # Use the default value if a value is not provided
    #
    foreach (@paramnames) {
        $params{$_} = $defaults{$_} unless (defined($params{$_}));
    }

    my $self = { content => new PostScript::TextBlock,
                 header  => new PostScript::TextBlock,
                 footer  => new PostScript::TextBlock,
                 %params };

    bless($self,$class);
    return $self;
}
```

The *addText()* method will add an element of text with a given font, size, and leading to the document. Because the document's content is a single TextBlock, the *addText()* method simply calls the *addText()* method of the TextBlock. The *addHeader()* and *addFooter()* methods add text to the document header and footer in a similar fashion.

```perl
sub addText {
    # Add text to the document
    #
    my $self = shift;
```

```
    my %params = @_;

    # Call the PostScript::TextBlock::addText method
    #
    $self->{'content'}->addText(%params);
}

sub addHeader {
    # Add a textual header to the document
    #
    my $self = shift;
    my %params = @_;

    $self->{'header'}->addText(%params);
}

sub addFooter {
    # Add a textual footer to the document
    #
    my $self = shift;
    my %params = @_;

    $self->{'footer'}->addText(%params);
}
```

The *Write()* method will create the PostScript code for the document and return it
as a string. The method calls the *Write()* method for the TextBlock representing
the content and, if the block does not fit on one page, takes the remainder, creates a new page, and iteratively draws the text and creates new pages until there is
no more text to draw. The *Write()* method will also print appropriate structure
comments in compliance with the Document Structuring Conventions. The
printHeader() and *printFooter()* methods are called to draw the header and footer
text with the creation of each new page.

```
sub Write {
    # The Write() method is called without parameters. It
    # returns a string containing the complete PostScript code
    # for the Document.
    #
    my $self = shift;
    my $pages = 1;

    # Should follow the Document Structuring Conventions
    #
    my $returnval = "%!PS-Adobe-3.0\n".
                    "%%Creator: The Perl PostScript Package\n".
                    "%%Pages: (atend)\n".
                    "%%BoundingBox: 0 0 $self->{'width'} $self->{'height'}\n".
                    "%%EndComments\n".
                    "%%BeginProlog\n".
                    "%%EndProlog\n";

    my $w = $self->{'width'} - $self->{'rmargin'} - $self->{'lmargin'};
```

```perl
    my $h = $self->{'height'} - $self->{'tmargin'} - $self->{'bmargin'};
    my $x = $self->{'lmargin'};
    my $y = $h + $self->{'bmargin'};

    $returnval .= "%%Page: 1\n";

    $returnval .= $self->printHeader($pages);
    $returnval .= $self->printFooter($pages);

    my ($code, $remainder) = $self->{content}->Write($w, $h, $x, $y);
    $returnval .= $code;
    $returnval .= "showpage\n";

    # Print the rest of the pages, if any
    #
    while ($remainder->numElements) {
        $pages++;
        $returnval .= "%%Page: $pages\n";
        $returnval .= $self->printHeader($pages);
        $returnval .= $self->printFooter($pages);

        ($code, $remainder) = $remainder->Write($w, $h, $x, $y);
        $returnval .= $code;
        $returnval .= "showpage\n";
    }
    $returnval .= "%%Trailer\n".
                  "%%Pages: $pages\n".
                  "%%EOF\n";
    return $returnval;
}


sub printHeader {
    # Create the PostScript code to generate the header
    # Always starts .25 inches (18 pts) from the top edge of paper
    #
    my $self = shift;
    my $pagenum = shift;

    # Do a search for the ##Page meta string that specifies a page number
    # and replace it with the page number...
    #
    my $header = $self->{'header'};
    foreach my $element (@$header) {
        $element->{'text'} =~ s/##Page/$pagenum/g;
    }

    my ($code, $remainder) =
        $self->{'header'}->Write( $self->{'width'} -
                                  $self->{'rmargin'} - $self->{'lmargin'},
                                  $self->{'tmargin'} - 18,
                                  $self->{'lmargin'},
                                  $self->{'height'}-18
                                  );
```

```
        # We should put a save/restore pair around the code so that
        # it doesn't disrupt the current graphics state
        #
        return "/savedpage save def\n".$code."savedpage restore\n";
    }

    sub printFooter {
        # Create the PostScript code to generate the footer
        # Always starts 2 pts from the bottom margin, otherwise same as header.
        #
        my $self = shift;
        my $pagenum = shift;

        my $footer = $self->{'footer'};
        foreach my $element (@$footer) {
            print STDERR $pagenum;
            $element->{'text'} =~ s/##Page/$pagenum/g;
        }

        my ($code, $remainder) =
            $self->{'footer'}->Write( $self->{'width'} - $self->{'rmargin'} -
                                      $self->{'lmargin'},
                                      $self->{'bmargin'} - 18,
                                      $self->{'lmargin'},
                                      $self->{'bmargin'} - 2
                                     );
        return "/savedpage save def\n".$code."savedpage restore\n";
    }

    1;
```

The PostScript::Document module implements five methods, which are described in detail below:

new() — *create a new PostScript::Document object*

```
$doc = PostScript::Document->new( paper   => $paper,
                                  width   => $width,
                                  height  => $height,
                                  rmargin => $rmargin,
                                  lmargin => $lmargin,
                                  tmargin => $tmargin,
                                  bmargin => $bmargin );
```

This method instantiates a new object of class PostScript::Document. There are seven attributes that may be optionally set when a new object is created; a **paper** attribute that can be one of the valid paper size strings (e.g., Letter, Legal, etc.), the width and height of the page (in points), and the four margins of the page (also in points). Note that if you specify the **paper** attribute, you do not have to include the width and height attributes (and vice versa). The default values are Letter paper (612×792 points) and margins of .5 inches (36 points).

addText() — *add a new element to a document*

```
$doc->addText( text=>$text,
               font=>$font,
               size=>$size,
               leading=>$leading )
```

The *addText()* method performs just like the *PostScript::TextBlock::addText()* method described in the previous section. In fact, the Document simply calls the *addText()* method of its *content* TextBlock. If the `font`, `size`, or `leading` attributes are not provided, the default attributes for the TextBlock object are used.

addHeader() — *add a textual header to a document*

```
$doc->addHeader( text=>$text,
                 font=>$font,
                 size=>$size,
                 leading=>$leading  )
```

The *addHeader()* method allows you to specify a header that will appear at the top of each page of the document. This header will be drawn in the top margin of the page, with the same right and left margins as the page. Only that portion of the header that fits in the top margin will be printed. If the `font`, `size`, or `leading` attributes are not provided, the default attributes for the TextBlock object are used.

The page numbers of individual pages may be included in the header by the use of the string `##Page` within the header's text string. The `##Page` string will be replaced at runtime with the appropriate page number. For example, the following will add the appropriate page number in the upper left corner of each page in the default font, size, and leading:

```
$doc->addHeader( text => "Page ##Page" );
```

addFooter() — *add a textual footer to a document*

```
$doc->addFooter( text=>$text,
                 font=>$font,
                 size=>$size,
                 leading=>$leading  )
```

The *addFooter()* method allows you to specify a footer that will appear at the bottom of each page of the document. This footer will be drawn in the bottom margin of the page, with the same right and left margins as the page. Only that portion of the footer that fits in the bottom margin will be printed. If the `font`, `size`, or `leading` attributes are not provided, the default attributes for the TextBlock object are used.

The page numbers of individual pages may be included in the footer with the `##Page` string, as described for the *addHeader()* method.

Write() — *return the PostScript code for a document*

```
$doc->Write()
```

The *Write()* method will generate the PostScript code for the document and return
it as a string. In general, you will want to use the *Write()* method to write the code
to a file that can be sent to a printer or other PostScript interpreter. You could do
this like in the following, which writes the PostScript code to a file called
psoutput.ps:

```
open OUT, '>psoutput.ps' or die "Couldn't open psoutput.ps: $!";
my $code = $doc->Write();
print OUT $code;
```

The PostScript::Elements Module

Finally, we will need to incorporate some sort of support for drawing vector
graphics in the form of lines, arcs, and boxes. This will be the job of the Post-
Script::Elements module. It provides routines to draw any of these three shapes,
and can be easily extended to encapsulate other shapes or more complex forms.
The methods allow you to control the width of the line, the tint of the line (a percentage of gray), and a tint with which to fill the shape (a percentage of gray or
transparent). The Elements module can be used as in this example, which will
draw a random number of arbitrary lines, boxes, and arcs (see Figure 11-6):

```
#!/usr/bin/perl -w
# Generate a random collection of lines, boxes, arcs
#
use strict;
use PostScript::Elements;

my $e = new PostScript::Elements;

my $r = rand(25);
for (my $i=0; $i<= $r; $i++) {
    $e->addArc(points  => [rand(612), rand(792),
                           rand(200), rand(360), rand(360)],
             linewidth => rand(8) );
    $e->addBox(points  => [rand(612), rand(792), rand(200), rand(200)],
             linewidth => rand(8) );
    $e->addLine(points => [rand(612), rand(792), rand(200), rand(200)],
             linewidth => rand(8) );
}

open OUT, ">example.ps" or die "Couldn't open example.ps: $!";
print OUT $e->Write();
close OUT;
```

In each case, the `points` attribute passes on the description of the points in the
line, box, or arc. It should be in the form of an anonymous list of points, the
length of the list depending on which method is being called (`arc` takes 5 points,

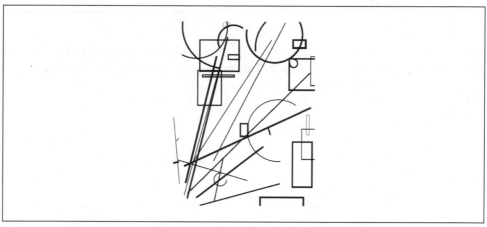

Figure 11-6. The PostScript::Elements module offers an abstract interface for representing arcs, lines, and boxes that may be strung together to form complex objects

for example, and `line` takes 4). The Elements module can be easily expanded to represent other shapes by adding an appropriate method name (e.g., *addCube()*) that can call the *addType()* method with a descriptive type attribute (e.g., `type="cube"`). The *Write()* method must also be updated with the code to generate the appropriate PostScript.

Here's the implementation of PostScript::Elements:

```
# Elements.pm
# A Perl object for representing lines, arcs, and boxes
# such that they can be easily output as PostScript code.
#
package PostScript::Elements;
use strict;

# @paramnames is the list of valid parameters,
# %defaults is the hash of default values for those parameters.
#
my @paramnames = qw( type points linewidth linetint filltint );
my %defaults = (
                linewidth => 1, # in points
                filltint  => -1,# -1 represents transparent
                linetint  => 0, # 0 == black, 1 = white
              );

sub new {
    # The constructor method.
    # An Element object can be one or more lines, arcs, or boxes
    #
    my $proto = shift;                # allow use as a class or object method
    my $class = ref($proto) || $proto;# see perltoot man page
    my $self = [];
```

```
        bless($self,$class);
        return $self;
}
```

The *addType()* method is a general means of adding new shapes to an Elements object. It handles assigning default values if attributes are not specified, and pushes the new shape onto the Elements object.

```
sub addType {
    my $self = shift;
    my %params = @_;

    # If a parameter is not specified, use the default...
    #
    foreach (@paramnames) {
        $params{$_} = $defaults{$_} unless (defined($params{$_}));
    };

    # Add the object to the current element
    #
    push @$self, { type      => $params{'type'},
                   points    => $params{'points'},
                   linewidth => $params{'linewidth'},
                   filltint  => $params{'filltint'},
                   linetint  => $params{'linetint'},
                 };
}
```

The *addArc()*, *addBox()*, and *addLine()* methods act as an intermediary between the user and the *addType()* method.

```
sub addArc {
    # Add an arc to the Element.
    # A points parameter is required, consisting of a reference to
    # list specifying the center coordinate, the radius
    # of the arc, and two numbers specifying the starting angle
    # and the ending angle describing the sweep of the arc.
    #
    my $self = shift;
    $self->addType(type => 'arc', @_);
}

sub addBox {
    # Add a Box to the Element.
    # The points parameter should consist of the upper left coordinate
    # of the box, its width, and its height.
    #
    my $self = shift;
    $self->addType(type => 'box', @_);
}

sub addLine {
    # Add a Line to the Element.
    # The points parameter should contain the starting coordinate and
```

```
            # the end coordinate.
            #
            my $self = shift;
            $self->addType(type => 'line', @_);
    }
```

The *Write()* method implements a case for each shape known to the Elements object. In the case of arcs, lines, and boxes, the PostScript code is very simple and should be self-explanatory at this point:

```
sub Write() {
        # A method to create the PostScript code that will render the
        # objects in the Element.
        #
        my $self = shift;
        my $returnval = "";
        my ($width, $height);


        foreach my $element (@$self) {
            # Generate the appropriate PostScript based on the
            # type attribute.
            # Arc:
            if ($element->{type} =~ /arc/i) {
                # First save the current path (if any),
                # then create the path of the arc
                #
                $returnval .= "gsave\n".
                                $element->{'points'}->[0]." ".    # x value
                                $element->{'points'}->[1]." ".    # y value
                                $element->{'points'}->[2]." ".    # radius
                                $element->{'points'}->[3]." ".    # start angle
                                $element->{'points'}->[4]." ".    # end angle
                                "arc\n";
                # Don't fill the arc if filltint attribute is -1
                # otherwise fill the current path with the tint specified by
                # the filltint attribute. Save the path so it can be restored
                # after the fill and it can be used by the stroke function.
                #
                if ($element->{'filltint'} >= 0 ) {
                $returnval .= $element->{'filltint'}." setgray\n".
                                "gsave \nfill \ngrestore\n";
            }

            # Stroke the arc with the width indicated by linewidth
            # and a greyscale percentage specified by linetint
            #
            $returnval .= $element->{'linetint'}." setgray\n".
                            $element->{'linewidth'}." setlinewidth\n".
                            "stroke\n".
                            "1 setgray\n".
                            $defaults{'linewidth'}." setlinewidth\n".
                            "grestore\n";
            # Box:
            #
```

```
    } elsif ($element->{type} =~ /box/i) {
        # A box is described by the upper left corner, a width
        # and a height
        #
        $width = $element->{'points'}->[2];
        $height = $element->{'points'}->[3];

        $returnval .= "gsave\n";
        $returnval .= $element->{'points'}->[0]." ".    # x value
                      $element->{'points'}->[1]." ".    # y value
                      "moveto\n".
                      # now draw it clockwise...
                      #
                      "$width 0 rlineto\n".
                      "0 ".(0-$height)." rlineto\n".
                      (0-$width)." 0 rlineto\n".
                      "0 $height rlineto\n".
                      "closepath\n";
        # Don't fill the box if filltint attribute is -1
        #
        if ($element->{'filltint'} >= 0 ) {
        $returnval .= $element->{'filltint'}." setgray\n".
                         "gsave \nfill \ngrestore\n";
    }
    $returnval .= $element->{'linetint'}." setgray\n".
                      $element->{'linewidth'}." setlinewidth\n".
                      "stroke\n".
                      "1 setgray\n".
                      $defaults{'linewidth'}." setlinewidth\n".
                      "grestore\n";
    # Line:
    #
    } elsif ($element->{type} =~ /line/i) {

        $returnval .= "gsave\n";
        $returnval .= $element->{'points'}->[0]." ".    # start x
                      $element->{'points'}->[1]." ".    # start y
                      "moveto\n".
                      $element->{'points'}->[2]." ".    # end x
                      $element->{'points'}->[3]." ".    # end y
                      "lineto\n".
                      $element->{'linetint'}." setgray\n".
                      $element->{'linewidth'}." setlinewidth\n".
                      "stroke\n".
                      "1 setgray\n".
                      $defaults{'linewidth'}." setlinewidth\n".
                      "grestore\n";
    } else {
      # Do nothing
    }
  }
  return ($returnval);
}


1;
```

The five methods implemented by PostScript::Elements are described here in greater detail:

new() — *create a new PostScript::Elements object*

```
$e = new PostScript::Elements
```

This method instantiates a new object of class PostScript::Elements.

addArc() — *add an arc to the object*

```
$e->addArc( points    => [ $x, $y, $r, $startangle, $endangle],
            linewidth => $linewidth,
            linetint  => $linetint,
            filltint  => $filltint )
```

The *addArc()* method will add an arc segment to the Elements object. It takes up to four parameters, of which only the **points** parameter is required:

points

A **points** parameter is required, consisting of a reference to a list specifying the center coordinate, the radius of the arc, and two numbers specifying the starting angle and the ending angle describing the sweep of the arc. For example:

```
addArc(points=>[50,50,25,0,360])
```

would add a complete circle centered at 50, 50 with a radius of 25. Note that the list of points is in the same form as the PostScript *arc* function.

linewidth

The **linewidth** attribute can be used to specify the point size of the line with which the arc is to be stroked. If no value is given, the default line width is 1 point.

linetint

The **linetint** attribute should be a number between 0 and 1 representing a percentage of gray, with 1 as black and 0 as white. Therefore, .8 would be the equivalent of a 20% gray screen. If no value is given, the line will be stroked in black (**linetint=1**).

filltint

The **filltint** attribute should be either –1 or a number between 0 and 1 representing a percentage of gray, with 1 as black and 0 as white. If the value is –1, the shape will not be filled in; it will be transparent. Otherwise, the shape will be opaque. The default value is –1.

addBox() — *add a box to the object*

```
$e->addBox( points    => [ $x, $y, $width, $height],
            linewidth => $linewidth,
            linetint  => $linetint,
            filltint  => $filltint )
```

The *addBox()* method adds a square box to the Elements object. It takes up to four parameters, of which only the `points` parameter is required:

points
> The `points` attribute should be an anonymous list with the coordinate of the upper left corner of the box followed by the width and height of the box. Remember that the coordinate system used by PostScript uses the lower left corner of the page as its origin.

linewidth
> The `linewidth` attribute functions as described for *addArc()*.

linetint
> The `linetint` attribute functions as described for *addArc()*.

filltint
> The `filltint` attribute functions as described for *addArc()*.

addLine() — *add a line to the object*

```
$e->addArc( points    => [ $startx, $starty, $endx, $endy],
            linewidth => $linewidth,
            linetint  => $linetint )
```

The *addLine()* method will draw a line between two points. It takes up to three `parameters (note that a filltint parameter is simply ignored)`:

points
> The `points` attribute should be given an anonymous array with the coordinate of the starting point (*startx, starty*) and the end point (*endx, endy*).

linewidth
> The `linewidth` attribute functions as described for *addArc()*.

linetint
> The `linetint` attribute functions as described for *addArc()*.

Write() — *return the PostScript code for an Element object*

```
$tb->Write()
```

The *Write()* method will generate the PostScript code that will render any lines, boxes, or arcs that have been added to the Elements object. The *Write()* method returns a string containing the PostScript code, which may be written to a file, piped to a process, or appended to other PostScript code.

References

PostScript Language Tutorial and Cookbook:

The so-called "Blue Book," with many examples and recipes, Adobe Systems, Inc., Addison-Wesley, 1985

PostScript Language Reference Manual, 2nd Edition:

The so-called "Red Book," the official language reference, Adobe Systems, Inc., Addison-Wesley, 1990

PostScript by Example:

A good introduction to PostScript, similar in purpose to the Blue Book, McGilton, Henry, and Mary Campione, Addison-Wesley Publishing Company, 1992

The Ghostscript Home Page:

http://www.cs.wisc.edu/~ghost

Adobe's Technical Resources Page:

http://www.adobe.com/supportservices/devrelations/

Adobe's Document Structuring Conventions:

http://www.adobe.com/supportservices/devrelations/PDFS/TN/5001.DSC_Spec_v3.0.pdf

The *html2ps* HTML-to-PostScript converter:

http://www.tdb.uu.se/~jan/html2ps.html

IV

Appendixes

A Simple PNG Decoder
in Perl

The PNGObject Perl module will only parse the critical chunks, and will skip (and identify) ancillary chunks. You can use the PNGObject module to dump a listing of the chunks of a PNG file. It can be used like this:

```perl
use PNGObject;
my $png = new PNGObject;
$png->readPNG('some_image.png');
```

Here is the code for a simple PNG decoder module:

```perl
# -*- Perl -*-
# PNGObject.pm
# A Perl module that will decode the chunks of a PNG formatted file and
# dump a printout of the various fields.
#
package PNGObject;

use strict;

# This hash defines the ordering of fields within the critical chunks
#
my %png_fields = (
    # Critical chunks
    #
    header =>
            [qw( width height bit_depth color_type
             compression filter interlace )],

    palette =>
            [qw( red green blue )],

    image_data =>
            [qw( data )]
);
```

```
# This will create a string which can be used for
# valid signature comparisons
#
my $png_signature = pack "H16", "89504E470D0A1A0A";

# A list of the standard ancillary chunks for use in a later
# regular expression.
#
my $ancillary_chunks =
    join "|",
    qw( bKGD  cHRM  gAMA  hIST  pHYs  sBIT  tEXT
        tIME  tRNS  oFFs  sCAL  tIME );

# This hash may be referenced to determine the length of
# each field (in bytes) for a particular chunk.
#
my %png_format = (

    # Every chunk has an 8 byte header and a 4 byte trailer
    #
    all => {
        'length'    => 4,
        type        => 4,
        # Chunk-specific data goes here
        #
        crc         => 4
    },

    header => {
        width       => 4,
        height      => 4,
        bit_depth   => 1,
        color_type  => 1,
        compression => 1,
        filter      => 1,
        interlace   => 1,
    },

    palette => {
        red         => 1,
        green       => 1,
        blue        => 1,
    },

    image_data => {
        data        => undef,
    },

    image_trailer => {
        type        => 4,
    }
)

# Three variables for storing the decoded values
#
```

An Important Note About Byte-Ordering

GIF, PNG, and JPEG files each contain some fields of numbers that span more than one byte. Unfortunately, which of the bytes is to be read as the most significant and which as the least differs from format to format. The GIF format is said to store its multi-byte numbers in *little-endian format*. PNG and JPEG store their numbers in *big-endian order*.[a] In little-endian formats the least significant byte is the lower byte in memory, and in big-endian, it is the highest byte.

Different platforms have different byte-ordering also. Low-level I/O routines used for reading binary data will read the data in the native format of the system. Intel machines, for example, are little-endian, while Motorola's 68XXX line is big-endian.

In Perl, a single byte can be converted to an integer with the *ord* function. Two or four bytes in little-endian format (on a little-endian system) can be changed to an unsigned integer with the functions:

```
unpack 'v', $two_bytes;     # a little-endian short integer (16 bits)
unpack 'V', $four_bytes;    # a little-endian long integer (32 bits)
```

The "v" in the **unpack** statement stands for VAX, which is a little-endian system. Two or four bytes in big-endian format (sometimes called "network" format) can be changed to a number with:

```
unpack 'n', $two_bytes;     # a big-endian short integer (16 bits)
unpack 'N', $four_bytes;    # a big-endian long integer (32 bits)
```

---

a. The terminology "little-endian" and "big-endian" was coined by Jonathan Swift, who used the terms in *Gulliver's Travels* to describe two factions of politicians pontificating over which orientation an egg should have when it is broken.

```
my $header;
my @image;
my @palette;

# The new method is the constructor for the PNGObject.
# It creates an anonymous array which may be used to store the
# decoded chunk data.
#
sub new {
   my $class = shift;
   my $self = [];
   bless ($self, $class);
   return $self;
}

sub readPNG {
    my $self = shift;
```

```perl
my $filename = shift;
my ($nextlength, $nexttype) = (0, '');
my ($crc, $imagedata);

open PNG, $filename || return 1000;   # Error 1000 = couldn't open file
binmode(PNG);

# Read and check signature
#
my $signature;
sysread(PNG, $signature, 8);
unless ($signature eq $png_signature) {
    return 2000;                      # Error 2000 = not a valid PNG file
}


# The sysread() function returns the number of bytes read.
#
while (sysread(PNG, $nextlength, $png_format{'all'}->{'length'})) {
    # The length field is more than one byte so we must worry about the
    # byte ordering. PNG is saved in big-endian order so we
    # can use Perl's unpack function with the 'N' option (N for
    # 'network' or big-endian order) to convert it into a long integer.
    #
    $nextlength =unpack "N", $nextlength;
    unless (sysread(PNG, $nexttype, $png_format{'all'}->{'type'})) {
        print "Premature end-of-file!\n";
        return 3000;   # Error 3000 = premature end of file
    }

    # Now check to see what the type of the next field is
    #
    if ($nexttype eq 'IHDR') {
        # A Header chunk
        #
        print "Found a Header Chunk!\n";
        $header = $self->readChunk(*PNG, 'header');
        # The data in CRC can be used to determine whether the
        # data in $header has been corrpted
        #
        sysread(PNG, $crc, $png_format{'all'}->{'crc'});

    } elsif ($nexttype eq 'PLTE') {
        # A Palette chunk
        #
        print "Found a palette!\n";
        my $size = $nextlength/3;
        print "Color table with $size entries:\n";
        for (my $index=0; $index < $size; $index++) {
            print "Index $index:\n";
            push @palette,
                $self->readChunk(*PNG, 'palette');
            print " \n";
         }
        sysread(PNG, $crc, $png_format{'all'}->{'crc'});
```

```
        } elsif ($nexttype eq 'IDAT') {
            # An Image Data chunk
            #
            print "Found an image data chunk!\n";
            print "Read ".sysread(PNG, $imagedata, $nextlength)." bytes.\n";

            # The @image list of image data must still be decoded
            #
            push @image, $imagedata;
            sysread(PNG, $crc, $png_format{'all'}->{'crc'});

        } elsif ($nexttype eq 'IEND') {
            # An Image Trailer chunk
            #
            print "Found the image trailer chunk!\n";
            return 1;

        } elsif ($nexttype =~ /$ancillary_chunks/) {
            # One of the standard ancillary chunks.
            # A more robust decoder should recognize all of these.
            #
            print "Skipping an ancillary chunk of type $nexttype.\n";
            print "  This chunk is a standard part of the PNG 1.0 spec,\n";
            print "  but is not supported by this decoder. Sorry.\n";
            skipChunk(*PNG, $nextlength);

        } else {
            # An unrecognized chunk. It should be skipped.
            #
            print "Skipping a chunk of type $nexttype.\n";
            print "  This chunk is not recognized as a standard part of the\n";
            print "  PNG 1.0 spec, but it could be a private or\n";
            print "  special purpose public chunk.\n";
            skipChunk(*PNG, $nextlength);
        }
    }
    print "Premature end of file (no IEND chunk encountered)...\n";
    return 3000;          # Error 3000 = premature end of file
}

sub skipChunk {
    my ($fh, $bytes) = @_;
    my $skip;

    # Skip the chunk, throwing the data away.
    # The number of bytes to skip is +4 because of CRC bytes
    #
    for (my $count=0; $count < $bytes + 4; $count++) {
        sysread($fh, $skip, 1);
    }
}

sub readChunk {
    # A convenience routine to read in generic chunk data.
```

```perl
    # Note that 'chunk data' does not include the chunk header or
    # the CRC trailer. This method returns a hash containing
    # the data. It also prints each field as it is read as an
    # appropriate sized integer for easy reading.
    #
    my $self = shift;
    my $fh = shift;          # the filehandle
    my $chunkname = shift;     # a string that is the key to the png_format
hash
    my @fields = @{$png_fields{$chunkname}};

    my %returnhash = ();

    foreach my $field (@fields) {
        sysread($fh,
                $returnhash{$field},
                $png_format{$chunkname}->{$field});

        print "$field: ";

        # If the field is more than four bytes long, we must unpack
        # it as a 'network' (big-endian) long integer.
        # If it is a two byte field, it must be unpacked as a
        # 'network' short integer.
        # Otherwise it is only a single byte and we can make it an
        # integer with ord.
        #
        if ($png_format{$chunkname}->{$field} == 4) {
            print unpack("N", $returnhash{$field});
        }elsif ($png_format{$chunkname}->{$field} == 2) {
            print unpack("n", $returnhash{$field});
        } else {
            print ord($returnhash{$field});
        }
        print "\n";
    }
    return { %returnhash };
}
1;    # All Perl modules should return true
```

B

Quick Reference Guide to the Gimp

This appendix serves as a quick tour of the many menus and dialog boxes of the Gimp. Each group of functions is described in brief, and information such as command key combinations for the various tools is provided where appropriate. It is organized in three sections:

- "The Gimp Toolbox," which describes the tools available in the floating toolbox (and from the *<Image>* → *Tools* menu).

- "The Toolbox Menu Hierarchy," which describes the menus accessible via the Toolbox and the functions associated with them.

- "The Image Menu Hierarchy," which describes the menus that are associated with an image window. This menu group is accessed by clicking the right mouse button within the image window.

The Gimp Toolbox

Each tool has a Tool Options dialog box associated with it that may be accessed by double-clicking on the tool's icon in the Toolbox. These options vary from tool to tool; generally they provide access to parameters, or they may put the tool in different modes which affect its behavior.

The Selection Tools

All of the selection tools are operated in a similar manner. To start drawing a selection, hold down the left mouse button and drag the mouse to define the selection area. To cancel a selection while drawing it, hold down the right mouse button while drawing and release the left button. To add to the existing selection, hold down the Shift key before drawing the selection.

To subtract from the current selection, hold down the Control key before drawing the selection.

To create a selection area that is the union of two selections, hold down the Shift and Control keys before drawing the second selection.

To constrain the selection image (for a perfect square or a circle, for example), hold down the Shift key while drawing the selection. To draw an area that is centered on the initial click point, hold down the Control key while drawing the selection.

Once an area is selected, it may be moved by holding down the Alt key, clicking on the selection area with the left mouse button, and dragging it to the desired position.

The Tool Options dialog for each of the selection tools allows you to specify whether you want to feather the selection area, which will result in a smoother selection.

The first six tools in the Toolbox are the selection tools:

The rectangular selection tool
> Allows you to select a rectangular region.

The elliptical selection tool
> Allows you to select an elliptical region.

The hand-drawn selection tool
> Allows you to draw an arbitrary region. The tool will automatically connect the first point and the last point on the path when you release the mouse.

The Magic Wand tool
> The Magic Wand will select a region based on all of the contiguous pixels of the same color as the pixel that was clicked. The Tool Options dialog box offers a *Sample Merged* option which, if on, will cause the magic wand to operate on all visible layers. If *Sample Merged* is off, the selection is only made on the current layer.

Bezier selection tool
> This tool allows you to define a selection area with curves or lines using a "Bezier drawing tool" similar to those found in most drafting programs. You can adjust the curves of the selection after it has been drawn by moving the handles associated with each point on the curve.

The Intelligent Scissors tool
> The Intelligent Scissors tool is similar to the hand-drawn selection tool, but it is easier to use in that it will attempt to guess the outlines of the region that you are trying to select. This selection region is then converted to a Bezier selection region which may be further tweaked to get it just right.

The Move Tool

The Move tool will move a layer or a selection, depending on which keys are held down when the tool is used:

No keys
> The tool will move the current layer when the mouse is clicked and dragged.

Shift + Up, Down, Left, or Right cursor keys
> The tool will move the current layer in the direction specified by the cursor key by 25 pixels.

Control + Up, Down, Left, or Right cursor keys
> The tool will move the current layer in the direction specified by the cursor key by 1 pixel. Useful for minute adjustments.

Alt + Up, Down, Left, or Right cursor keys
> The tool will move the current selection in the direction specified by the cursor key by 1 pixels.

Alt + Shift + Up, Down, Left, or Right cursor keys
> The tool will move the current selection in the direction specified by the cursor key by 25 pixels.

The Magnifying Glass Tool

Clicking on a coordinate with the Magnifying Glass will increase the magnification of the current view and center the window on the clicked point. The Tool Options dialog provides options that will resize the window to fit the image.

The Crop Tool

The Crop tool allows you to select part of an image and discard the rest.

The Transform Tool

The Transform tool is actually a collection of four tools. More accurately, the Transform tool can be in one of four tool modes: Rotation, Scaling, Shearing, and Perspective. The tool mode is set via the Transform tool's Tool Options dialog box.

Rotation mode
> In this mode the Transform tool acts a free rotation tool on the current selection. You can hold down the Control key to constrain the rotation angle to 15-degree increments.

Scaling mode

In this mode the Transform tool will scale (enlarge or shrink) the current selection. You can hold down the Control key to constrain scaling to the y dimension, or the Shift key to constrain in the x dimension. Holding down both the Shift and Control keys will make the scaling proportional.

Shearing mode

In this mode the Transform tool will "shear" the image (i.e., shift all the pixels in a plane).

Perspective mode

In this mode the Transform tool will allow you to shift the pixels of the image to get a perspective effect.

The Flip Tool

The Tool Options dialog determines whether the Flip tool will reflect the image on the horizontal or vertical axis.

Text Tool

This tool allows you to place text on the image, with the upper left corner of the text box placed at the clicked point. Once the text is placed on the image, it ceases to become editable text and becomes an image of text. The text dialog box allows you to specify the vertical size of the text in pixels and a font. The color of the text will be the current selected color.

The Color Picker

The Color Picker tool will set the current selected color to the color of the clicked pixel. It will also bring up a dialog with the values for the Red, Green, Blue, and Alpha channels of the color.

The Bucket Fill Tool

The Bucket Fill tool behaves differently if there is an active selection than if it is used on an image without an active selection. If there is an active selection, the Bucket tool will fill the selection with the foreground color. If there is not an active selection, the tool will fill the contiguous area around the clicked pixel with the foreground color. If the Shift key is held down in either case, the background color is used for the fill instead of the foreground color.

The Tool Options dialog for the Bucket tool also has a number of options of note:

Fill Opacity

Allows you specify a percentage value for the opacity of the fill.

Fill Threshold

A range of values used to determine whether a pixel is part of the area to be filled. A pixel is part of the area if it is within this many values of the clicked pixel.

Mode

Allows you to choose a paint mode.

Fill Type

If this option is set to *Color Fill*, the tool will use the foreground or background color to fill. If it is set to *Pattern Fill*, it will use the current active pattern to fill.

Sample merged

If this option is selected, the area to be filled will be determined using the merged image of all the visible layers. Otherwise it will perform on the current layer (the default setting).

Blend Tool

The Blend tool, also called the Gradient tool, allows you to fill an area with a gradient. The start and end points of the gradient are determined by mouse movements; click on the starting point and drag the mouse to the end point. The Tool Options dialog provides the following gradient controls of note:

Opacity

A percentage value specifying the overall opacity of the gradient.

Offset

A percentage value indicating at what point to start the gradient. A value of 20, for example, would start the gradient a fifth of the way through.

Mode

The paint mode that should be used to apply the gradient.

Blend

The *Blend* option allows you to specify whether the colors in the gradient should run from the foreground to background color (or vice versa), from 100% opaque foreground color to 100% transparent foreground color, or whether a custom gradient (provided by the Gradient Editor) should be used.

Gradient

> The *Gradient* option allows you to choose from one of nine gradient types: Linear, Bi-linear, Radial, Square, Conical (Symmetric or Asymmetric), or Shapeburst (Angular, Spherical, or Dimpled).

Repeat

> Allows you to specify whether the gradient should repeat if it does not fill the entire area.

The Pencil Tool

The Pencil tool will draw pixels in the current selected color with the current selected brush. Unlike the Paintbrush tool, the pencil will draw in a single solid color. If you draw fast with the Pencil tool, you may find that the Gimp has trouble keeping up with the cursor and will hedge the line a bit by simplifying the pencil line and making it more choppy. You can avoid this behavior by holding down the Alt key while you draw. This will store the cursor events in a buffer that will let the Gimp catch up with your fast drawing without losing information. To draw a straight line between two points, hold down the Shift key when drawing.

The Paintbrush Tool

The Paintbrush tool is similar to the Pencil tool, except it will draw in the currently selected brush using all the colors of the brush. You can use the Alt and Shift keys with the Paintbrush as you would with the Pencil tool. In addition, the Tool Options dialog offers a *Fade Out* option that specifies the distance in pixels you can paint before the paint "runs out" and you must release the mouse and click again to start a new brushstroke. The default value for *Fade Out* is 0, which indicates that the brush has an infinite supply of paint.

The Eraser Tool

The Eraser tool behaves differently on images with an alpha channel. If the image does not have an alpha channel, the Eraser will draw the background color with the currently selected brush. If the image has an alpha channel, the Eraser will draw in a transparent color with the current brush. The Alt and Shift keys operate the same as for the Pencil tool.

The Airbrush Tool

The Airbrush tool will paint using the current brush like the Paintbrush tool, but the paint will be applied gradually in a semi-transparent spray. The Rate and Pressure tool options let you control how quickly the paint flows and how quickly the transparency of the spray decreases. The Alt and Shift keys operate for the Airbrush tool as for the Pencil tool.

The Clone Tool

The Clone tool (whose icon is a stamp and stamp pad) allows you to paint using the current brush filled in with the currently selected pattern or with a region of pixels within the same image.

The Convolver Tool

The Convolver tool is similar to the Smudge tool in Adobe Photoshop. It allows you to soften sharp edges in an image. The Tool Options dialog allows you to control the pressure (intensity), and whether the area under the cursor should be blurred or sharpened.

The Toolbox Menu Hierarchy

These menus are available at the top of the floating toolbox. A few of the options have equivalent menus associated with the image window, such as *New* or *Open* from the *File* menu. The commands accessible from these menus generally create new images or perform administrative functions such as setting user preferences or starting services. Typically these menus are referred to by the notation *<Toolbox>* → *menu* → *submenu*.

The File Menu

New

> Start a new image. Dialog allows you to specify a new width and height and the initial background color.

Open

> Open an existing image.

About

> Brings up a dialog box with a scrolling message bar featuring the names of all the Gimp developers.

Preferences

> Provides a dialog box that gives access to the user's preferences for the display, user interface, memory usage, and default colormap settings, and the paths to Gimp resources such as plug-ins, palettes, and gradients. This information is stored in the *.gimprc* file in the *.gimp* subdirectory of the user's *home* directory.

Tip of the Day

> Brings up a dialog box with a "tip of the day." This box also pops up when the Gimp is first started.

Dialogs

> This menu provides access to the Gimp's dialog boxes. There are five:

> *Brushes*

>> Select a brush from the brush collection, or set the paint mode, opacity and spacing of a brush.

> *Patterns*

>> Select a pattern from the pattern collection to be used by the fill tools or other tools that use patterns.

> *Palettes*

>> Select a palette from the palette collection or create a new palette.

> *Gradient Editor*

>> Select a built-in custom gradient or create a new custom gradient for use by the Blend tool.

> *Tool Options*

>> This menu item will bring up the Tool Options dialog for the currently selected tool.

Quit

> Quit the Gimp.

The Xtns Menu

DB Browser

> The *DB Browser* opens a window that contains information culled from the Gimp's internal Procedural Database. It is a very handy tool for writing plug-ins and scripts, or even just gleaning hints about the usage of some obscure function. Each of the Gimp's internal functions, as well as plug-ins, scripts and extensions are all listed in the browser. You may pull out groups of functions with the Search by Name and Search by Blurb buttons.

Screen Shot

> This extension will allow you to snap an image of a single window or the whole screen, and it will return a new Gimp image with the screenshot. The *Include Decorations* option controls whether window trimmings (such as window names and close boxes) are to be included in the screenshot.

Script-Fu

Console

This option provides a command-line interface to the SIOD (Scheme in One Day) Scheme interpreter on which Script-Fu is built. You can type a Scheme instruction on the Current Command line and the interpreter will execute it; try (+ 2 2) and see what you get.

Server

This menu option allows you to select a port for the Gimp to communicate with Script-Fu scripts, and to specify an optional log file that will capture errors and messages generated by scripts. The default Script-Fu port is 10008.

Refresh

This command allows you to add scripts to the Gimp while it is running. The *Refresh* option will re-read the list of available scripts and will register new entries.

Web Browser

The *Web Browser* submenu contains bookmarks to online Gimp documentation resources such as the FAQs, Gimp News, the plug-in registry, the manual, tutorials, and the bug report page. The *Open URL* option allows you to type in a specific URL with which the Gimp will launch an external web browser such as Netscape.

The Image Menu Hierarchy

These menus are available by clicking the right mouse button within an image window. In general, the commands accessible via these menus all operate on the image (or on a layer of the image, or on a selection area) from which they were called. Typically these menus are referred to by the notation *<Image>→ menu → submenu*.

The File Menu

New

Start a new image. Dialog allows you to specify a new width and height and the initial background color. This is functionally equivalent to the *New* option under the *Toolbox→ File* menu.

Open

Open an existing image. This is functionally equivalent to the *Open* option under the *Toolbox→ File* menu.

Save

    Save the current image.

Save As

    Save the current image and specify a filename and format. Some image for-
mats require a certain type of image. (To save as a GIF, for example, the
image must be in Indexed mode.) Only the formats applicable to the current
image will be shown in the file type selector of the Save As dialog. If the *By
extension* option is selected (it is the default option), the Gimp will attempt to
guess the file format based on the filename extension provided (e.g., given the
name *quahog.png*, it will try to save as a PNG file).

Preferences

    Equivalent to the *Preferences* option under the *Toolbox → File* menu.

Close

    Close the image.

Quit

    Quit the Gimp.

Mail image

    A somewhat gratuitous (but actually kind of nice) feature; the *Mail image*
option will mail the current image (either Uuencoded or as a multi-part MIME
message) to a specific email address.

Print

    Print the image to a PostScript file or printer.

The Edit Menu

Cut

    Remove the selection from the image and place it in the paste buffer, from
which it may be retrieved with the Paste command. Note that anything currently in the paste buffer will be lost. If a selection is Cut from a layer with an
alpha channel, the selected area will be replaced with 100% transparent pixels. If the layer does not have an alpha channel, the selected area will be
replaced with the current background color.

Copy

    Place a copy of the selected pixels in the paste buffer. Anything previously in
the paste buffer will be lost.

Paste

    Place a copy of whatever is in the paste buffer (from a previous Cut or Copy)
on the image.

Paste Into

Place a copy of whatever is in the paste buffer on the image. *Paste Into* will position the pasted image within the current selection area and crop the pasted image to the selection.

Clear

Remove the selected area from the image. If a selection is cleared from a layer with an alpha channel, the selected area will be replaced with 100% transparent pixels. If the layer does not have an alpha channel, the cleared area will be replaced with the current background color.

Fill

Fill the selected area with the currently selected background color.

Stroke

Draw an anti-aliased line that follows the border of the currently selected area with the currently selected brush. This command may be used in conjunction with the circular selection tool to draw circles, for example.

Undo

Undo the last action. Note that most actions and commands are undoable, even some that you wouldn't necessarily expect (such as moving guidelines). The number of levels of undo may be set in the Preferences dialog box (the default is 5 levels of undo).

Redo

Perform the opposite of an Undo (i.e., re-do the action that was last undone). Note that this must be done immediately after an Undo for it to have an effect.

Cut Named

Perform the same action as *Cut*, but allow the user to associate a name tag with the paste buffer. This allows you to maintain many off-screen paste buffers from which to pull image pixels with *Paste Named*.

Copy Named

Perform the same action as *Copy*, but allow the user to associate a name tag with the paste buffer.

Paste Named

Perform the same action as *Paste*, but allow the user to choose the paste buffer from which to paste. Only selections cut or copied with *Cut Named* or *Copy Named* will show up in this list.

Copy Visible

Copy an image consisting of the current visible layers flattened into a single layer. Useful for obtaining a flattened image from a multi-layered file without flattening the source image.

The Select Menu

Toggle

Turns the "marching ants" of a selection on or off but keeps the selection area active.

Invert

Selects the negative area around the current selection (you might say that it "omits" the currently selected area from a larger selection).

All

Selects the entire image.

None

Any areas that are currently selected will be deselected.

Float

This command will create a "floating selection" from the current selection. A floating selection is a moveable selection area that occupies a layer of its own. The anchor command from the Layers & Channels dialog box will merge a floating selection with the layer it was originally associated with.

Sharpen

This command will remove the fuzziness from the edges of a selection, resulting in a sharp-edged selection area.

Border

This command will create a new selection area that consists of the specified number of pixels surrounding the border of the current selection area.

Feather

A feathered selection is a selection with a "soft edge." The pixels of the selection region grow progressively more transparent toward the edge of the selection. The Tool Options dialog for each of the selection tools allows you to specify the number of pixels near the edge that are feathered. Feathering will help a selection blend in with a background better than an unfeathered selection.

Grow

Expand the current selection area by a given number of pixels in each direction. Along with *Shrink*, this allows very fine control over the extent of a selection area.

Shrink

Contract the current selection area by a given number of pixels in each direction.

Save to Channel

This command will create a "selection mask" which will appear in the Layers & Channels dialog box. This is essentially a way of saving selection regions for later use.

By Color

This command will allow you to select all of the pixels in the image of a certain color or within a certain range of colors.

The View Menu

Zoom In

Increases the magnification of the image displayed in the current window.

Zoom Out

Decreases the magnification of the image displayed in the current window.

Zoom

Provides a list of magnification ratios at which you may view the image (ranging from 16:1 to 1:16).

Window Info

Provides information about the image in the current window, including its size, display ratio, color mode, the color depth at which it is currently displayed, and the number of bits used for the red, green, and blue channels of the image.

Toggle Rulers

Turns the rulers on or off.

Toggle Guides

Guide lines may be added to an image by clicking on the ruler and dragging a guide into place. This option turns these guides on or off.

Snap to Guides

This will cause selections to "snap" to a guide line when it is moved close to it. It is useful for easily aligning several selection areas.

New View

This will open another window on the same image. Changes made to this new view will be reflected in any other open views also. The *Close* command will close a view (window). When the last view on an image is closed, the Gimp will ask you if you wish to save the image if you have not already done so.

Shrink Wrap

If *Shrink Wrap* mode is selected, the size of the window of the current view will expand if you zoom in on the image, so that the entire image fits within the window.

The Image Menu

Colors

This menu option provides access to a number of commands for manipulating the color levels in an image. All of these commands are applied to the currently selected area.

Equalize

Equalize is a color filter that may be used to correct an image that is either over- or under-exposed.

Invert

This will invert all of the pixels within the current selection. For color images, "inversion" means that the value of each channel (R, G, B) is subtracted from the maximum value (255) to give the "inverted" value.

Posterize

This command will quantize the color values within the current selection to a given number of color levels. It is used more as a special effect than for anything else.

Threshold

This command calls up a dialog box with a histogram showing the frequency of intensity values in an image. Selecting an intensity value (or range of values) will display only those pixels of the given intensity.

Color Balance

This option allows you to control the values of each of the red, green, and blue channels relative to the current values. The values can be adjusted individually for the shadow, midtone, and highlight areas of the image.

Brightness-Contrast

This command allows you to control the brightness and contrast of the currently selected area by adjusting a sliding scale that indicates a range of –127 to 127 levels in relation to the current brightness and contrast.

Hue-Saturation

Allows you to control the hue (the color's place in the spectrum) and saturation (the intensity of the color) of all the colors in the current selection. Note that this will only work for RGB mode images.

Curves

This command will bring up a dialog box that provides a fine degree of control over the color and brightness levels of the currently selected area. You can define custom curves for each of the red, green, blue, and alpha channels in the image.

Levels

This command will display a histogram like that of the *Threshold* command, and will let you control the minimum and maximum values for each of the individual channels of the image. The *Levels* command is useful for accentuating the highlighted and shadowed areas of an image.

Desaturate

Removes the color information from the selected area, but keeps the image in RGB mode.

Auto-Stretch Contrast

This is an enhancement technique that will find the minimum and maximum values of each of the red, green, and blue channels for a selected area and "stretch" them so that they span the full range of values. It is a good tool for enhancing muddy photos or scans of poor quality.

Auto-Stretch HSV

This is an enhancement technique that will find the minimum and maximum values of Hue, Saturation, and Value for a selected area and "stretch" them so that they span the full range of values.

Normalize

This filter is a variation of *Auto-Stretch Contrast* that performs the "stretching" of value a bit more intelligently.

Channel Ops

Duplicate

Creates a copy of the image with layers and channels preserved.

Offset

Shifts the current layer by a given amount in the x and y directions. The image will wrap around if the appropriate option is set.

Compose

The *Compose* command will assemble three or four images that are the result of a *Decompose* action into a single new image created by using the individual images as the appropriate channels. The mapping of images to channels may be specified by the user within the Compose dialog box.

Decompose

This command will separate each channel of the current layer into a separate image file. The image may be decomposed in several different color spaces: RGB, HSV, CMY, CMYK, or Alpha. In CMYK color space, for example, the Cyan, Magenta, Yellow, and Black channels will each be copied into their own separate image.

Alpha

> *Add Channel*
>> Adds an alpha channel to the image. An image must have an alpha channel if it is to have transparency.

> *Threshold Alpha*
>> Allows you to specify an alpha channel threshold in the range 0 to 255.

RGB

> Converts the image to RGB mode (the default mode for a new image) which allows millions of colors. Each pixel is saved as individual red, green, and blue values. RGB mode images may not be saved directly as certain color mapped file formats such as GIF.

Grayscale

> Converts the image to grayscale mode. In grayscale mode, each pixel is one of 256 shades of gray. Grayscale images may be saved directly as GIF files.

Indexed

> Converts the image to Indexed mode, with a color table of user-defined size. In Indexed mode, each pixel in the image is stored as an index to a color table. When converting an RGB image to an Indexed image, the color quantization is performed intelligently and dithering may be applied to create a better image. Most filters will not work directly on Indexed mode images, because they must often generate new colors that are not necessarily in the images color table (the Blur filter, for instance). You can view the resulting color table by selecting the *Dialogs* → *Indexed Palette* dialog box.

Resize

> Resizes the borders of the image, but does not scale the pixels of the image.

Scale

> Resizes the image and scales the pixel data to fit the new image dimensions. The new size may be indicated in absolute pixels, or in proportion to the image's original size.

Histogram

> This command brings up a dialog box with a histogram graph showing the values and frequency of occurrence of the intensity of each pixel in each channel of the current selection. The horizontal axis of the histogram is the intensity value (in the range 1 to 255). The vertical "spikes" represent the number of pixels in the image with that particular intensity level. The histogram window also shows specific information such as the mean, standard deviation, and the actual number of pixels with a certain intensity level.

Save palette

This command allows you to save the color table of an Indexed mode image as a palette that will appear in the Palettes dialog box.

Transforms

Autocrop

This command will crop the unused background from the edges of an image. That is, it will crop the image to the bounding box of the actual content of the image.

Image

This submenu provides the options of rotating the entire image 90 or 270 degrees (clockwise in both cases).

Layer

This submenu provides the options of rotating the currently selected layer 90 or 270 degrees (clockwise in both cases).

Rotate

This is another rotate tool that will allow you to rotate either the entire image or the currently selected layer by 0, 90, 180, or 270 degrees clockwise.

Zealous Crop

This command will crop the unused background from the edges and middle of an image.

The Layers Menu

Layers & Channels

Opens the Layers & Channels dialog box.

Raise Layer

Moves a layer up one level in the layer stack. The background layer can be neither raised nor lowered.

Lower Layer

Moves a layer down one level in the layer stack.

Anchor Layer

This will merge a floating selection with the layer the selection was originally associated with.

Merge Visible Layers

Combine all visible layers into a single layer. The position of the resulting layer in the layer stack will be the same position as the lowest original visible layer. All layers not marked as visible will remain as separate layers.

Flatten Image

> Combine all visible layers into a single layer and discard all non-visible layers. This command takes alpha information into account when combining layers, but it removes the alpha channel from the final image. The result is an image with a single layer and no alpha channel.

Alpha to Selection

> This will create a new selection region consisting of the alpha channel for the current layer.

Mask to Selection

> This command will retrieve a previously saved selection mask and mark it as the current active selection region.

Add Alpha Channel

> Adds an alpha channel to only the currently selected layer.

Align Visible Layers

> This command will align all of the visible layers based on a variety of parameters.

Figure B-1. This cute photo of a cat playing with Gumby is used by several plug-ins as a random image data seed. It is the file named beavis.jpg in your plug-in directory.

The Tools Menu

Provides access to all the tools in the Toolbox.

The Filters Menu

All of the filters available from this menu will be applied to the currently selected area. Most of the filters have custom dialog boxes that allow you to modify many input parameters.

Repeat Last

Re-applies the last action chosen from the *Filters* menu with the same parameters.

Re-show Last

Re-applies the last action chosen from the *Filters* menu, but allows you to reset the input parameters.

Animation

Animation Optimize

This plug-in applies various optimizations to a Gimp layer-based animation.

Animation Playback

This plug-in allows you to preview a Gimp layer-based animation.

Animation UnOptimize

This plug-in "reconstructs" a Gimp layer-based animation that has been optimized with *Animation Optimize*. This makes the animation much easier to work with if, for example, the optimized version is all you have.

Artistic

Apply Canvas

This function applies a canvas texture map to the drawable.

Cubism

A special effect filter that converts the image into a collection of arbitrarily rotated squares.

Mosaic

A special effect filter that converts the image into a pattern of simulated tiles, using the colors of the original image.

Oilify

A filter that applies the familiar (and much abused) "oil paint" special effect.

Blur

Blur

This function randomly blurs the specified drawable, using a 3×3 blur. The type and percentage are user-selectable.

Gaussian Blur (IIR)

> Applies a gaussian blur to the drawable, with specified radius of effect (in pixels). Horizontal and vertical blurring can be independently invoked by specifying one or the other. The IIR gaussian blurring works best for large radius values and for images which are not computer-generated.

Gaussian Blur (RLE)

> Similar to the previous *Gaussian Blur*, but the RLE blurring performs most efficiently on computer-generated images or images with large areas of constant intensity.

Motion Blur

> This plug-in adds copies of the image and displaces them to achieve the effect seen when photographing a moving object at a slow shutter speed.

Pixelize

This plug-in causes the image to be pixelized in blocks of the given dimensions.

Colors

Alien Map

> A special effects filter.

Color Exchange

> Swap two colors in an image, with an optional threshold setting.

Colorify

> Averages the RGB colors in the image and uses this information to change the colors in the image.

Gradient Map

> This plug-in calculates the luminosity of each pixel and replaces each pixel by the sample of the active gradient (chosen with the Gradient Editor) proportional to that luminosity. In other words, a completely black pixel would be replaced with the leftmost color of the gradient, and a complete white pixel would be replaced with the rightmost color of the gradient.

Hot

> This plug-in scans the image for "hot" pixels. A "hot" pixel is one with a value of chrominance or composite signal amplitude that is too high when encoded into an NTSC or PAL video signal. This plug-in allows you to blacken each hot pixel, or reduce its luminance or saturation.

Max RGB

> This plug-in returns an image in which each pixel holds only the channel that has the maximum value of each of the red, green, and blue channels.

Scatter HSV

This plug-in scatters the pixel values in HSV (Hue, Saturation, Value) space.

Semi Flatten

This plug-in flattens pixels that aren't completely transparent against the current Gimp background color and retains those pixels that are completely transparent (see Chapter 7, *Web Graphics with the Gimp*). Operates on an RGB image with Alpha.

Smooth Palette

This plug-in returns an image that acts as a palette from an RGB image.

Value Invert

This plug-in effectively inverts the brightness of each pixel while leaving its color and saturation unchanged. It does this by taking an Indexed or RGB image and inverting its Value in HSV (Hue, Saturation, Value) space.

Combine

Depth Merge

This plug-in takes two RGBA images and two corresponding grayscale depth maps, and combines the two images based on which has a lower depth value for each pixel.

Film

A special effects filter that composes several layers or images onto a simulated roll of film.

Distorts

Blinds

This plug-in adds the effect of opening or closing a set of window blinds on the image.

Emboss

This plug-in applies an embossing effect on the given drawable. The user may specify the angle and elevation of the light source.

Engrave

A filter that creates an effect similar to old wood engravings.

Iwarp

A plug-in that allows you to "interactively warp" a given image.

Pagecurl

This plug-in creates the popular page curling effect.

Polar Coords

This plug-in remaps an image from rectangular coordinates to polar coordinates (or vice versa).

Ripple

This plug-in will shift the pixels of each row or column by a certain number of pixels coinciding with the shape of the user-specified wave form.

Shift

This plug-in displaces the pixels of the specified drawable, where each row is shifted a random number of pixels.

Value Propagate

This plug-in will propagate the values of the current layer.

Waves

Similar to *Ripple*, this plug-in will shift the pixels of each row or column by a certain number of pixels to give a waving effect.

Whirl and Pinch

This plug-in distorts the image by whirling and pinching it around its center. Whirling is achieved by rotating each pixel through a certain angle around the center, and pinching is akin to the effect of pulling the center of the image mapped to a 3-D elastic surface.

Edge-Detect

Edge

This plug-in detects the edges in an image by applying a 3×3 convolution kernel.

Laplace

This plug-in creates one-pixel wide edges from the image. The image should first have a Gaussian Blur (IIR) applied in the range 1.5–5.0 for the filter to work properly.

Sobel

This plug-in detects the edges of an image in one or both directions using a "Sobel operator."

Enhance

Deinterlace

This plug-in is useful for processing images from video capture cards. When only the odd or even fields get captured, *Deinterlace* can be used to interpolate between the existing fields.

Despeckle

This plug-in selectively performs a median or adaptive box filter on an image to remove "speckles."

Destripe

This may be used to remove vertical stripes caused by the uneven light source of a cheap scanner.

NL Filter

A Nonlinear "Swiss army knife" filter.

Sharpen

A filter that may be used to "sharpen" a photographic image by performing a convolution filter on the image.

Generic

Convolution Matrix

This filter provides a 5×5 convolution matrix.

Glass Effects

Apply Lens

This plug-in uses Snell's law to draw an ellipsoid lens on top of the image.

Glass Tile

This plug-in divides the image into squares that have the look of glass blocks.

Light Effects

FlareFX

This filter adds an effect similar to a flash of light reflecting from a piece of glass (a lens flare).

Sparkle

Adds sparkles with diffraction effects to the image.

SuperNova

This plug-in produces an effect like a supernova burst. The amount of the light at each point is in inverse proportion to the distance from the center of the burst.

Map

Bump Map

This creates an embossing effect using a grayscale image as a bump map to be applied on the source image.

Displace

This plug-in takes two images, a source image and a "displace map image." It then displaces each pixel of the source image by the given x and y offsets multiplied by the intensity of corresponding pixels in the displace map image.

Fractal Trace

This plug-in transforms an image by mapping it around the Mandelbrot Fractal.

Illusion

A special effects filter.

Make Seamless

This plug-in creates a seamlessly tileable image from the input image.

Map Object

This plug-in maps a picture to a plane or sphere, with many user-customizable options.

Paper Tile

This plug-in cuts and slides an image.

Small Tiles

This plug-in will make the image a composite of smaller versions of itself.

Tile

This plug-in creates a new image with a single layer sized to the specified dimensions. The input image is then tiled into this layer.

Misc

Video

This plug-in simulates the degradation of an old low-dot-pitch RGB video monitor.

Noise

Noisify

This plug-in adds random noise to the channels of an image.

Randomize

This plug-in randomly modified the drawable, either by "Hurling" (throwing random colors), picking from nearby pixels, or "Slurring" (a melting effect).

Spread

This plug-in causes pixels to be randomly moved to another location whose distance varies from the original by the given horizontal and vertical spread amounts.

Render

CML Explorer

This plug-in creates an image of a Coupled-Map Lattice (CML), a kind of Cellular Automaton.

Checkerboard

This plug-in adds a checkerboard pattern to an image.

Diffraction Patterns

This will generate customizable diffraction patterns

Gfig

A robust plug-in that allows you to generate geometric shapes for inclusion in Gimp images.

Grid

This draws a user-defined grid on the image.

IfsCompose

This plug-in will create an Iterated Function System fractal from an interactive user interface.

Maze

This plug-in generates a maze using either the depth-first search method or Prim's algorithm. It can make tileable mazes too. See *http://www.poboxes.com/kevint/gimp/maze-help.html* for more help.

Plasma

This creates a "plasma cloud" image.

Qbist

This plug-in generates modern art pictures from a random genetic formula, based on an article by Jörn Loviscach.

Sinus

This plug-in generates different textured patterns.

Solid Noise

This creates a grayscale noise texture.

The Script-Fu Menu

One important thing to remember when applying scripts is that they often cannot be undone all at once. Scripts are sequences of commands that will be undone individually when you select *Undo*. Often there will be more commands performed than your Undo buffer will hold (the default is 5 levels of Undo). It is best to apply scripts to a copy of your original image when possible (usually the script will offer this as an option).

Version 1.0 of the Gimp was distributed with a separate Script-Fu menu hierarchy for scripts written in Script-Fu. This menu structure will probably become less relevant in the future, as scripts should really be placed next to their functional counterparts (e.g., a script that combines other images should go in the *<Image>→ Filters→ Combine* menu rather than *<Image>→ Script-Fu→ Combine*). This is not to say that you cannot create new subgroups within the menu hierarchy; it's just that the criteria for organizing the workflow should not necessarily be the language in which the plug-in was written. That said, the following are scripts written in ScriptFu:

Decor

Add Bevel

This script adds a beveled edge of a given size to an image.

Circuit

This script fills the current selection area with something that looks vaguely like a circuit board.

Coffee Stain

This adds a realistic-looking coffee stain to your image.

Fuzzy Border

This script will gradually fade out the edges of the source image (similar to the *Old Photo* script).

Lava

This script fills the current selection with a lava effect.

Old Photo

This gives the image the appearance of an old, yellowed photograph.

Predator

This script fills the current selection with an interesting pattern.

Round Corners

This script rounds the corners of an image and adds an optional drop-shadow.

Slide

This script gives the image the appearance of a photographic slide, with an optional label and number markings.

Xach Effect

This creates a starburst effect, as seen on the Gimp News web page.

Modify

Add Border

This script adds a colored border of user-defined size to the image.

Utils

ASCII 2 Image Layer

This script will read text from a file and compose it in a given font on the image.

Draw HSV Graph

This script returns a new image that is a graph of the Hue, Saturation, and Value values of the given image.

Show Image Structure

This script creates a three-dimensional simulation of the layer structure of the image.

Stencil Ops

Carve-It

This script takes a grayscale and a source image and uses the grayscale as a stencil to carve from the source image.

Chrome-It

This script takes a grayscale and a source image and uses the grayscale as a stencil on which to run the chrome effect.

Alchemy

Clothify

This script creates a textured cloth effect using the source image.

Erase every other row

This script will remove either the even or odd rows or columns of pixels from an image.

Unsharp Image

A script that acts like a sharpen filter on the current selection.

Weave

This creates a basket weave effect.

Selection

Distress Selection

This script will make the borders of a selection region less regular.

Fade Outline

This script will crop the image to the selected area and fade edges of the region outside the selection.

To Brush

This script will convert the current selection region to a brush that may be made available via the Brushes dialog.

To image

This script will create a new image from the current selection.

Round

This will round off the edges of an active rectangular selection.

Shadow

Drop-Shadow

This script adds a drop shadow of a given length to the current selection or alpha channel.

Perspective

This scripts adds a "perspective shadow" of the selection.

Render

Make Grid System

This creates a grid on top of the image with a user defined number of rows and columns, using the current brush settings.

Line Nova

This draws a series of lines in the foreground color from the center of the image to its edges.

C

Procedure Reference for the Gimp

This appendix provides a reference to the interface to the Gimp's internal Procedural Database (PDB). The Gimp's API says that all procedures and plug-ins must contain some sort of documentation about themselves, and this documentation gets logged in the PDB when the procedure is registered. There are several ways of accessing this information while you are programming. The most helpful is the DB Browser extension, which provides a searchable interface to the PDB from within the Gimp.* The DB Browser has certain limitations for the Gimp-Perl programmer, however. In the DB Browser, all procedure names are delimited by hyphens (gimp-image-new, for example), while Perl uses underscores (gimp_image_new). The reference tables in this appendix list the Gimp procedure names with underscores. The names of several constants are also different when working with the Gimp Perl module than they appear in the DB Browser (the paint modes, for example). These are noted in the following tables also.

The purpose of this reference is to give you another way of looking at the Gimp's procedures. It is ordered by functional category. This reference should be used in conjunction with the DB Browser, because the Browser provides you with a look inside the version of Gimp that you are currently running and is by definition more up-to-date. There are also several scripts and filters that are not documented here.

The following tables are broken down into ten sections, ordered loosely by the order in which you may typically use them:

1. *Procedural database information*: procedures for obtaining information about the Gimp's PDB.

2. *File operations*: procedures for loading and saving files.

---

* The other way to access this information is via one of the PDB query procedures.

3. *Painting, drawing, and transform*: procedures for drawing on an image.

4. *Color control, palettes, and patterns*: procedures for managing color.

5. *Selection*: procedures that create selection regions.

6. *Layers and channel management*: procedures that manipulate layers and channels.

7. *Undo and redo control*: procedures for managing the Gimp's Undo stacks.

8. *Image information and management*: procedures for obtaining information about an image.

9. *User interface procedures*: procedures that control user interface gadgets.

10. *Extensions*: Gimp extensions available under the *Xtns* menu.

Script-Fu scripts often have hyphens in their names rather than underscores.[*] When calling Script-Fu scripts from Perl, you must use this syntax for hyphenated procedure names:

```
"script-fu-old-photo"->(RUN_INTERACTIVE, $image, $drawable, 1, 1, 1, 1, 1);
```

Most of the procedures may be called using procedural-style syntax, or by using a more sophisticated object-oriented approach. The Gimp-Perl module defines several Perl objects that may be used to simplify procedure calls. In general, a "procedural style" call such as:

```
$height = gimp_drawable_height($drawable);
```

may be re-written as:

```
$height = $drawable->height;
```

if the scalar **$drawable** contains a *Drawable*. Note that in the latter case you do not have to include **gimp_drawable_** as part of the procedure call, and you also do not have to send the drawable as a parameter. Gimp::Fu will go a step further when using an object, and let you leave off the **image** and the **drawable** if they are the first two parameters. The procedure call:

```
gimp_image_by_color_select( $image, $drawable,
                            [255, 0, 0], 10,
                            SELECTION_REPLACE, 1, 0, 0, 0 );
```

could be written using an object as:

```
$image->by_color_select( [255, 0, 0], 10, SELECTION_REPLACE, 1, 0, 0, 0 );
```

---

[*] To make matters worse, these scripts are not distinguished from their underscored counterparts in the DB Browser. You have to guess by the "script-fu-" prepended to the procedure's name.

To create a new object, use the appropriate constructor procedure. For example, to create a new Layer object, call *gimp_layer_new* in an object-oriented manner:

```
# See the listing for gimp_layer_new for the description
# of the parameters necessary to create a new layer
#
my $layer = new Layer($image, $width, $height,
                      RGB_IMAGE, "Nice Layer",
                      100, NORMAL_MODE);
```

Some objects pull double duty; they may be used to call a number of types of procedures. The valid objects, and the prefixes for the types of procedures that they may call, is:

Object	Prefixes	Object	Prefixes
Gimp	gimp_	Selection	gimp_selection_
Layer	gimp_layer_ gimp_drawable_ gimp_image_ gimp_	Drawable	gimp_drawable_ gimp_layer_ gimp_image_ gimp_
Image	gimp_image_ gimp_drawable_ gimp_	Channel	gimp_channel_ gimp_drawable_ gimp_image_ gimp_
Display	gimp_display_ gimp_	Palette	gimp_palette_
Gradients	gimp_gradients_	Plugin	plug_in_
Edit	gimp_edit_	Tile	gimp_tile_
Progress	gimp_progress_	PixelRgn	gimp_pixel_rgn_
Region	none	GDrawable	gimp_drawable_
Brushes	gimp_brushes_	Patterns	gimp_patterns_

All of the following tables are divided into three columns. The first is the procedure's name, the second is a brief description (the procedure's "blurb" from the PDB), and the third is an ordered list of the arguments that the procedure takes. If a procedure returns values, they are listed in column three under "Returns".

Procedural Database Information

Use *gimp_procedural_db_dump* to log the entire database to a file. Use *gimp_procedural_db_proc_info* to retrieve information about a specific procedure. The *gimp_procedural_db_query* function will allow you to query the database using regular expressions to find groups of similar entries.

See also the sidebar "The Gimp is a Self-Documenting System" in Chapter 7 for a full example using these procedures.

Table C-1. Procedures Providing Access to the Gimp's Internal Procedural Database

Name	Description	Arguments
gimp_ procedural_ db_dump	Dumps the current contents of the procedural database	`filename` (*String*) The dump filename
gimp_ procedural_ db_get_data	Returns data associated with the specified identifier	`identifier` (*String*) The identifier associated with data **Returns:** `bytes` (*Integer*) The number of bytes in the data `data` (*IntArray*) A byte array containing data
gimp_ procedural_ db_proc_arg	Queries the procedural database for information on the specified procedure's argument	`procedure` (*String*) The procedure name `arg_num` (*Integer*) The argument number **Returns:** `arg_type` (*Integer*) The type of argument (PDB_INT32, PDB_INT16, PDB_INT8, PDB_FLOAT, PDB_STRING, PDB_INT32ARRAY, PDB_INT16ARRAY, PDB_INT8ARRAY, PDB_FLOATARRAY, PDB_STRINGARRAY, PDB_COLOR, PDB_REGION, PDB_DISPLAY, PDB_IMAGE, PDB_LAYER, PDB_CHANNEL, PDB_DRAWABLE, PDB_SELECTION, PDB_BOUNDARY, PDB_PATH, PDB_STATUS) `arg_name` (*String*) The name of the argument `arg_desc` (*String*) A description of the argument
gimp_ procedural_ db_proc_info	Queries the procedural database for information on the specified procedure	`Procedure` (*String*) The procedure name **Returns:** `blurb` (*String*) A short blurb `help` (*String*) Detailed procedure help `author` (*String*) Author(s) of the procedure `copyright` (*String*) The copyright `date` (*String*) Copyright date `proc_type` (*Integer*) The procedure type (INTERNAL, PROC_PLUGIN, PROC_EXTENSION) `num_args` (*Integer*) The number of input arguments `num_rvals` (*Integer*) The number of return values

Table C-1. Procedures Providing Access to the Gimp's Internal Procedural Database

Name	Description	Arguments
gimp_ procedural_ db_proc_val	Queries the procedural database for information on the specified procedure's return value	procedure (*String*) The procedure name val_num (*Integer*) The return value number **Returns:** val_type (*Integer*) The type of return value (PDB_INT32, PDB_INT16, PDB_INT8, PDB_FLOAT, PDB_STRING, PDB_INT32ARRAY, PDB_INT16ARRAY, PDB_INT8ARRAY, PDB_FLOATARRAY, PDB_STRINGARRAY, PDB_COLOR, PDB_REGION, PDB_DISPLAY, PDB_IMAGE, PDB_LAYER, PDB_CHANNEL, PDB_DRAWABLE, PDB_SELECTION, PDB_BOUNDARY, PDB_PATH, PDB_STATUS) val_name (*String*) The name of the return value val_desc (*String*) A description of the return value
gimp_ procedural_ db_query	Queries the procedural database for its contents using regular expression matching	name (*String*) The regex for procedure name blurb (*String*) The regex for procedure blurb help (*String*) The regex for procedure help author (*String*) The regex for procedure author copyright (*String*) The regex for procedure copyright date (*String*) The regex for procedure date proc_type (*String*) The regex for procedure type **Returns:** num_matches (*Integer*) The number of matching procedures procedure_names (*StringArray*) The list of procedure names
gimp_ procedural_ db_set_data	Associates the specified identifier with the supplied data	identifier (*String*) The identifier for association with data bytes (*Integer*) The number of bytes in data data (*IntArray*) The data

File Operations

All of the file operations performed by the Gimp are handled by plug-ins. To support a new file format, all you have to do is write a "file load" procedure and a "file save" procedure, and register them with the Gimp. Each format's load procedure follows a similar format, taking three arguments and returning an image. The *run_mode* specifies whether the Gimp should prompt the user for information (if *RUN_INTERACTIVE*) or simply perform the action with the supplied arguments (if *RUN_NONINTERACTIVE*). The *filename* and *raw_filename** arguments should both contain the path and name of the file to load. The first five arguments of the save procedure for a file format are also generally standard: the *run_mode*, the *image* to save, the *drawable* for the image, the *filename* to save it as, and the *raw_filename*. Most formats have additional arguments to the save procedure (*file_png_save*, for example, allows you to specify a compression level and whether the image is to be interlaced).

The *gimp_temp_name* function will return a unique filename in the user's *.gimp* directory. Here's an example of saving an image as a temporary GIF file:

```
# Save as a temporary GIF file
#
gimp_convert_indexed_palette($img, 1, 2, 0, 0);   # Use web palette
my $tmpfile = gimp_temp_name('gif');
file_gif_save(RUN_NONINTERACTIVE, $img, $drawable,
              $tmpfile, $tmpfile, 1, 0, 100, 0);
```

There are actually many more file formats supported by the Gimp; only those specifically applicable to web graphics have been listed in Table C-2. Check the DB Browser for the full list of file formats supported by your version of the Gimp.

Table C-2. Procedures for Loading and Saving Files

Name	Description	Arguments
file_gif_load	Loads files of Compuserve GIF file format	run_mode (*Integer*) RUN_INTERACTIVE or RUN_NONINTERACTIVE filename (*String*) The name of the file to load raw_filename (*String*) The name entered **Returns:** image (*Image*) Output image

---

* The *raw_filename* parameter is there as a convenience for certain applications, to allow the name that was entered to differ from the actual path to the file, as in a URL string, for example.

Table C-2. Procedures for Loading and Saving Files (continued)

Name	Description	Arguments

file_gif_save	Saves files in Compuserve GIF file format	run_mode (*Integer*)
		    RUN_INTERACTIVE or RUN_NONINTERACTIVE
		image (*Image*)
		    Image to save
		drawable (*Fo*)
		    Drawable to save
		filename (*String*)
		    The name of the file to save the image in
		raw_filename (*String*)
		    The name entered
		interlace (*Integer*)
		    Save as interlaced
		loop (*Integer*)
		    Loop infinitely if an animated GIF
		default_delay (*Integer*)
		    Default delay between frames in milliseconds for animated GIF
		default_dispose (*Integer*)
		    Default disposal type for animated GIF:
		    0 Don't care
		    1 Combine
		    2 Replace

file_jpeg_load	Loads files of the JPEG file format	run_mode (*Integer*)
		    RUN_INTERACTIVE or RUN_NONINTERACTIVE
		filename (*String*)
		    The name of the file to load
		raw_filename (*String*)
		    The name entered
		Returns:
		image (*Image*)
		    Output image

file_jpeg_save	Saves files in the JPEG file format	run_mode (*Integer*)
		    RUN_INTERACTIVE or RUN_NONINTERACTIVE
		image (*Image*)
		    Image to save
		drawable (*Drawable*)
		    Drawable to save
		filename (*String*)
		    The name of the file to save the image in
		raw_filename (*String*)
		    The name entered
		interlace (*Integer*)
		    Save as interlaced
		quality (*Float*)
		    Quality of saved image (Q factor) in the range 0 to 1
		smoothing (*Float*)
		    The smoothing factor for the saved image in the range 0 to 1
		optimize (*Integer*)
		    Optimization of entropy encoding parameters

Table C-2. Procedures for Loading and Saving Files (continued)

Name	Description	Arguments
file_png_load	Loads files of the Portable Network Graphics format	run_mode (*Integer*) RUN_INTERACTIVE or RUN_NONINTERACTIVE filename (*String*) The name of the file to load raw_filename (*String*) The name entered **Returns:** image (*Image*) Output image
file_png_save	Saves files in the Portable Network Graphics format	run_mode (*Integer*) RUN_INTERACTIVE or RUN_NONINTERACTIVE image (*Image*) Image to save drawable (*Drawable*) Drawable to save filename (*String*) The name of the file to save the image in raw_filename (*String*) The name entered interlace (*Integer*) Save as interlaced compression (*Integer*) The compression level in the range 0 to 9 (9=most)
file_ps_load	Load file of PostScript/PDF file format	run_mode (*Integer*) RUN_INTERACTIVE or RUN_NONINTERACTIVE filename (*String*) The name of the file to load raw_filename (*String*) The name of the file to load **Returns:** image (*Image*) Output image
file_ps_load_ setargs	Set additional parameters for procedure file_ ps_load	resolution (*Integer*) Resolution to interpreted image (dpi) width (*Integer*) Desired width height (*Integer*) Desired height check_bbox (*Integer*) 0. Use width/height 1. Use BoundingBox information pages (*String*) Pages to load (e.g., 1,3,5-7) coloring (*Integer*) 4. Black and white 5. Gray 6. Color image 7. Automatic

Table C-2. Procedures for Loading and Saving Files (continued)

Name	Description	Arguments
file_ps_load_ setargs (*cont'd*)		TextAlphaBits (*Integer*) The number of pixels of alpha to use for anti-aliasing (1, 2, or 4) GraphicsAlphaBits (*Integer*) The number of pixels of alpha to use for anti-aliasing (1, 2, or 4)
file_ps_save	Save file in PostScript file format	run_mode (*Integer*) RUN_INTERACTIVE or RUN_NONINTERACTIVE image (*Image*) Input image drawable (*Drawable*) Drawable to save filename (*String*) The name of the file to save the image in raw_filename (*String*) The name of the file to save the image in width (*Float*) Width of the image in PostScript file height (*Float*) Height of image in PostScript file x_offset (*Float*) X-offset to image from lower left corner y_offset (*Float*) Y-offset to image from lower left corner unit (*Integer*) Unit for width/height/offset. 0 inches, 1 millimeter keep_ratio (*Integer*) 0. Use width/height, 1. Keep aspect ratio rotation (*Integer*) Degrees to rotate (0, 90, 180, 270) eps_flag (*Integer*) 0. PostScript 1. Encapsulated PostScript preview (*Integer*) 0. No preview >0. Max. size of preview
file_psd_load	Loads files of the Photo-Shop™ PSD file format	run_mode (*Integer*) RUN_INTERACTIVE or RUN_NONINTERACTIVE filename (*String*) The name of the file to load raw_filename (*String*) The name of the file to load **Returns:** image (*Image*) Output image

Table C-2. Procedures for Loading and Saving Files (continued)

Name	Description	Arguments
file_url_load	Loads files given a URL	run_mode (*Integer*) RUN_INTERACTIVE or RUN_NONINTERACTIVE filename (*String*) The name of the file to load raw_filename (*String*) The name entered **Returns:** image (*Image*) Output image
gimp_file_load	Loads a file by extension	run_mode (*Integer*) RUN_INTERACTIVE or RUN_NONINTERACTIVE filename (*String*) The name of the file to load. raw_filename (*String*) The name entered. **Returns:** image (*Image*) Output image.
gimp_file_save	Saves a file by extension	run_mode (*Integer*) RUN_INTERACTIVE or RUN_NONINTERACTIVE image (*Image*) Input image drawable (*Drawable*) Drawable to save filename (*String*) The name of the file to save the image in raw_filename (*String*) The name of the file to save the image in
gimp_xcf_load	Loads file saved in the .xcf file format	dummy_param (*Integer*) Dummy parameter filename (*String*) The name of the file to load raw_filename (*String*) The name of the file to load **Returns:** image (*Image*) Output image
gimp_xcf_save	Saves file in the .xcf file format	dummy_param (*Integer*) Dummy parameter image (*Image*) Input image drawable (*Drawable*) Active drawable of input image filename (*String*) The name of the file to save the image in raw_filename (*String*) The name of the file to load

Table C-2. Procedures for Loading and Saving Files (continued)

Name	Description	Arguments

gimp_gimprc_ query	Queries the gimprc file parser for information on a specified token	token (*String*)
		    The token to query for
		Returns:
		value (*String*)
		    The value associated with the queried token

gimp_image_ get_filename	Return the file-name of the image	image (*Image*)
		    The image
		Returns:
		filename (*String*)
		    The image's filename

gimp_image_ set_filename	Set the image's filename	image (*Image*)
		    The image
		filename (*String*)
		    The image's filename

gimp_register_ load_handler	Registers a file load handler procedure	procedure_name (*String*)
		    The name of the procedure to be used for loading
		extensions (*String*)
		    Comma-separated list of extensions this handler can load (e.g., "jpeg, jpg")
		prefixes (*String*)
		    Comma-separated list of prefixes this handler can load (e.g., "http:, ftp:")

gimp_register_ magic_load_ handler	Registers a file load handler procedure	procedure_name (*String*)
		    The name of the procedure to be used for loading
		extensions (*String*)
		    Comma-separated list of extensions this handler can load (e.g., "jpeg, jpg")
		prefixes (*String*)
		    Comma-separated list of prefixes this handler can load (e.g., "http:, ftp:")

gimp_register_ save_handler	Registers a file save handler procedure	procedure_name (*String*)
		    The name of the procedure to be used for saving
		extensions (*String*)
		    Comma separated list of extensions this handler can save (e.g., "jpeg, jpg")
		prefixes (*String*)
		    Comma separated list of prefixes this handler can save (e.g., "http:, ftp:")

gimp_temp_ name	Generates a unique file-name	extension (*String*)
		    The extension the file will have
		Returns:
		name (*String*)
		    The temporary filename

Painting, Drawing, and Transforms

In the Gimp, a Drawable is a layer, a channel, or an image. You can use the Gimp::Drawable object to simplify the use of most of these drawing procedures. Procedures to get information about drawables are listed later in this appendix, in Table C-8.

For more information on operating directly on the raw pixels of an image, check out the Gimp::Pixel manpage that is distributed with the Gimp-Perl module.

Table C-3. Procedures for Drawing and Painting on Images, Controlling Brushes, and Performing Transformations

Name	Description	Arguments
gimp_airbrush	Paint in the current brush with varying pressure. Paint application is time-dependent	image (*Image*) The image drawable (*Drawable*) The drawable pressure (*Float*) The pressure of the airbrush strokes in the range 0 to 100 num_strokes (*Integer*) Number of stroke control points (count each coordinate as 2 pts) strokes (*FloatArray*) Array of stroke coordinates (stroke$_{x1}$, stroke$_{y1}$, ... stroke$_{xn}$, stroke$_{yn}$)
gimp_blend	Blend between the starting and ending coordinates with the specified blend mode and gradient type	image (*Image*) The image drawable (*Drawable*) The affected drawable blend_mode (*Integer*) The type of blend (FG_BG_RGB, FG_BG_HSV, FG_TRANS, CUSTOM) paint_mode (*Integer*) The paint application mode (NORMAL_MODE, DISSOLVE_MODE, BEHIND_MODE, MULTIPLY_MODE, SCREEN_MODE, OVERLAY_MODE, DIFFERENCE_MODE, ADDITION_MODE, SUBTRACT_MODE, DARKEN_ONLY_MODE, LIGHTEN_ONLY_MODE, HUE_MODE, SATURATION_MODE, COLOR_MODE, VALUE_MODE) gradient_type (*Integer*) The type of gradient (LINEAR, BILINEAR, RADIAL, SQUARE, CONICAL_SYMMETRIC, CONICAL_ASYMMETRIC, SHAPEBURST_ANGULAR, SHAPEBURST_SPHERICAL, SHAPEBURST_DIMPLED) opacity (*Float*) The opacity of the final blend in the range 0 to 100

Table C-3. Procedures for Drawing and Painting on Images, Controlling Brushes, and Performing Transformations (continued)

Name	Description	Arguments
gimp_blend (*cont'd*)		offset (*Float*) Offset relates to the starting and ending coordinates specified for the blend. This parameter is mode-dependent. repeat (*Integer*) Repeat mode (REPEAT_NONE, REPEAT_ SAWTOOTH, REPEAT_TRIANGULAR) supersample (*Integer*) Do adaptive supersampling (true/false) max_depth (*Integer*) Maximum recursion levels for supersampling threshold (*Float*) Supersampling threshold x1 (*Float*) The x coordinate of this blend's starting point y1 (*Float*) The y coordinate of this blend's starting point x2 (*Float*) The x coordinate of this blend's ending point y2 (*Float*) The y coordinate of this blend's ending point
gimp_brushes_ get_brush	Retrieve information about the currently active brush mask	**Returns:** name (*String*) The brush name width (*Integer*) The brush width height (*Integer*) The brush height spacing (*Integer*) The brush spacing (% of maximum width and height)
gimp_brushes_ get_opacity	Get the brush opacity	**Returns:** opacity (*Float*) The brush opacity in the range 0 to 100
gimp_brushes_ get_paint_ mode	Get the brush paint_mode	**Returns:** paint_mode (*Integer*) The paint mode (NORMAL_MODE, DISSOLVE_ MODE, BEHIND_MODE, MULTIPLY_MODE, SCREEN_MODE, OVERLAY_MODE, DIFFERENCE_ MODE, ADDITION_MODE, SUBTRACT_MODE, DARKEN_ONLY_MODE, LIGHTEN_ONLY_MODE, HUE_MODE, SATURATION_MODE, COLOR_MODE, VALUE_MODE)
gimp_brushes_ get_spacing	Get the brush spacing	**Returns:** spacing (*Integer*) The brush spacing in the range 0 to 1000

Table C-3. Procedures for Drawing and Painting on Images, Controlling Brushes, and Performing Transformations (continued)

Name	Description	Arguments
gimp_brushes_list	Retrieve a complete listing of the available brushes	**Returns:** num_brushes (*Integer*) The number of brushes in the brush list brush_list (*StringArray*) The list of brush names
gimp_brushes_refresh	Refresh current brushes if a new brush has been added while the Gimp has been running	
gimp_brushes_set_brush	Set the specified brush as the active brush	name (*String*) The brush name
gimp_brushes_set_opacity	Set the brush opacity	opacity (*Float*) The brush opacity in the range 0 to 100
gimp_brushes_set_paint_mode	Set the brush paint_mode	paint_mode (*Integer*) The paint mode (NORMAL_MODE, DISSOLVE_MODE, BEHIND_MODE, MULTIPLY_MODE, SCREEN_MODE, OVERLAY_MODE, DIFFERENCE_MODE, ADDITION_MODE, SUBTRACT_MODE, DARKEN_ONLY_MODE, LIGHTEN_ONLY_MODE, HUE_MODE, SATURATION_MODE, COLOR_MODE, VALUE_MODE)
gimp_brushes_set_spacing	Set the brush spacing	spacing (*Integer*) The brush spacing in the range 0 to 1000
gimp_bucket_fill	Fill the area specified either by the current selection if there is one, or by a seed fill starting at the specified coordinates	image (*Image*) The image drawable (*Drawable*) The affected drawable fill_mode (*Integer*) The type of fill (FG_BUCKET-FILL, BG_BUCKET_FILL, PATTERN_BUCKET_FILL) paint_mode (*Integer*) The paint application mode (NORMAL_MODE, DISSOLVE_MODE, BEHIND_MODE, MULTIPLY_MODE, SCREEN_MODE, OVERLAY_MODE, DIFFERENCE_MODE, ADDITION_MODE, SUBTRACT_MODE, DARKEN_ONLY_MODE, LIGHTEN_ONLY_MODE, HUE_MODE, SATURATION_MODE, COLOR_MODE, VALUE_MODE) opacity (*Float*) The opacity of the final bucket fill in the range 0 to 100

Table C-3. Procedures for Drawing and Painting on Images, Controlling Brushes, and Performing Transformations (continued)

Name	Description	Arguments
gimp_bucket_ fill (*cont'd*)		threshold (*Float*) The threshold determines how extensive the seed fill will be. Its value is specified in terms of intensity levels in the range 0 to 255. This parameter is only valid when there is no selection in the specified image. sample_merged (*Integer*) Use the composite image, not the drawable x (*Float*) The x coordinate of this bucket fill's application. This parameter is only valid when there is no selection in the specified image. y (*Float*) The y coordinate of this bucket fill's application. This parameter is only valid when there is no selection in the specified image.
gimp_clone	Clone from the source to the dest drawable using the current brush	image (*Image*) The image drawable (*Drawable*) The drawable src_drawable (*Drawable*) The source drawable clone_type (*Integer*) The type of clone (IMAGE_CLONE, PATTERN_CLONE) src_x (*Float*) The x coordinate in the source image src_y (*Float*) The y coordinate in the source image num_strokes (*Integer*) Number of stroke control points (count each coordinate as 2 pts) strokes (*FloatArray*) Array of stroke coordinates (stroke$_{x1}$, stroke$_{y1}$, ... stroke$_{xn}$, stroke$_{yn}$)
gimp_convolve	Convolve (blur or sharpen) using the current brush	image (*Image*) The image drawable (*Drawable*) The drawable pressure (*Float*) The pressure in the range 0 to 100 convolve_type (*Integer*) Convolve type (BLUR, SHARPEN) num_strokes (*Integer*) Number of stroke control points (count each coordinate as 2 pts) strokes (*FloatArray*) Array of stroke coordinates (stroke$_{x1}$, stroke$_{y1}$, ... stroke$_{xn}$, stroke$_{yn}$)

Table C-3. Procedures for Drawing and Painting on Images, Controlling Brushes, and Performing Transformations (continued)

Name	Description	Arguments
gimp_crop	Crop the image to the specified extents	image (`Image`) 　The image new_width (`Integer`) 　New image width in the range 0 to current width new_height (`Integer`) 　New image height in the range 0 to current height offx (`Integer`) 　X offset in the range 0 to current width – **new_width** offy (`Integer`) 　Y offset in the range 0 to current height – **new_height**
gimp_drawable_set_pixel	Sets the value of the pixel at the specified coordinates	drawable (`Drawable`) 　The drawable x_coordinate (`Integer`) 　The x coordinate y_coordinate (`Integer`) 　The y coordinate num_channels (`Integer`) 　The number of channels for the pixel pixel (`IntArray`) 　The pixel value
gimp_edit_clear	Clear selected area of drawable	image (`Image`) 　The image drawable (`Drawable`) 　The drawable to clear from
gimp_edit_copy	Copy from the specified drawable	image (`Image`) 　The image drawable (`Drawable`) 　The drawable to copy from
gimp_edit_cut	Cut from the specified drawable	image (`Image`) 　The image drawable (`Drawable`) 　The drawable to cut from
gimp_edit_fill	Fill selected area of drawable	image (`Image`) 　The image drawable (`Drawable`) 　The drawable to fill from
gimp_edit_paste	Paste buffer to the specified drawable	image (`Image`) 　The image drawable (`Drawable`) 　The drawable to paste from paste_into (`Integer`) 　Clear selection if 0, or paste behind it if 1 **Returns:** floating_sel (`Layer`) 　The new floating selection

Table C-3. Procedures for Drawing and Painting on Images, Controlling Brushes, and Performing Transformations (continued)

Name	Description	Arguments
gimp_edit_stroke	Stroke the current selection	image (*Image*) The image drawable (*Drawable*) The drawable to stroke to
gimp_eraser	Erase using the current brush	image (*Image*) The image drawable (*Drawable*) The drawable num_strokes (*Integer*) Number of stroke control points (count each coordinate as 2 pts) strokes (*FloatArray*) Array of stroke coordinates (stroke$_{x1}$, stroke$_{y1}$, ... stroke$_{xn}$, stroke$_{yn}$)
gimp_eraser_extended	Erase using the current brush	image (*Image*) The image drawable (*Drawable*) The drawable num_strokes (*Integer*) Number of stroke control points (count each coordinate as 2 pts) strokes (*FloatArray*) Array of stroke coordinates (stroke$_{x1}$, stroke$_{y1}$, ... stroke$_{xn}$, stroke$_{yn}$) hardness (*Integer*) SOFT(0) or HARD(1) method (*Integer*) CONTINUOUS(0) or INCREMENTAL(1)
gimp_flip	Flip the specified drawable about its center either vertically or horizontally	image (*Image*) The image drawable (*Drawable*) The affected drawable flip_type (*Integer*) Type of flip (HORIZONTAL (0), VERTICAL (1)) **Returns:** drawable (*Drawable*) The flipped drawable
gimp_image_add_channel	Add the specified channel to the image	image (*Image*) The image channel (*Channel*) The channel position (*Integer*) The channel position

Table C-3. Procedures for Drawing and Painting on Images, Controlling Brushes, and Performing Transformations (continued)

Name	Description	Arguments
gimp_image_ resize	Resize the image to the specified extents	image (*Image*) The image new_width (*Integer*) New image width new_height (*Integer*) New image height offx (*Integer*) X offset between upper left corner of old and new images (new − old) offy (*Integer*) Y offset between upper left corner of old and new images (new − old)
gimp_image_ scale	Scale the image to the specified extents	image (*Image*) The image new_width (*Integer*) New image width new_height (*Integer*) New image height
gimp_paint- brush	Paint in the current brush with optional fade out parameter	image (*Image*) The image drawable (*Drawable*) The drawable fade_out (*Float*) Fade out parameter >0 num_strokes (*Integer*) Number of stroke control points (count each coordinate as 2 pts) strokes (*FloatArray*) Array of stroke coordinates (stroke$_{x1}$, stroke$_{y1}$, ... stroke$_{xn}$, stroke$_{yn}$)
gimp_ paintbrush_ extended	Paint in the current brush with optional fade out parameter	image (*Image*) The image drawable (*Drawable*) The drawable fade_out (*Float*) Fade out parameter >0 num_strokes (*Integer*) Number of stroke control points (count each coordinate as 2 pts) strokes (*FloatArray*) Array of stroke coordinates (stroke$_{x1}$, stroke$_{y1}$, ... stroke$_{xn}$, stroke$_{yn}$) method (*Integer*) CONTINUOUS (0) or INCREMENTAL (1)

Table C-3. Procedures for Drawing and Painting on Images, Controlling Brushes, and Performing Transformations (continued)

Name	Description	Arguments
gimp_pencil	Paint in the current brush without sub-pixel sampling	image (*Image*) The image drawable (*Drawable*) The drawable num_strokes (*Integer*) Number of stroke control points (count each coordinate as 2 pts) strokes (*FloatArray*) Array of stroke coordinates (stroke$_{x1}$, stroke$_{y1}$, ... stroke$_{xn}$, stroke$_{yn}$)
gimp_perspective	Perform a possibly non-affine transformation on the specified drawable	image (*Image*) The image drawable (*Drawable*) The affected drawable interpolation (*Integer*) Whether to use interpolation x0 (*Float*) The new x coordinate of upper left corner of bounding box y0 (*Float*) The new y coordinate of upper left corner of bounding box x1 (*Float*) The new x coordinate of upper right corner of bounding box y1 (*Float*) The new y coordinate of upper right corner of bounding box x2 (*Float*) The new x coordinate of lower left corner of bounding box y2 (*Float*) The new y coordinate of lower left corner of bounding box x3 (*Float*) The new x coordinate of lower right corner of bounding box y3 (*Float*) The new y coordinate of lower right corner of bounding box **Returns:** drawable (*Drawable*) The newly mapped drawable
gimp_posterize	Posterize the specified drawable	image (*Image*) The image drawable (*Drawable*) The drawable levels (*Integer*) Levels of posterization in the range 2 to 255

Table C-3. Procedures for Drawing and Painting on Images, Controlling Brushes, and Performing Transformations (continued)

Name	Description	Arguments
gimp_rotate	Rotate the specified drawable about its center through the specified angle	image (*Image*) The image drawable (*Drawable*) The affected drawable interpolation (*Integer*) Whether to use interpolation angle (*Float*) The angle of rotation (radians) **Returns:** drawable (*Drawable*) The rotated drawable
gimp_scale	Scale the specified drawable	image (*Image*) The image drawable (*Drawable*) The affected drawable interpolation (*Integer*) Whether to use interpolation x1 (*Float*) The x coordinate of the upper left corner of newly scaled region y1 (*Float*) The y coordinate of the upper left corner of newly scaled region x2 (*Float*) The x coordinate of the lower right corner of newly scaled region y2 (*Float*) The y coordinate of the lower right corner of newly scaled region **Returns:** drawable (*Drawable*) The scaled drawable
gimp_shear	Shear the specified drawable about its center by the specified magnitude	image (*Image*) The image drawable (*Drawable*) The affected drawable interpolation (*Integer*) Whether to use interpolation shear_type (*Integer*) Type of shear (HORIZONTAL (0), VERTICAL (1)) magnitude (*Float*) The magnitude of the shear **Returns:** drawable (*Drawable*) The sheared drawable

Table C-3. Procedures for Drawing and Painting on Images, Controlling Brushes, and Performing Transformations (continued)

Name	Description	Arguments
gimp_text	Add text at the specified location as a floating selection or a new layer	image (*Image*) 　The image drawable (*Drawable*) 　The affected drawable (−1 for a new text layer) x (*Float*) 　The x coordinate for the left side of text bounding box y (*Float*) 　The y coordinate for the top of text bounding box text (*String*) 　The text to generate border (*Integer*) 　The size of the border >= 0 antialias (*Integer*) 　Generate anti-aliased text size (*Float*) 　The size of text in either pixels or points size_type (*Integer*) 　The units of the specified size (**PIXELS**, **POINTS**) foundry (*String*) 　The font foundry, "*" for any family (*String*) 　The font family, "*" for any weight (*String*) 　The font weight, "*" for any slant (*String*) 　The font slant, "*" for any set_width (*String*) 　The font set-width parameter, "*" for any spacing (*String*) 　The font spacing, "*" for any **Returns:** text_layer (*Layer*) 　The new text layer
gimp_text_ext	Add text at the specified location as a floating selection or a new layer	image (*Image*) 　The image drawable (*Drawable*) 　The affected drawable (−1 for a new text layer) x (*Float*) 　The x coordinate for the left side of text bounding box y (*Float*) 　The y coordinate for the top of text bounding box text (*String*) 　The text to generate border (*Integer*) 　The size of the border >= 0 antialias (*Integer*) 　Generate anti-aliased text

Table C-3. Procedures for Drawing and Painting on Images, Controlling Brushes, and Performing Transformations (continued)

Name	Description	Arguments
gimp_text_ext (*cont'd*)		size (*Float*) The size of text in either pixels or points size_type (*Integer*) The units of the specified size (PIXELS, POINTS) foundry (*String*) The font foundry, "*" for any family (*String*) The font family, "*" for any weight (*String*) The font weight, "*" for any slant (*String*) The font slant, "*" for any set_width (*String*) The font set-width parameter, "*" for any spacing (*String*) The font spacing, "*" for any registry (*String*) The font registry, "*" for any encoding (*String*) The font encoding, "*" for any **Returns:** text_layer (*Layer*) The new text layer
gimp_text_get_ extents	Get extents of the bounding box for the specified text	text (*String*) The text to generate size (*Float*) The size of text in either pixels or points size_type (*Integer*) The units of the specified size (PIXELS, POINTS) foundry (*String*) The font foundry, "*" for any family (*String*) The font family, "*" for any weight (*String*) The font weight, "*" for any slant (*String*) The font slant, "*" for any set_width (*String*) The font set-width parameter, "*" for any spacing (*String*) The font spacing, "*" for any **Returns:** width (*Integer*) The width of the specified text height (*Integer*) The height of the specified text ascent (*Integer*) The ascent of the specified font descent (*Integer*) The descent of the specified font

Table C-3. Procedures for Drawing and Painting on Images, Controlling Brushes, and Performing Transformations (continued)

Name	Description	Arguments
gimp_text_get_ extents_ext	Get extents of the bounding box for the specified text	text (*String*) The text to generate size (*Float*) The size of text in either pixels or points size_type (*Integer*) The units of the specified size (PIXELS, POINTS) foundry (*String*) The font foundry, "*" for any family (*String*) The font family, "*" for any weight (*String*) The font weight,"*" for any slant (*String*) The font slant, "*" for any set_width (*String*) The font set-width parameter, "*" for any spacing (*String*) The font spacing, "*" for any registry (*String*) The font registry, "*" for any encoding (*String*) The font encoding, "*" for any **Returns:** width (*Integer*) The width of the specified text height (*Integer*) The height of the specified text ascent (*Integer*) The ascent of the specified font descent (*Integer*) The descent of the specified font

Color Control, Palettes, and Patterns

A color is represented by an anonymous array of three elements representing the red, green, and blue values:

```
my $red = [ 255, 0, 0 ];
```

The Gimp comes with several default patterns, palettes, and gradients, all of which may be referred to by name:

```
# Set the current pattern
my $pattern = "Blob1";
gimp_patterns_set_pattern($pattern);

# Convert $image to an indexed palette
my $palette = "Reds_And_Purples";
gimp_convert_indexed_palette($image, 1, 4, 0, $palette);
```

```
# Set the active gradient
my $gradient = "Mexican_flag_smooth";
gimp_gradients_set_active($gradient);
```

Table C-4. Procedures for Manipulating the Colors in an Image, and Managing Palettes and Patterns

Name	Description	Arguments
gimp_ brightness_ contrast	Modify bright- ness/contrast in the specified drawable	image (*Image*) 　　The image drawable (*Drawable*) 　　The drawable brightness (*Integer*) 　　Brightness adjustment in the range −127 to 127 contrast (*Integer*) 　　Constrast adjustment in the range −127 to 127
gimp_color_ balance	Modify the color balance of the specified draw- able	image (*Image*) 　　The image drawable (*Drawable*) 　　The drawable transfer_mode (*Integer*) 　　Transfer mode 　　0　Shadows 　　1　Midtones 　　2　Highlights preserve_lum (*Integer*) 　　Preserve luminosity values at each pixel cyan_red (*Float*) 　　Cyan-Red color balance in the range −100 to 100 magenta_green (*Float*) 　　Magenta-Green color balance in the range −100 to 100 yellow_blue (*Float*) 　　Yellow-Blue color balance in the range −100 to 100
gimp_color_ picker	Determine the color at the given drawable coordi- nates	image (*Image*) 　　The image drawable (*Drawable*) 　　The drawable x (*Float*) 　　X coordinate of upper-left corner of rectangle y (*Float*) 　　Y coordinate of upper-left corner of rectangle sample_merged (*Integer*) 　　Use the composite image, not the drawable save_color (*Integer*) 　　Save the color to the active palette **Returns:** color (*Color*) 　　The return color

Table C-4. Procedures for Manipulating the Colors in an Image, and Managing Palettes and Patterns (continued)

Name	Description	Arguments
gimp_ convert_gray- scale	Convert specified image to grayscale (256 intensity lev- els)	image (*Image*) The image
gimp_ convert_ indexed	Convert specified image to indexed color	image (*Image*) The image dither (*Integer*) Floyd-Steinberg dithering num_cols (*Integer*) The number of colors to quantize to
gimp_ convert_ indexed_pal- ette	Convert specified image to indexed color	image (*Image*) The image dither (*Integer*) Floyd-Steinberg dithering palette_type (*Integer*) The type of palette to use: 0 Optimal 1 Reuse 2 Web 3 Mono 4 Custom num_cols (*Integer*) The number of colors to quantize to, ignored unless palette_type set to 0 (optimal) palette (*String*) The name of the custom palette to use, ignored unless palette_type is set to 4 (Custom)
gimp_ convert_rgb	Convert specified image to RGB color	image (*Image*) The image
gimp_curves_ explicit	Modifies the intensity curve(s) for specified drawable	image (*Image*) The image drawable (*Drawable*) The drawable channel (*Integer*) The channel to modify (VALUE, RED, GREEN, BLUE, GRAY) num_bytes (*Integer*) The number of bytes in the new curve (always 256) curve (*IntArray*) The explicit curve

Table C-4. Procedures for Manipulating the Colors in an Image, and Managing Palettes and Patterns (continued)

Name	Description	Arguments
gimp_curves_ spline	Modifies the intensity curve(s) for specified drawable	image (*Image*) The image drawable (*Drawable*) The drawable channel (*Integer*) The channel to modify (VALUE_CHANNEL, RED_ CHANNEL, GREEN_CHANNEL, BLUE_CHANNEL, ALPHA_CHANNEL, GRAY_CHANNEL) num_points (*Integer*) The number of values in the control point array (4 to 32) control_pts (*IntArray*) The spline control points (cp_{x1}, cp_{y1}, ... cp_{xn}, cp_{yn})
gimp_desatu- rate	Desaturate the contents of the specified draw- able	image (*Image*) The image drawable (*Drawable*) The drawable
gimp_equal- ize	Equalize the con- tents of the speci- fied drawable	image (*Image*) The image drawable (*Drawable*) The drawable mask_only (*Integer*) Equalization option
gimp_ gradients_ get_active	Retrieve the name of the active gra- dient	No arguments required **Returns:** name (*String*) The name of the active gradient
gimp_ gradients_ get_list	Retrieve the list of loaded gradients	No arguments required **Returns:** num_gradients (*Integer*) The number of loaded gradients gradient_names (*StringArray*) The list of gradient names
gimp_ gradients_ sample_cus- tom	Sample the active gradient in custom positions	num_samples (*Integer*) The number of samples to take positions (*FloatArray*) The list of positions to sample along the gradi- ent **Returns:** array_length (*Integer*) Length of the color_samples array (4 * num_ samples) color_samples (*FloatArray*) Color samples (R_1, G_1, B_1, A_1, ... R_n, G_n, B_n, A_n)

Table C-4. Procedures for Manipulating the Colors in an Image, and Managing Palettes and Patterns (continued)

Name	Description	Arguments
gimp_ gradients_ sample_uni- form	Sample the active gradient in uniform parts	num_samples (*Integer*) The number of samples to take **Returns:** array_length (*Integer*) Length of the color_samples array (4 * num_ samples) color_samples (*FloatArray*) Color samples (R_1, G_1, B_1, A_1, ... R_n, G_n, B_n, A_n)
gimp_ gradients_ set_active	Sets the specified gradient as the active gradient	name (*String*) The name of the gradient to set
gimp_histo- gram	Returns information on the intensity histogram for the specified drawable	image (*Image*) The image drawable (*Drawable*) The drawable channel (*Integer*) The channel to modify (VALUE_CHANNEL, RED_ CHANNEL, GREEN_CHANNEL, BLUE_CHANNEL, GRAY_CHANNEL) start_range (*Integer*) Start of the intensity measurement range end_range (*Integer*) End of the intensity measurement range **Returns:** mean (*Float*) Mean intensity value std_dev (*Float*) Standard deviation of intensity values median (*Float*) Median intensity value pixels (*Float*) Alpha-weighted pixel count for entire image count (*Float*) Alpha-weighted pixel count for range percentile (*Float*) Percentile that range falls under
gimp_hue_ saturation	Modify hue, lightness, and saturation in the specified drawable	image (*Image*) The image drawable (*Drawable*) The drawable hue_range (*Integer*) Range of affected hues (ALL_HUES, RED_HUES, YELLOW_HUES, GREEN_HUES, CYAN_HUES, BLUE_HUES, MAGENTA_HUES) hue_offset (*Float*) Hue offset in degrees in the range -180 to 180 lightness (*Float*) Lightness modification in the range -100 to 100 saturation (*Float*) Saturation modification in the range -100 to 100

Table C-4. Procedures for Manipulating the Colors in an Image, and Managing Palettes and Patterns (continued)

Name	Description	Arguments
gimp_image_ get_cmap	Returns the image's colormap	image (*Image*) The image **Returns:** num_bytes (*Integer*) Number of bytes in the colormap array in the range 0 to 768 cmap (*IntArray*) The image's colormap
gimp_image_ get_ component_ active	Returns whether the specified component is active	image (*Image*) The image component (*Integer*) The image component (RED_CHANNEL, GREEN_ CHANNEL, BLUE_CHANNEL, GRAY_CHANNEL, INDEXED_CHANNEL) **Returns:** active (*Integer*) 1 for active, 0 for inactive
gimp_image_ get_ component_ visible	Returns whether the specified component is visible	image (*Image*) The image component (*Integer*) The image component (RED_CHANNEL, GREEN_ CHANNEL, BLUE_CHANNEL, GRAY_CHANNEL, INDEXED_CHANNEL) **Returns:** visible (*Integer*) 1 for visible, 0 for invisible
gimp_image_ set_cmap	Sets the entries in the image's color-map	image (*Image*) The image num_bytes (*Integer*) Number of bytes in the new colormap in the range 0 to 768 cmap (*IntArray*) The new colormap values
gimp_image_ set_ component_ active	Sets the specified component's sen-sitivity	image (*Image*) The image component (*Integer*) The image component (RED_CHANNEL, GREEN_ CHANNEL, BLUE_CHANNEL, GRAY_CHANNEL, INDEXED_CHANNEL) active (*Integer*) Active if 1, inactive if 0
gimp_image_ set_ component_ visible	Sets the specified component's visi-bility	image (*Image*) The image component (*Integer*) The image component (RED_CHANNEL, GREEN_ CHANNEL, BLUE_CHANNEL, GRAY_CHANNEL, INDEXED_CHANNEL) visible (*Integer*) Visible if 1, not visible if 0

Table C-4. Procedures for Manipulating the Colors in an Image, and Managing Palettes and Patterns (continued)

Name	Description	Arguments
gimp_invert	Inverts the contents of the specified drawable	image (*Image*) The image drawable (*Drawable*) The drawable
gimp_levels	Modifies intensity levels in the specified drawable	image (*Image*) The image drawable (*Drawable*) The drawable channel (*Integer*) The channel to modify(VALUE_CHANNEL, RED_ CHANNEL, GREEN_CHANNEL, BLUE_CHANNEL, GRAY_CHANNEL) low_input (*Integer*) Intensity of lowest input in the range 0 to 255 high_input (*Integer*) Intensity of highest input in the range 0 to 255 gamma (*Float*) Gamma correction factor in the range 0.1 to 10 low_output (*Integer*) Intensity of lowest output in the range 0 to 255 high_output (*Integer*) Intensity of highest output in the range 0 to 255
gimp_palette_get_background	Get the current Gimp background color	No arguments required **Returns:** background (*Color*) The background color
gimp_palette_get_foreground	Get the current Gimp foreground color	No arguments required **Returns:** foreground (*Color*) The foreground color
gimp_palette_refresh	Refreshes current palettes	
gimp_palette_set_background	Set the current Gimp background color	background (*Color*) The background color
gimp_palette_set_default_colors	Set the current Gimp foreground and background colors to black and white	
gimp_palette_set_foreground	Set the current Gimp foreground color	foreground (*Color*) The foreground color
gimp_palette_swap_colors	Swap the current Gimp foreground and background colors	

Table C-4. Procedures for Manipulating the Colors in an Image, and Managing Palettes and Patterns (continued)

Name	Description	Arguments
gimp_ patterns_get_ pattern	Retrieve information about the currently active pattern	No arguments required **Returns:** name (*String*) The pattern name width (*Integer*) The pattern width height (*Integer*) The pattern height
gimp_ patterns_list	Retrieve a complete listing of the available patterns	No arguments required **Returns:** num_patterns (*Integer*) The number of patterns in the pattern list pattern_list (*StringArray*) The list of pattern names
gimp_ patterns_set_ pattern	Set the specified pattern as the active pattern	name (*String*) The pattern name
gimp_threshold	Threshold the specified drawable	image (*Image*) The image drawable (*Drawable*) The drawable low_threshold (*Integer*) The low threshold value in the range 0 to 255 high_threshold (*Integer*) The high threshold value in the range 0 to 255

Selection Procedures

Table C-5. Procedures for Creating Selection Regions

Name	Description	Arguments
gimp_by_ color_select	Create a selection by selecting all pixels (in the specified drawable) with the same (or similar) color to that specified	image (*Image*) The image drawable (*Drawable*) The drawable color (*Color*) The color to select threshold (*Integer*) Threshold in intensity levels in the range 0 to 255 operation (*Integer*) The selection operation (SELECTION_ADD, SELECTION_SUB, SELECTION_REPLACE, SELECTION_INTERSECT) antialias (*Integer*) Anti-aliasing On/Off feather (*Integer*) Feather option for selections

Table C-5. Procedures for Creating Selection Regions (continued)

Name	Description	Arguments
gimp_by_ color_select (*cont'd*)		feather_radius (*Float*) Radius for feather operation sample_merged (*Integer*) Use the composite image, not the drawable
gimp_ellipse_ select	Create an ellip- tical selection over the speci- fied image	image (*Image*) The image x (*Float*) X coordinate of upper left corner of ellipse bounding box y (*Float*) Y coordinate of upper left corner of ellipse bounding box width (*Float*) The width of the ellipse height (*Float*) The height of the ellipse operation (*Integer*) The selection operation (SELECTION_ADD, SELECTION_SUB, SELECTION_REPLACE, SELECTION_INTERSECT) antialias (*Integer*) Anti-aliasing On/Off feather (*Integer*) Feather option for selections feather_radius (*Float*) Radius for feather operation
gimp_floating_ sel_anchor	Anchor the specified float- ing selection to its associated drawable	floating_sel (*Layer*) The floating selection
gimp_floating_ sel_remove	Remove the specified float- ing selection from its associ- ated drawable	floating_sel (*Layer*) The floating selection
gimp_floating_ sel_to_layer	Transform the specified float- ing selection into a layer	floating_sel (*Layer*) The floating selection
gimp_free_ select	Create a polyg- onal selection over the speci- fied image	image (*Image*) The image num_pts (*Integer*) Number of points (count 1 coordinate as two points) segs (*FloatArray*) Array of points (p1.x, p1.y, p2.x, p2.y, ..., pn.x, pn.y)

Table C-5. Procedures for Creating Selection Regions (continued)

Name	Description	Arguments
gimp_free_ select (*cont'd*)		operation (*Integer*) The selection operation (SELECTION_ADD, SELECTION_SUB, SELECTION_REPLACE, SELECTION_INTERSECT) antialias (*Integer*) Anti-aliasing option for selections feather (*Integer*) Feather option for selections feather_radius (*Float*) Radius for feather operation
gimp_fuzzy_ select	Create a fuzzy selection start- ing at the spec- ified coordi- nates on the specified draw- able	image (*Image*) The image drawable (*Drawable*) The drawable x (*Float*) X coordinate of initial seed fill point (image coor- dinates) y (*Float*) Y coordinate of initial seed fill point (image coor- dinates) threshold (*Integer*) Threshold in intensity levels in the range 0 to 255 operation (*Integer*) The selection operation (SELECTION_ADD, SELECTION_SUB, SELECTION_REPLACE, SELECTION_INTERSECT) antialias (*Integer*) Anti-aliasing On/Off feather (*Integer*) Feather option for selections feather_radius (*Float*) Radius for feather operation sample_merged (*Integer*) Use the composite image, not the drawable
gimp_image_ get_selection	Return the selection of the specified image	image (*Image*) The image **Returns:** selection_mask_ID (*Selection*) The ID of the selection channel
gimp_image_ floating_selec- tion	Return the floating selec- tion of the image	image (*Image*) The image **Returns:** floating_sel (*Layer*) The image's floating selection

Table C-5. Procedures for Creating Selection Regions (continued)

Name	Description	Arguments
gimp_rect_ select	Create a rect-angular selec-tion over the specified image	image (*Image*) The image x (*Float*) X coordinate of upper-left corner of rectangle y (*Float*) Y coordinate of upper-left corner of rectangle width (*Float*) The width of the rectangle height (*Float*) The height of the rectangle operation (*Integer*) The selection operation (SELECTION_ADD, SELECTION_SUB, SELECTION_REPLACE, SELECTION_INTERSECT) feather (*Integer*) Feather option for selections feather_radius (*Float*) Radius for feather operation
gimp_ selection_all	Select all of the image	image (*Image*) The image
gimp_ selection_bor-der	Border the image's selec-tion	image (*Image*) The image radius (*Integer*) Radius of border (pixels)
gimp_ selection_ bounds	Find the bounding box of the current selection	image (*Image*) The image **Returns:** non-empty (*Integer*) True if there is a selection x1 (*Integer*) X coordinate of upper left corner of selection bounds y1 (*Integer*) Y coordinate of upper left corner of selection bounds x2 (*Integer*) X coordinate of lower right corner of selection bounds y2 (*Integer*) Y coordinate of lower right corner of selection bounds
gimp_ selection_clear	Set the selec-tion to none, clearing all previous con-tent	image (*Image*) The image
gimp_ selection_ feather	Feather the image's selec-tion	image (*Image*) The image radius (*Float*) Radius of feather (in pixels)

Table C-5. Procedures for Creating Selection Regions (continued)

Name	Description	Arguments
gimp_ selection_float	Float the selection from the specified drawable with initial offsets as specified	image (*Image*) 　The image drawable (*Drawable*) 　The drawable from which to float selection offset_x (*Integer*) 　X offset for translation offset_y (*Integer*) 　Y offset for translation **Returns:** layer (*Layer*) 　The floated layer
gimp_ selection_grow	Grow the image's selection	image (*Image*) 　The image steps (*Integer*) 　Pixels to enlarge the selection
gimp_ selection_ invert	Invert the selection mask	image (*Image*) 　The image
gimp_ selection_is_ empty	Determine whether the selection in empty	image (*Image*) 　The image **Returns:** is_empty (*Integer*) 　1 if the selection is empty
gimp_ selection_ layer_alpha	Transfer the specified layer's alpha channel to the selection mask	image (*Image*) 　The image layer (*Layer*) 　Layer with alpha
gimp_ selection_load	Transfer the specified channel to the selection mask	image (*Image*) 　The image channel (*Channel*) 　The channel
gimp_ selection_none	Deselect the entire image	image (*Image*) 　The image
gimp_ selection_save	Copy the selection mask to a new channel	image (*Image*) 　The image **Returns:** channel (*Channel*) 　The new channel
gimp_ selection_ sharpen	Sharpen the selection mask	image (*Image*) 　The image
gimp_ selection_ shrink	Shrink the image's selection	image (*Image*) 　The image radius (*Integer*) 　Pixels to shrink the selection

Table C-5. Procedures for Creating Selection Regions (continued)

Name	Description	Arguments
gimp_ selection_trans- late	Translate the selection by the specified offsets	image (*Image*) The image offset_x (*Integer*) X offset for translation offset_y (*Integer*) Y offset for translation
gimp_ selection_value	Find the value of the selection at the speci- fied coordi- nates	image (*Image*) The image x (*Integer*) X coordinate of value y (*Integer*) Y coordinate of value **Returns:** value (*Integer*) Value of the selection, between 0 and 255

Layers and Channels

Table C-6. Creating, Manipulating, and Managing Layers and Channels

Name	Description	Arguments
gimp_channel_ copy	Copy a chan- nel	channel (*Channel*) The channel to copy **Returns:** Channel_copy (*Channel*) The newly copied channel
gimp_channel_ delete	Delete a chan- nel	channel (*Channel*) The channel to delete
gimp_channel_ get_color	Get the com- positing color of the specified channel	channel (*Channel*) The channel **Returns:** color (*Color*) The channel's composite color
gimp_channel_ get_name	Get the name of the specified channel	channel (*Channel*) The channel **Returns:** name (*String*) The channel name
gimp_channel_ get_opacity	Get the opacity of the specified channel	channel (*Channel*) The channel **Returns:** opacity (*Float*) The channel opacity

Table C-6. Creating, Manipulating, and Managing Layers and Channels (continued)

Name	Description	Arguments
gimp_channel_ get_show_ masked	Get the composite type for the channel	channel (`Channel`) The channel **Returns:** show_masked (`Integer`) composite method for channel
gimp_channel_ get_visible	Get the visibility of the specified channel	channel (`Channel`) The channel **Returns:** visible (`Integer`) The channel visibility
gimp_channel_ new	Create a new channel	image (`Image`) The image to which to add the channel width (`Integer`) The channel width (must be > 0) height (`Integer`) The channel height (must be > 0) name (`String`) The channel name opacity (`Float`) The channel opacity in the range 0 to 100 color (`Color`) The channel compositing color **Returns:** channel (`Channel`) The newly created channel
gimp_channel_ ops_duplicate	Duplicate the specified image	image (`Image`) The image **Returns:** new_image (`Image`) The new, duplicated image
gimp_channel_ ops_offset	Offset the drawable by the specified amounts in the X and Y directions	image (`Image`) The image drawable (`Drawable`) The drawable to offset wrap_around (`Integer`) Wrap image around or fill vacated regions fill_type (`Integer`) Fill vacated regions of drawable with background or transparent (`OFFSET_BACKGROUND`, `OFFSET_` `TRANSPARENT`) offset_x (`Integer`) Offset by this amount in X direction offset_y (`Integer`) Offset by this amount in Y direction
gimp_channel_ set_color	Set the compositing color of the specified channel	channel (`Channel`) The channel color (`Color`) The composite color

Table C-6. Creating, Manipulating, and Managing Layers and Channels (continued)

Name	Description	Arguments
gimp_channel_ set_name	Set the name of the specified channel	channel (*Channel*) The channel name (*String*) The new channel name
gimp_channel_ set_opacity	Set the opacity of the specified channel	channel (*Channel*) The channel opacity (*Float*) The new channel opacity in the range 0 to 100
gimp_channel_ set_show_ masked	Set the composite type for the specified channel.	channel (*Channel*) The channel show_masked (*Integer*) The new channel **show_masked** value
gimp_channel_ set_visible	Set the visibility of the specified channel.	channel (*Channel*) The channel visible (*Integer*) The new channel visibility
gimp_image_ add_layer	Add the specified layer to the image	image (*Image*) The image layer (*Layer*) The layer position (*Integer*) The layer position
gimp_image_ add_layer_ mask	Add a layer mask to the specified layer	image (*Image*) The layer's image layer (*Layer*) The layer to receive the mask mask (*Channel*) The mask to add to the layer
gimp_image_ flatten	Flatten all visible layers into a single layer and discard all invisible layers	image (*Image*) The image **Returns:** layer (*Layer*) The resulting layer
gimp_image_ free_shadow	Free the specified image's shadow data (if it exists)	image (*Image*) The image ID
gimp_image_ get_active_ channel	Returns the active channel of the specified image	image (*Image*) The image **Returns:** channel_ID (*Channel*) The ID of the active channel
gimp_image_ get_active_ layer	Returns the active layer of the specified image	image (*Image*) The image **Returns:** layer_ID (*Layer*) The ID of the active layer

Table C-6. Creating, Manipulating, and Managing Layers and Channels (continued)

Name	Description	Arguments

gimp_image_ get_channels	Returns the list of channels contained in the specified image	image (*Image*)
		   The image
		Returns:
		num_channels (*Integer*)
		   The number of channels contained in the image
		channel_ids (*IntArray*)
		   The list of channels contained in the image

gimp_image_ get_layers	Returns the list of layers contained in the specified image	image (*Image*)
		   The image
		Returns:
		num_layers (*Integer*)
		   The number of layers contained in the image
		layer_ids (*IntArray*)
		   The list of layers contained in the image

gimp_image_ lower_channel	Lower the specified channel in the image's channel stack	image (*Image*)
		   The image
		channel (*Channel*)
		   The channel to lower

gimp_image_ lower_layer	Lower the specified layer in the image's layer stack	image (*Image*)
		   The image
		layer (*Layer*)
		   The layer to lower

gimp_image_ merge_visible_ layers	Merge the visible image layers into one	image (*Image*)
		   The image
		merge_type (*Integer*)
		   The type of merge (EXPAND_AS_NECESSARY, CLIP_TO_IMAGE, CLIP_TO_BOTTOM_LAYER)
		Returns:
		layer (*Layer*)
		   The resulting layer

gimp_image_ pick_correlate_ layer	Find the layer visible at the specified coordinates	image (*Image*)
		   The image
		x (*Integer*)
		   The x coordinate for the pick
		y (*Integer*)
		   The y coordinate for the pick
		Returns:
		layer (*Layer*)
		   The layer found at the specified coordinates

gimp_image_ raise_channel	Raise the specified channel in the image's channel stack	image (*Image*)
		   The image
		channel (*Channel*)
		   The channel to raise

gimp_image_ raise_layer	Raise the specified layer in the image's layer stack	image (*Image*)
		   The image
		layer (*Layer*)
		   The layer to raise

Table C-6. Creating, Manipulating, and Managing Layers and Channels (continued)

Name	Description	Arguments
gimp_image_ remove_chan- nel	Remove the specified chan- nel from the image	image (*Image*) The image channel (*Channel*) The channel
gimp_image_ remove_layer	Remove the specified layer from the image	image (*Image*) The image layer (*Layer*) The layer
gimp_image_ remove_layer_ mask	Remove the specified layer mask from the layer	image (*Image*) The layer's image layer (*Layer*) The layer from which to remove mask mode (*Integer*) Removal mode (APPLY, DISCARD)
gimp_image_ set_active_ channel	Sets the speci- fied channel as active in the specified image.	image (*Image*) The image channel (*Channel*) The channel to be set active
gimp_image_ set_active_ layer	Sets the speci- fied layer as active in the specified image.	image (*Image*) The image layer (*Layer*) The layer to be set active
gimp_image_ unset_active_ channel	Unsets the active channel in the specified image.	image (*Image*) The image
gimp_layer_ add_alpha	Add an alpha channel to the layer if it doesn't already have one.	layer (*Layer*) The layer
gimp_layer_ copy	Copy a layer	layer (*Layer*) The layer to copy add_alpha (*Integer*) Add an alpha channel to the copied layer **Returns:** layer_copy (*Layer*) The newly copied layer
gimp_layer_ create_mask	Create a layer mask for the specified speci- fied layer	layer (*Layer*) The layer to which to add the mask mask_type (*Integer*) The type of mask (WHITE_MASK, BLACK_MASK, ALPHA_MASK) **Returns:** mask (*Channel*) The newly created mask

Table C-6. Creating, Manipulating, and Managing Layers and Channels (continued)

Name	Description	Arguments
gimp_layer_delete	Delete a layer	layer (*Layer*) The layer to delete
gimp_layer_get_apply_mask	Get the apply mask setting for the layer	layer (*Layer*) The layer **Returns:** apply_mask (*Integer*) The layer's apply mask setting
gimp_layer_get_edit_mask	Get the edit mask setting for the layer	layer (*Layer*) The layer **Returns:** edit_mask (*Integer*) The layer's edit mask setting
gimp_layer_get_mode	Get the combination mode of the specified layer	layer (*Layer*) The layer **Returns:** mode (*Integer*) The layer combination mode (NORMAL_MODE, DISSOLVE_MODE, BEHIND_MODE, MULTIPLY_MODE, SCREEN_MODE, OVERLAY_MODE, DIFFERENCE_MODE, ADDITION_MODE, SUBTRACT_MODE, DARKEN_ONLY_MODE, LIGHTEN_ONLY_MODE, HUE_MODE, SATURATION_MODE, COLOR_MODE, VALUE_MODE)
gimp_layer_get_name	Get the name of the specified layer	layer (*Layer*) The layer **Returns:** name (*String*) The layer name
gimp_layer_get_opacity	Get the opacity of the specified layer	layer (*Layer*) The layer **Returns:** opacity (*Float*) The layer opacity
gimp_layer_get_preserve_trans	Get the preserve transparency setting of the layer	layer (*Layer*) The layer **Returns:** preserve_trans (*Integer*) The layer's preserve transparency setting
gimp_layer_get_show_mask	Get the show mask setting for the layer	layer (*Layer*) The layer **Returns:** show_mask (*Integer*) The layer's show mask setting

Table C-6. Creating, Manipulating, and Managing Layers and Channels (continued)

Name	Description	Arguments
gimp_layer_ get_visible	Get the visibility of the specified layer	layer (*Layer*) The layer **Returns:** visible (*Integer*) The layer visibility
gimp_layer_is_ floating_sel	Is the specified layer a floating selection?	layer (*Layer*) The layer **Returns:** is_floating_sel (*Channel*) Non-zero if the layer is a floating selection
gimp_layer_ mask	Get the specified layer's mask if it exists	layer (*Layer*) The layer **Returns:** mask (*Channel*) The layer mask
gimp_layer_ new	Create a new layer	image (*Image*) The image to which to add the layer width (*Integer*) The layer width (must be > 0) height (*Integer*) The layer height (must be > 0) type (*Integer*) The layer type (RGB_IMAGE, RGBA_IMAGE, GRAY_IMAGE, GRAYA_IMAGE, INDEXED_IMAGE, INDEXEDA_IMAGE) name (*String*) The layer name opacity (*Float*) The layer opacity in the range 0 to 100 mode (*Integer*) The layer combination mode (NORMAL_MODE, DISSOLVE_MODE, BEHIND_MODE, MULTIPLY_MODE, SCREEN_MODE, OVERLAY_MODE, DIFFERENCE_MODE, ADDITION_MODE, SUBTRACT_MODE, DARKEN_ONLY_MODE, LIGHTEN_ONLY_MODE, HUE_MODE, SATURATION_MODE, COLOR_MODE, VALUE_MODE) **Returns:** layer (*Layer*) The newly created layer

Table C-6. Creating, Manipulating, and Managing Layers and Channels (continued)

Name	Description	Arguments
gimp_layer_resize	Resize the layer to the specified extents	layer (*Layer*) The layer new_width (*Integer*) New layer width new_height (*Integer*) New layer height offx (*Integer*) X offset between upper left corner of old and new layers (new – old) offy (*Integer*) Y offset between upper left corner of old and new layers (new – old)
gimp_layer_scale	Scale the layer to the specified extents	layer (*Layer*) The layer new_width (*Integer*) New layer width new_height (*Integer*) New layer height local_origin (*Integer*) Use a local origin, or the image origin?
gimp_layer_set_apply_mask	Set the apply mask parameter for the specified layer	layer (*Layer*) The layer apply_mask (*Integer*) The new layer apply mask setting
gimp_layer_set_edit_mask	Set the edit mask parameter for the specified layer	layer (*Layer*) The layer edit_mask (*Integer*) The new layer edit mask setting
gimp_layer_set_mode	Set the combination mode of the specified layer	layer (*Layer*) The layer mode (*Integer*) The new layer combination mode
gimp_layer_set_name	Set the name of the specified layer	layer (*Layer*) The layer name (*String*) The new layer name
gimp_layer_set_offsets	Set the layer offsets	layer (*Layer*) The layer offx (*Integer*) Offset in x direction offy (*Integer*) Offset in y direction
gimp_layer_set_opacity	Set the opacity of the specified layer	layer (*Layer*) The layer opacity (*Float*) The new layer opacity in the range 0 to 100

Table C-6. Creating, Manipulating, and Managing Layers and Channels (continued)

Name	Description	Arguments
gimp_layer_ set_preserve_ trans	Set the preserve transparency parameter for the specified layer	layer (*Layer*) The layer preserve_trans (*Integer*) The new layer preserve transparency setting
gimp_layer_ set_show_ mask	Set the show mask parameter for the specified layer	layer (*Layer*) The layer show_mask (*Integer*) The new layer show mask setting
gimp_layer_ set_visible	Set the visibility of the specified layer	layer (*Layer*) The layer visible (*Integer*) The new layer visibility
gimp_layer_ translate	Translate the layer by the specified offsets	layer (*Layer*) The layer offx (*Integer*) offset in x direction offy (*Integer*) offset in y direction

Undo and Redo

Table C-7. Procedures for Enabling and Disabling Undo/Redo, and Managing Undo Groups

Name	Description	Arguments
gimp_image_ enable_undo	Enable the image's undo stack	image (*Image*) The image **Returns:** enabled (*Integer*) True if the image undo has been enabled
gimp_image_ disable_undo	Disable the image's undo stack	image (*Image*) The image **Returns:** disabled (*Integer*) True if the image undo has been disabled
gimp_undo_ push_group_ end	Finish a group undo	image (*Image*) The ID of the image in which to pop an undo group
gimp_undo_ push_group_ start	Starts a group undo	image (*Image*) The ID of the image in which to pop an undo group

Image Information and Management

Table C-8. Procedures for Getting Information About an Image, Creating and Deleting Images, and Managing Drawables

Name	Description	Arguments
gimp_display_delete	Delete the specified display	`display` (Display) The display
gimp_display_new	Creates a new display for the specified image	`image` (*Image*) The image **Returns:** `display` (Display) The new display
gimp_displays_flush	Flush all internal changes to the user interface	
gimp_drawable_bytes	Returns the bytes per pixel	`drawable` (*Drawable*) The drawable **Returns:** `bytes` (*Integer*) Bytes per pixel
gimp_drawable_channel	Returns whether the drawable is a channel	`drawable` (*Drawable*) The drawable **Returns:** `channel` (*Integer*) Non-zero if the drawable is a channel
gimp_drawable_color	Returns whether the drawable is an RGB based type	`drawable` (*Drawable*) The drawable **Returns:** `color` (*Integer*) Non-zero if the drawable is an RGB type
gimp_drawable_fill	Fill the drawable with the specified fill mode	`drawable` (*Drawable*) The drawable `fill_type` (*Integer*) Type of fill (`BG_IMAGE_FILL`, `WHITE_IMAGE_FILL`, `TRANS_IMAGE_FILL`)
gimp_drawable_get_pixel	Gets the value of the pixel at the specified coordinates	`drawable` (*Drawable*) The drawable `x coordinate` (*Integer*) The x coordinate `y coordinate` (*Integer*) The y coordinate **Returns:** `num_channels` (*Integer*) The number of channels for the pixel `pixel` (*IntArray*) The pixel value

Table C-8. Procedures for Getting Information About an Image, Creating and Deleting Images, and Managing Drawables (continued)

Name	Description	Arguments

gimp_ drawable_gray	Returns whether the drawable is an grayscale type	drawable (*Drawable*)
		   The drawable
		Returns:
		gray (*Integer*)
		   Non-zero if the drawable is a grayscale type

gimp_ drawable_has_ alpha	Returns non-zero if the drawable has an alpha channel	drawable (*Drawable*)
		   The drawable
		Returns:
		has_alpha (*Integer*)
		   Does the drawable have an alpha channel?

gimp_ drawable_ height	Returns the height of the drawable	drawable (*Drawable*)
		   The drawable
		Returns:
		height (*Integer*)
		   Height of drawable

gimp_ drawable_ image	Returns the drawable's image	drawable (*Drawable*)
		   The drawable
		Returns:
		image (*Image*)
		   The drawable's image

gimp_ drawable_ indexed	Returns whether the drawable is an indexed type	drawable (*Drawable*)
		   The drawable
		Returns:
		indexed (*Integer*)
		   Non-zero if the drawable is a indexed type

gimp_ drawable_layer	Returns whether the drawable is a laycr	drawable (*Drawable*)
		   The drawable
		Returns:
		layer (*Integer*)
		   Non-zero if the drawable is a layer

gimp_ drawable_ layer_mask	Returns whether the drawable is a layer mask	drawable (*Drawable*)
		   The drawable
		Returns:
		layer_mask (*Integer*)
		   Non-zero if the drawable is a layer mask

gimp_ drawable_ mask_bounds	Find the bounding box of the current selection in relation to the specified drawable	drawable (*Drawable*)
		   The drawable
		Returns:
		non-empty (*Integer*)
		   True if there is a selection
		x1 (*Integer*)
		   X coordinate of upper left corner of selection bounds
		y1 (*Integer*)
		   Y coordinate of upper left corner of selection bounds

Table C-8. Procedures for Getting Information About an Image, Creating and Deleting Images, and Managing Drawables (continued)

Name	Description	Arguments
gimp_ drawable_ mask_bounds (*cont'd*)		x2 (*Integer*) X coordinate of lower right corner of selection bounds y2 (*Integer*) Y coordinate of lower right corner of selection bounds
gimp_ drawable_ merge_shadow	Merge the shadow buffer with the specified drawable	drawable (*Drawable*) The drawable undo (*Integer*) push merge to undo stack?
gimp_ drawable_off-sets	Returns the offsets for the drawable	drawable (*Drawable*) The drawable **Returns:** offset_x (*Integer*) X offset of drawable offset_y (*Integer*) Y offset of drawable
gimp_ drawable_type	Returns the drawable's type	drawable (*Drawable*) The drawable **Returns:** type (*Integer*) The drawable's type (RGB_IMAGE, RGBA_IMAGE, GRAY_IMAGE, GRAYA_IMAGE, INDEXED_IMAGE, INDEXEDA_IMAGE)
gimp_ drawable_ type_with_ alpha	Returns the drawable's type with alpha	drawable (*Drawable*) The drawable **Returns:** type_with_alpha (*Integer*) The drawable's type with alpha (RGBA_IMAGE, GRAYA_IMAGE, INDEXEDA_IMAGE)
gimp_ drawable_ update	Update the specified region of the drawable	drawable (*Drawable*) The drawable x (*Integer*) X coordinate of upper left corner of update region y (*Integer*) Y coordinate of upper left corner of update region w (*Integer*) Width of update region h (*Integer*) Height of update region
gimp_ drawable_ width	Returns the width of the drawable	drawable (*Drawable*) The drawable **Returns:** width (*Integer*) Width of drawable

Table C-8. Procedures for Getting Information About an Image, Creating and Deleting Images, and Managing Drawables (continued)

Name	Description	Arguments
gimp_image_active_draw-able	Get the image's active draw-able	image (*Image*) The image **Returns:** drawable (*Drawable*) The active drawable
gimp_image_base_type	Get the base type of the image	image (*Image*) The image **Returns:** base_type (*Integer*) The image's base type (RGB_IMAGE, GRAY_IMAGE, INDEXED_IMAGE)
gimp_image_clean_all	Set the image dirty count to 0	image (*Image*) The image
gimp_image_delete	Delete the specified image	image (*Image*) The image ID
gimp_image_height	Return the height of the image	image (*Image*) The image **Returns:** height (*Integer*) The image's height
gimp_image_new	Creates a new image with the specified width, height, and type	width (*Integer*) The width of the image height (*Integer*) The height of the image type (*Integer*) The type of image (RGB_IMAGE, GRAY_IMAGE, INDEXED_IMAGE) **Returns:** image (*Image*) The ID of the newly created image
gimp_image_width	Return the width of the image	image (*Image*) The image **Returns:** width (*Integer*) The image's width
gimp_list_images	Returns the list of images currently open	No arguments required **Returns:** num_images (*Integer*) The number of images currently open image_ids (*IntArray*) The list of images currently open

User Interface

Table C-9. Procedures for Controlling User Interface Objects

Name	Description	Arguments
gimp_message	Displays a dialog box with a message	message (*String*) Message to display in the dialog
gimp_progress_init	Initializes the progress bar for the current plug-in	message (*String*) Message to use in the progress dialog
gimp_progress_update	Updates the progress bar for the current plug-in	percentage (*Float*) Percentage of progress completed
gimp_quit	Causes the gimp to exit gracefully	kill (*Integer*) Flag specifying whether to kill the gimp process or exit normally

Extensions

Table C-10. Gimp Extensions Available Under the Xtns Menu

Name	Description	Arguments
extension_db_browser	List available procedures in the PDB	run_mode (*Integer*) RUN_INTERACTIVE or RUN_NONINTERACTIVE
extension_screenshot	Create a screenshot of a single window or the whole screen	run_mode (*Integer*) RUN_INTERACTIVE or RUN_NONINTERACTIVE root (*Integer*) Root window (TRUE, FALSE) window_id (*String*) Window ID **Returns:** image (*Image*) Output image
extension_script_fu	A scheme interpreter for scripting Gimp operations	
extension_script_fu_console	Provides a console mode for script-fu development	run_mode (*Integer*) RUN_INTERACTIVE or RUN_NONINTERACTIVE

Table C-10. Gimp Extensions Available Under the Xtns Menu (continued)

Name	Description	Arguments
extension_ script_fu_ server	Provides a server for remote script-fu operation	run_mode (*Integer*) RUN_INTERACTIVE or RUN_NONINTERACTIVE port (*Integer*) The port on which to listen for requests logfile (*String*) The file to log server activity to
extension_ web_browser	Open URL in Netscape	run_mode (*Integer*) RUN_INTERACTIVE or RUN_NONINTERACTIVE url (*String*) URL of a document to open new_window (*Integer*) Create a new window or use existing one?

Index

About the Author

Shawn Wallace is a programmer, artist, and managing director of the AS220 (*http://www.as220.org*) artist community in downtown Providence, RI. He has been applying computers to graphics problems for the past twelve years, and has been having fun recently by applying Perl to all sorts of problems.

He studied computer engineering at the University of Rhode Island and participated in the construction of an early (mid-1980s) hypermedia delivery system at HyperView Systems in Middletown, RI. Shawn is a cofounder of the SMT Computing Society, as well as a member of the Rhode Island chapter of the Perl Mongers. Other current software projects include the Bolero open source music notation system (http://*www.as220.org/shawn/bolero*) and the Institute for Folk Computing, a program to inform and inspire the use of open software by the general public in Providence.

Colophon

The animal on the cover of *Programming Web Graphics with Perl and GNU Software* is a collared titi, a small, capuchin-like monkey found in South America. The word "titi" means "little cat" in the language of the Aymara Indians of Peru and Bolivia, and it's not hard to see why it was so named. The titi is one of the smallest of the monkeys, measuring 12–16 inches long, with a long, bushy tail measuring 13–20 inches. Titis have long, silky fur, and long, claw-like nails. Despite their short legs, they are extremely agile jumpers. They feed on insects, lizards, fruit, leaves, blossoms, and occasionally small birds.

Titis live in pairs, perhaps with one or two young. They are believed to mate for life. Females give birth to one offspring at a time, who is then carried and cared for by the male until reaching maturity. Although titis are extremely nervous monkeys who seem to be in constant motion, it is not uncommon for the pair to take a break and rest on a tree branch huddled close together, with their tails intertwined. When it comes to protecting their territory, titis are very aggressive, and often start the day by patrolling the edge of their territory and jumping up and down and screaming at the titi in the adjoining territory, who is engaged in a similar security patrol.

Jane Ellin was the production editor for *Programming Web Graphics with Perl and GNU Software*. Kim Brown was the copyeditor; Lynn Hutchinski wrote the index with support from Seth Maislin; Nicole Gipson Arigo, Sarah Jane Shangraw, and

Sheryl Avruch provided quality control; and Betty Hugh, Kimo Carter, and Sebastian Banker provided production support.

Edie Freedman designed the cover of this book, using a 19th-century engraving from the Dover Pictorial Archive. The cover layout was produced with Quark XPress 3.3 using the ITC Garamond font. Whenever possible, our books use RepKover™, a durable and flexible lay-flat binding. If the page count exceeds RepKover's limit, perfect binding is used.

The inside layout was designed by Edie Freedman and implemented in FrameMaker by Mike Sierra. The text and heading fonts are ITC Garamond Light and Garamond Book. The illustrations that appear in the book were created in Macromedia Freehand 7.0 by Robert Romano. This colophon was written by Clairemarie Fisher O'Leary.

How to stay in touch with O'Reilly

1. Visit Our Award-Winning Web Site

http://www.oreilly.com/

★ "Top 100 Sites on the Web" —*PC Magazine*
★ "Top 5% Web sites" —*Point Communications*
★ "3-Star site" —*The McKinley Group*

Our web site contains a library of comprehensive product information (including book excerpts and tables of contents), downloadable software, background articles, interviews with technology leaders, links to relevant sites, book cover art, and more. File us in your Bookmarks or Hotlist!

2. Join Our Email Mailing Lists

New Product Releases

To receive automatic email with brief descriptions of all new O'Reilly products as they are released, send email to:
listproc@online.oreilly.com
Put the following information in the first line of your message (*not* in the Subject field):
subscribe oreilly-news

O'Reilly Events

If you'd also like us to send information about trade show events, special promotions, and other O'Reilly events, send email to:
listproc@online.oreilly.com
Put the following information in the first line of your message (*not* in the Subject field):
subscribe oreilly-events

3. Get Examples from Our Books via FTP

There are two ways to access an archive of example files from our books:

Regular FTP

- ftp to:
  ftp.oreilly.com
  (login: anonymous
  password: your email address)
- Point your web browser to:
  ftp://ftp.oreilly.com/

FTPMAIL

- Send an email message to:
  ftpmail@online.oreilly.com
  (Write "help" in the message body)

4. Contact Us via Email

order@oreilly.com
To place a book or software order online. Good for North American and international customers.

subscriptions@oreilly.com
To place an order for any of our newsletters or periodicals.

books@oreilly.com
General questions about any of our books.

software@oreilly.com
For general questions and product information about our software. Check out O'Reilly Software Online at **http://software.oreilly.com/** for software and technical support information. Registered O'Reilly software users send your questions to: **website-support@oreilly.com**

cs@oreilly.com
For answers to problems regarding your order or our products.

booktech@oreilly.com
For book content technical questions or corrections.

proposals@oreilly.com
To submit new book or software proposals to our editors and product managers.

international@oreilly.com
For information about our international distributors or translation queries. For a list of our distributors outside of North America check out:
http://www.oreilly.com/www/order/country.html

O'Reilly & Associates, Inc.
101 Morris Street, Sebastopol, CA 95472 USA
TEL 707-829-0515 or 800-998-9938
(6am to 5pm PST)
FAX 707-829-0104

International Distributors

UK, EUROPE, MIDDLE EAST AND AFRICA (EXCEPT FRANCE, GERMANY, AUSTRIA, SWITZERLAND, LUXEMBOURG, LIECHTENSTEIN, AND EASTERN EUROPE)

INQUIRIES

O'Reilly UK Limited
4 Castle Street
Farnham
Surrey, GU9 7HS
United Kingdom
Telephone: 44-1252-711776
Fax: 44-1252-734211
Email: josette@oreilly.com

ORDERS

Wiley Distribution Services Ltd.
1 Oldlands Way
Bognor Regis
West Sussex PO22 9SA
United Kingdom
Telephone: 44-1243-779777
Fax: 44-1243-820250
Email: cs-books@wiley.co.uk

FRANCE

ORDERS

GEODIF
61, Bd Saint-Germain
75240 Paris Cedex 05, France
Tel: 33-1-44-41-46-16 (French books)
Tel: 33-1-44-41-11-87 (English books)
Fax: 33-1-44-41-11-44
Email: distribution@eyrolles.com

INQUIRIES

Éditions O'Reilly
18 rue Séguier
75006 Paris, France
Tel: 33-1-40-51-52-30
Fax: 33-1-40-51-52-31
Email: france@editions-oreilly.fr

GERMANY, SWITZERLAND, AUSTRIA, EASTERN EUROPE, LUXEMBOURG, AND LIECHTENSTEIN

INQUIRIES & ORDERS

O'Reilly Verlag
Balthasarstr. 81
D-50670 Köln
Germany
Telephone: 49-221-973160-91
Fax: 49-221-973160-8
Email: anfragen@oreilly.de (inquiries)
Email: order@oreilly.de (orders)

CANADA (FRENCH LANGUAGE BOOKS)

Les Éditions Flammarion ltée
375, Avenue Laurier Ouest
Montréal (Québec) H2V 2K3
Tel: 00-1-514-277-8807
Fax: 00-1-514-278-2085
Email: info@flammarion.qc.ca

HONG KONG

City Discount Subscription Service, Ltd.
Unit D, 3rd Floor, Yan's Tower
27 Wong Chuk Hang Road
Aberdeen, Hong Kong
Tel: 852-2580-3539
Fax: 852-2580-6463
Email: citydis@ppn.com.hk

KOREA

Hanbit Media, Inc.
Sonyoung Bldg. 202
Yeksam-dong 736-36
Kangnam-ku
Seoul, Korea
Tel: 822-554-9610
Fax: 822-556-0363
Email: hant93@chollian.dacom.co.kr

PHILIPPINES

Mutual Books, Inc.
429-D Shaw Boulevard
Mandaluyong City, Metro
Manila, Philippines
Tel: 632-725-7538
Fax: 632-721-3056
Email: mbikikog@mnl.sequel.net

TAIWAN

O'Reilly Taiwan
No. 3, Lane 131
Hang-Chow South Road
Section 1, Taipei, Taiwan
Tel: 886-2-23968990
Fax: 886-2-23968916
Email: benh@oreilly.com

CHINA

O'Reilly Beijing
Room 2410
160, FuXingMenNeiDaJie
XiCheng District
Beijing, China PR 100031
Tel: 86-10-86631006
Fax: 86-10-86631007
Email: frederic@oreilly.com

INDIA

Computer Bookshop (India) Pvt. Ltd.
190 Dr. D.N. Road, Fort
Bombay 400 001 India
Tel: 91-22-207-0989
Fax: 91-22-262-3551
Email: cbsbom@giasbm01.vsnl.net.in

JAPAN

O'Reilly Japan, Inc.
Kiyoshige Building 2F
12-Bancho, Sanei-cho
Shinjuku-ku
Tokyo 160-0008 Japan
Tel: 81-3-3356-5227
Fax: 81-3-3356-5261
Email: japan@oreilly.com

ALL OTHER ASIAN COUNTRIES

O'Reilly & Associates, Inc.
101 Morris Street
Sebastopol, CA 95472 USA
Tel: 707-829-0515
Fax: 707-829-0104
Email: order@oreilly.com

AUSTRALIA

WoodsLane Pty., Ltd.
7/5 Vuko Place
Warriewood NSW 2102
Australia
Tel: 61-2-9970-5111
Fax: 61-2-9970-5002
Email: info@woodslane.com.au

NEW ZEALAND

Woodslane New Zealand, Ltd.
21 Cooks Street (P.O. Box 575)
Waganui, New Zealand
Tel: 64-6-347-6543
Fax: 64-6-345-4840
Email: info@woodslane.com.au

LATIN AMERICA

McGraw-Hill Interamericana
Editores, S.A. de C.V.
Cedro No. 512
Col. Atlampa
06450, Mexico, D.F.
Tel: 52-5-547-6777
Fax: 52-5-547-3336
Email: mcgraw-hill@infosel.net.mx

O'REILLY®

O'REILLY™

O'Reilly & Associates, Inc.
101 Morris Street
Sebastopol, CA 95472-9902
1-800-998-9938

Visit us online at:
http://www.ora.com/
orders@ora.com

O'REILLY WOULD LIKE TO HEAR FROM YOU

Which book did this card come from?

_____

Where did you buy this book?
- ❏ Bookstore
- ❏ Direct from O'Reilly
- ❏ Bundled with hardware/software
- ❏ Other _____
- ❏ Computer Store
- ❏ Class/seminar

What operating system do you use?
- ❏ UNIX
- ❏ Windows NT
- ❏ Other _____
- ❏ Macintosh
- ❏ PC(Windows/DOS)

What is your job description?
- ❏ System Administrator
- ❏ Network Administrator
- ❏ Web Developer
- ❏ Other _____
- ❏ Programmer
- ❏ Educator/Teacher

❏ Please send me O'Reilly's catalog, containing a complete listing of O'Reilly books and software.

Name _____   Company/Organization _____

Address _____

City _____   State _____   Zip/Postal Code _____   Country _____

Telephone _____   Internet or other email address (specify network) _____

Nineteenth century wood engraving
of a bear from the O'Reilly &
Associates Nutshell Handbook®
Using & Managing UUCP.

BUSINESS REPLY MAIL

FIRST CLASS MAIL   PERMIT NO. 80   SEBASTOPOL, CA

Postage will be paid by addressee

O'Reilly & Associates, Inc.
101 Morris Street
Sebastopol, CA 95472-9902